TRASH ANIMALS

Trash Animals

HOW WE LIVE WITH NATURE'S FILTHY, FERAL, INVASIVE, AND UNWANTED SPECIES

Kelsi Nagy and Phillip David Johnson II, Editors

Foreword by *Randy Malamud*

University of Minnesota Press

Minneapolis

London

Copyright 2013 by the Regents of the University of Minnesota

All rights reserved. No part of this publication may be reproduced, stored in a retrieval system, or transmitted, in any form or by any means, electronic, mechanical, photocopying, recording, or otherwise, without the prior written permission of the publisher.

Published by the University of Minnesota Press
111 Third Avenue South, Suite 290
Minneapolis, MN 55401-2520
http://www.upress.umn.edu

ISBN 978-0-8166-8054-2 (hc)
ISBN 978-0-8166-8055-9 (pb)

A Cataloging-in-Publication record for this book is available from the Library of Congress.

Printed in the United States of America on acid-free paper

The University of Minnesota is an equal-opportunity educator and employer.

20 19 18 17 16 15 14 13   10 9 8 7 6 5 4 3 2 1

This book is dedicated to our families.
We appreciate your support beyond measure.

We also dedicate this book to all
insignificant, unwanted, or despised creatures of this world.

Contents

Foreword

Randy Malamud

THERE IS A RANGE OF NONHUMAN ANIMALS who are despised or feared or mocked because we have constructed them as the disgusting "other" in our anthropocentric fantasies of existence.

We like to imagine that we are in control of our homes, gardens, forests, parks, landscapes, and urban spaces, and we are determined to serve as gatekeepers, or wardens, adjudicating which species are allowed and which are banned, which are prized and which are denigrated. These decisions are often based on our prejudices, our taste, and our habits.

Cats, for example, are lovely, as long as they are suitably domesticated, registered, or commodified. But a pack of feral cats in a junkyard, scrawny and mewling, strikes us as verminous. Eagles and raptors circling overhead evoke our admiring awe, while pigeons shuffling underfoot are shooed or kicked away. Why—because they don't fly as much or as high? Do we see them as lazy? Do they lose cachet because they poop too much? (How much does a pigeon poop compared to an eagle?) Do we denigrate some animals because they're too common, too adaptable to human society? Do we disdain animals who proliferate too easily? Are we threatened by them? Are we prone to fetishize the rarer animals, the eagles and pandas, precisely because they are endangered and thus serve as evidence of our superior skills of survival over them, indicating our greater power, while we seem powerless to control prairie dogs and rats?

In the essays brought together here, readers will note a keenly personal, idiosyncratic, subjective focus embodying each individual writer's own experiences with a range of animals that have gotten the short end of the stick. This is an antidote to the predominant unexamined presuppositions about

certain species. Cultural prejudices, like any effective propaganda, are gener-
alized, mass market, lowest-common-denominator caricatures. These stories
are precise, detailed, and honest in order to resist the half-truths of propaganda (which is how I would characterize the trash-labeling of certain species, a parallel to the historical phenomenon of trash-labeling certain racial,
ethnic, and religious human cultures).

The narratives are engaging and inviting. While they often suggest global,
theoretical, and macroecological insights, they begin with the local and the
particular, an encounter between two distinct animals: one is armed with a
word processor to initiate a dialogue in a textual realm; the other is patho-
logically underdetermined, framed, and subjectified ad absurdum but perhaps positioned here to be invited into a more welcoming discourse. When
Carolyn Kraus talks about pejoratively constructed images of cockroaches
and makes a connection to the role of negative stereotyping in promoting
genocide, we realize how insidious are the cultural pathways that convince
the masses to buy into the cheap, thoughtless caricatures perpetuated about
certain species. The writers in *Trash Animals* encourage us to dismiss much of
what we have "learned" and confront coyotes, Mormon crickets, starlings,
and a host of other real, vital, important animals as if we were meeting
them for the first time.

"Trash," in "trash animals," is of course ironic. The writers collected here
don't really think these animals, or any animals, are trash: dirty, unwanted,
useless detritus. That's what the world at large thinks, and these writers want
to rescue these animals from that characterization. Trash, *real* trash, is a
big problem today. We make too much of it, and we don't do a very good
job of figuring out how to dispose of it. Its toxic runoffs threaten our ecological safety. It is an indicator of our overconsumption: wasted food, excessive packaging, thoughtlessly discarded by-products of our living habits. It
smells bad; it is an eyesore; it overwhelms our civic utilities. We need to do
a better job with regard to trash: generating less of it, recycling it, disposing
of it more intelligently. We have more than enough real trash; we certainly
don't need to include in our trash heaps things that aren't really trash. Part
of our problem, living in the world, is properly understanding and valuing
all the elements that coexist with us.

What cultural forces are complicit in relegating certain animals to the
trash heap? What are the consequences of devaluing (and of valuing) certain
animals, attaching labels? There are authentic reasons for regarding some
species as important, dangerous, or particularly worthy of our attention. But
the criteria for such assessments should be guided by ecology not culture.

Perhaps there are indeed alignments between some of our cultural and ecological assessments; certainly there are valid biological reasons for shunning waste, threat, excessive predation, and invasiveness. And so perhaps by analyzing the roots and causes of our knee-jerk cultural responses to some animals, we may in fact arrive at a clearer sense of why we may reject and spurn some of our *earthmates.*

Good anthrozoology (such as the reader will confront in the following essays) makes us look at the same animals we've always looked at but see complexities that we never thought about. Gavan Watson does this in his essay about Toronto's gulls, ubiquitous and misperceived. These writers remind us that the more we find out about these animals, the better suited we are to deal with them. Kraus literally enacts this in her essay when, beset with an invasion of cockroaches, her first and finest instinct is to run out and spend the day in the library finding out everything she doesn't know about them: the first thing she seems to realize that she does know about them is how much she doesn't know. Michael Branch does the same thing when faced with a packrat infestation.

As Watson explains, we have a tendency to project our own neuroses about living in our own habitats onto the animals that share the landscape with us. In our most honestly self-reflective moments, I believe, we are all aware to some extent that we are not, as a culture, the best custodians, or even inhabitants, of our ecosystem; and in our more venal moments, as we try to sublimate our ecological transgressions and minimize the cognitive dissonance we must feel for fouling our nests, we shirk sole responsibility for this state of affairs: we try to share the blame, spread the blame. We try to implicate the other animals—especially "trash animals"—in our own misbehavior; we want to drag them down with us.

This higher state of enlightenment that readers may achieve after studying these essays isn't a utopian paradise; animals will continue to be killed, displaced, overwritten. Such is life. But still, in *Trash Animals* we are afforded a necessary corrective. In our status quo cultural experiences, we are induced to see animals simply, neatly, in frames (or cages or tight, concise categories): an animal is a pet or meat or a charismatic megafauna or a cartoon. We don't allow a great deal of variety, complexity, or nuance in the limited amount of our attention we set aside for nonhuman animals, and we don't want to work very hard to problematize or reconceptualize our received ideas. Hence, it seems obvious that the animals that don't fit into some more convenient (for us) category in terms of how we use them, how they might appeal to us, end up in the category of "trash." And if we think of this process in relation to other kinds of trash—spoiled food, broken cell phones and computers, packaging, car carcasses—we can see that that, too, is being categorized, conveniently, as something we don't want around us, don't want to think about, don't want to deal with, don't want to integrate into a more challenging eco-vision. And so other trash, too, is becoming a big problem, piling up, seeping toxically into water tables. We need to learn to deal with trash, and part of that is recognizing that some of what we consider trash isn't trash—it is useful, important, and shouldn't be thrown on the trash heap.

The word *trash* is derogatory—white trash, trailer trash, talking trash—and we shouldn't be disparaging parts of our ecosystem because (as Barry Commoner preaches) everything is connected to everything else, and everything has to go somewhere. The essays that follow help us to think about what it means to denigrate an animal—why we might be inclined to have done so in the first place, and why it might be more intelligent, more responsible, to stop doing so. Trash is in the eye of the beholder. If anyone deserves the epithet of trash animal, it's us! We create more trash, and we hierarchically arrange (pervert, destroy) the world according to a scale of values that is often directly antagonistic to environmental sanity. In the introduction to his wry survey *Trash,* John Knechtel writes that we "are embedded in our trash . . . To purge the earth of garbage would be to destroy our own reflection."[1] We are what we trash, and the "trash" animals, the cockroaches and pigeons and all, are closer to us than we would like to think. We need to rehabilitate and rediscover what we are prone to toss aside.

James Bishop asks in his essay about magpies: Do we consider them trash because they're pests? Because they're "ugly"? Or for some other unexamined reason emanating from our cultural stereotypes and prejudices? The point is to interrogate and reconfigure these stereotypes. With an engaging and inspiring personal account of how he met magpies in Korea and learned to admire them, Bishop typifies the power of culture to undo and revise received ideas. Simply put, all the writers herein try, in one way or another, to tell us a story that supplants the other stories we've told or heard or inferred about these dirty, useless animals.

Probably we can't help approaching animals with stories, prejudices, misconceptions, and putting animals in (and seeing them through) cultural frames. But we might as well at least try to make sure that the stories we tell and the frames we create are relatively better than the ones that have led us to establish an imperial and hubristic superiority over the other animals, a hierarchical and regrettable ecological (mis)vision that facilitates the kinds of attitudes toward animals that make us less receptive to the idea of a symbiotic harmony with other species and more inclined to wall ourselves inside away from "them," on our own or perhaps with a few cute furry species.

It's not simply that we need to learn to love all the animals that we are now taught to loathe and shun—sometimes this is what these essays describe, and sometimes (as in the essay on lubbers) the essayists do not conclude with an epiphany of communion—but still, it's an *essay* (from the French: an attempt, trying something on), and it gives the subject animals the benefit of the doubt. It tries to encounter them, to come to terms with them, and to understand them more richly than we have done when we condemn these animals to the realm of trash.

We need to appreciate the dignity of these animals—of *all* animals, who are equally possessed of integrity and importance and spirit—in order to preserve our own dignity and to exist as good citizens of the planet.

Note

1. John Knechtel, ed., *Trash* (Cambridge, Mass.: MIT Press, 2006), 9.

Acknowledgments

THE EDITORS OF THIS VOLUME would like to thank all those who had a hand in putting this book together. We reserve our sincerest thanks and gratitude to all of our contributors for trusting and distrusting our editorial advice, finally shaping their animal essays into the niches we envisioned in this collection.

We thank SueEllen Campbell, professor of English at Colorado State University, for suggesting we pursue this project and whose valuable advice and editorial savvy set us on a straight path and pushed this book along; John Calderazzo, professor of English at Colorado State University, for his generous support and encouragement; and Laura Pritchett for her advice on the Introduction and whose comments we took to heart. We extend special thanks to Randy Malamud, professor of English at Georgia State University, for being excited about this project, reading the essays, and agreeing right away to write the Foreword; and Michael P. Branch, professor of literature and environment at the University of Nevada, Reno, for his tireless support, advice, and encouragement, particularly during the long summer days of digging drainage ditches at his desert home. We also thank everyone who discussed the project with us at conferences, attended our panel discussions, and asked good questions, especially our colleagues of the Western Literature Association and the Association for the Study of Literature and Environment.

Of our contributors, we thank the following scholars and writers for allowing us to reprint their stories and essays, some of whom heard about the project and sought us out: Bruce Barcott, Charles Bergman, Andrew Blechman, Lisa Couturier, Carolyn Kraus, Kathleen Dean Moore, Charles

Mitchell, and Bernard Quetchenbach. We extend heartfelt thanks to Gavan P. L. Watson, Catherine Puckett, Christina Robertson, Michael P. Branch, James E. Bishop, Kyhl Lyndgaard, and Jeffrey A. Lockwood for contributing original work to our uncommon collection.

This volume would not be what it is without the generous support and enthusiasm of Richard Morrison and Erin Warholm-Wohlenhaus at the University of Minnesota Press.

Phillip David Johnson II would especially like to thank his family—his wife, Inger, and his children, Seth and Allar—for putting up with the long hours he spent in the office with the door locked while reading over manuscripts, editing essays, and writing letters. "Yes, Daddy will be out of the office in five minutes—*truthfully this time.*"

Kelsi Nagy especially thanks her parents, Patricia Zibell-Nagy and Dan Nagy, for encouraging her to walk the path less traveled, literally and figuratively. She could never thank them enough for their generous support. She thanks her mentors at Colorado State University's philosophy department, in particular Holmes Rolston III and Jane Kneller, as well as Paul Waldau and Michael Noonan at Canisius College for allowing her to become a student of anthrozoology at the last minute. She extends special thanks to her colleagues in Canisius College's anthrozoology program for all the discussions about the relationships between human and nonhuman animals that benefited her contribution to the Introduction. Thanks to Patrick Harbula and Chris Fry for their advice and help with the manuscript, and special thanks to Liz Gaylor for being a longtime friend and editor—everyone should have a friend like you.

Introduction

Kelsi Nagy and Phillip David Johnson II

WORTHLESS, THREATENING, DANGEROUS, destructive, and ugly. Varmints, vermin, pests, scavengers, nuisances, and exotics or invasive alien species— these terms come to mind, without much reflection, when we think about certain animals or, heaven forbid, when we actually encounter them. These terms make us think of animals like snakes, coyotes, carp, starlings, pigeons, prairie dogs, rats, mice, cockroaches, and locusts, to name just a few, and there are many, many others. It is common to think of these animals as harmful, filthy, despicable, or useless. We take it for granted that these and other animals are perceived as having little or no value. These "worthless" species are often associated with, treated like, and called "trash."

Hunters, anglers, scientists, suburbanite homeowners, and zoo-goers alike fear, despise, and ignore animals for a number of conflicting, arbitrary reasons. Some devalue animals because they are common and uninteresting, like gull species that hover over supermarket parking lots. Others denigrate animals with nonnative origins, such as carp or starlings in North America or any animals classified as "exotics" or "invasive alien species." Some animals are especially despised for being ugly or for inspiring fear and disgust.

Reactions like these do not always come from animal haters. Passionate advocates for wildlife view some animals as enemies, a justification for extermination. It is not uncommon for literature written by birders, hunters, anglers, nature and environmental writers, and scientists to classify out-of-place and undesirable animals as disposable, particularly when those species compete with more desirable ones. Birders feel joy or angst, depending on the species of sparrow they see from a distance, and deem unwanted birds "garbage" birds. Hunters revere the lives of deer and elk but consider the shooting of prairie dogs and coyotes as a useful service to ranchers or simply as target practice. Anglers wax poetic about the virtues of brook trout but toss carp on the shores of lakes to die, though neither fish is likely to be native to the waters where it was caught. Scientific studies lose objectivity when describing "invasive alien species," using terms such as "bio-pollution" and unwittingly incorporating the long history of xenophobic discourses surrounding unwelcome *human* immigrants. Pet owners may call predators like foxes and coyotes "urban terrorists" if they are the cause of a beloved companion animal's demise.[1]

These attitudes and engagements with animals often reveal assumptions about what nature ought to be, or what nature was at one time. Many of us believe that certain species do not belong in certain natural or human-built spaces, like prairie dogs on ranches, Canadian geese on golf courses, or unwanted starlings or carp in natural areas. These animals may reveal the manner in which we project expectations onto the landscape, what some geographers call geographies of human imagination. Ranches, golf courses, and even national parks or public lands are examples of landscapes where nonhuman animals' habitat may come into conflict with human ideas of property, utility, or what nature is or should be—exposing their place in our human-ordered world. Instead of evaluating whether human expectations of nature are incorrect or inadequate, these animals slide into roles as symbols of human fears or frustrations.

In *Wild Echoes,* Charles Bergman argues that endangered animals have two faces: one symbolic, the other real.[2] The same is true of "trash" animals (including some that are extinct or endangered), who carry the myths, symbolism, stories, and violence of human history, because they have historically resisted domestication, because they transgress the boundary of domesticated or wild, or because they have been a hindrance to larger human efforts to reorganize the landscape. Some trash animals thrive on the coattails of human colonization and imperialism; some continue to thrive in spite of human resource management and ongoing efforts to eradicate them. The majority of these species are viewed as having no economic value or, worse, as disrupting human enterprise. We think it is important to think carefully about wildlife, even problematic or "worthless" species, and to carefully consider the conceptual and practical problems that arise from equating animals with what we discard.

That so-called trash animals abound in human consciousness is no astonishing fact, and the purpose of *Trash Animals* is not simply to point out that some animals are maligned by humans. The real purpose lies much deeper, questioning not only the implications of calling an animal "trash" but also what we can understand about the personal and cultural phenomenon of the trash animal.

This collection explores trash animals through a variety of genres, from cultural studies and journalism to creative nonfiction; each essay explores human relationships with an animal believed to be worthless or, for a number of reasons, undesirable, animals inspiring human violence or indifference. The contributors discuss the natural (and human) history of each animal while they explore the historical and cultural reasons that have assigned the species a lowly order in our modern bestiary. Often, writers find scientific objectivity hopelessly entangled in culture, or they find science can dispel myths or taboos about species despised on the basis of their reputation. For example, when Lisa Couturier muses on the biology of coyotes in chapter 5, "One Nation under Coyote, Divisible," that they are in fact far less dangerous to humans and agriculture than what is commonly believed, she argues that the violence done to coyotes is unwarranted: "I want to say to those willing to shoot at the unknown—to shoot at what is perceived as a threat—that perhaps certain explicit information would calm their fears." In many cases, by looking more closely at a certain species, contributors see in the animal something to appreciate, perhaps even to revere, something that alters their perspective on the world shared with other animals.

What Is a Trash Animal?

In order to understand our question, "What does it mean to call an animal trash?," we must understand where the term comes from and what "trash" means when we use it as a category for animals. Animals have been referred to as trash for hundreds of years. The earliest print reference, according to the *Oxford English Dictionary,* is in 1749, when *The Wealth of Great Britain in the Ocean* reported, "There are three kinds of mark'd herring among the Dutch, each less than the other, and of prices proportionate, the last sort are called trash."[3] This association of trash and animal places the awareness of an animal's monetary worth within the historical emergence of capitalism in the eighteenth century. Currently, the term "trash animal" is sometimes used by fur trappers to refer to a nontarget animal—for example, when a skunk is caught in place of a bobcat.[4] Then and now, assigning value to animals based on their economic worth, or conversely on how they affect human enterprise for good or ill, appears innate, normal, or "God-given" in human–animal engagements, but the assigned financial values of animals say far more about human desires, and other tangled values, than the inherent worth of a species.

"Trash" describes an animal as worthless, useless, and disposable, none of which are inherent qualities of an animal itself; rather, it defines an animal's relationship to humans or attitudes about how humans understand the way an animal fits into our worldview. In the twenty-first century, assigning value in terms of monetary worth feels innate or instinctual. However pervasive or powerful this concept happens to be in our collective consciousness, money is also only an idea, one that lies at the center of a social contract. But economic value is not a true or inherent value.

Aldo Leopold warned about the short-sightedness of assigning economic value to plants, animals, and even biotic habitats more than once in his seminal work, *Sand County Almanac*. Leopold wrote, "Of the 22,000 higher plants and animals native to Wisconsin, it is doubtful whether more than 5 per cent can be sold, fed, eaten, or otherwise put to economic use." Does that, therefore, make the remaining 95 percent of wild flowers, songbirds, rodents, and wolves worthless? Far from it. These "members of the biotic community" contribute to the "stability" and "integrity" of the ecosystem and are "entitled to continuance."[5] Leopold argued that even the wolves (arguably more unpopular during Leopold's time than they are today) were integral to the overall functioning of ecosystems. The wild lands that Leopold himself helped depopulate of wolves became diminished by erosion when deer populations exploded and the hillsides were denuded of vegetation. The wolves, which had previously been seen as competition for deer hunters, became valued by Leopold because of their role in the continuance of a vital ecosystem. The trash fish thrown overboard by Dutch fishermen in the eighteenth century and the unlucky trash animals that stumble into fur hunters' traps today also have a worth that extends beyond our economic markets and cultural conditioning. Calling these animals "trash" can lull us into a kind of complacency. Because they are of no economic significance or sometimes harm human enterprise, they are described as worthless and therefore treated as if they are disposable. That humans place values on animals, values that reflect human-centered activities and concepts, is understandable, but seeing beyond our anthropocentric conditioning can be useful and meaningful.

It is important to understand that "trash" is not just a label but a concept that shapes individual and communal perception of the world—what cultural studies scholars refer to as a cultural metaphor, not just the comparison of two dissimilar things (as in literary works) but a figurative way of understanding some complex phenomenon or process. Trash is not just the material stuff we throw away, but a classification that defines for us the ways we understand and act toward certain inanimate or animate objects. Trash masquerades as an objective and unquestionable category in society, but, looking closely, trash does so much more.

Who we imagine ourselves to be, our identity, is tied up with the way we understand the world around us, and our understanding of trash reveals more about us than the things we throw away. You don't have to go much further than the colloquial saying, "one man's trash is another man's treasure," to see that what qualifies as trash is defined by the individual using the word, the person's attachments to personal prejudices and religious beliefs, and their culture's worldview. "Trash" commonly designates objects considered no longer useful or that have ceased to fulfill their intended purpose or benefit. However, what humans designate as trash becomes a far more complicated matter, attested to by the recent explosion of trash studies in anthropology, history, cultural and literary studies, and the arts. Studies of trash and all of its variants—garbage, refuse, filth, rubbish, and waste— have shown that the connotations and symbolism of trash are deeply embedded in identity—the ways we imagine ourselves and our communities.

One of the first scholars to examine how undesirable categories relate to human identity, anthropologist Mary Douglas argued in her influential work *Purity and Danger* that "dirt is matter out of place." "Dirt," she contends, "is never a unique, isolated event. Where there is dirt there is system. Dirt is the by-product of a systematic ordering and classification of matter, insofar as ordering involves rejecting inappropriate elements." For Douglas, dirt exists outside of a culture's "normal" or "safe" worldview. Dirt is not inherently dangerous until it becomes "pollution," a "dangerous kind of dirt."[6] Even in today's secular world, dirt, pollution, and trash account for all that we find ambiguous and anomalous. Trash is dumped on the margins of society, often in undesirable landscapes or where marginalized people who are too poor or powerless to fight against the poisoning of their environment live. We call people we find strange or disorderly "trash," and we wage campaigns against animals that are alien, invasive, or destructive to human enterprise and identify them with or treat them as trash.

Douglas's theory shows that we fear what we find dirty or polluted, in many cases because these dangerous kinds of filth cannot be easily defined, controlled, or dismissed. It is no wonder plants, animals, and insects that we find difficult to define, contain, or control are deemed trash animals. Donna Haraway, in her book *When Species Meet,* echoes Douglas's theory when she discusses the plight of wolf–dog hybrids bred in South Africa during the apartheid era that failed to be useful as attack dogs. They were hard to train and failed to take orders, deferring to their human pack leader rather than taking the lead when ordered to do so. After apartheid ended, the "useless" hybrid dogs had no place to call home. Haraway writes, "Both epidemiologically and genetically categorically 'impure,' these canids enter the cultural category of the disposable 'homeless,' or in ecological terms 'nicheless.' The new state could not care less what happens to these animate tools of a former racist regime."[7] The wolf–dog hybrids aren't easily categorized, they aren't useful as work dogs, and their unpredictable nature disqualifies them as desirable companion animals. A mix of North American wild wolf and South African domestic canines, these creatures also do not belong in the wild on either continent. Their association as mascots of apartheid and their unpredictable behavior certainly qualify them as dangerous. Haraway identifies the prevailing sentiment toward these animals as trash when she describes them as "disposable" and "homeless." Even the privately funded shelters that were set up to help some of the wolf–dogs only accepted "pure" animals. Ultimately, through no fault of their own, Haraway concludes, without a proper niche within the cultural psyche these animals faced a grim future. In this collection, coyotes making their way into new territories on the East Coast of the United States and pigeons, once highly regarded domestic birds but now viewed as feral nuisances, are also disdained for these same reasons.

Outside of cultural studies, trash animals lurk in scientific studies and writing as well. Invasive species, like carp, are called "biological pollution" without a second thought by supposedly objective scientists working in the growing field of invasion biology. Invoking the metaphor of pollution to describe a species is qualitatively different from phrases like "nonnative" or "exotic," but it reveals the frustration that invasion biologists feel when they cannot manage or control species that damage human property or, worse, endanger the lives of other species. We cannot predict which nonnative animals and plants will disturb ecosystems, farms, or urban landscapes. Not only do these species like carp "trash" landscapes, invading what was once beautiful or pristine, they are difficult or impossible to control or eradicate.[8] The failure to manage many of these animals with the best scientific research and control methods reveals our all-too-human limits and makes us confront the fact that much of the natural world remains a mystery to us.

It is no wonder we justify violent actions when attempting to control plants and animals that are viewed as both worthless, dangerous, and out of control. These pests, vermin, and plagues can kindle a deep desire to squash, crush, and destroy animal–enemies. Philosopher Greg Kennedy takes a closer look at the connection between trash and violence. In his book *An Ontology of Trash* (2007), he writes:

> "Trash" connotes violence. We sometimes apply the word to people as a particularly venomous pejorative. As a verb it can be used synonymously with "to destroy," as in "the thugs trashed the place." In this sense, "trash" means a manner of physically relating to other beings. It is a mode of comportment, treating things without care, negatively, and destructively. . . . We exist, for the most part, in a way that violently negates beings rather than takes care of them.[9]

As Kennedy notes, when we classify objects as trash, we impose inherently negative qualities on those objects. Value, in other words, does not simply label; value engages with the world. For Kennedy, the label "trash" sets aside an object, a person, or an animal for violence. Though Kennedy never takes up questions about animals, his observations about the central cultural importance of trash are immediately relevant to negative human–animal relationships where disposability is built a priori into objects of our world. Animals associated with the effluvia and by-products of mainstream society take on all of the symbolisms and stigmas of trash. Many of the essays in *Trash Animals* discuss the kinds of violence committed on these unwanted or despised species. As far as human actions toward wildlife are concerned, deeming an animal trash justifies most kinds of violent actions toward wildlife.

Neither the editors nor the contributors would agree that any animal can or should be inherently, objectively classified as trash. Nor would we wish to dispose of them. We contextualize the essays in this collection by combining current work on trash theory with animal studies. By looking closely at the "trash" label, we find that our focus recenters on people. Historian Susan Strasser, in *Waste and Want: A Social History of Trash*, writes: "If we focus on the categorizing process that defines trash, our attention will be drawn away from the rubbish heap and concentrated on human behavior."[10] Consequently, the trash animal as an idea becomes a tool for analysis, revealing these deep human conflicts, inconsistencies, and constructed boundaries.

Trash, as such, does not exist outside human culture. In the nonhuman world there is no trash, only transformation—even when there is excess. Trash is a human creation both literally and figuratively. Trash is also an idea that changes based on culture, society, geography, religion, history, personal beliefs, and circumstance. At the heart of this collection is this question: what does it mean to call an animal "trash"? And because trash is inherently a subjective category, what does using the phrase "trash" to describe animals say about human desires and fears about filthy, worthless, or despised animals? These questions challenge biological, psychological, economic, aesthetic, and ethical engagements with the more-than-human world, asking for a reexamination of human values and assumptions that operate unchecked, guiding both sentiment and science, policy and management.

Moral Worth and Trash Animals

Once we recognize that naming an animal "trash" justifies human violence toward those animals viewed as dangerous or worthless, the question becomes, "*should* we treat animals like trash?" Even creepy-crawly, ugly, threatening, or insignificant animals live as sentient creatures, not inanimate objects to be thrown on the trash heap without a second thought. Discussions about animal welfare or rights can ignore these "insignificant" and often numerous species. But what separates the moral worth of a carp, pigeon, or prairie dog from livestock, lab animals, endangered species, and house pets—all groups of animals that inspire discussion and activism about animal rights? Many essays in the collection touch on the moral status of trash animals and the confusing or frustrating moral gray area that underlies our relationship with these unwanted animals. The authors find that wrestling with these uncomfortable questions is trying at times, but there is a significant amount to be learned from questioning personal prejudices concerning wildlife.

Many of the essays here challenge the irrational ways humans perceive and treat animals. Since the inception of the animal rights movement, there has been a growing awareness and concern for the welfare of animals, such as laboratory animals, farm and zoo animals, and endangered species. Not all animals have benefited from the animal rights or environmental movements, but they are not outside the scope of animal rights. For example, the high-profile animal rights organization PETA includes "pest" species in its mission statement:

> PETA focuses its attention on the four areas in which the largest numbers of animals suffer the most intensely for the longest periods of time: on factory farms, in the clothing trade, in laboratories, and in the entertainment industry. We also work on a variety of

other issues, including the cruel killing of beavers, birds, and other "pests" as well as cruelty to domesticated animals.[11]

The Humane Society of the United States also advocates for pest species through various humane education programs. Even though there are many that feel compassion for so-called trash animals, these creatures do not often figure prominently in the animal rights movement as they may not motivate as many people to donate money to animal rights campaigns as puppies, bunny rabbits, and poorly treated livestock do. Advocating for unwanted wildlife may also incite controversy in an already controversial arena.

Though many consider humans to be morally better or more entitled than animals because we possess the faculty of reason, human attitudes and actions toward animals continue to be erratic. For example, *Audubon* magazine reported on farmers who poisoned red-winged blackbirds that were snacking on their sunflower seed crops.[12] When these farmers sold their crops, a portion of the sunflower seeds ended up as bird food. On the farm, the birds are animal enemies, but when perched on the backyard feeder these same birds may be seen as charming. While the scenario is understandable, it still reveals a deep irony about how North Americans assign moral value to birds. People often act as if we expect animals to evaluate which human environments are good and which are bad and act accordingly. *Rationally* it is unrealistic to expect animals to behave this way.

Prejudice against animals does not confine itself to those viewed as economic threats. "Environmentally minded" citizens, such as birders, often refer to common birds, such as pigeons and Canadian geese, as "garbage" or "trash" birds, exposing a deeper prejudice invoked by some ubiquitous birds even in so-called nature lovers. Anglers also refer to fish that don't have any recreational or economic value as "trash" fish. A fisherman who lovingly sets free a cutthroat trout he has caught may very well toss a bullhead catfish on the bank to die. Both fish are native inhabitants of North America. Why should we revere one fish and abhor the other? Even among so-called nature and animal lovers, the term "trash" opens up a moral loophole through which slip the creatures that are deemed ugly, gross, problematic, alien, or insignificant.

In his book, *Some We Love, Some We Hate, Some We Eat: Why It's So Hard to Think Straight about Animals,* psychologist Hal Herzog discusses the numerous ways our thoughts about animals defy logic: "Much of our thinking is a mire of instinct, learning, language, culture, intuition, and our reliance on mental shortcuts." Research shows humans instinctually respond more favorably to animals that remind us of human infants. This "cute response" explains why it is easier for wildlife protection agencies to raise funding for "cute" animals and why we rarely hear about the sixty insects listed under the Endangered Species Act. It is no coincidence that the World Wildlife Fund's mascot is the adorable, doe-eyed, fuzzy giant panda bear and not a lizard or a snake. But instincts are just a part of the complex network of beliefs and idea that inform our relationship with animals. Herzog writes:

> Genes and experience conspire to make it easy for us to learn to fear some animals but not others. Our culture tells us which species we should love, hate, and eat. Then there are the conflicts between reason and emotion, our reliance on hunches and empathy, and our propensity to project our own thoughts and desires into the heads of others [meaning animals].[13]

It is difficult indeed to think straight about animals, but if we attempt to see animals apart from our anthropocentric projections and desires, might we be able to see these animals with some sort of clarity? If we understand animals on their own terms, could we then minimize or end conflicts with problematic wildlife or find a way to humanely end their lives when necessary? If, in fact, our false beliefs about a species are the cause for conflicts between humans and animals, might we find a better way to be neighbors simply by changing our minds and then our behaviors?

The authors of these essays on trash animals are aware of the various taboos that cultural indoctrination breeds—Mormon crickets, a kind of locust, are harbingers of the apocalypse; magpies molest livestock; snakes are evil; and prairie dogs spread the plague—assumptions that may continue to prevail even if they are untrue. While examining these creatures' cultural identities, the authors are also curious about the "real" or biological animal apart from any beneficial or harmful relationship the animal might have personally or with other humans. As Thomas Nagel reminds us in his essay "What Is It Like to Be a Bat?," it is unlikely that we will ever know the true experience of any animal—bat, rat, or feral cat—because we lack the physiological mechanisms to inhabit these animals' phenomenological experiences. Still, there is merit in making an effort to shift to an animal's point of view given our rudimentary understanding of their behaviors, habits, and biology/physiology. This shift in perspective from human to nonhuman animal allows us to analyze our behaviors in relationship with the animals' realities from a less anthropocentric point of view.

By looking at an animal's biology in conjunction with its natural and cultural history, some of the taboos fall away. For example, James E. Bishop, in chapter 12, "Kach'i: Garbage Birds in a Hybrid Landscape," states that magpies may be beneficial to ranchers by removing ticks and other parasites from livestock, and Kelsi Nagy, in chapter 6, "Prairie Dog and Prejudice," discovers prairie dogs are victims, not carriers, of the plague. Other authors reveal that some control methods used to reduce species populations are unnecessarily inhumane or flat-out ineffective. Andrew D. Blechman, in chapter 13, "Flying Rats," documents the huge arsenal of poisons, spikes, and glue that are the accepted methods of pigeon "control." He discovers, ironically, the most effective way to manage pigeons happens to be the most humane. Christina Robertson, in chapter 4, "Managing Apocalypse: A Cultural History of the Morman Cricket," reveals a further irony when she documents the widespread use of pesticides to manage insects. Ultimately, the efforts to control species may be more harmful to humans than the threat of the animals themselves. The violent campaigns waged against some insects, birds, and mammals such as coyotes (all animals that are commonly poisoned), result in yet another manner of polluting the environment and ultimately our own bodies. How we respond to conflicts with animals reveals our larger relationship with the environment as a whole.

Other chapters reveal the limits of science as an objective arbiter of nature. Charles Bergman, in chapter 2, "Hunger Makes the Wolf," shows that the studies conducted about wolf populations in Alaska are driven by a desire to create abundant moose populations for hunters. He finds that science cannot ultimately answer all our questions about value and management of species. As Bergman says, "Science cannot tell us how to relate to wild animals, how to treat them, what place to make for them in our lives." He suggests humans would live diminished lives without creatures like wolves, which signify qualities like wildness, freedom, lust, and hunger, and that animals can also serve as totems of our partially understood fears and desires. Jeffrey A. Lockwood, in chapter 16, "A Six-legged Guru: Fear and Loathing in Nature," also shows us that disgust can be an aesthetic experience when he illuminates the life of the prairie lubber grasshopper, which has a rather disgusting escape tactic. Life is full of beauty, but it is also full of feces, filth, and decay. Lockwood shows us that even creatures that disgust us can lead us into wonder.

The essays in *Trash Animals* reveal that human relationships with animals, even animals that seem ecologically or economically worthless (oftentimes, a harmful assumption) or that do us harm, can be imagined in new ways. And if we can see animals in a different light, our ethics of engagement will certainly follow. It is vitally important to engage in a moral dialogue about "insignificant" creatures because invertebrates, insects, fish, and rodents compose the majority of animal life.[14] *Trash Animals* offers a timely analysis of human attitudes toward animals and the environment and begins a new dialogue about our relationship with animals in an increasingly postpristine world.

The Collection

Each essay in this collection explores the history and biology of an individual trash animal and, emphasizing the inherent value of each, proposes a unique thesis about that animal's representation in culture and science. The first section, "The Symbolic Trash Animal," examines cultural and psychological constructs of species, in effect revealing more about human fears than of the animals themselves. The middle sections, "The Native Trash Animal," "The Invasive Trash Animal," and "The Urban Trash Animal," shift from the symbolic to the biological animal and ask whether conflicts with humans are unavoidable or are a result of unrealistic desires to dominate animals and environments. The closing section, "Moving beyond Trash," focuses on ways to reimagine human relationships with animals regarded as having little or no value, suggesting ultimately that the concept of the trash animal, not the animal itself, is what we should discard.

Part I, "The Symbolic Trash Animal," looks to animals that are symbolically associated with what Western people—North Americans primarily—find filthy, dangerous, or evil. These essays make clear that it is human misunderstanding of animals such as the ring-billed gull, wolf, and Mormon cricket that places them in the category of trash. By investigating the narratives, symbols, fears, and other cultural baggage associated with these species and, as Bergman says, "the space to make for them in our lives," these authors challenge us to perceive these animals in new ways. These essays construct the varied ways species come to be maligned and question if these animals deserve the consequences of human prejudice.

In chapter 1, "See Gull: Cultural Blind Spots and the Disappearance of the Ring-Billed Gull in Toronto," Gavan P. L. Watson asks the reader to consider the nature of our relationship with a species that is both ubiquitous and maligned, the ring-billed gull, although it is rarely called that. Watson argues that though the bird is prevalent in the urban environment of Toronto, the fact that residents of the city do not know the bird's actual name or its natural history makes it virtually invisible. This impedes a nuanced understanding of this species, creating a psychological distance between human and bird. By identifying the ring-billed gull as a seagull or "shit hawk," residents do not engage with this bird's unique natural history, a story that could inspire appreciation of this creature that was at one time nearly extinct. Instead, ring-billed gulls are viewed as the ultimate trash bird, disturbing the peace with their raucous calls, defecating on human-built spaces, and thriving in the wake of excess trash produced by the city's human inhabitants. Ultimately, Watson warns that it is not this "seagull" that should be blamed for its irritating success as a species; rather, the residents themselves and the trash produced by their lifestyles of excess must be recognized as the real problem.

In chapter 2, "Hunger Makes the Wolf," Charles Bergman reflects on the ways humans need animals we perceive as dangerous, like wolves. In his personal quest to see wolves in the wild, Bergman interviews scientists, crawls into a den to come face to face with the wild animal, and presents a multitude of cultural interpretations of the wolf that includes wolf as mother, lover, nurturer, devil, sexual deviant, thief, insatiable hunger, symbol of the untamable wild, vermin, scourge, and murderer. As such, the wolf has been much maligned. Even "the great conservationist president," Theodore Roosevelt, called the wolf "the beast of waste and desolation." Bergman looks critically at the efforts that are made by wildlife biologists to objectively understand the wolf and its role in the landscape, but concludes that wolf management is ultimately left to humans and their desires to neuter the landscape and tame wolves. Even in one of the wildest and most untamed places in the world, the Arctic, the author observes wolves scavenging at the dump, a scene that fills him with a sense of loss. The fact that wolves may harm the interests of hunters or livelihoods of ranchers makes them loathsome for many, but Bergman argues these conflicting creatures are necessary to our wildlands and our spirits. The wolf as metaphor resonates in our psyches in deep and meaningful ways that can't be quantified by science or sit easily in our domestic lives. Wolves connect us to the primal call of the wild, the wilderness within.

Catherine Puckett looks at a creature more maligned than the wolf and equally endangered, the eastern diamondback rattlesnake, in chapter 3, "Beauty and the Beast." A biologist who has studied reptiles on different continents, Puckett understands the snake from a scientist's perspective but journeys beyond a scientific understanding of the species of rattlesnake she encounters at her home in Florida. Puckett looks at the cultural stigma surrounding snakes in the South informed by religion, myth, and family and recounts the harms that are inflicted on creatures that, while poisonous, are also "more polite than people." Rattlesnakes, like snakes everywhere, are mythological animals as much as they are real animals; they are perceived as worthless, dangerous, and evil and are treated accordingly. As a biologist, Puckett understands the snake presents few dangers if one has an understanding of its habits and does not intentionally mess with these creatures, which are worthy of respect. She also sees the snake as an ally, one who has a secret knowledge of the wilderness she loves. The rattlesnake is an outsider in its own habitat, as she finds herself to be—an unconventional Southern woman living with her husband's all-too-conventional family as she enters middle age.

Christina Robertson asks readers to deconstruct their fears and prejudices of locusts and questions if toxic campaigns to control these insects are warranted in chapter 4, "Managing Apocalypse: A Cultural History of the Mormon Cricket." A symbol of the apocalypse, overwhelming to the human senses when they swarm but a natural citizen of the Great Plains nonetheless, these locusts are targets of toxic eradication campaigns. Robertson examines the history of insect eradication campaigns in the West, which continue today despite negligible results and toxic consequences up the food chain from birds to predators and livestock, to humans. Mormon crickets serve as a symbol for misguided land management policies and a silent apocalypse—the slow poisoning of our environment and ourselves.

Part II, "The Native Trash Animal," reconsiders engagements with coyotes, prairie dogs, and packrats and reframes the nature of these conflicts from a biological and historical perspective. When the biological behavior of an animal is weighed against human-imposed psychological associations, discourse, and cultural symbolism, the real causes of human–animal conflicts are exposed. These essays scrutinize the conventional way people view conflicts with wildlife and propose new ways of thinking about and handling inevitable conflicts with animals.

In chapter 5, "One Nation under Coyote, Divisible," Lisa Couturier contemplates the migration of coyotes into the eastern urban landscapes surrounding her home near Washington, D.C. Even though Couturier has never seen a coyote, she identifies with the creature making a home in the urban and agrarian landscapes of the East. She is drawn to the creature to fulfill "a need . . . the origins of which . . . had grown from the attempts we all make to understand the misunderstood creatures in one's life, whether they be people or animals." The coyote is feared because it is both unfamiliar and misunderstood by many. Couturier discusses the violence that is strategically enacted on coyotes by government organizations even though coyotes rarely molest livestock and serve as natural and free rodent control on the landscape. As coyotes migrate east, filling the niche the extirpated wolves left behind, the author welcomes the wild and unknown into her suburban landscape and life.

When Kelsi Nagy decides to turn her horse out on a pasture inhabited by prairie dogs, she explores the national controversy surrounding prairie dogs. In chapter 6, "Prairie Dog and Prejudice," she examines general perceptions of prairie dogs, which have caused people to assume these creatures are invaders that destroy the landscape, harm cattle, and spread the plague. Nagy learns that the prejudice surrounding prairie dogs has generated unfounded myths about these creatures that are actually an important part of the prairie ecosystem. Even though prairie dogs provide the only food and shelter for the most endangered mammal in North America, measures to control prairie dogs continue on public lands. The battle between ranchers and environmentalists has made prairie dogs the most controversial wildlife species in North America. Nagy shows that imposed prejudices toward unwanted wildlife reveals imposed values toward wildlife that are difficult to overcome no matter how valuable prairie dogs are to the Great Plains ecosystem.

In chapter 7, "Nothing Says Trash like Packrats: Nature Boy Meets Bushy Tail," Michael P. Branch does battle with the wily packrats living in the crawl space of his desert home and challenges us to reconsider the kind of neighbors we are for wildlife. Once packrats move into his newly built home outside Reno, Nevada, Branch looks to his own ignorance and agency in creating habitat for packrats. His solutions work with the animal's behavior but not without first having blood on his hands. Even though a packrat can be considered one of the worst kinds of invader—a messy, smelly rodent that carries off house keys and baby pacifiers—the author learns that there is a value to the rodent's hoarding behaviors. A native mammal in North America, packrats have been bringing artifacts of nature (and now culture) to their middens for centuries. Their nests, some of them in continuous use for fifty thousand years, are time capsules of the natural history of the Great Desert Basin and a treasure trove for climate researchers that use plant and animal artifacts preserved in ancient middens to analyze past climate trends. Branch concludes that these creatures have become the ultimate trash animal, having turned trash—animal droppings, twigs, leaves, bones, and berries—into scientific treasures, a window into the biologic past.

The essays in Part III, "The Invasive Trash Animal," explore the introduction of species to North America as part of the larger colonial desire to remake landscape. These essays treat animals that were too successful in acclimating, attesting to the unforeseen consequences of human attempts to manipulate the nonhuman world. The animals represented in this section—Canada geese, starlings, and common carp—highlight the current politically and rhetorically charged issue of invasive alien species. These authors point to the fact that human agency led to the release of these invasive species and reflect on how we as individuals make meaning with biologic forces far beyond our control.

In chapter 8, "Canadas: From Conservation Success to Flying Carp," Bernard Quetchenbach questions what it means to lose the wild rhythms of nature, like the migration of geese, and to have them replaced with year-round resident geese. While wild geese bring to mind iconic images of untamed nature and the changing seasons, resident geese are lumped into the category of nuisance animals with raccoons and gulls. Even birders make distinctions between migratory and urban geese. Like other nuisance species, human activity led to year-round populations of geese, by-products of twentieth-century hunters who bred captive geese as decoys. Once released, these semi-wild geese never took to the skies with their migrating kin and settled permanently in urban environments, fouling pristine and orderly sidewalks and golf courses. Quetchenbach looks closely at the dis-ease with which we live with Canadian geese and proposes that "the year-round presence of the once almost-exclusively migratory Canada goose testifies that our actions have far-reaching, unpredictable effects, causing apparently permanent disruptions in what we like to think of as serene, dependable nature."

Charles Mitchell reminds us in chapter 9, "The Bard's Bird; or, The Slings and Arrows of Avicultural Hegemony: A Tragicomedy in Five Acts," that sometimes nature is disturbed by humans for the most fickle reasons. Starlings, one of the most successful and arguably annoying invasives, were introduced as part of a Birds of Shakespeare project by the American Acclimatization Society with the intention of improving the landscape by introducing Old World species to the Americas and elevating the character of the nation's immigrant populations through songbirds mentioned in the famous bard's plays. Today starlings are considered pests that disturb the peace with raucous calls and alfresco gatherings with bird droppings and disrupt agriculture and air travel. Half of all planes that hit flocks of birds crash into murmurations of starlings. While extreme measures are undertaken to control these much-maligned immigrants, including heavy poisoning with a toxin often referred to as starlicide, Mitchell wonders what we are fighting against when we wage campaigns against this successful alien species. Starlings mirror the progress of human immigrants across the continent, they continue to thrive in our environments, and they are here to stay. Mitchell ponders the starling's role in a new world that we have adapted for our own use where starlings thrive through no fault of their own. Might they have filled the niche of other avian predecessors before them? They are an echo of the great flocks of passenger pigeons that they will never replace on the landscape except in our imaginations.

Phillip David Johnson II meditates on fly fishing for carp, invasive species, sport fishing, and what wilderness means in an increasingly post-pristine world in chapter 10, "Fly-Fishing for Carp as a Deeper Aesthetics." The carp is the quintessential trash fish, an exotic, invasive bottom-feeder that thrives in polluted environments. Its reputation often clouds the fact that it was introduced in the United States to restock overfished, polluted waters in the wake of manifest destiny. Though the carp industry continues to thrive, the association of carp with trash and marginalized human groups remains. As sport fish, Johnson finds them worthy adversaries—big, strong, and difficult to catch. Fishing for them in irrigation ditches, city park ponds, and golf courses, he finds solitude that has vanished on the pristine yet crowded trout streams near his home in Colorado. Ultimately, Johnson asks if it is possible to find value fishing for an invasive species in a trashed landscape and what carp reveal about other attitudes toward nature, wilderness, and our relationship with animals.

Part IV, "The Urban Trash Animal," follows animals that thrive in urban spaces and take on the ambivalent attitudes people hold regarding cities. In places, these essays reveal the irony inherent when the biological success of some species would have never been possible without the city and other human-built spaces. This section challenges readers to look beyond cultural constructs that pit humans against animals or that place animals within anthropocentric systems of value.

Carolyn Kraus examines exactly how far a pacifist can be pushed by the cockroaches that have moved into her home in chapter 11, "Metamorphosis in Detroit." Ashamed that the house she shares with her two sons becomes infiltrated by cockroaches, Kraus tries to deal with the problem on her own by learning about cockroach behavior and natural history. While cockroaches are a longtime citizen of the planet and a marvel of survival, Kraus finds they have been loathed for centuries. Throughout history, different cultures have used "cockroach" to belittle or vilify other humans. For example, what we call the German cockroach was called the Russian roach by the

Prussians and the Prussian roach by the Russians. It is a word unfortunately associated with genocide—a metaphor of eradication. Enamored with the fascinating biology of roaches, Kraus finds that it is easier to love the theoretical animal than the insects scurrying through her home. Some conflicts between humans and animals cannot be avoided no matter how many facts are known about them.

In chapter 12, "Kach'i: Garbage Birds in a Hybrid Landscape," James E. Bishop recounts his time living in a crowded city in South Korea. During his tenure in a hyperurban environment, Bishop finds wonder in these magpies, which, unlike North Americans, Koreans admire or see as auspicious omens of good luck. Seeking nature in the city, Bishop discovers how magpies evoke nostalgia for the wild that the city has replaced. He finds beauty in the raucous birds' resourcefulness and in the creatures themselves, gaining an appreciation that replaces the negative perception of the magpie he was taught as a child.

Andrew D. Blechman analyzes the varied campaigns waged against urban pigeons, whose excrement is blamed for destroying a city's beauty, in chapter 13, "Flying Rats," taken from his book *Pigeons: The Fascinating Saga of the World's Most Revered and Reviled Bird* (2006). While pigeons pose no more of a health threat than an average house cat, many people view them as vile and disgusting creatures. Like other trash birds, they are loathed for their ubiquity, their waste, and their ability to thrive in human-built environments. This change in attitude toward pigeons is a recent phenomenon in human history, and Blechman examines their perceived harms and the peculiar place the feral creature holds in Western society. He finds that not everyone loathes pigeons. A handful of people are dedicated advocates to the plight of rock doves. For these modern-day feral pigeon fanciers, the pigeon may serve as a symbol of their own outcast or misfit natures. Ironically, those who are most concerned about pigeon welfare, the feeders, may also be the people standing in the way of effective and humane pigeon management.

The essays in Part V, "Moving beyond Trash," shift emphasis from the critique of human–animal conflicts to the reimagining of peaceful coexistence with problematic animals. If no peaceful way can be found to coexist with some animals, at least much can be learned from a thorough understanding of the conflict, not only about the nature of species but also about human aesthetics, evolution, and the limits of moral thought and action.

In chapter 14, "Kill the Cat That Kills the Bird?," Bruce Barcott writes about the controversy surrounding feral cats and asks some tough questions about the rights of individual animals versus the existence of endangered bird species. Barcott travels to Galveston, Texas, to meet the most notorious cat killer in the United States, Jim Stevenson, an avid birder arrested for shooting feral cats. An exotic species in the United States, house cats that have turned wild are the second-leading cause of wild bird deaths in North America. As urban development creates island ecosystems, bird populations are becoming increasingly sensitive to predation by these unmanaged creatures. Some environmentalists think they should be captured and killed by any means necessary, but opposition by cat lovers to this management strategy is so severe it even has the U.S. legal system in a quandary. Barcott asks us to consider if there are humane ways to manage feral cats and effectively save bird populations.

Kyhl Lyndgaard challenges our perception of a species most people find ugly—the bullhead catfish—in chapter 15, "An Unlimited Take of Ugly: The Bullhead Catfish." Like carp, bullheads are a fish often thrown away by fishermen. Not only do these bottom-feeders have an unsightly appearance, they can thrive in habitats with low oxygen and even radiation. We often disdain creatures that can survive in the habitats we pollute, and in the process we vilify a species with impressive adaptations. The author proposes that an understanding of this native fish's biology and natural history may aid in an aesthetic appreciation of a fish "so ugly, he is, in a way, attractive."

In chapter 16, "A Six-legged Guru: Fear and Loathing in Nature," Jeffrey A. Lockwood engages the reader to find the value of disgust in his meditation on prairie lubber grasshoppers, a sensation that other species deemed trash elicit from humans. The prairie lubber is particularly unique in this category. The insect evades capture by vomiting and defecating on its captor, tapping into the deep and primal instinct of revulsion. Lockwood examines the value that this reaction, akin to fear, may have for humans. While science strives to sanitize our lives, experiences of disgust connect us to our instinctual natures. As much as we would like all our interactions with nature to be clean, safe, and cuddly, "nature . . . is as likely to shit on us as to embrace us." Lockwood asks us to search for value in this experience that both attracts and repels us, revealing our animal natures in all their moral complexity.

Kathleen Dean Moore appeals to both our intellect and our emotion to live lives of compassion and deliberation toward all of creation in chapter 17, "The Parables of the Rats and Mice." Taken from her book *The Pine Island Paradox: Making Connections in a Disconnected World* (2004), Moore examines her own encounters with rats and mice and shares moments of guilt and wonder for animals that many people poison without a second thought.

She exposes the notion of utility inherent in the cost-benefit analysis of the moral theory of utilitarianism and challenges the reader to reexamine what extending moral compassion to these often overlooked creatures might feel like. Ultimately, Moore offers the view that like a pebble thrown into the water, human actions ripple far beyond us, affecting the lives of other species and the environment. Because we are capable of making choices, we also have a moral obligation to recognize there are consequences to our actions. Moore encourages readers to reflect on their behaviors in the natural world and try to minimize harm. This essay shows one way we can reimagine our moral actions toward problematic wildlife.

Confronting the Trash Animal Within

"There is a magpie in all of us," quotes James E. Bishop in his essay for this collection. In this instance, the magpie—a species that caches nonfood items, a behavior it shares with humans—represents the tendency to hoard and becomes a disparaged symbol of human extravagance. Other animals in the collection, notably wolves, rattlesnakes, carp, and cockroaches, may also symbolize unwelcome aspects of human behavior. Representations of maligned species can serve to remind us that our mysterious and occasionally unruly animal natures shape human identities as much as rationality or the ability to use symbolic language does. For better or for worse there exist aspects of any one of these creatures, from carp to cockroaches, in the human psyche. This is because our identity is intertwined with attitudes and beliefs about the nonhuman animals we share our world with. As Laurence Simmons and Philip Armstrong write in *Knowing Animals,*

> The very idea of the human—the way we understand and experience
> ourselves as humans—is closely tied up with ideas about animals.
> Many of the concepts, dispositions and sensibilities that comprise
> "human nature" rely upon perceived differences and similarities
> between nature and culture, reason and instinct, mind and body;
> commonly invoked traits such as humaneness, inhumanity, beast-
> liness, compassion and sentiment.[15]

While there is much to be learned about the animals themselves from these essays, what the authors learn about human beliefs and actions, as well as our culture, can teach us much about the ways nonhuman animals factor into human communities, worldviews, and the many ways animals inform individual identity. For these reasons *Trash Animals* will be of special interest to those who study human–animal relationships in animal-cultural studies, anthrozoology, geography, philosophy, environmental literature, ecocriticism, and animal rights.

Species deemed trash animals are beginning to figure more prominently in the fields of animal-cultural studies and anthrozoology, disciplines that to date have focused primarily on human–animal relationships with companion animals, lab animals, and animals in zoos. The booklets in the Reaction Animal series, full of cultural and biological history and beautifully rendered art, feature an eclectic list of species, some of them— *Mosquito, Pigeon, Rat, Fly*—clear trash animal candidates. This is evidence that species previously considered harmful or insignificant are gaining more attention from authors writing about culture and animals.[16] Articles such as "Getting Their Hands Dirty: Raccoons, Freegans, and Urban 'Trash'"[17] (which focuses on the rhetoric of scavenging used to negatively describe both dumpster divers and urban raccoons, even though scavenging is an economically and ecologically efficient behavior) are being published with growing frequency in journals like *Critical Animal Studies* and *Anthrozoöz. Antennae: The Journal of Nature in Visual Culture* has dedicated three volumes to representations of insects in art, media, literature, and human cuisine. And the books *Insect Poetics* (2006) and *Poetics of the Hive: The Insect Metaphor in Literature* (2001) both look at the way our understanding of insects and their communities has shaped how we use language and understand our own communities.[18] Trash species confront us with our often-conflicted perceptions of the natural world as well as attitudes about aesthetics and ethics, all vital to how we create and understand human communities and identity. As problems with pollution, extinction, and the loss of wild landscapes intensify, species that flourish in a postpristine environment will continue to factor more prominently into discussions about animals, identity, and worldviews. *Trash Animals* adds to the growing conversation about conflict species in culture and opens the door for further conversations and scholarship in this field.

The animals and ideas discussed in *Trash Animals* are also of conceptual value to the field of geography. Questions about the literal and figurative space we make for animals are already being considered in this discipline. Human attitudes toward unwanted or problematic wildlife provide a conceptually rich topic of inquiry for this field. In his essay "How Pigeons Became Rats: The Cultural-Spatial Logic of Problem Animals," Colin Jerolmack analyzes the negative rhetoric used toward certain species, pigeons and house sparrows in particular. The vehement language used toward these urban dwellers reveals far more than the fact that they are unpopular city residents. He writes, "Tracing the problematization of animals signifies how the nature/culture boundary is conceived, negotiated, and protected."[19] Confronting species that don't abide by human-conceived boundaries: nature/culture, wild/domestic, human property / animal habitat, our conception of the world is a function of our culture and not inherent in the world.

If these categories are not inherent in the world but are on some level a choice—a choice perpetuated by one's culture—then understanding the human values embodied in these categories tell us something about our moral behavior in the world. In the collection *Animal Spaces, Beastly Places: New Geographies of Human–Animal Relations,* the essay "(Un)Ethical Geographies of Human–Non-human Relations: Encounters, Collectives, and Spaces" discusses the way in which we create categories for animals to inhabit on the landscape—in homes or on farms, in nature preserves or zoos—which reveals our moral attitudes toward the natural world.[20] If we are aware our categories have a moral impact on these creatures' lives, is the world we created the world we would choose to live in? These concepts also become less rigid and more fluid when we recognize that conceptual maps applied to human–animal relationships differ in various cultures and historical times. For instance, magpies are revered in Korea; in China carp are seen as both auspicious and delicious; pigeons, coyotes, and starlings have all been revered at different moments in history. People of the Jain religion continue to recognize the moral importance of even the tiniest insect. Even as our attitudes toward animals and the landscape are revealed as projections of our imaginations, scholars of geography question our moral agency toward non-human animals because, as Jerolmack states, "While the modernist understanding of the nature/culture relationship is certainly contested by scholars and activist, it is still a powerful organizing principle that is not merely a matter of utility but is also a moral and ontological matter."[21] Regarding trash animals, it appears the fields of cultural studies and geography will grow in dialogue with philosophy and the disciplines of environmental and animal ethics.

Many of the creatures in *Trash Animals* reveal the limits of human moral agency: spiders, cockroaches, and rattlesnakes to name a few. Invasive species, such as carp and feral cats, that threaten the habitat or survival of other native species reveal tensions inherent in the fields of environmental and animal ethics. In particular, the question of whether the rights of individual animals (championed by philosophers of animal rights) are more important than the survival of a species (the rights of a species are often valued above the rights of individual animals for environmental ethicists) is touched on in chapter 14, "Kill the Cat That Kills the Bird?" by Bruce Barcott. Feral cats, a nonnative species in North America, are a significant factor in declining populations of some native birds. When philosopher Holmes Rolston III is asked which species is of more value, he replies that the suffering of an exotic feral cat is irrelevant to the survival of a native species. Is the suffering of feral cats truly irrelevant? On a practical level, does this rationale appear moral or appealing to those who manage wildlife or to volunteers who work with feral cats? Questions like these are raised throughout this collection as invasive species come into direct conflict with the rights of native animals. Even problematic native species like wolves and prairie dogs make us question how humans assign natural value to certain species and not to others.

While the topic of trash animals lends itself to creating philosophic dichotomies like this environmental ethics versus animal rights conundrum, we hope that *Trash Animals* creates a conversation where people can conceive of solutions that move beyond dichotomies. *The contributors* challenge readers to reimagine our relationships with nonhuman animals and advocate for better, more intelligent, more humane management strategies. Environmental and animal ethics can play a central role in this endeavor. Questions of value, aesthetics, animal autonomy, and human moral agency toward problematic wildlife are all topics that are fertile philosophical ground, touched on throughout the book.

Environmental literature—fiction, poetry, and creative nonfiction—can also help us grasp these complex topics regarding wildlife through the use of narrative. The essays in *Trash Animals* are based in narrative to draw together the personal and the theoretical issues addressed in the collection. Some are taken from literature that focuses on animals: *Wild Echoes* (chapter 2), *The Hopes of Snakes* (chapter 5), *Pigeons* (chapter 13), and *Pine Island Paradox* (chapter 17) are all books that address complexities of human–animal relationships from a personal point of view. Trash animals may also be found in some literature that focuses specifically on urban nature, such as *City Wilds: Essays and Stories about Urban Nature* and *Urban Nature: Poems about Wildlife in the City*.[22] Even in human-built landscapes, untamed creatures live autonomous lives. These creatures may breed fear, disgust, or loathing in some urban residents, but they may also inspire joy, wonder, and compassion in other city dwellers. Literature can also illuminate the lives of nonhuman animals through our imaginations in ways that other, more theoretical disciplines cannot or choose not to invoke.

The species in *Trash Animals,* and other species like them, have carved a small but growing niche for themselves in a variety of disciplines that focus on human–animal relationships. Exploring the limitations and tension of our relationships with animals, especially those we come into conflict with, reveals both human limitation and transcendence. On a personal level one cannot read these essays without being confronted by their own problematic relationship with the natural world and having to face the trash animal within.

Conclusion

We are aware that conflicts between humans and nonhuman animals are inevitable—at times unavoidable. The contributors to this collection ask readers to set aside their preconceived notions and anthropocentric concerns for a moment and consider the realities of other living beings in a new light. This exercise draws on our capacities as moral creatures. But this may not be as much a feat of moral imagination as it is of common sense. In Robert Sullivan's delightful book *Rats: Observations on the History and Habitat of the City's Most Unwanted Inhabitant,* he describes an alley full of trash bags as "pristine rat habitat" and likens rats rifling through trash bags in a New York City alley to grizzly bears fishing for spawning salmon in a wild stream.[23] It is no mystery that species flourish with so many resources at their disposal. Gavan Watson, in chapter 1, "See Gull," asks, "If the ring-billed gull is hated for its scavenging on our own urban leftovers, why are we not implicating ourselves in the lifestyle that leads to creation of the waste?" Instead of vilifying scavengers that capitalize on an efficient survival strategy, we could assume responsibility for the vast amount of food thrown away every year. According to the U.S. Environmental Protection Agency, as of 2010 food waste represents the single-largest component of municipal solid waste reaching landfills and incinerators.[24] Are animals to blame for flourishing in the abundant habitat we create?

The essays here ask us to consider other acts of moral imagination and common sense to conceive of better, more effective, more humane solutions for human–wildlife conflicts. What if building houses for urban pigeons and collecting their eggs were the solution to effective pigeon management in cities? What if embracing prairie dogs as a keystone species was the most effective means to preserving other rare species of native wildlife on the Great Plains? What if more people took the time to learn about the behavior of species like packrats to minimize conflicts before they set out poison? What if the money spent poisoning or shooting unwanted species like starlings and coyotes by Wildlife Services (a branch of the USDA) were instead given to farmers to supplement lost crops or livestock due to wildlife? These essays invite readers to consider new relationships between humans and conflict species and the realities of these relationships.

Conceiving of new attitudes toward unwanted wildlife requires, at bare minimum, an understanding of the values and meanings inherent in the language used to discuss them. Perhaps new rhetoric and cultural metaphors need to be created for a different future with these species to evolve. At the very least we need to tell new stories about so-called trash animals and their habitats. Jenny Price echoes this sentiment in her essay, "Thirteen Ways of Seeing Nature in L.A.," in which she identifies the "core trouble" with contemporary nature writing. She proposes, "Nature writers have given endless paeans to the wonders of wildness since Thoreau fled to Walden Pond, but need to tell us far more about our everyday lives in the places we actually live."[25] Of course wild animals are a part of our lives, especially in city wilds. The essays in this collection can be counted among the new stories being told about nature. We may be reluctant to embrace these new stories about wildlife and their habitats because many of these species remind us that we are living in a postpristine world, one that is arguably a diminished one from the world our ancestors lived in. Instead of vilifying the creatures that thrive in this increasingly urbanized and polluted environment, it behooves us to first understand how we have participated in its creation and how we might go about improving our shared world while we can.

While people passionately debate the usefulness, worthlessness, or the destructiveness of certain species, those species continue to forge lives on the margins—in rivers and lakes, on prairies and mountains, in cities, in our backyards, and under our kitchen sinks. As many of the essays in this collection point out, the more one learns about a trash animal, the more that animal seems prophetically similar to the human species. Animals that successfully inhabit new environments, alter landscapes, and disrupt ecosystems remind us, uncomfortably, of ourselves. This likeness demonstrates that important social questions underlay animal issues. These essays force us to ask who we are as humans and where we fit into a world that existed billions of years before the arrival of *Homo sapiens* and will last billions of years into the future. One thing, though, will be for certain. Our species will be outlived by more than one of the animals treated in this collection.[26]

Notes

1. Jenny Price, "Thirteen Ways of Seeing Nature in L.A.: We Need to Rewrite the Stories We Tell about Nature, and L.A. Is the Best Place to Do It," *Believer* 33 (April 2006): 8.

2. Charles Bergman, *Wild Echoes: Encounters with the Most Endangered Animals in North America* (New York: McGraw-Hill, 1990), 10.

3. *Oxford English Dictionary*, 2nd ed., s.v., "Trash"; House of Commons, *The Wealth of Great Britain in the Ocean* (London, 1749), 51.

4. Tom Reed, "A Wyoming Trapper Seeks Pelts and Beauty," *High Country News*, April 12, 1999, http://www.hcn.org/issues/152/4919. Though some claim the term "trash animal" was invented by animal-rights activists, it has been documented on multiple occasions that trappers use the term as well.

5. Aldo Leopold, *Sand County Almanac* (New York: Oxford University Press, 1949), 210.

6. Mary Douglas, *Purity and Danger* (New York: Routledge, 1966), 44, 45.

7. Donna Harroway, *When Species Meet* (Minneapolis: University of Minnesota Press, 2008), 37.

8. See Alan Burdick, *Out of Eden* (New York: Farrar, Strauss, Giraux, 2005).

9. Greg Kennedy, *An Ontology of Trash: The Disposable and Its Problematic Nature* (Albany: State University of New York Press, 2007), xvi–xvii.

10. Susan Strasser, *Waste and Want: A Social History of Trash* (New York: Metropolitan Books), 5.

11. PETA mission statement, http://www.peta.org/about/default.aspx.

12. Ted Williams, "Red Baiting," *Audubon*, November–December 2001, http://archive.audubonmagazine.org/incite/incite0111.html.

13. Hal Herzog, *Some We Love, Some We Hate, Some We Eat: Why It's So Hard to Think Straight about Animals* (New York: Harper Collins, 2010), 66.

14. David Quammen, "The Face of a Spider," in *Flight of the Iguana: A Sidelong View of Science and Nature* (New York: Touchstone, 1988), 7–8.

15. Laurence Simmons and Philip Armstrong, eds., *Knowing Animals* (The Netherlands: Koninklijke Brill NV, 2007), 1–2.

16. All published by Reaktion Books, London: Richard Jones, *Mosquito* (2012); Barbara Allen, *Pigeon* (2009); Jonathan Burt, *Rat* (2005); Steven Connor, *Fly* (2006).

17. Lauren Corman, "Getting Their Hands Dirty: Raccoons, Freegans, and Urban 'Trash,'" *Critical Animal Studies* 9, no. 3 (2011): 28–61.

18. Eric C. Brown, ed., *Insect Poetics* (Minneapolis: University of Minnesota Press, 2006); Christopher Hollingsworth, *Poetics of the Hive: Insect Metaphor in Literature* (Iowa City: University of Iowa Press, 2001); "Insect Poetics," 2 vols., special issue, *Antennae: The Journal of Animals in Visual Culture*, no. 3 (Autumn 2007), http://www.antennae.org.uk; "Insectia," special issue, *Antennae: The Journal of Animals in Visual Culture*, no. 11 (Autumn 2009), http://www.antennae.org.uk.

19. Colin Jerolmack, "How Pigeons Became Rats: The Cultural-Spatial Logic of Problem Animals," *Social Problems* 55, no. 1 (February 2008): 72–94.

20. Chris Philo and Chris Wilbert, *Animal Spaces, Beastly Places: New Geographies of Human–Animal Relations* (London: Routledge, 2000).

21. Jerolmack, "How Pigeons Became Rats," 5.

22. Terrell F. Dixon, ed., *City Wilds: Essays and Stories about Urban Nature* (Athens: University of Georgia Press, 2002); Laure-Anne Bosselaar, ed., *Urban Nature: Poems about Wildlife in the City* (Minnespolis: Milkweed Editions, 2000).

23. Robert Sullivan, *Rats: Observations on the History and Habitat of the City's Most Unwanted Inhabitant* (London & New York: Bloomsbury, 2004), 70–71.

24. http://www.epa.gov/osw/conserve/materials/organics/food/fd-basic.htm.

25. Price, "Thirteen Ways of Seeing Nature in L.A.," 5.

26. This point is made by Carolyn Kraus in chapter 11, "Metamorphosis in Detroit."

I. THE SYMBOLIC TRASH ANIMAL

1 See Gull

Cultural Blind Spots and the Disappearance of the Ring-Billed Gull in Toronto

Gavan P. L. Watson

FOR MOST TORONTONIANS, the organism known as a ring-billed gull *(Larus delawarensis)* does not exist. This is an impressive feat for a large (mostly), white bird considered to be the most abundant gull in North America. In Toronto, gulls are some of the bigger birds that are regularly seen, and ring-bills are no exception. Beak to tail, their size is equivalent to the diameter of a discarded automobile tire, and with their wings spread in anticipation of flight, ring-bills have a foot to spare on either side of a typical city sidewalk. Though they are considered large birds in the spectrum of their greater avian family, ring-bills are still spry, weighing in the range of two quarter-pound hamburgers,[1] but they are of average size and weight when compared to other gull species.

Plastic in their behavior, ring-bills are opportunistic feeders that have adapted well to human-manipulated environments. One such place is the city of Toronto, home to many ring-billed gulls and my home, too. Historically, ring-bills have had a fish-based diet.[2] Attracted by the promise of a fish dinner, ring-billed gulls have always had a presence along the shoreline of Lake Ontario (and its various postglacial incarnations), including the land now occupied by Toronto. Since ring-billed gulls are omnivorous, their diet, in an urban area like Toronto, has changed, now consisting of 7 percent fish, 22 percent insects, 23 percent earthworms, and 42 percent waste.[3] It seems as though ring-bills eat whatever they can easily get their black-ringed beaks on.

The ring-billed gull was likely named because of the presence of that small black ring around the tip of its yellow bill. Both male and female adults look the same with brilliant white heads and underparts, light gray backs, black wingtips, yellow legs, and webbed feet. The plumage combination of white, gray, and black is beautiful, but their eyes are striking: a sulfur-yellow iris surrounds a jet-black pupil, and around the eye is a small margin of featherless skin that is a brilliant blood-orange. Together, the colors create a concentrated flash of color that I find captivating. Since moving to Toronto, ring-bills have become a part of my travels throughout the city. I see them walking along the shore of Lake Ontario; as a flying flash of white contrasting with the tall, dark-hued buildings of the downtown core; as soaring specks high above my midtown apartment building; and even nine miles from the lake, swimming in the various water features located throughout the York University campus. When I look around, ring-billed gulls are everywhere in my Toronto.

It is obvious that these birds have been successful in their adaptation to the human-manipulated environment—too successful, perhaps. When thinking of birds and urban spaces, cities and metropolises, the rock dove (*Columba livia*) is often considered the quintessential urban inhabitant because of its ubiquity (and these birds are maligned in the eyes of many because of it). In Toronto's case, the ring-billed gull fills the niche of the maligned, omnipresent urban avian.

Part of their ever-presence is due to the fact that, during the summer months, Toronto's waterfront is home to, at last count, approximately sixty thousand nesting pairs of ring-bills.[4] Since the discovery of nine nesting pairs in the early 1970s[5] on a three-mile, 617-acre peninsula created in Toronto Harbour popularly known as the Leslie Street Spit, ring-billed gulls have had an important relationship with this particular landscape. Created from the urban tailings of the city's growth during the last half-century, the Leslie Street Spit was originally intended by the Toronto Harbour Commission to act as a breakwater for an improved Outer Harbour.[6] Known then as the Eastern Headland, the spit was terraformed with "sandy dredged spoil" from the bottom of the Outer Harbour and "fill" (vernacular for waste) from the city's construction sites.[7] As you walk along the spit today, in between the fields of goldenrod (*Solidago*) and coppices of poplar (*Populus*), evidence of these origins emerge from the cairns of discarded concrete and dunes made of rebar. The anticipated increase in shipping that the Eastern Headland was intended to facilitate never materialized, and this peninsula's identity as a breakwater began to disappear. In its place, Tommy Thompson Park emerged, now managed by the local conservation authority,[8] and with it a new, popular identity as the largest "area of existing natural habitat on the waterfront of Canada's largest city."[9] Perhaps less well known is the spit's status as home to 10 percent of the Canadian population of breeding ring-bills and approximately one-third of the ring-bill nesting pairs in the Great Lakes region.[10]

And yet for the majority of those living in Toronto, ring-bills disappear. When Torontonians notice a ring-billed gull, they likely see a seagull instead. At first, this may not seem like such an egregious error—they are at least still identifying these birds as gulls. However, I suggest that there is power in the way we see and know organisms. How and what we call the others in the more-than-human world provides a powerful indication of the state of relations with these organisms. In the case of ring-billed gulls, it is their urban ubiquity, their everydayness, that has led to their disappearance and speaks of a relationship that, quite simply, does not exist.

"Seagull" is a tricky name to use, as around Toronto there is not a drop of seawater to be found. To reach the Atlantic Ocean and to be true seagull, a ring-bill would have to travel over 430 miles (and I am measuring *as the gull flies*) across Lake Ontario, upper New York State, and the length of Massachusetts before being able to land in the briny water of Boston Harbor. "Lakegull" may be a more appropriate moniker, but even this classification is problematic. While there may be thousands of ring-billed gulls living close to Toronto, they are not the only gull species to be found. The two most common gulls in Toronto are the ring-billed gull and the herring gull *(L. argentatus)*. Superficially similar, these two gull species differ in size, with the larger of the two, the herring gull, averaging twenty-five inches in length, four inches larger than the ring-bill. These two gulls also differ in the coloration of their legs and bills: the herring gull has pink legs and a bright red dot on the bill's lower mandible.

Most people do not realize that the seagull they are familiar with does not really exist. While it can be said that adults of both species of common Toronto gulls have light gray backs and similar shapes, when one knows what to look for and attends to the organism in front of them, it takes little effort to distinguish between ring-billed and herring gulls.

Members of our urban community misidentify ring-billed and herring gulls due to their distance from these birds. However, rather than physical space, the distance that I am describing is psychological space, manifesting itself in the observers' lack of interest. Psychological distance can mean that no matter how closely or frequently we see these birds, ring-billed and herring gulls' identities are homogenized as seagulls. In this act, the individual distinctiveness of these species disappears and a generic seagull emerges. More important, this loss of identity prematurely forecloses any opportunity to know more about these birds. Stereotypes, or overgeneralized referents, emerge in dominant discourse that reinforces anthropocentric ideals of what nature should be: meek, unusual, melodious, and accessible on our terms.

Ring-billed gulls suffer guilt by association because they are seen as birds that will steal food and defecate on you. Further implicating ring-bills as pests are those birds found near restaurants foraging through discarded fast-food containers. Often experienced as "that screeching bird," the ring-billed gull's vocalizations are interpreted as annoying and harsh. In a setting (such as a communal nesting location, landfill site, or location of available food) where there are many ring-bills, the noise is a "disturbance."[11] Ring-billed gulls are social and vocal and often, in pursuit of food, will "squabble" and "fight"—anthropocentric interpretations that reinforce negative caricatures of ring-bills. Their perceived stereotypical performance is filled with actions that do not endear them to us: ring-billed gulls are often seen as the "seagull" that flies into parking lots and bickers with other gulls in the effort to devour our urban flotsam and jetsam. At their worst, ring-billed gulls have come to be known by the crass moniker "shithawks." While we tend to find birds of prey, such as hawks, charismatic and engaging (witness the multitude of images of majestic raptors, soaring overhead, nary a piece of guano in sight), the name "shithawk" belittles: the wide variety of behaviors and actions that ring-billed gulls undertake are ignored, and the ring-billed gull's behavioral variety is condensed into a bird that hunts humans down with the intent to shit on them. Often observed as the most numerous species at landfill sites,[12] ring-billed gulls are implicated, literally, as "garbage" birds: they eat it, they excrete it, they are it.

Rather than being dismissed as (a) waste, the thousands of ring-billed gulls found in Toronto should be cause for celebration. At one time in the not-so-distant past, ring-billed gulls were not such a fixture of the Toronto waterfront. Rather, they were emblems of fashion (literally), with their bright white feathers and wings fastened to hats. Throughout the nineteenth century and into the early twentieth century, milliners worked to meet consumer demand calling for bird plumage affixed to hats.[13] A globalized trade, economies of scale required that birds were killed in exceedingly high numbers (up to 200 million birds a year at the beginning of the twentieth century) throughout the world, and feathers were shipped to meet the needs of what was in vogue in the cities of Paris, London, and New York.[14] As victims of this trade, ring-billed gulls were extirpated from portions of their range,[15] and Eastern North American populations of gulls, terns, and herons were depressed to such a point that people feared that their populations would never recover.[16] In response, a groundswell of support emerged in the conservation of these species. Laws protecting nongame birds were passed; organizations promoting bird conservation, such as the Audubon Society, were founded; and partly due to the vivid descriptions of plume hunters' methods, bird feathers fell out of fashion.[17] Populations of these so-called plumage species increased, and with them, ring-billed gulls began to re-populate areas of their historical range.

Colonial nesters, these birds often return to breed at the colony where they hatched; adults can often be found within feet of their last nest, sur-rounded by thousands of other ring-bills.[18] The breeding population of ring-billed gulls on the Leslie Street Spit reached an estimated high of seventy thousand pairs in 1984.[19] This reestablishment of (an exceedingly) viable ring-billed gull breeding population should be seen as a success of conserva-tion. This success is a part of the spit's transformation from *paene insula* to *panae natura*: what was once an isthmus of waste is now a three-mile-long peninsula thriving with life.[20] In this change of space, the home of the ring-bill's nesting colony is gaining status, both culturally as one of Toronto's larg-est green spaces available for recreation (as evidenced by the transformation of "the Eastern Headland" into "Tommy Thompson Park") and biologically as a recognized "Important Bird Area" by Bird Life International.[21] In turn, the ring-bill has come under the watchful eye of those intent on manag-ing this space. It was decided that the ring-billed gull was doing *too* well in their recovery and that these birds should now be seen as a threat to that newly emerging nature. With as many as a quarter million ring-billed gulls[22] in Toronto at the end of a breeding season, management efforts have been undertaken since 1984 to limit the size of their colony. These control mea-sures have included a falconer and falcon (given the presence of a predator, either the birds are scared away or the falcon chases, captures, and kills the ring-bills); pyrotechnics (noise-making firecrackers that go off randomly, which is meant to disturb the ring-bills enough to discourage nesting); ar-tificial owls; and collecting and oiling eggs (which effectively kills the devel-oping bird by suffocation).[23]

When the few nesting pairs of ring-billed gulls along with other related species were found on the Leslie Street Spit in the late 1970s, it was suggested that the conservation of these colonies was "desirable."[24] Now, in their turn from conservation success to biological nuisance, ring-bills are seen as a menace to the other important birds found on the Leslie Street Spit due to the colony's consumptive nature—consumption in this case being breeding habitat. If the ring-billed gull colony was left unmanaged, it is suggested the colony could grow as large as 180,000 breeding pairs[25] and claim breeding territory from other (more important, reads the subtext) birds. In the call to limit the expansion of the ring-billed gull's colony, new value is placed on the created landscape of the Leslie Street Spit. No longer considered garbage, the land has been transformed into a valuable space for conservation and recreation, but at the expense of species that, with their presence, helped to create the Leslie Street Spit. In this turn, we fall prey to a kind of double movement that is evidence of our own fickle memory: the ring-billed gull now becomes the waste on the Leslie Street Spit, an overabundant bird limiting the richness of this so-called accidental wilderness.[26]

In my experience, we project our own neuroses about urban living onto the birds that share the landscape with us. The ring-billed gull has come to represent the results of our own contested urban living arrangements. What we find problematic with these birds, we should find problematic about our own city existence. If the ring-billed gull is loathed for their large numbers and success in spreading across North America, what does that say about our own colonial actions? If the ring-billed gull is hated for its scavenging on our own urban leftovers, why are we not implicating ourselves in the lifestyle that leads to creation of the waste? In vilifying an organism that readily adapts itself to new locations, easily takes advantage of new sources of food, and through little claim to happenstance becomes a roaring biological success, we are vilifying our own ecological record. While it is not surprising to discover our limited perspective when it comes to characterizing ring-billed gulls, it is problematic that we ignore our own animality, that which makes us human, reflected by such a similar organism.

So why are ring-billed gulls flourishing? Ring-bills not only reflect human behavior, they depend on it. Simply put, their success is due to our presence. Regardless of our contested past with these birds, ring-bills in the last century have developed a relationship with us that is of great benefit to them. There is no question that the Toronto experience of ring-billed gulls is by any measure unique: their success in reestablishing and expanding their historical range has come with our (unwitting or not) assistance. It is, in fact, these successes in adapting and flourishing in human-manipulated environments that have fated ring-bills to their status of maligned species. Humans and ring-billed gulls are well suited for each other, so much so that I envision that ring-billed gulls operate as the smaller member of a symbiotic relationship: the benefits that Toronto ring-billed gulls have gained from our presence are obvious—land on which to create a breeding colony and easy access to food are two of the most important. As distasteful as we might find it, we also benefit from the ring-bill's apparent eagerness to eat our waste.

But ring-bills provide us something a little more subtle. Regardless of our personal preference, their presence is inextricably interwoven into what is Toronto. Just as it would be no less a disaster today if ring-billed gulls disappeared from our urban setting as they did a century ago, ring-bills are part of the complex set of relationships that exist (often hidden) within the living city. If we are open to their presence and, in turn, an awareness of the heterogeneity of living beings in an urban setting, we can include the ring-billed gull in the making and telling of our city stories—our own lives. In ring-billed gulls' representation as disgusting or dirty, it is made that much more difficult for those who find themselves with a ring-billed gull to see their intrinsic animality and value. In beginning to understand the ring-billed gull as something more than garbage, we begin to engage with the more-than-human world from a different ethical alignment. It is an ethic that begins with the assumption that there is value in difference and worth in the unexpected and openness to discovering value in otherness, be that bird, animal, or human.

Notes

1. Cornell Lab of Ornithology, "Ring-Billed Gull: Detailed Page," Cornell Lab of Ornithology, http://www.allaboutbirds.org/guide/Ring-billed_Gull/lifehistory/nc.

2. Jennifer L. Newbrey, Michael A. Bozek, and Neal D. Niemuth, "Effects of Lake Characteristics and Human Disturbance on the Presence of Piscivorous Birds in Northern Wisconsin, USA," *Waterbirds* 28, no. 4 (2005): 478–86.

3. William G. Wilson and Edward D. Cheskey, "Leslie Street Spit, Tommy Thompson Park: Important Bird Area Conservation Plan" (Bird Life Canada, 2001), 57.

4. Ibid.

5. H. Blokpoel and P. M. Fetterolf, "Colonization by Gulls and Terns of the Eastern Headland, Toronto Outer Harbour," *Bird Banding* 49, no. 1 (1978): 59–65.

6. Wilson and Cheskey, "Leslie Street Spit, Tommy Thompson Park."

7. Blokpoel and Fetterolf, "Colonization by Gulls and Terns of the Eastern Headland, Toronto Outer Harbour," 59.

8. Toronto and Region Conservation Authority, "Spit Construction," http://www.tommythompsonpark.ca/.

9. Wilson and Cheskey, "Leslie Street Spit, Tommy Thompson Park," 7.

10. Ibid.

11. Hans Blokpoel and Gaston Tessier, "Control of Ring-Billed Gulls and Herring Gulls Nesting at Urban and Industrial Sites in Ontario, 1987–1990," paper presented at the Eastern Wildlife Damage Control Conferences, University of Nebraska, 1991.

12. Hillary Boyle Cressey, *The Comparative Foraging Ecologies of a Scavenging*

Guild of Birds at Two Northern Virginia Landfills (Fairfax, Va.: George Mason University, 2002), 109.

13. Robin W. Doughty, *Feather Fashions and Bird Preservation* (Berkeley: University of California Press, 1975).

14. Ibid.

15. Cornell Lab of Ornithology, "Ring-Billed Gull: Detailed Page."

16. Doughty, *Feather Fashions and Bird Preservation.*

17. Ibid.

18. Cornell Lab of Ornithology, "Ring-Billed Gull: Detailed Page."

19. Wilson and Cheskey, "Leslie Street Spit, Tommy Thompson Park."

20. Jennifer Foster and L. Anders Sandberg, "Friends or Foe? Invasive Species and Public Green Space in Toronto," *Geographical Review* 94, no. 2 (2004): 178–98.

21. Wilson and Cheskey, "Leslie Street Spit, Tommy Thompson Park."

22. Ibid.

23. Ibid.

24. Blokpoel and Fetterolf, "Colonization by Gulls and Terns of the Eastern Headland, Toronto Outer Harbour," 65.

25. Wilson and Cheskey, "Leslie Street Spit, Tommy Thompson Park."

26. Toronto and Region Conservation Authority, "Spit Construction."

2 Hunger Makes the Wolf

Charles Bergman

This essay was originally published in 1990 in Bergman's Wild Echoes. *The controversy and management of gray wolves have undergone significant changes since then, as noted at the end of the chapter.*

THE WOLVES HAD DUG THEIR DEN into the crest of a small ridge in a dense stand of spruce trees. We meandered toward the den site, keeping to the thin line of one of the many wolf trails, past several lifeless beaver ponds and through the wet underbrush. High in the Alaska Range, the soggy clouds hung off the sides of the surrounding peaks like wet clothes, loose and heavy. We emerged from the dark spruce into a clearing where the wolves had trampled the dirt around their den into a hard pack. A small hole in the ground, the opening of the den looked like a dirty mouth puckered into a belch, and around the mouth was scattered the gnawed litter of former meals—four beaver skulls from the nearby ponds, moose bones well chewed by teething pups, an antler, a ram's horn from a Dall sheep, duck feathers.

Though the wolves were gone, and though there was a calm in the darkness of the shaded den site, it took little imagination to feel the intimations of ferocity and passion in the marks of the fangs on these bones. I found myself thinking not of comfortable domesticity but of Francisco Goya and his painting *Chronos Devouring His Children*—an image of savagery and hunger. And I realized, for the first time, that one aspect of living in time and nature is to live with hunger.

Carl Jung associated Saturn, the Roman name for the Greek time deity Chronos, with the *Sol niger* of alchemists, the dark or shadow side of the sun, and claimed that the ancients knew this destructive aspect of the sun. That's why Apollo, god of the sun, was also associated with mice and rats. And with wolves.

I found an image of wolves at this den site that could not be easily domesticated, a threat always hovering on the edges of our lives, on the borders of our consciousness. The wolf has long been an image of this frightening hunger, both in nature and in the human spirit. In *Troilus and Cressida,* Shakespeare looked inside and found "appetite, an universal wolf," that devours "an universal prey." Instead of facing this dark aspect of the wolf and other animals, we have in this country and this century worked to domesticate nature. Both scientists and environmentalists have contributed: scientists, by working to reduce animals to rational and objective terms, to numbers and formulae and laws; environmentalists, by making nature into a mirror of our middle-class, comfortable culture, a realm of tidy homes and nurturing families. In both cases, we remain alienated from some deep and primal power in the wolf, a power not accessible to reason and not necessarily conformable to culture. As I stood by the mouth of the wolves' den, I felt stirrings of this power.

I had come to this wolf den with Danny Grangaard, a biological technician for the Alaskan Department of Fish and Game. We had been helicoptered deep into the Alaska mountains to a place too remote and rugged for a regular plane. Danny was taking part in a long-term study to gain a scientific understanding of the relationships between wolves and their prey. Shortly after we walked to the den, Danny slipped on rubber gloves and began collecting the bones and other litter in a plastic garbage bag.

I let myself go with my feelings. The wolf has always evoked powerful passions in humans. Very few Americans, for example, have ever seen a wolf, yet the animal lives in all our imaginations. Every animal wears a double face: it is both creature and symbol, fact and analogy. Seeing a wolf as an animal, as Danny was trying to do in this study, tells what the wolf *is;* it helps us see the wolf rationally, objectively, with a certain kind of distance. Seeing a wolf as a symbol tells us what it *means;* it helps us see the wolf imaginatively, often with a confusing intimacy. The symbol shows the wolf that lives inside, and much that it reveals is not only cultural but personal. It connects us to our childhood dreams, to our most basic needs and desires, and to the demonic.

In a strange way, the images of hunger around the den did not frighten so much as exhilarate me. Looking at the mouth of the den, I could feel the wolf inside. Like Alice in Wonderland, I had an impulse to crawl in and see the pups—an irresistible urge to see the wolf face-to-face, to confront the beast in its den.

Danny said he thought it would be all right. I grabbed a flashlight and dropped to my hands and knees. The hole was only fourteen inches wide, and I could barely fit through. Still, I wormed my way in up to my hips. The burrow dropped straight down and then angled hard right. It was crowded inside; my arms were cramped; I was barely able to reach ahead and shine the light. The dirt walls were wet, dripping, stinking of wolf piss and damp fur.

In the beam of the flashlight, about seven feet away from me, three wolf pups cowered in the far corner of the den, a protoplasmic pile of bluish-gray fur. One brownish ear, I remember, was crushed against the top of the den. A couple of huge rust-colored paws poked out from the pile, precise owners unknown. The pups had small snouts on adorable faces, giving only faint hints of the fangs to come. Their eyes reflected a dull blue from the flashlight, expressionless and completely impersonal, inhuman. The pups growled at me in low, menacing tones, the snarling edge of the unknown. Those throaty growls were the fiercest threats I've ever heard.

This was as close to the pure experience of the alien and the wild as I have ever come in nature, as raw as the bones the wolves themselves had chewed. These wolves were untamable. Facing them in their den, I found myself at the borders of the irrational, staring in awe at its power. The wolves in the den—a world beyond reason and culture.

I thought later of one of La Fontaine's fables, of the wolf that preferred a life of hunger in the wild to the well-fed life of a dog wearing a collar. At some barely accessible level, this is the wolf that lives in the American psyche, part of the fabric of our daily language:

Hunger makes the wolf.
We wolf down our food.
The wolf at the door.
We cry wolf.
A man who loves women and sex? A wolf, of course.

These images unconsciously shape the way we see wolves; most of them are full of fear, defined by hunger and sex and a sense of intrusion. Fantasy is always a precondition for our perception of reality. The wolf in our imagination describes an interior landscape of fearful and alien impulses, projected onto the beast beyond. But there is more to this wild wolf.

When we are crazy, on the edge of madness or uncontrollable passion, then what? In the irresistible urge for freedom and that unrestrainable wildness, we howl with the wolves at the moon.

Such wildness wears a horrifying mask, too. One manifestation is lycanthropy, which once was considered a medical condition. Overcome by melancholy, a person could be transfigured into a wolf; stealing into cemeteries and churchyards at the dark hour of midnight, the afflicted person digs up corpses like a wolf. It is a gruesome association of death and hunger and the travesty of the sacred. The mistake is to take all this literally. It is psychology. A man-wolf, or werewolf, might howl fearfully, but the fur is not really on the outside. The more horrifying fur grows beneath the skin, creepy and itching, felt invisibly.

Here—in the human soul—is the second true wilderness. Animals like wolves can give us some of that wild energy that William Blake called "the opposite of reason." The wolf den, and the experience of crawling into it, evoked for me this deeper layer of meaning. We all have the right to construct our own meanings out of our experiences in nature: nature is not only an objective world but also a world we create.

More is at stake in saving a wild wolf than we realize. We need to save both the literal and the symbolic creatures. Part of the reason so many animals are endangered, in this rational and empirical age, is precisely that we have forgotten the two faces of every creature. We have forgotten what animals *mean*. I don't want to settle for only half the animal. Already, we are learning to accept diminished beasts and diminished selves. In facing those wolf pups in the den, I entered nature in a new way, engaged and passionate. My experiences with endangered animals have become for me an ongoing struggle to discover new ways of perceiving these creatures, to respond more immediately to animals, and to explore a much wider range of possibilities in living.

After we finished at the den site—after I crawled back out of the den and Danny gathered up all the prey remains—we hid in a blind in the woods. We hoped to have one of the rarest experiences in wildlife study—seeing the parent wolves with their pups at the den. I wanted especially to see the mother.

Endangered animals are, largely though not completely, the victims of our culture, martyrs of the cult of progress. Each species has traced its own narrative toward its precarious status, and the particularities of its story are determined mostly by the nature of its relationship with our culture. Like individual people, each species has its own vulnerabilities, its own ways of suffering. And you feel, after studying endangered species, that you are growing expert in the permutations of inflicted suffering, a kind of displaced, biological sadism. If the animals themselves weren't so wonderful, so compelling to seek and so exhilarating to encounter, following their stories would be like documenting a disaster. The scope of the enterprise would be narrow, like medicine reduced to the specialty of autopsy.

The wolf in North America is one knot in the weave of our relationships with wild animals, and it shows us one way that science has taught us to see and treat animals.

When I came to Alaska, I joined a number of biologists working on wolf research for the Alaska Department of Fish and Game. Danny Grangaard, who was with me at the wolf den, was working on one of the research projects around Tok, Alaska, near the Canada–Alaska border and the Alaska Range of mountains. The point of the research, and the reason that Danny collected the bones by the den, is to understand the effects of wolves on populations of moose, caribou, sheep, and other prey. In more technical terms, the research is on predator–prey relations.

The research on wolves is both very sophisticated and extremely controversial. The controversy stems from the fact that the research does not simply satisfy the theoretical curiosity of the researchers. For the last decade and a half, the wolf research in Alaska, Canada, and Minnesota has also been used to justify "wolf control," the official euphemism for government-sponsored killing of wolves to manage their populations. The larger question this research raises is how pure or objective wildlife biology can be in the understanding it gives us of animals, in this case of wolves and their prey. Put another way, what is the intersection here of science and politics, objective knowledge and self-interest? Everything about wolf research stirs fierce emotions. Beneath the passions and the politics, the wolf as an animal remains elusive, with matters as basic as its North American population debated intensely among experts. Yet the wolf has been studied intensively in North America for almost half a century.

Wary and intelligent, *Canis lupus* is called both timber wolf and gray wolf. The pelt color in the species varies widely, from almost snow white to black. Usually, an individual wolf's coat blends several shades of fur—grays, blacks, whites. The wolf is found throughout the Northern Hemisphere and is considered by most experts to be a single species, although there are twenty-four recognized subspecies in North America and eight in Europe and Asia. The rare red wolf, which is currently being reintroduced to the wild in the southeastern United States, may be a variant of the gray wolf, though opinions on that differ.

In the contiguous United States, the gray wolf survives only in vestigial populations. The largest remnant, about 1,000 to 1,200 animals, lives in the wilderness of northeastern Minnesota, in and around the Boundary Waters Canoe Area and Voyageur National Park. Some of these wolves have wandered into Wisconsin, where there are now about twenty or thirty wolves. Mainland Michigan supports a half dozen or so wolves, mostly lone wolves; transplant efforts into the state have been largely unsuccessful. Currently, about twelve wolves live and roam on Michigan's Isle Royale in Lake Superior, a number that fluctuates up and down over the years. About a dozen haunt the forests of Montana, and proposals to reintroduce the wolf to Yellowstone National Park continue to arouse anger on both sides of the issue. All the wolves in the contiguous United States are protected by the Endangered Species Act.

In Alaska and Canada, even the most basic aspect of wolf biology is an area of contention. The current official population estimate of wolves in Alaska, for example, is 6,000 to 10,000. Such figures not only mean the wolf is not in immediate danger of extinction but also are used to show that the population is healthy and that wolves can be shot, or "controlled." Critics of these numbers, and the census that produces them, claim that the wide range in the estimated numbers is itself a sign of their dubious value, rendering them unreliable at best and, some say, meaningless. Canada gives an official estimate of 50,000 wolves, but since the country has no formal census for wolves, the figure is an extrapolation, and some call it a guess.

Despite a range of attitudes, the majority of wolf biologists find the evidence compelling: wolves, they say, can and do decimate the populations of their prey, especially deer, moose, and caribou. A number of factors seem to be involved in several recent drastic declines—the biologists call them "crashes"—of prey species, especially severe winters, overhunting, and predation. The debate among biologists hinges on how to weigh the impact of each of these factors on, say, a region's moose population. Those conducting the studies feel they have isolated the wolf as a main culprit in many regions, and they maintain that wolf control is guided by their research.

In 1975, arguing that it would help to restore depressed populations of moose, caribou, and deer, game managers in Alaska resumed a discontinued program of killing wolves. In the winter of 1977–78, for example, 920 wolves were killed by trapping and aerial shooting. (This figure represents the total "harvest." Fewer than 150 wolves were taken in the "control" program.) In Canada, three of the nine provinces conduct wolf control programs. In British Columbia, using planes and helicopters to locate the packs, government agents in 1983–84 shot 330 wolves. The killings provoked mountains of hostile letters, public protests, and court actions that still continue.

Until three decades ago, the federal government paid hunters to kill wolves. When wolf bounties were dropped in Alaska in 1959, the numbers of both wolves and prey increased dramatically. Biologists for the Alaska Department of Fish and Game thought the situation was reaching a stable balance. Then a series of severe winters hit Alaska in the late sixties and early seventies, and wolves crashed in numbers along with their prey.

In order to understand what was happening, Bob Stephenson and several colleagues in the Alaska Department of Fish and Game began what was some of the most important research on wolves and their prey. I met Stephenson in Fairbanks, a cheerful, friendly man with a sense of humor, and joined him several times in the field. According to Stephenson, their studies forced them to rethink the relationship between wolves and prey. Their main study area was in the Tanana Flats. During the devastating winters of the late sixties and early seventies, moose dropped from a previous high of about 20,000 in 1965 to a low of 3,000 in 1975. Caribou numbers crashed, too, from 5,000 in 1970 to 2,000 in 1975.

Most of us cut our ecological teeth on the concept of the balance of nature, a concept enshrined until recently in graduate schools of wildlife management. The notion is that predators and prey live in a delicate harmony, exquisitely sensitive to each other. They form a kind of contained system, with self-regulating mechanisms to keep their populations healthy. On the basis of this theory, researchers like Stephenson expected the populations of moose and caribou, as well as of wolves, to rebound vigorously. They did not, despite a succession of mild winters after the harsh winters. The biologists were forced to rethink what was going on.

Stephenson acknowledges that one pressure was overhunting. But he argues that in 1973 the state took action by closing the caribou season to hunters in the area, and it squeezed the moose harvest down to less than 3 percent of the herd. Nevertheless, according to Stephenson, biologists were surprised that the populations of ungulates (hooved mammals such as deer, caribou, and moose) did not rebound. In this particular area of Alaska, a wolf pack will take a moose every five days or so. To the biologists in Alaska, the wolf seemed to be one reason for the low numbers of moose and caribou.

They decided to test that hypothesis. Each year between 1975 and 1979, the Alaska Department of Fish and Game experimentally killed 38 to 60 percent of the wolves in Tanana Flats by trapping and shooting from planes. Compared with a control population in the Nelchina Basin near Mount Denali, moose and caribou calf survival jumped twofold to fourfold almost immediately. Today, moose populations in the area are high. This experiment and similar experiences elsewhere in North America convinced the people in the Alaska Department of Fish and Game, and many of the other biologists I have met, that wolves can limit the numbers of prey.

To use biological language, the wolves create a "predator pit," shorthand for a sharp drop in prey numbers either induced or maintained by predators. Both wolves and predators suffer. The pits weaken the wolves through hunger; on rare occasions a wolf may turn to cannibalism. But the wolves don't decline to the point where prey can quickly recover. The smaller numbers of wolves subsist on prey like beavers, muskrats, ducks, and hares—enabling the wolves to maintain low ungulate numbers. Both wolves and prey remain far below an area's carrying capacity, and these lows can persist for decades.

By this logic, the biologists are convinced that wolf control not only helps prey rebound but actually is good for the wolves too. Reducing wolf numbers allows prey to rebound, and then wolf numbers can also climb back up.

The most intensive long-term research on wolves and prey has been conducted in Minnesota and on Isle Royale, Michigan. L. David Mech (his last name rhymes with "beach"), a preeminent expert on wolves, has conducted research in both places for over thirty years. A wolf biologist for the U.S. Fish and Wildlife Service for over twenty years, he has focused his studies on the wolves and white-tailed deer of northeastern Minnesota. Mech was one of the first to document the effects wolves can have on prey over time, although he generally takes a more moderate position on wolf control than do Stephenson and his colleagues in Alaska.

In the late 1960s, Mech's study area supported a large wolf population, and he estimates that on average a wolf kills about fifteen deer per year, though the number can go twice as high. Several severe winters with deep snow—just as in Alaska at the same time—made it easier for wolves to catch and kill deer. As wolf numbers increased, the white-tailed deer went into a steep decline. Soon the wolves were running out of prey.

In the early 1970s, wolves began to trespass into other packs' territories, searching for scarce deer. Wolf litter size shrank. Pups starved. Mech even began to find cannibalized wolves. By the winter of 1974–75, wolf numbers had dropped as much as 55 percent.

For Mech, this research anticipated the findings in Alaska. His major criticism of the Alaska research, however, is that these lows do not necessitate wolf control programs. He claims that the problem with the research in Alaska is that it has not followed the wolf-prey populations over a long enough period of time. Pointing to over three decades of studying the wolves and moose on Isle Royale, a 210-square-mile island in Lake Superior that may be the single best natural laboratory for wolf studies in the world, he argues that these predator lows are the down curves of long-term cycles or fluctuations. In time, in natural circumstances, both wolves and prey rebound. Wolf control simply speeds up the cycles.

Mech's research has led him to rethink his view of the balance of nature. The problem with the concept of the balance of nature is that it creates too static an image of the relationships among the animals. He prefers to think of the relationship as a "dynamic equilibrium"—fluctuating over time as the result of built-in tensions and pressures.

Despite the studies of the Alaska Department of Fish and Game and L. David Mech, not all wolf biologists are convinced either that wolves depress prey numbers or that wolf control is justified. Gordon Haber, a biologist who studied wolves for many years at Denali National Park, is an intensely outspoken critic of the research and the killing of wolves. During the early seventies, when prey were crashing in Alaska, Harber did not see such an abrupt crash in wolves or moose in Denali National Park. This has led him to conclude that the wolf-moose system outside the park in the Tanana Flats had been stretched too thin by overhunting and thus was vulnerable to the catastrophes of severe winters.

To many critics of wolf control, it's not the wolves causing the crash in prey, but an artificial factor—overhunting. This is where biology crashes head-on with politics. These critics turn to the decimation of Alaska's western Arctic caribou herd for further corroboration of their view. Once the largest herd in North America, it numbered 242,000 in 1972. With an annual harvest, mainly by native subsistence hunters, of about 25,000 caribou, the herd had plunged to 75,000 by 1976. The game limit was cut to 3,000 a year, and the western Arctic caribou herd began to recover. By 1979, it had risen to 119,000—without formal wolf control. The Alaska Department of Fish and Game estimates, however, that 200 wolves may have been killed by rural residents—mainly Eskimos—angry at hunting restrictions. The issue of native subsistence hunting, often on snowmobiles, complicates an already raw debate.

As the debate flares—in the press, in the courts, in people's living rooms— it easily turns into a fight between hunters and wolf advocates. As one environmentalist said to me, "It's our position that Fish and Game is managing for people. They're trying to meet hunting demand by killing wolves. But Alaska is not an exclusive club for hunters."

Though this seems to be how the political boundaries get drawn, most people, like Stephenson and Haber, stress that the lines of demarcation are not so clear. Stephenson says that such a portrayal of the situation is an oversimplification. According to Haber, well-monitored hunting is not inconsistent with populations of wolves. I personally met several hunters and trappers in Alaska who were by no means fanatical wolf haters. Still, even Bob Stephenson admits that the question of hunting is an important factor: "People up here," he told me, "need their moose, want game in their freezers. In Alaska and Canada, we have to factor people into the equation. Twenty to thirty years in a natural cycle is a long time to wait for a hunter to get his moose."

There seems to be no question that the recent biological research has sharpened our view of the wolf as predator. We are less likely now to see the wolf as innocuous in its impacts on prey, aware as we have become of prey crashes and predator-prey cycles. Yet the disputes among biologists over factual matters—the exact cause of crashes, the census figures, the illegal hunting of wolves, and more—all show that the issue cannot be resolved by biology alone. We know we can give short-term benefits to hunters through wolf control. But we don't know the long-term implications of humans displacing wolves in the ongoing cycles between predator and prey.

It is clear that even a documented decline in prey numbers is not a necessary signal for wolf control. Biology here tells us what we *can* do. It does not tell us what we *should* do. It is also clear to me that what is at stake in the issue of wolf control is not biological research—the ability of science to somehow show us what to do. What is at stake is how we will relate to wolves. What place will we offer them on our last frontier, as well as in the contiguous United States? This is a complicated question of politics and ethics. The attraction of trying to define wolf control as a biological problem is that we might be able to reduce our quandaries to empirical certainties, with an objective, external standard of right and wrong. We could absolve ourselves of the responsibility of choosing what to do, of deciding how to treat the wolves.

But the fact is we cannot absolve ourselves of responsibility. Science cannot tell us how to relate to wild animals, how to treat them, what place to make for them in our lives. Our relationships with animals cannot be reduced, or confined, to the comforting absolutes of a biologist's graph. In fact, the virtue of seeing our relationships with animals, both personal and cultural, as something we can choose, as a scenario created by us rather than determined for us, is that we are not bound by what has been. This view gives us the hope of freedom and change in our relations with animals.

What about wolf control? While it may be an oversimplification to see the conflict in terms of wolves versus hunters, I doubt there would be any interest in wolf control if humans were not part of the picture. Still, *which* biological arguments we find convincing—*for* wolf control or *against* it— are likely to be determined by how we answer one question: in a crunch, does a human being have more right to a moose than a wolf?

This abstract and sophisticated research on wolves as predators is more than mere science. I want to consider it from another perspective, suggested by the curious intersection of scientific research and the politics of wolf control. If we learn to widen the focus, to increase the depth of field, when we view our interactions with endangered species, maybe we can begin to appreciate some of the subjective realities that shape even the most apparently objective view of a creature as controversial as the wolf.

I want to look briefly at the research on wolves not as science but as a cultural parable. In the context of history, the research on wolves as predators is not so much the formulation of knowledge as it is the reformation of social values.

An eerie sense of déjà vu haunts the debate over wolves and wolf control in Alaska. There is a real question whether the killing of wolves in Alaska and Canada—sponsored by government agents, however sincere—is a repeat in another key of the environmental travesties of the lower forty-eight states. Is it a modulated twentieth-century attempt to do what the pioneers and colonists in our earlier centuries did with chilling thoroughness and an almost religious zeal in the contiguous United States? Then, the argument was to eliminate the wolf. Now, the argument is to reduce or "control" the wolf.

The historical evidence of the wolf's systematic persecution in the contiguous United States is overwhelming and is abundantly documented by Barry Lopez in *Of Wolves and Men* (1978, 2004). In the colonial United States, the wolf must have once been very numerous, even allowing for the exaggerations in contemporary reports. In 1630, the Massachusetts Bay Company established the first bounty system in the New World—one penny per wolf. About then, William Wood wrote in *New England's Prospect,* "There is little hope of their [wolves'] utter destruction, the Countrey being so spacious, and they so numerous, travelling in Swamps by Kennells." According to Michael Wigglesworth, in "God's Controversy with New England" (1662), the world outside the colonial settlements of the Puritans was a place of devils, and his imagery evokes wolves:

A waste and howling wilderness
Where none inhabited
But hellish fiends and brutish men.

This howling wilderness needed to be tamed. The colonists succeeded: by 1800, the wolf was eliminated from New England, lingering in eastern Canada in just a few pockets.

The history of wolves in New England comes as a sobering reminder of how quickly, how easily, how irrevocably we can destroy a species. As Peter Matthiessen's *Wildlife in America* (1987) shows, the early colonists looked on a continent containing, to them, seemingly inexhaustible abundance. The teeming moose and wolves, waterfowl and fish staggered the imagination of early writers and explorers and left them certain the wealth could never be depleted. Matthiessen writes of "the Spaniards who extended the explorations of Columbus to the mainland . . . greeted by a variety of wildlife which will not be seen on the continent again." Yet the history of these animals—their quick disappearance—is a slap to our confidence in a country's abundance. And the parallel with Alaska, and its wolves, needs to be drawn. Alaska is often described as a land so large that it is beyond our poor powers to destroy—yet that is exactly how the colonists felt about New England.

According to Barry Lopez, the worst carnage against wolves took place on the Great Plains. In their westward drive into the wilderness, the pioneers portrayed themselves as conquerors of the continent, bringing civilization into the darkness. This rationale extended to the clearing of forests and killing of animals. As Barry Lopez notes, Theodore Roosevelt, the great conservationist president, called the wolf "the beast of waste and desolation." The wolf was viewed as vermin, a scourge, a frightening predator, to be systematically persecuted. When white men destroyed the great herds of bison on which the Plains wolf lived, the wolves turned to cattle. How serious the threat actually was is not clear, but the defense of cattle became the rationale for a full-scale campaign against the wolf. When the bounty system alone failed to kill all the wolves, the federal government underwrote a kind of zoocide using bounties, trapping, hunting, and poison. Between 1883 and 1918, Montana alone recorded 80,730 wolves killed, with bounty payments of $342,764, according to Barry Lopez. By 1920, wolves were virtually eliminated throughout the West, their carcasses littering the path of manifest destiny.

Some of the frontier mentality also underlies the modern effort to control wolves. The man who led me to wolf dens, in fact, was an Alaskan frontiersman. Danny Grangaard not only works for Alaska Fish and Game on wolf research projects but is also a triggerman in the wolf control programs around Tok. He rides shotgun in planes and shoots packs of wolves in the winter snow. He is convinced that the wolf research ensures that wolves are being managed, not persecuted. As he said around the campfire one night, "No way are wolves gonna go tits up in Alaska."

Over twenty years ago, Danny left his ranch in South Dakota and settled in Tok, where he became a trapper. For two weeks I camped with him in mountains and marshes, warm sun and snow. The whole time, he wore the same boots—cowboy boots. His idea of packing for a long outing? One extra pair of socks, a pair of leaky hip waders, and a carton of Marlboro cigarettes thrown into an old green Kelty pack. He is a thin man, with blue eyes that jump with intelligence.

I liked him—for his wildness, for his love of nature, and for his knowledge of wolves. I liked him especially when he tried to shock me. "Ya know what's a kick in the ass?" he asked me one evening, as he piled the campfire high with spruce branches. "Burnin' spruce trees. Ya get drunked up, go out in the snow at thirty below, and ya jest put a lighter on one o' the trees. Poof."

He said wolves were his favorite "critter," largely because they're so smart. When I asked him how he felt about shooting wolves in the control programs, he replied with ambivalence: "It's a bummer. But Mother Nature's a cruel sucker. Got to have some kind of management, 'cuz can't jest leave it to Mother Nature. She's tough."

Despite our political differences—he called me a "Sa-hara clubber"— I found Danny's personality engaging and clearly defined, and I tried to understand how he saw things. His perspective on wolf control fit with his view of nature as challenging and cruel. His description of the wolf as smart and tough was also a good description of himself, projected outward. His wolf was a reflection of himself, as is the case for all of us.

Which comes first, culture or science, is a tough issue. But it is hard *not* to see in all these views of the wolf the validation of cultural values. The interpretations of the wolf from earlier centuries—the frontier views— imposed moral values onto the wolf. Even the more recent, more objective views of this century reflect culture as well. The interpretations mirror particular historical moments, each with definite political implications when it comes to relating to wolves, to managing them.

How an objective science conditions our relations to wild animals came alive for me when I spent several days with L. David Mech on his research

project in northeastern Minnesota. His book, *The Wolf* (1981) remains defini-
tive on nearly all aspects of wolf biology, and when I visited him he had radio
collars on wolves in thirteen packs as part of his studies. Mech is highly
articulate, very intelligent, and enormously stimulating to be around. He
speaks with darting quickness, punctuated by active hands and flashing
brown eyes. Over his many years working with wolves, he has acquired a
forceful, authoritative tone.

Speaking with him about the disagreements among wolf biologists, I
asked for his opinion on why there are so many points of view. He described
his own position this way: "As a scientist, I subscribe to one method of determining truth in this world—the scientific one. I believe I'm the one objective
scientist. Whatever happens, I just want to find out. I'm more of a scientist
than a conservationist. I'm not attached. I try to minimize my personal in-
teraction with the wolves." The power of this assertion, so direct and blunt,
was refreshing. But I found myself pondering his words—"the one objective
scientist"—for days.

Objectivity in science is a relatively easy target to knock off; the wonder
is how tenaciously we continue to believe in it. As Susanne K. Langer writes
in *Philosophy in a New Key* (1979, 1996), "The formulation of experience
which is contained within the intellectual horizon of an age and a society
is determined, I believe, not so much by events and desires, as by the *basic
concepts* at a people's disposal for analyzing and describing their adventures
to their own understanding. . . . These same experiences could be seen in
many different lights, so the light in which they do appear depends on the
genius of a people as well as the demands of the external occasion" (italics
in original).

What I am suggesting is that objectivity is itself a cultural assumption,
that it is one way among many of knowing an animal. Objectivity in studying nature requires a particular posture, a particular attitude toward animals. Objectivity, even rigorously applied, does not redeem us from the
imposition of a point of view on nature. As Langer says, "The problem of
observation is all but eclipsed by the problem of *meaning*. And the triumph
of empiricism in science is jeopardized by the surprising truth that our
sense-data are primarily symbols" (italics in original).

In other words, even the empirical observations we believe in as fact are
made, not simply recorded. All phenomena, like crashes of prey or cycles of
wolves and moose, have to be interpreted, given a history of cause and effect.
Some ordering principle, some paradigm, has to be used to make sense out
of experience, and the Western mind has turned largely to science.

Though it is true that the study of wolves and other animals as creatures has enabled us to see them better, it also imposes its own distance and limitations. Regardless of the knowledge it may produce, objectivity requires that we treat an animal as an object and not as a living creature that struggles, thinks, and feels just as we do. It necessarily separates us from animals, yet we're surprised that we don't feel more connected. The blindness of empiricism is that it gives us too much faith in the illusions of our eyes. We come to believe that what we see is real. Meanwhile, we have grown illiterate in the unconscious attachments to trees and rocks, and we are unaware of the deeper strategies and motives that shape our objective relationships to the world.

René Descartes, the seventeenth-century philosopher, was one of the founders of the scientific method. He is famous for bequeathing to posterity the concept that animals are to be viewed as mechanisms, *automata*—a paradigm we still labor under in trying to understand animals through general laws and statistical formulas. In Discourse 6 of the *Discourse on Method,* published in 1763 in France, he made clear the goals of this new philosophy of science:

> Knowing the power and the effects of fire, water, air, the stars, the heavens and all the other bodies which surround us . . . , we might put them . . . to all the uses for which they are appropriate, and thereby make ourselves, as it were, masters and possessors of nature.

I have come to see wolf control as a case study, in extremis, of the kinds of effects we can expect in knowing animals objectively: distance from and power over nature. Managing wildlife is, after all, a contradiction in terms.

Some of these ideas were seething in my mind as I joined Mech in a small plane to fly over the winter snow of northern Minnesota to look for wild wolves. He was expert at finding the wolves. He used radiotelemetry, following the beeps in his earphones as well as the wolves' tracks in the snow. At the time, I had never before seen a wild wolf, but in one day Mech showed me seventeen of them, most of them sleeping on southern exposures to get as much warmth from the winter sun as possible. I was thrilled.

I have no doubt that the plane, flying over spruce bogs and frozen lakes, zeroing in on wolf packs I would never have seen from the ground, offers perhaps the best hope for keeping track of the wolves, for studying their populations and gaining information useful in managing this endangered species. But the plane also seems to be a metaphor for a certain kind of relationship with wild animals. It offers the view from on high: commanding, expansive, and aloof. It is precisely here that the politics of wolf control and the politics of objective science intersect—both imply a kind of superiority to nature and a need to control it when it gets unruly. For all the pure motives of most of our wildlife managers—and I honor and respect their good intentions—wolf control nevertheless derives from the same worldview that has enabled Americans to dominate nature wherever they have gone. Humans are superior to nature. If we no longer try to conquer or eliminate wolves, we at least try to control them. This is the same premise that lies behind the conservationists' notion of stewardship in managing animals. The very idea of human stewardship, however, implies that we are in control of nature and responsible for it. We are flying above it, so to speak, striving for commanding views.

In the afternoon, we flew over a single wolf crossing a frozen lake. The low winter sun stretched the wolf's shadow long and blue across the ice and snow. The wolf turned to look up at the plane, raised its snout into the air, opened its mouth, and seemed to howl. We couldn't hear it. For an instant I felt myself rise above the normal and muddled course of my life. I wanted to hear a wolf howl; I wanted to see a wild adult wolf on the ground. I wanted, as it were, to see with my feet, connected to the earth.

It takes courage to admit that we are not absolved of our own particular points of view, that we all must look out upon the world from a particular time and place that involves us in distortions, that even our science is shaped by history, and that wolves are more than our poor projections, whether those projections derive from the moral view that exterminated wolves or the scientific view that controls them.

The pilot flew the plane in tight circles above the wolf so that we could watch it longer. The aircraft turned on one wing in a dizzying spiral. Looking down on the wolf, I tried to focus on it. I was happy for the view but aware, too, of the distance between it and me—of the distance we've put between ourselves and animals. We've rationalized nature and made ourselves superior to it in the process. I realized also that we cannot do to nature anything we are not already doing to ourselves.

The three wolf pups shuffled out of their den, one by one, and plopped onto their haunches with a kind of sweet canine gracelessness. This was the same den I had earlier crawled into, staring so closely into the pups' wild eyes, transfixed in the glare of the Other, only now I was hidden in the spruce trees, in a blind some distance away. I watched the pups for three days.

They tramped around the den site, schlepping their way through the days, bumbling into each other, and often tripping over their own oversized paws. They nuzzled each other with their little pug noses, bit faces and ears, and licked each other all over. In mock assaults, they even laid ambushes for one another, acting out playful rivalries as they pounced and sent each other rolling into the den, pencil-thin tails wagging furiously. They were irresistibly clumsy and, unable to stay away from each other, alive with body contact. For hours each day, they would sleep, lounging on top of each other in a rich puppy pile of bluish-gray fur.

As both Freudians and voyeurs know, looking can be an act of power. I have often had the vague sense that watching wildlife is a type of voyeurism. I know I like to watch. I was watching these pups at their den, grabbing glimpses from a distant blind, with that eerie and invulnerable sense of seeing but not being seen. There was something superior in my watching, as the pups played in the intimacy of their den, unaware of me. I had much the same pleasure that an audience has at a play, spectators who are always somehow superior to the characters on stage.

And like a play on the stage, the play of the pups was also a text to be read. Their play was anything but aimless. It was filled with meaning. Through play, these pups were learning to live in a pack. Wolves are intensely social animals, living in packs that are structured in rigid hierarchies. In the chain of power, each wolf has a defined place on a ladder of dominance and submission. In addition to developing distinct personalities, these wolf pups were also learning a complex vocabulary of gestures and postures for expressing their status relative to each other.

One of the pups, for example, was bigger than the others, easily identifiable by a bold white star on its chest. A leader, it was always the first one to emerge from the den in the morning. One morning, it poked out of the den but paused at the mouth for ten minutes until the others appeared, too. Then it padded off down a small trail into nearby grass. The other two followed. It chewed some grass with its head turned sideways, attacked an unsuspecting moose bone, disappeared into some spruce to the left of the den, and reappeared on a small ridge behind the den. Here, it sat down and scratched an ear, the quintessence of puppiness.

The smallest pup had returned to the mouth of the den, where it sat with its back to the pup with the white star. The starred pup suddenly began to get worked up with anticipation, spotting an opportunity. Pawing the ground, its rear end and little tail wagging in growing excitement, it looked like a dog eager for its owner to throw a ball. And then—a sudden spring, bowling the smaller, more timid littermate snout over tumbling tail into the den.

The triumphant pounce was only one of several ways the starred pup expressed its superiority over the others. Frequently, it would mount the other pups from the side, front paws on their backs, in a posture of dominance that biologists call "riding up." The other pups would respond with the classic pose of submission—head lowered, ears back, tail curled between hind legs. The starred pup would also assert itself by "standing across" another pup, which would curl on its back, stomach up, tail tucked between its legs.

Numbers in a wolf pack can vary greatly, from four to fifty wolves, but most packs contain six to fifteen. It's unclear how a pack comes into being, but most members are related. Normally, the dominant male and female, the alpha pair, are the only ones to mate. Biologists believe most pups join their parents' pack.

Breeding starts as early as January through March, the farther north the later. Pups are born in April or May, weighing a pound. Blind and deaf at birth, they open their eyes at about fifteen days and are out of the den, exploring, by the fourth week. Sometime between the sixth and eighth week, the parents move the pups to a rendezvous site—a sort of lupine hub—where the whole pack helps raise them. The pups live at the rendezvous site while the pack goes off to hunt—in essence, all the adult wolves now become parents. The pups will beg for food from any member of the pack; the food is carried back to the pups in the adults' stomachs and regurgitated.

The deep bonds between members of a pack begin at birth and are reinforced throughout the wolves' lives. They teach a powerful lesson: the pack is family. But a single text can always be read in multiple ways, and much of what I saw watching the wolf pups over the days was not natural history. In fact, I saw most of the natural history that I did only because I had learned it from reading or talking with wolf biologists. I could only partly view the pups as "things." They were other lives. I saw creatures that play, have babies, take care of them, live and die, think and feel—creatures that face the same problems life poses for us and that have all the dignity of doing what they must do to live. These pups had a secret and undescribed story—and this part of an animal, its *life*, is only apprehensible by wonder. The powerful pull I feel toward animals comes from deep inside me. They stir feelings in me that lie below words, a primitive power. I found myself responding to these pups not out of a sense of superiority or distance but in a more empathic and intimate way.

Often in the afternoon, in the blind, I slipped in and out of naps as the wolves slept, and day naps for me swim with my most vivid dreams. In this unguarded state, I realized that the pups, playing and waiting for their parents to return—as I was waiting for the wolf parents to return—evoked in me a recurring scene from my childhood. Before a bitter divorce, my parents separated several times. My two sisters and I often entertained ourselves alone while my mom or dad was gone; we would eat candy corn, I remember, and watch *The Untouchables* or *The Roaring Twenties* on TV on Saturday nights. And just before I came to Alaska to watch the wolves, my wife and I had separated for the second time, and my two sons had asked me frequently when I would be coming back home. I felt this intense and irrational identification with the wolf pups waiting for their parents' return—a bridge contained in the image of the absent parent and the children on their own. At some moments, I honestly could not have told you for sure where I ended and the wolves began. This is not mysticism—not oneness—though it is a breaking down of boundaries through feelings. At this level, when inner responds to outer, I feel most caught up in life, most in love with what the world holds.

Make no mistake, however. Moments like these at the wolf den are not pure release. I suddenly realized that all this longing I carry around with me—to see wild wolves, to crawl into their den—stems from a sense of loss. It reflects an emptiness, a sense of absence, that can probably never be filled.

Though the lyric form seems to dominate in most nature writing, I have to admit that I turn to nature not only to find the beautiful and healthy. My longings in nature lie close to pain and personal struggles. It is not easy to find positive images of the wolf in Western culture, but probably the most famous wolf story stresses the mother wolf as nurturer. According to Roman historian Livy, Romulus and Remus were the illegitimate twin sons of Mars and a vestal virgin. The two boys were abandoned to die, but a she-wolf found them and suckled them so that they grew and became the founders of a great civilization.

I love this myth, for it holds the promise of a nurturing nature and it tells of the power that even lost children can draw from the wild wolf. It offers a concept I believe in not only for myself, when I feel most like a lost and motherless child, but also for all the endangered and threatened animals on our continent: that what has been lost under the domination of our civilization can be found and reclaimed.

Charles Perrault, the French writer of fairy tales, wrote the classic and original version of "Little Red Riding Hood" in the late seventeenth century. Stressing the sexual danger of the wolf, Perrault depicts a dramatic confrontation between young girl and wolf in bed, and he does not have a hunter rescue Red Riding Hood (as do the Brothers Grimm). The end of the story comes swiftly, full of ominous threat and innuendo:

> "Grandmother dear, what big teeth you have!"
> "The better to eat you with!"
> With these words the wicked Wolf leapt upon Little Red Riding Hood and gobbled her up.

Perrault even provides a moral for French girls growing up in the age of Louis XIV: Don't listen to strangers, he warns urbanely, for even gentle wolves are of all creatures the "most dangerous." They follow "young maids in the streets, even to their homes."

In illustrating the tale, Gustave Doré pictures Little Red Riding Hood in bed with the wolf. Doré picks the dramatic moment of recognition, when the virginal Little Red Riding Hood, wide-eyed and in bed with the wolf, seems suddenly to realize exactly what the wolf wants—the epiphany of sexuality. This association between sex and wolves is no accident. In France, even today, people speak idiomatically of losing virginity as "seeing the eyes of the wolf."

For the most part though, we've neutered nature. To adapt Lady Macbeth's great phrase, we have "unsexed" nature. We're not going to have some toothy, drooling wolf following us home from a trip through the woods or from our weekend camping trip to the national park. The nature photography in our magazines almost never acknowledges the sexual energy in nature. Instead, it seduces us with purely aesthetic or domestic images. Sometimes it presents the violent, which accords with the Darwinian view of nature as a struggle. Never, like the Greeks, do we show images of Pan, the god of nature, in his sexual guise—with his phallus huge and erect, too large to be hidden or controlled.

The Middle Ages taught us to moralize nature, and the Renaissance taught us to rationalize it. Still, when I turn to the medieval bestiaries—compiled before our distance from nature was as great as it is now—I can feel immediately the emotional concerns, the passions and vitality, and the energy of sex within the descriptions only barely contained by medieval morality. A preoccupation with animals as images of lust, lasciviousness, and sexual infidelity is repeated in the descriptions of creature after creature. Those wanton beasts. The sexual and the emotional in nature, and in humans, had to be controlled. The entries on the wolf in the bestiaries are especially exemplary of these anxieties.

Derived from an early Greek text called *Physiologus* (The Naturalist), the bestiaries of the Middle Ages reached an apex in the twelfth and thirteenth centuries. They are compilations of natural history, Christian morals, and what we now call pseudoscience. As the scholar Florence McCullough describes them in her major study *Medieval Latin and French Bestiaries* (1962), "From the early centuries of our era through the Middle Ages the *Physiologus* and its later, expanded form, the bestiary, were among the most popular and important of Christian didactic works."

The bestiary tradition has, I think, been badly misinterpreted and maligned. From a post-Renaissance worldview, most scholars look back on the bestiaries and scour them for an emerging interest in objective natural history, the creatures themselves. There is not very much literal realism in the bestiaries, so the bestiaries are often treated with disdain or an embarrassed apology. The bestiaries reveal a different consciousness. For the Middle Ages, the bestiaries *were* natural history, and they reveal the way one historical period made sense of its relationship to the world. Often, contemporaries did lose sight of the creature itself and mistook the bestiaries' lore for literal fact. Monastic clerks in their cells offer encyclopedic descriptions of both beasts and monsters, with nothing to distinguish fact from fantasy— lions and lizards, hyenas and hydras, onagers and aspidochelones.

But the clerk writing a bestiary did not offer literal facts because he was not concerned about them. The mind behind the entries in, say, T. H. White's *The Book of Beasts* (1984), is not literal. It sees in different ways. White's book is a translation of a twelfth-century Latin manuscript now, according to White, in the Cambridge University Library. The imagination that wrote these entries sees the world as metaphorical. Nature is the text of God, and it should be read to reveal God's mysteries and the moral order that informs His creation. Call it a sacramental vision: the world of nature offers analogies to the human spirit. As T. H. White remarks, "The meaning of symbolism was so important to the medieval mind that St. Augustine stated in so many words that it did not matter whether certain animals existed; what did matter was what they meant." Beneath the didacticism and the moralizing, what the bestiaries give us is not pseudoscience but psychology encoded in the imagery of animals.

Amid a wealth of lore on wolves, the bestiaries stress the wolf's wildness, hunger, rapacity, and uncontrollable passions—the image of the demonic. In T. H. White's translation, the monastic writer summarizes the spirit of the wolf in the first chapter: "The word 'beasts' should properly be used about lions, leopards, tigers, wolves, foxes, dogs, monkeys and others which rage about with tooth and claw—with the exception of snakes. They are called Beasts because of the violence with which they rage, and are known as 'wild' *(ferus)* because they are accustomed to freedom by nature and are governed *(ferantur)* by their own wishes. They wander hither and thither, fancy and free, and they go wherever they want to go." Desire and freedom and fearful wildness—much of this is associated with emotions, especially rage. One bestiary text gives the etymological origin of the Greek for wolf, *lycos,* as a word meaning "rage."

The wolf is especially revealed in its hunger, particularly its rapacity. Again in White's translation: "Moreover, the wolf is a rapacious beast, and hankering for gore. He keeps his strength in his chest and jaws: in his loins there is really very little." This is the wolf that stalked the lambfolds of medieval shepherds, one of the hounds of hell. In another etymology from the same bestiary, wolves "are called *lycos* in Greek on account of the bites, because they massacre anybody who passes by with a fury of greediness." This rapacity was easily allegorized. Corrupt clergy were wolves; greedy barons were wolves. But in addition to representing greed or avarice, the wolf had religious significance for the medieval mind. Most especially, the wolf was like the devil: "The devil bears the similitude of a wolf . . . darkly prowling round the sheepfold of the faithful" says the bestiary. Jesus himself warned of the "ravening wolves" (Matt. 7:15) coming in sheep's clothing—false prophets preying on the unsuspecting. In John 10:12, Jesus called himself the shepherd protecting the sheep from the wolf.

Hunger and rapacity. The predatory wolf. For the medieval mind, sexual hunger was never far from the surface of the times moralizing. The imagination of the medieval natural historians makes a profound psychological connection between lust and death, between passion and predation—as if the bestiarist realized that our lives in nature subject us to both. Says the bestiarist: what a wolf tramples does not live; furthermore, "Wolves are known for their rapacity, and for this reason we call prostitutes wolves, because they devastate the possessions of their lovers" (White, *Book of Beasts*). In classical Rome, in fact, *lupa* meant prostitute as well as she-wolf, and the Lupercal temples became brothels. In some countries today, twilight at morning or night is still called "the hour of the wolf"— when prostitutes and thieves are at work.

The association between wildness and sexuality in the wolf is made even more explicit. According to the bestiarist, it was reported that on the backside of the wolf "there is a small patch of aphrodisiac hair, which it plucks off with its teeth if it happens to be afraid of being caught, nor is this aphrodisiac hair for which people are trying to catch it of any use unless taken off alive" (White, *Book of Beasts*). The aphrodisiac tuft of hair is only potent when taken from the wild, living wolf. In the bestiary tradition, the wolf is seen in intensely physical ways. Its character resides in parts of its body—mouth, feet, tufts of hair. The body seems to provide images for psychological impulses. In animals, we can see images of our relationship to ourselves, projected outward. Read the bestiary backward, as it were, from nature to ourselves, and you find in the medieval lore revelations of some of the emotional dramas we experience in our relations with nature.

This is clearly shown in one of the most insightful pieces of medieval wolf lore. Much of the wolf's power is concentrated in its eyes. At night, says the bestiarist, the wolf's eyes shine like lamps, like a demonic glowing out of the dark. If the wolf sees a man first, it strikes him dumb "and triumphs over him like a victor over the voiceless" (White, *Book of Beasts*), but if the wolf is seen first, it loses its own ferocity and cannot run. Here, perhaps more clearly than in other pieces of lore, is an allegory of control over the wild and dark in nature. Words and vision—two of our primary tools to steal the ferocity from the wolf. Our fear is that if the wolf sees us first, we lose our power of speech. We go mute and impotent. This, it seems to me, is a sort of primal fear of loss of identity, of the power of words to name things and give us control over them. Here is the fear that we may lose our power over nature, that we may lose ourselves in its power. The real beast feared in the bestiaries is the beast within. In the struggle for control, it is easier to blame the wolf in nature than it is to face ourselves. The price of such control is steep—alienation not only from animals but from the vital and frightening energy within.

Beneath our words and abstractions, there is another realm of experience. As the bestiarist knew, this realm is visible in the demonic glow of the wolf's eyes. It is in that dumb and frightening silence beyond the reach of words, beyond the reach of morality, and beyond the reach of science.

I once saw an adult wolf very close up, a young one in a captive colony in St. Paul, Minnesota. He bounded up at me, onto my chest, like an overgrown dog trying to lick my face. He threw himself on me, and I grabbed clumps of his fur in my hands. His yellow, depthless eyes were like bullets, fierce and wild even in captivity. Their intensity frightened me, disturbed me. When I leaned toward this wolf, one of his fangs gouged my forehead, drawing blood that trickled into my eye.

I don't want my life neutered and neat. I want to see those fierce yellow eyes and even to wrestle with the demonic and tear things open. I know the fear the medievals felt in the eyes and the fangs of the wolf. But I want also to hear the wolf inside, whose howls echo only dimly in the memory.

After all my traveling in North America, looking for wolves, the central question remains: What place will we make for the wolf in our culture? In our lives?

The wolf, like other big predators, evokes powerful fears and intense passions. Like grizzly bears and mountain lions, the wolf poses major challenges: Will we preserve what range it has left in the United States? Will we reintroduce it into parts of its historic range in the contiguous United States? I had two very different encounters with adult wolves in the wild, and they suggested two poles in our experience of these predators—two postures we can take.

In late April 1985, I flew to Eureka Weather Station, on Ellesmere Island, because this was reported to be the best place to see the Arctic race of wolf, *Canis lupus arctos*. At 80 degrees north latitude, it is a place that would appeal to any imagination in love with extremes. I went with a friend and photographer.

Located on the Fosheim Peninsula, the Canadian weather station where we stayed looked out on Slidre Fiord, a small arm off the Eureka Sound. In the afternoons, I could walk westward over the ice on the fiord, to the edge of the sound, and see Axel Heiberg Island rolling into high hills in the cold, diaphanous light. The sun no longer set at night but rolled around the sky like a glowing ring, turning the snow and the Arctic foxes into pastel shades of pink in its low and slanting light. But the cold was still strong. Icebergs lay trapped in the frozen fiord like huge hulks, images of arrested motion, as if the world had simply ground to a halt.

On my walks around the island, I felt as though I had come to the edge of some austere absolutes—intense cold, a timeless and blinding light, immeasurable miles of blank snow. A white silence brooded over the ice and snow. There isn't that much snow on Ellesmere—in the polar desert, it gets about fifteen inches a year, which doesn't melt until June. It was an immense void, swept clean and empty by the wind. I found myself thinking of Arctic explorers and of how some people will go such a long way to get a glimpse of the untouched and the ultimate.

It would be easy to romanticize my trip to Eureka, but that would be partly illusion. Other compelling images remain. The weather station compound reminded me vaguely of a sprawling, self-contained cocoon: low buildings hunkered against the cold. The main building, where the six or so men lived while stationed at Eureka, was a vast dormitory complex with all the current accoutrements of comfort: wide-screen TV, VCR, library of movies (I saw *The Right Stuff* and *Gorky Park* while I was there), pool table, weight room. There was also a full-time cook and baker who kept us supplied with more food than we could eat—huge meals and a constant spread of cakes and cookies. I felt less that I was confronting the remote High Arctic than that I was insulated from it.

The first night, after dinner, one of the guys offered to give us a ride to the dump. Arctic wolves hang out there, feeding off the garbage. We scraped our leftovers into a bunch of plastic buckets, loaded them into the back of a pickup, and drove up the small hill between the bunkhouse, the airport runway, and the dump. We drove slowly, honking the horn like mad. Looking to our right, out over the fiord, I spotted three white wolves a few hundred yards away. They moved superbly, their legs barely moving, in an ankle trot. Against the cool white world of ice and snow, they were like white ghosts, like white shadows drifting by.

A Russian proverb says, "The wolf is fed by its feet." Wolves travel all winter, and the urge to travel is probably related to the need to hunt. The wolf's chest is narrow and strong, its legs are long, and its paws are huge— all adaptations for a life on the move, even through deep winter snow. A wolf can cover a mile in about five minutes, effortlessly it seems, and keep the pace up for hours. It can cover up to 120 miles per day. When it spots quarry, the wolf prefers a short chase, a quick burst of about 100 yards, lips curled back, fangs out, snarling and barking.

When the three wolves heard us blasting away on the horn, they bolted toward us as if it were a hunt. All three of them caught up with us, fell in behind the truck, and followed us to the dump. I have vivid memories, poignant yet almost comical, of us driving, the horn blaring, and the wild wolves racing behind the truck like Pavlovian dogs after their dinner, ears pressed back against their heads, big snouts and heads pressed forward, long legs bounding under arching white backs.

At the garbage dump, we emptied the buckets and retreated. The wolves went straight for the food. Up close, through binoculars, their snouts and paws were smudged and greasy from eating at the dump, their white coats bleary with soot.

These were not the wild wolves I had come so far to see. Though they were all wild, they seemed nearly tame. I found in these wolves an example of one way the Western mind accommodates all those disturbing impulses we find in the wolf—sex and violence, wildness and passion. We train it. We control it, as we "control" the wolves of Alaska. Both the literal and the symbolic wolf are left to live along the margins of our lives, feeding on our leftovers, as it were. It was a sad image, an image of loss.

But I have another image of wolves that counters this one and reveals a different way of relating to wolves. It comes from the den I watched with Danny Grangaard in the mountains around Tok, Alaska. The one I crawled into. The other where I watched the pups. The one where I got the urge to see the mother wolf.

After watching the den from the blind for some time, we decided we weren't going to see the parents come in while we were so close. Wild wolves are elusive. You have to be extremely clever, and lucky, to see one. Danny suggested we go up onto a bluff above the den, where we could camp and watch without the wolves' seeing, smelling, or hearing us. The bluff was very high, several hundred feet, and overlooked a gravel bar and several small ponds along Bone Creek. We made our camp under several big spruce trees. From our campfire, we could watch the bar below, though the actual den was out of sight in the trees.

We watched for four days, an almost constant vigil. I knew the scene below by heart. I could close my eyes and picture the creek entering the open gravel bar, rushing past and bending right in the distance between two very steep slopes that led straight up to mountain peaks. In my mind's eye, I knew just where the poplars were, at the base of the bluff; I could see the line of spring-fed ponds on the right, like milky-blue beads on a string, full of Dolly Varden trout rippling the surface as they fed in the evenings. Several times, I even imagined seeing an adult wolf step out of the bush and onto the clearing of the gravel bar. The watching only intensified my desire to see the mother wolf.

At three in the morning of the fourth night, a wolf woke me with its howling. I'd never heard anything like it before; its eerie notes were emphasized by the remote mountains and the smoldering ember of our fire. The howl was a manic moaning, rising and falling in pitch until it railed off on a haunted, mournful note. I sat up in my sleeping bag and woke Danny.

A wolf howls to assert territory, to call meetings with other wolves, to entertain itself, or, as this one seemed to be doing, to announce its presence. Deep in the Alaska Range, the bluff was ringed with rugged peaks. Sky-piercing and heart-piercing, snow-veined, relentless peaks. The howls and the mountains all around—the beauty of the unattainable. In the slow alembic of a pale summer dawn, the snowcaps glowed in Botticellian blues and pinks. From the den below, the pups answered the adult's howl, a yapping chorus, more tremulous and intensely high-pitched. The pups whined like a pack of coyotes. The adult answered them. The howls rolled down the mountainsides, echoing off the buttes and rock spires, the talus and cliffs, spilling out of distant recesses and inhuman reaches.

This was a true waking, wolf howls washing over me in waves, to something wild and summer-new. Danny looked at me across the campfire. "If you're gonna see a wild wolf, this is your chance." We got up, stood out on the bluff, and scanned the bar. Both of us breathed shallow, short heaves of expectation, alive to the imminent promise of satisfied hopes. And then the wolf appeared on the gravel bar in the grayish shadows below. She stepped from the greenish puff of aspens into the open, walking slowly, aimlessly, nonchalantly.

"That's the bitch," Danny whispered. He'd seen her several times before. She was all white, except for a steel-gray saddle on her haunches.

A few feet onto the gravel, she stopped and looked back over her shoulder, Bette Davis–style, toward the den. She sniffed the air, padded on across the bar to the right, and wandered slowly toward our bluff. Her indolence was delicious to watch. Almost out of sight she stopped, raised her snout, and howled again, a kind of hysteria in the voice at odds with her casual pace. And as if she were merely a specter, she vanished as phantomlike as she had appeared, into the timber at the base of the bluff.

Danny and I had been a rapt audience. A wild wolf. We can make room for them; we can let them live their own lives. The howl of the wolf speaks of regions in nature and in ourselves, that we can never tame, never control. But we can learn to live with it. Occasionally, even if for only a few minutes, we can hear that demonic music in their howls, feel the ecstasy of those haunting echoes.

On the bluff, after she had gone, I let myself go in delirious surrender. I had gotten what I wanted, a look at the mother wolf. Sometimes we do get what we want; sometimes what is given is enough—like a mother/lover's breast in my mouth. Dancing like a dervish, lost in the euphoria of release, I was caught up in a sort of wolf madness, celebrating a wild wolf, feeling less like a spectator than, suddenly, a partner with this mother wolf in a dance I didn't for a minute understand.

Editors' Note

Notably, the reintroduction of wolves into Yellowstone National Park in 1995 reestablished the species' presence in the western United States. The presence of wolves as a keystone predator has had a significant positive impact on the ecology of the park. The elk changed their foraging behaviors, and areas previously overgrazed were restored. The regular presence of elk carcasses also benefited scavenging species including eagles, ravens, and bears. The successful reintroduction culminated with the species being delisted in Montana, Idaho, Washington, and Oregon in 2011. Wyoming followed suit in 2012. These states are now responsible for managing wolf populations with some oversight from U.S. Fish and Wildlife Services. The legalization of wolf hunting in Montana, Idaho, and Wyoming has caused an outcry from concerned citizens and environmental groups. Others consider the delisting of wolves in western states a conservation success story.

Wolf management in Alaska, the setting for much of Bergman's essay, also remains controversial. Wolves continue to be hunted and trapped in the state. It remains legal to hunt wolves by airplane and helicopter, a management strategy that is motivated by the desire to keep populations of ungulates high for sport and subsistence hunters. The Alaska Department of Fish and Game reports that populations of wolves across the state are between 7,000 and 10,000, but in 1993 and 2012 various environmental groups filed petitions to list southeast Alaska's population of gray wolves as threatened under the Endangered Species Act. Defenders of Wildlife's 2011 report on Alaska predator control programs gives a detailed list of aggressive programs targeting wolves that are not strictly based on a scientific understanding of populations of deer, moose, or caribou. Wolf management in Alaska may be even more transparently governed by the whims of hunters and government officials than it was twenty-five years ago, when Bergman conducted his research for this essay.

The wolf population on Isle Royale, Michigan, another topic of this essay, has also changed. Over the past twenty years, inbreeding, gender disparity, and climate change all threaten the wolves' survival on the island. Due to unseasonably warm winters, no stable ice bridge has formed between the island and mainland Ontario in several years, and the last time a new individual was introduced to the population was in 1997. The population of the wolf pack is dangerously low: as of 2012, there are nine individuals, and only three of them have been documented to be female. Wildlife managers must decide if human intervention is needed to reintroduce new wolves into the population and whether to continue the study of Isle Royale wolves that has been conducted for the past fifty years.

3 Beauty and the Beast

Catherine Puckett

OUR CHILDHOOD WORLD at home in north Florida was one of women mostly alone while their husbands were at war, at sea, in the air. And while we children were scared of the wildness, we were thrilled by it, too. We lived in a new neighborhood mucked out of a swampy area near the Jacksonville coast. Snakes were divided into two groups: garter snakes or poisonous snakes, nothing else. We didn't know enough to call them venomous then, and the only venomous snakes we could recognize for sure (kind of) were the rattlesnake and the cottonmouth (the moccasin, which came up from the swamps behind our houses to sun on the sidewalks or the warm cement of our carports).

Sometimes we'd see swarms of tiny snakes slithering around the sidewalks after a rainstorm. All moccasin or rattler babies, our mothers announced firmly, forbidding us to go out then, but when they were cooking or folding laundry or watching *The Edge of Night*, we would sneak outside and challenge each other to races across the sidewalk, the obstacles being the dozens of "poisonous" baby snakes that one had to hop over to reach the goal.

How many times did we hear our own mother or a neighbor woman scream in that precise pitch that announced one thing only: "Snake! Poisonous Snake!" Then one of us would fetch Mr. Joe from his house, and he'd follow us, shuffling and stooped and older than sin but nevertheless one of the men of the neighborhood while the husbands were out at sea. We all had a large, flat-edged shovel leaning against the wall of the carport, and the sole purpose of this shovel was to kill snakes.

Mr. Joe would take the shovel and smash it down on the snake's head to stun it. And then there was the next sound, the sound I will forever associate with the slaying of snakes, that loud, echoing, scraping sound of metal being struck hard against concrete, the splatting sound of a shovel blade going through a soft body. Suddenly that wide, cottony mouth would close in utter surprise (it seemed to us), and then it would open again, the snake's true vicious nature apparent even in death, even though its head was now separated from its still-moving body.

Sometimes the snake's head and its body would move toward each other as though seeking to be joined again, as if the serpent's body knew where its soul was. Mr. Joe, standing back now, would tell us to stand back, too, that the snake could still bite us after its head had been chopped off. "They that malicious," he would say, reinforcing what we had learned at church.

Once, babies poured out of the severed body part of a snake, and our mothers pointed to them, saying they told us so. In our dreams we imagined snake heads chasing us, the bodies following behind, as merciless and as disjointed as our fatherless lives.

Snakes, of course, were not only part and parcel of our actual world in the South but also at church, where we learned that the evil serpent was part of all of us and where nature, like a loose woman ("joked" some men), could be controlled only so long. I was around seven years old when I started to associate the outdoors world with the freedom to write and think. I'd ride my bike to a large oak tree and climb as high as I could, a book and a diary clutched under my arm. I was a girl on the loose in the world. From my perch high in the tree, I looked around at the wild world, and I saw that it was good.

Elegy to a Snake

This is an elegy, an elegy to a snake—the eastern diamondback rattlesnake, the largest rattlesnake in the world, whose skin is coveted but whose presence is not tolerated in most places.

Although only limited scientific information exists about diamondback numbers, it reveals that these snakes are disappearing as alarmingly fast as the farms around me in north Florida. Despite this, diamondbacks are protected only in North Carolina and not in any other state they have called home for the last five million years. It's hard, after all, to get people all lathered up about legally protecting rattlesnakes.

"No other wild animal in the United States," says the Humane Society of America, "is as extensively exploited and traded without regulation or oversight as the rattlesnake." They are hunted for boot and belt and purse leather, for sport, for religion, for fun and out of fear, and for rattlesnake roundups (where, as both herpetologists and the Humane Society note, many round-ups violate the most basic fundamentals of the humane treatment of animals).[1] They are the living centerpiece of snake-handling Christian fundamentalist sects that believe that sinless Christians, the ones filled with the spirit of the Holy Ghost, will not be bitten by the serpent. They are an object of machismo for young men who are the most apt to get bit and to die (usually while drunk or taking a dare). They are the subject of considerable mythology and legends, here at home among my husband's farming family and in Florida culture.

Some of us treat snakes the same way we treat homeless people. We aren't willing to get to know them, let alone look at them or touch them—our eyes slide away; we walk faster (or run); we don't want to think about (or read about) them; we don't want to see them; we definitely do not want them in our territory. Some of us are willing to beat them to death.

Even at home, even among many of my friends and family, I am considered odd (the kindest word they can come up with) for my desire to see these animals become protected, to not want them killed on the farm that I live on. I am not impractical, and I am too old to be starry-eyed. I know—very well—that the rattlesnakes that still live on our farm and in its woods can hurt or kill our family dogs, can even (God forbid) bite or kill my twelve-year-old daughter or stepdaughter, or me or my husband. Yet I want them to survive here on the farm's four hundred acres. I know, despite contrary belief, these snakes are not aggressive, are not likely to bite unless you are messing with them. Isn't there enough room for all of us?

I've learned, though, that if I see one, especially within a mile of the house, that I'd better remain quiet about it or someone—even my husband—will try to find and kill the snake. So I have made a silent bargain with these snakes—I'll remain quiet and you stay out of sight from everyone but me (and please let me see you first, I add). I carefully teach my children about rattlesnake habits and where not to stick their hands and feet. In rattlesnake season, which is from about March through November here in north Florida, I don't wander the woods as much with my dogs; instead I walk them on the farm roads.

Time

I measure time and seasons by snakes, not by trees with new leaves or butterflies in my garden or the restless incoherence of cardinals winging low through the trees in desire. Spring—that inchoate chaos of spring—arrives when the first snake crawls all the way out of its winter haven to catch the rays of the spring sun. Warmth first, then food. In snake season, the first thing I must do before stepping off the sandy farm roads to enter into the woods is pause and make sure the tall grasses bordering the woods aren't harboring an eastern diamondback rattlesnake—a Charon to keep me out. Just a stone's throw from here, I came too close to a five-foot diamondback one day while out with one of my dogs. When I walk by that place, my calves still involuntarily quiver with the remembrance of how fast the snake transformed from a long, thick rope to a coiled one, hissing and rattling at me, so close to my legs that all the nerves in them vibrated, it seemed, as fast as that rattle. *Move*, they sang in unison. *Move*. My dog, not leashed, wisely did not rush for the snake, and I reached down to grab her collar and back off.

If I see no venomous snake, then comes what feels to me like a small blessing that I offer before entering into another world so different from the one in my home a third of a mile from here: I lift my arms and part the leaves of a beauty berry so I can pass underneath and into the woods. In snake season, I am watchful—rattlesnakes can blend in well, and I worry about the dogs, who are invariably with me. (A friend's dog recently was bitten by a young rattlesnake; it survived but is still, a month later, not back to normal.) But I am almost magnetically drawn to the woods, to the shifting balance of my world when I enter the woods. I am, it seems to me, entering the domain of others.

The farm, about four hundred acres (forty of which belong to us, the rest to my husband's siblings) is about half woods and half pastures; coyotes, foxes, and an occasional bobcat prowl at night, and bats loop through warm evening skies, snapping up mosquitoes. Flocks of wild turkeys still roam here, and gopher tortoises burrow deep in sandy soils from oceans long ago, creating havens for rattlesnakes and other animals who share their burrows with them. In the woods, I find old clay turpentine pots, which I take home and plant flowers in.

The first year of my marriage to my husband was so hard I often wanted to run away—what we hoped would be a gentle melding of families was instead a clashing of wills and desires, strangers living together on this farm with different expectations and rules. My solace, as always, was in the natural world—it reminds me of the daily gift of being alive, of the fact that each day holds the promise of holiness. I delight in getting reacquainted with the landscape I had never left behind in my imagination, even though I had been away from Florida for twenty years until getting remarried. For six of those years, I lived on the coast near Oregon in Humboldt County, California, home of redwoods, spectacular seaside cliffs, few people, and a lot of illegally grown pot. There were no venomous snakes, something I could never get used to. There is something humbling and right about being in a place where animals still exist that are more powerful than you, that under the right circumstances can even kill you. This right ordering of nature makes me realize my proper place in the scheme of things—not the apex predator after all, not all the time.

My husband claims that already I know this land better than any of his family, including him. So I wander the woods, the eccentric lady that Emerson married, sometimes by myself, sometimes with my daughter, noting the caves where the bats come from, guessing the size of a tortoise by the diameter of its burrow entrance, and learning which trees the hawks favor.

One day, I caught a hog-nosed snake (locals call them the spreadin' adder) and showed my youngest daughter how it will, when bothered (as I was bothering it), puff itself up with air to look bigger, all the while hissing and flattening its head so it resembles a cobra. If that doesn't scare the bejeezus out of the potential predator, the snake will flip over and play dead, its mouth gaping open, its tongue hanging out, for all the world looking as though it's dead and that flies will start gathering at any moment. If you flip it over, it promptly turns right back over again, playing possum *(I'm really dead!)*. As soon as you look away, flip, it's over again and slithering off into the grass.

My daughter and I pause on a walk one day to watch a smashed, seemingly dead toad staggering across the road like a drunk on a bender. Peering underneath, we see two black-and-orange beetles carrying the toad. The small dramas of wildlife, my twenty-one-year-old eldest daughter calls these kinds of minutiae.

My ancestors must have crawled out of damp southern earth, red musky soil clinging to their skin, vines plaited like snakes in their hair. My circadian rhythms are southern. I am the Southeast in some primeval way. A wet, humid, sun-drenched place, full of screaming birds, thin paths leading to unexplored land, tangled vines, fanciful painted creatures, sometimes primitive thoughts. Sudden darkness, sudden light. When I lived away from here for several decades, I would close my eyes and summon my landscape, a panther scream in the dark, delicate butterfly wings flitting across my mind, a rattlesnake rustling in the grass.

Looking for Snakes

Every chance I get, I wander the farm, looking for snakes, hoping to see another diamondback. I peer into woodpiles, use a stick to turn over logs and old boards and sheet metal at the barn. As best I can, I peer down stump holes and gopher tortoise burrows. But although I find innumerable other kinds of nonvenomous snakes, I never saw another live eastern diamondback on the farm, although I did see two dead ones on the dirt road that leads to our farm. I suspected my husband's family of killing them, but by then I knew better than to ask.

Two days ago, Ken Dodd and his wife Marian Griffey came to the farm to search for rattlesnakes with me. Ken is a retired USGS herpetologist who has spent decades in Florida, mostly working on turtles and salamanders but always with an eye to snakes. He is the person his neighbors call when they need a rattlesnake removed from their property.

Rattlesnakes see worlds we don't even know exist, Ken reminds me as we sit at my kitchen table eating blueberry muffins and talking about the natural history of rattlesnakes. One of these worlds is the chemical-sensory world of prey. "We see woods," says Ken, "and they see scent. They see the world in a heat sense, almost an infrared sense."

This thought makes me happy. I like to think of this huge, mysterious chemical-sensory world that we don't see or smell but that is there, a huge pheromone presence that we walk through, ride our bikes through; we are oblivious to the "talk," the silent words being spoken all around us, moths finding each other in the night, male rattlers finding females.

Ken turns philosophical with words that remind me of Walt Whitman's poem, "I Think I Could Turn and Live with the Animals." "Rattlesnakes," muses Ken, "don't hate other rattlers, they don't start wars, they aren't trying to hoard all the mice. The one that lives under the Presbyterian church does not take umbrage with the one under the Baptist church. Most of the rattlesnakes I know are a lot more polite than people I know. Their mamas didn't teach them manners—they are just innately polite."

Catching Snakes

I have seen and caught many snakes, although I do not consider myself a herpetologist. When you hang around with herpetologists, the norm becomes skewed—one rides the roads at night in places that snakes like, with the car door open, looking at the road. When you see a snake crossing the road, you slam on the brakes, leap out, and either catch the snake or move it off the road. One collects rare dead snakes from the road (and trust me, there's almost no smell equivalent to a dead snake in a small VW beetle) and freezes them until the scientist can dissect the snake or it gets buried amid the frozen food, to be excavated some years later.

I cannot count how many times I have seen rattlesnakes, but I believe that even as someone who knows how to find snakes, I've probably seen only about twenty to thirty rattlesnakes in my wanderings. Some occasions were memorable, usually those when I was *not* looking for snakes and happened across one. I've caught snakes in Venezuela and Belize, in Florida, and in all the other states I have lived in as an adult. I saw a sidewinder (once), beautiful and thick-bodied in pale moonlight in the Sonoran Desert. I saw several western timber rattlesnakes when looking for rock art with friends in the Colorado mountains. I saw a Mojave rattlesnake in the desert, and I've seen many pygmy rattlers. Once I saw an eastern diamondback sunning near the mouth of a gopher tortoise burrow, another time one slid quickly over my snake boot when I was helping track pine snakes, and I often saw them in the eighties while riding the remote back roads for my master's thesis about the Suwannee River.

Yet I Am Not Innocent: A Man, a Woman, and a Snake in the Jungle

Once, a scientist asked me to marry him as we bathed in a small stream's pool in the remote jungles of Venezuela's Guyana Shield. We were spending a month in Venezuela, searching most nights for critically endangered Orinoco crocodiles in the nearby river. Even for a Floridian, I felt surrounded by green—tender new greens and the dark greens of magnolia leaves; the sky, too, a green canopy of tree leaves with an occasional thin trail of blue "other sky" visible.

The heat, at midday, was palpably dense, bowing us down as we explored the jungle, finally stumbling upon the creek. It was shallow and clear, full of pebbles, with inviting, bluish, deep pools here and there. Trumpet-shaped flowers, fiesta-colored, swirled lightly in the water, twined skyward on vines. The scientist and I, sweaty and dirty, stripped off our clothes and carefully got in the water, shuffling our feet to guard against fearsome fresh-water stingrays. In the background, scarlet macaws screeched in a high tone, howler monkeys made a low bass rumble like a far-off tornado, and what I called the drum bird (I didn't know what it was) beat a second ancient pulse in my chest. I loved that sound, that unidentifiable bird, like Rima the Bird Girl's call. A venomous snake lay on a shelf in the creek's ravine above us, though we didn't know it yet.

Shortly after the proposal, the rains came, so we stood, took another shower, and then dressed again. A while later, as we sat by the creek, we heard our American bush pilot clambering through the trees and soon saw him above us, clad in shorts, his feet bare like the local Indians. He started climbing down the slope of the ravine, waving and shouting to us about finding a poison-arrow frog, and almost stepped on a large fer-de-lance— an extremely venomous snake—stretched out on his path.

He yelped in surprise, and the scientist, a herpetologist, called out a warning, and then we were climbing up toward the bush pilot and the snake. It was golden brownish and large, the triangular part of the jaws providing room for the venom glands. Water drops from the recent rain sparkled all over its body, and I remember thinking that this was probably what the famed river diamonds of Venezuela looked like.

After taking pictures of the snake, the man who proposed to me took a stick and forced the snake down the slope, where he broke its neck with a hard blow to what we would call its neck. He put it in a collecting bag; I could see it twitching now and then—not yet dead?—as we headed back to our camp, where he dissected it. It was a female, he said, calling out the measurements and other information for me to write down. I was the scribe, a scribe who was also adept at catching crocodiles and snakes and frogs. The snake had just shed—the old shed skin was still patchy on her face. No food in her stomach, the scientist noted, and I wrote that down, too.

Although I said "yes" in the jungle, we never did get married. But the scientist bestowed scientific names on a lot of animals, both before and after me. One of them, perhaps, was that female snake, with water droplets shining like diamonds on her skin, hungry after shedding, out hunting. Even though this was the man I had loved most in my life at that time, I grew to understand something that I couldn't articulate yet—I had to come to nature myself, on my own terms. Seeing and knowing some piece of the essence of an animal was more important to me than naming it. Though I tried, tried very hard sometimes, wanting to be a scientist, I could not come to nature on his terms.

Women and Snakes 1: Eve in the Garden with the Serpent, Talking

I like to think that Adam and Eve could both be called scientists of the natural world, and that the way they interacted with the natural world is still present today, with Adam's role—the traditional (male-dominated) scientific model—most respected and legitimized. Adam, of course, named all the animals that God presented before him, including Eve. Nowhere does the story say that Adam tried to intuit the nature of the animals before he named them or that he talked with them.

But Eve, I like to think, watched and came to *know* the plants and animals. She registered them as a part of her world, not separate from it, an intuitive kind of physics, the knowledge that all of us—whether star or worm, person or snake—are made of the same matter. She had a relationship with the animals *beyond* naming, or so I like to think. Perhaps the animals began to inhabit her dreams, her muscles and sinews, her very bones. Eve *saw* them, and maybe they *saw* her. Perhaps she saw that the snake is closest to the earth, that it inhabits that thin space where earth meets sky, where skin feels smooth, on cool limestone or the warty knots on hackberry trees, in the drowsy heat of warm sand in the first sunny days of spring.

As is obvious in her chats with the serpent, Eve also conversed with the animals, revealing her understanding that there is a diversity of languages beyond the human, beyond words. What is the consciousness of trees, insects, birds, snakes? she may have wondered. Perhaps trees speak in a language of pheromones wafting through the air and soil, telling each other secrets and having long philosophical discourses that we know nothing about. Birds see in infrared light and can detect the magnetism of the earth even when blindfolded. Snakes sense the smallest vibrations and know an animal through its movement and its chemical scents. The consciousness of trees gathers as indecipherable as dew gathers in the night—time on an unfathomable scale. Maybe Eve intuited that the touching of pollen to stamen is an orgasm of sorts, so slow and imperceptible to humans that we cannot see or sense it but that nevertheless is there.

Ruach is the word used for God in the Bible at first. God is breath, God is an invisible force or power seen only in how God affects the world. I like imagining God as breath (pheromones?), as wind—sometimes a sweet zephyr, other times a violent tornado-spawning wind. Perhaps God is simply the holy breath in all life, the transpiration of plants, the breathing skin of a frog, the air bubbles of a diving spider, or the slither of a rattlesnake through fallen leaves.

"So the Lord God said to the serpent, 'because you have done this, cursed are you above all the livestock and all wild animals! You will crawl on your belly and you will eat dust all the days of your life. And I will put an enmity between you and the women and between your offspring and hers; he will crush your head, and you will strike his heel.'" The serpent, according to the church of my youth, represents temptation, evil, and knowledge, and out of this knowledge came sorrow and so to this day the curse of the serpent.

Eventually, however, I began to wonder if snakes are so feared because they are like women in some ways. Is it the contact that snakes and women have with the earth (women having always been more associated with nature than men—think Mother Nature) that some men (and women) really hate? Is it the vast difference (or the sameness) between women and snakes that repels and attracts? The undulating body, the sinuous curves, the language of silence and movement, the satiny, glistening skin, the knowledge of the power of snakes, of venom. Medusa redeemed, Medusa reclaimed. Eve in the garden with the serpent, talking; Eve in the wilderness with the serpent, talking; Eve in bed with the serpent, talking.

Contrary to the church teachings of my youth, I now believe that we didn't fall down but climbed up and out of the garden, thanks to Eve's act of civil disobedience. After being egged on by the serpent, Eve's action— eating the apple of the Tree of Wisdom—is what gave us the blessed (and sometimes cursed) gift of free will. I like to think that when Eve left the Garden (latching the gate firmly behind her because she was never going back there, even if nicely invited), she was both scared and thrilled because she was going outside, leaving the domestic garden to make her place in the real world of free will and wild nature, both human and animal. Perhaps, though frightened, she was glad for the knowledge she had acquired, glad for the gift of feeling sexuality and unexpected joy or even sorrow, glad for the ability to discern good from evil, that blessed and cursed knowledge that allows us to know our past and to perceive our future. I, for one, am glad it was the woman who said, "Eat and have knowledge." I am thankful that the snake gave us this.

Women and Snakes 2: Cassandra and Medusa

All myths, says comparative religion writer Karen Armstrong, contain some truth, or they won't work as myth any longer.[2] And snakes, everywhere, are mythological animals as much as real animals going about the daily business of whatever snake culture they hail from.

The fear of snakes and the worship of snakes, called opiolatreia, have occurred in most cultures, ancient and modern. Although snakes were "good" in some cultures (ancient Greeks, Egyptians), to most they were evil or the bearers of evil; in some cases they represented both good and evil. Native Americans usually left rattlesnakes alone; for the most part, they feared them and held them in esteem. Some called the rattlesnake "Grandfather," a term of respect, and even today, the Hopi use rattlesnakes as part of an elaborate ceremonial dance.

In parts of the South today, the handling of venomous snakes is how believers test their personal faith. Snake-handling sects started in 1906 by George Went Hensley (who died at age seventy in Florida from the bite of an eastern diamondback). His biblical justification for the taking up of snakes was from the Gospel of Mark, when Jesus, after his resurrection, said, "And these signs shall follow them that believe: in my name shall they cast out devils; they shall speak with new tongues; they shall take up serpents; and if they drink any deadly thing, it shall not hurt them; they shall lay hands on the sick, and they shall recover."

In contrast to these churches, which consider the snake evil, in the second century AD a gnostic ophite sect sprang up, continuing for several centuries. This sect believed that the serpent in the Garden of Eden liberated people from the unevolved God of the Old Testament; the snake was a hero because it urged Adam and Eve to leave the Garden. The snake, then, gave gnosis, or wisdom, to people. A snake was even part of their communion service—it rolled among the bread before it was eaten, and each participant kissed the snake on the mouth.

It's not just Western religions or myths that bestowed a central place on the snake; most premodern culture worshipped snakelike deities, not only in prehistoric Europe, where there were many snake cults, but in other places as well. Chinese mythology tells of Nüwa, the snake with a woman's head, who created the first people. The Aztecs had Quetzalcoatl, the feathered serpent creation god (Quetzalcoatl's evil opposite was the Serpent of Obsidian Knives). The Australian aborigines had the Rainbow Serpent, who was essential in the world's creation. Snakes also told the secrets of the universe to the Mayan sky goddess, and in ancient Indian tales, a serpent swallowed the first ocean but did not release the creatures within it until Indra used a lightning bolt to cleave the snake's stomach.

Some anthropologists speculate that throughout history the snake has been associated with women because of the similarity between a snake's ability to shed its skin and a woman's ability to shed "blood" each month through menstruation. According to one feminist anthropologist, Marija Gimbutas, as paraphrased on the *Salon* magazine Web site, "The sacred aspects of snakes were leached from cultural memory and the creature became a pop culture metaphor for the sneaky behavior exhibited by femmes fatales."[3]

Medusa, in particular, has fascinated me since I first read about her when I was an adolescent, discovering Greek mythology and having my worldview (southern, Christian) shattered with this thought that kept banging around in my head as I read: these people believed these Gods were their Gods, and they believed these stories as reality. Just like we do with Christianity.

Some years ago, I dressed up as Medusa for Halloween. In my adult life, I had never before dressed up for Halloween in a costume that required much forethought, but I wanted to be Medusa because (and I didn't tell anyone this) she turned men to stone. They could not *look* at her and so never really *saw* her. I had reached the age where I was a new member of the clan of aging women that many men no longer "look at." I wanted to say basically, "Screw this. I have a different kind of power."

Though I am no seamstress, nor am I skilled at the crafty arts (I was worried they would doom me to a lifetime of being sought out for bazaars and fund-raising endeavors), I was determined to be Medusa. I made my Medusa headdress by threading thin, flexible wire through fishing lures shaped like snakes and then sewing those onto my long, black witch wig (threaded with gray hair).

I couldn't name, then, why I found Medusa's power so intriguing, but by the time I put on her garb, I had thought about it a lot more. Medusa, with her tresses of moving snakes, was *powerful*—she could turn anyone to stone who looked at her. She was a warrior.

But she was also lonely, I imagine now. If one is invisible or never seen, isn't one lonely? Could women see her and not turn to stone? Did she talk to the snakes on her head? Did they, like Eve's snake, whisper truths to her about the world in which she lived? Did Medusa look in a mirror and have her heart break? Were her sisters, the fellow Gorgons, the only ones able to see her?

In yet another myth, snakes also imparted truths to a woman, truths no one heard or, if they did, believed. Cassandra, the most beautiful daughter of King Priam, according to one of the two legends about how she gained her gift of prophesy, spent the night in the Temple of Apollo. There, the snakes that lived in the temple came and licked her ears, telling her truths, for snakes told only the truth. They gave her the ability to foretell the future, but Apollo, furious, cursed Cassandra by preventing anyone from believing the truths she uttered. In Toni Morrison's *Beloved,* Sethe, the main character, turns into a snake after she realizes a white boy is following her in the woods, and she fears he will rape her. But here, too, the snake is not treacherous; instead, it is another truth-teller. "Down in the grass, like the snake she believed she was, Sethe opened her mouth, and instead of fangs and a split tongue, out shot the truth."

The Venom

There's no doubt about it—eastern diamondback rattlesnakes are the most dangerous snakes in North America, mostly because they are the largest rattlesnake in the world—because of their great size, they have larger venom glands and more venom. This means, of course, that if they do strike and envenomate a person, the dose of venom can be dangerously high.

Researchers estimate that two-thirds of those bitten by rattlesnakes in the United States (about eight thousand a year) are male. In the United States, 99 percent of venomous snakebites are caused by rattlesnakes; the eastern and western diamondback rattlesnakes are responsible for about 95 percent of deaths (twelve or fewer a year). Yet this is the important part: most of the people who get bitten have been messing with the snakes—usually young men (often inebriated) trying to capture or kill them. Bruce Means, the authority on eastern diamondbacks, has been bitten twice, on the same finger. He readily admits that he fits the profile of those likely to be bit (except the getting drunk part)—in both instances, he was messing with a snake.

Both times he was bitten, his legs went out first. "I asked the doctor why my arms didn't go out, and he said, 'You're a biologist, you ought to know the answer to that.' Well, the answer is that we have many more nerves going to our arms because of our dexterity with our fingers and all. We only have a few nerves governing our legs, but we have way more going to our arms. What this means is that the prey crawls off a short distance and can't move any longer, and then ultimately it dies."

Still, Means said that in more than 4,500 encounters with eastern diamondbacks in the wild, the rattling of a snake was a rarity—he and his research associates only noted rattling in seventeen snakes, and of those, nine were snakes that had been handled and released. "The eastern diamondback is likely to sound a warning rattle less than one-half a percent of the time when approached—if it is not disturbed by poking, prodding, or other threatening actions, including body posturing," he notes. In reality, one should look at these figures from the opposite perspective. Means said, "More than 99 percent of the time, an unthreatening encounter with a human being results in an eastern diamondback maintaining its cryptic behavior."

There were numerous instances when Means, who usually wore snake boots, found himself unexpectedly within striking range of a diamondback he had been looking for. "At first my field notes recorded these as dangerous close encounters. When it was apparent that finding myself within striking range was not especially courting death, my notes began to record a 'close call' only when my foot was nearly touching the snake's coils. By the third year it was apparent that even standing next to a study animal was not especially stressful for the snake. In all my encounters with these snakes, neither I nor my assistants ever had a snake strike at us unless we had bothered it first by trying to capture it."

The venom of a rattlesnake is quite complex and is, basically, their equivalent of the weapons we people use to acquire meat safely, from a distance (arrows, bullets, poison-arrow darts) rather than in a close encounter with teeth, claws, or talons. Ironically, we use these same methods to kill rattlesnakes, which use their venom to sometimes kill us.

An eastern diamondback rattlesnake, according to Means, will find a stalking place and take up a hunting position: think of a deer hunter in a stand. But unlike that deer hunter, diamondbacks are much more patient—they may stay in the same place for as long as a week, barely moving. But first, they need to know where the best hunting places are. Like good human hunters, diamondbacks will scout out their territory, but unlike them, they are equipped with special sensory tools. (They don't need to go to the store and buy guns and bullets, or arrows and bows.)

So let's say we have a hungry eastern diamondback—it is spring, he is warmed up now, and he hasn't eaten for months. The snake sees worlds we don't even know exist, as Ken Dodd reminded me. They "see" rodent and rabbit highways (some of their most preferred food) in the grasses, the woods, and over the Los Angeles–style highways of the branches of a large fallen tree. (This is one reason why people sometimes encounter these snakes on the "other" side of the fallen log that a person is stepping over—the snake has simply staked out a good place to catch a rodent on its daily commute.)

All snakes have Jacobson's organs, which are an extremely souped-up version of a scent organ (such as our noses). The forked tongue of snakes, instead of being a sign of the devil, is in fact part of this marvelous mechanism for following chemical scent trails—not just of prey but, for that male diamondback, of females in mating season as well. Basically, it works like this: the snake uses its forked tongue to collect scent molecules in the air and on the ground and then puts the tongue back in its mouth, where the two forks fit neatly into two grooves that carry the "scent" information to the brain. It translates it into, say, *Wow, a lot of mice use this fallen log, but no rabbits.* Or, *There's a female rattlesnake over this way. Gotta get going.* (In the same way, we may smell freshly baked bread from a bakery several blocks over, and our feet lead the way.) This is why you see snakes' tongues flicking in and out so much; they are simply chemically sniffing the world around them to make a picture of it that is much more chemical-sensory than ours.

But rattlesnakes and other pit vipers—the most highly evolved snakes—also use two heat-seeking pits underneath their eyes as a kind of second set of eyes for mapping their world. I imagine it is similar to those infrared images that soldiers at night could see with the early versions of night-vision goggles, but scientists don't know precisely how the heat images translate in a pit viper's brain. Still, they do know the pits may have first evolved to help them assess a prey's size or threat: a human- or mammoth-sized image would be a threat instead of a possible dinner. There is also evidence that these pits may have evolved to help snakes with thermoregulation; in an experiment with western diamondbacks, researchers covered up the pits of some animals, and they subsequently had a hard time finding shelter. So the pits may, in fact, serve as a thermometer as well as a hunting scope and a safety alarm.

But back to our diamondback: He has found that good mouse highway and has coiled up on the far side of the log in its hunting pose. It's sit and wait time for him. Yawn for us because now it's a few days later; we would be bored silly, but the rattlesnake still waits in his snake yogic position. Then, early one evening, a cotton rat begins to scuttle over the log. Our snake "sees" the rat's heat image coming toward him. *It's not a person, not danger. It's food!* Once that happens, a rattler's third tool comes into play: its hypodermic-needle fangs loaded with venom.

The snake gets in striking position, nicely coiled. At the right time, probably using its heat-seeking pits to "see" where to strike, our rattler strikes out and envenomates the rat with (most of the time) Olympic target-shooter accuracy. The rat staggers, but moves on. The diamondback generally stays put—its venom will work soon enough. No need to get chewed up by a stressed-out rat. So the rat keeps going *(Gotta get out of here, outa here, away, back to my nest, away from danger, away, away)*, but its legs are giving out, and soon it falls. After a while, the diamondback will rather leisurely stretch out and begin to move, using its superb chemical-sensory capabilities to track the envenomated rat with incredible accuracy. One of Bruce Means's students showed, in fact, that a rattlesnake can distinguish his or her envenomated rat from any other, even other recently envenomated rats.

By now, the rat may be dead, but no matter what, it is down for the count. Special enzymes in the snake venom are already at work in the rat's body, helping the snake digest the food before the snake has even eaten it. (One reason rattlesnake venom causes such problems for people is that it does the same thing to us—we are being predigested for the snake.) When the snake finally gets to its meal, it has not had to suffer the torment of bites from sharp rodent teeth.

The Other Side of the Tracks

Once, when my eldest daughter was a Girl Scout in Louisiana, I was asked by some of the leaders to give a talk about nature at the annual campout on a bayou in the woods. They suggested that I talk about butterflies or flowers or something like that. Something girlie.

"I'll be damned," I thought to myself, and I borrowed a friend's two corn snakes to take to the campout. I don't think the leaders were particularly happy because—even though the snakes were tame and quite friendly (not to mention beautiful)—they insisted I stand on one side of a dirt road to talk about snakes while the girls were forced to stand on the other side. Still, I was delighted when some of the girls surged across the road to get closer to the snakes, which were winding pleasantly around my forearm. And it pleased me even more when, throughout the day, a number of different girls, one by one or two by two, sidled up to me and asked if they could touch the snakes.

Quite recent research shows that, for whatever reason (and there is debate on this), toddler girls are more afraid of snakes (and spiders) than toddler boys. The researcher, male, suggested that perhaps this is because of the investment that females make in their young. Another "fear" researcher, a woman, said maybe so, but couldn't it also be that girls "read" faces better than boys, that they've learned to fear snakes and spiders because of watching the faces of those they love as they see these animals?

A fear of snakes, according to preeminent scientist E. O. Wilson, may be one of only a few human instinctual fears. Perhaps, he said, it came from the birth of our species in Africa so many millions of years ago—a landscape replete with venomous snakes—and when people radiated from there to other places, other landscapes, they brought their practical fear of snakes with them.

Interesting. One part of the myth of Medusa says that when Perseus flew over the continents, holding Medusa's head after he had severed it, that the drops of blood that fell from the severed snake hair onto the earth below caused snakes—venomous snakes—to spring forth from the earth, in this case, Africa.

Perhaps, as Wilson suggests, one of the reasons for our (maybe) instinctual fear of snakes is that God's breadbasket for human evolution was Africa, where venomous snakes were fairly common, including rear-fanged snakes such as puff adders. It makes sense, then, why we didn't develop a fine discrimination of snakes. Snakes slid easily into the realm of mythology because of this lack of close contact and because of their ability to inflict death, and they became the other, associated with the spirit world because of their immense power to cause death.

Trials and Tribulations

When talking with Bruce Means one day on his land in the panhandle of Florida, he said this to me: "These animals are way more complex than we give them any credit for—for example, after a year, they can find their way back to the exact same place they were a year before—and I mean the same tree! This just astounded me. Yet the usual human being makes subjective value judgments about animals—for instance, if it's furry or feathered, it's better than—or higher than—the 'lower' forms that are scaly or slimy. But they've arrived at the same time and place as we have, and they probably are just as genetically as advanced in their own way as we are. And although they don't have the same adaptations that we have, they still have adaptations that are as advanced as ours for their time on this planet. They've gone through the same trials and tribulations over the same period of time as every other bit of life on this planet, including human beings. The only thing that puts us slightly apart from everything else is our cognition—and sometimes I wonder about that," he added, chuckling.

The Gate

In my mind, there is a gate. It is an old farm gate, like one of the gates I find now and then in the woods or near the old tobacco barns, rough boards of different sizes pegged together by hand, green and orange lichen and moss clinging to the wood. The rusty hinges of the gate creak when I lift the latch to get to the other side.

One part of my life occurs predominantly on one side of the gate, another part on the other side. Of course, these two lives are not really separate; they mingle and inform each other. But inside the gate is my domestic home, my yard and vegetable garden, the pollinator garden with nectar-drunk bees drowsing over flowers. Inside the gate are the people most important to me: my nearly eighteen-year-old son, whose deep voice and great height still surprise me as he nears his high-school graduation. He leans on his own gate now, one hand on the latch, ready to leave, the other hand raised in parting. My twelve-year-old daughter, born when I was forty, so like my mother with her dark hair and fiery eyes, and so determined that sometimes I imagine she was conceived and born by her sheer will alone—I was on birth control pills at the time she was conceived. *(You aren't leaving me in here; I've been waiting forty years as an egg. Ready or not, I'm coming into your life.)* Not long ago, I watched her flying a kite in the pasture, her blue-tiered skirt swirling against her legs, her voice, singing, carried to me on the wind. A voice so clear and sweet that perhaps, instead, she sang her way into this world like a Siren.

But outside the gate is another world, one where I am not housekeeper or cook or nanny or accountant or friend or lover or mom or teacher or where I do my professional science work. Outside the gate is the serpent.

Given the prominence of snakes in my childhood, perhaps it is no accident that I spent the early part of my professional life studying snakes and other reptiles—endangered crocodiles in remote rivers of Venezuela and Belize, gopher tortoises, pine snakes. I couldn't decide between being a writer and a scientist. Writer and anthropologist Loren Eiseley also struggled with this dichotomy, finally noting in a 1964 essay that the separation of "these two types of creation—the artistic and the scientific— . . . are an illusion, that they are a product of unreasoning fear, professionalism, and misunderstanding."[4] Forty years later, though, I still tussled with this separation. I had one leg planted in the world of science, the other in the world of words. I excelled at identifying snakes and other herps—reptiles and amphibians—because of a graduate-student job in the herpetological area of the Florida Museum of Natural History. There, I typed the scientific name, place of collection, and other information about any herp that had been collected and given to the museum. I had a cafeteria tray on which I would put my formaldehyde-preserved snake (or frog, lizard, or turtle), and after I had typed the label for each animal, I would tie it onto the ones that had legs. Using a large needle, I sewed the labels onto dead snakes or legless lizards. To this day, I consider taxonomy—the Adam-like naming of things—a vital and necessary part of science (with ever-shrinking funds), but I found myself wondering then—and still wonder now—what the daily lives of those animals had been like, and I wondered if sometimes that got missed in the excitement of collection, the hunt for specimens, a hunt that reminded me sometimes of hunts for game. Now and then I found myself saddened by how many of a particular species had been collected from some sites. It felt like slaughter, not science. The scientists I have invariably been drawn to have been the ones who cannot contain the passion of knowing in addition to naming—whether they thought of it this way or not—of wanting to see and register the other. These scientists, in some way, want to speak for the animal—not just the facts, but the being of the animal.

Don't get me wrong: I love science. I live and breathe the traditional world of science each day, writing about science findings objectively, hoping that somehow words and the images and thoughts they create can make a difference in our lives and may move someone to action or reverence or effective policies. This is our only world!

For a long time, I thought that to be a writer about the natural world meant I needed to be a scientist and act like what I thought a scientist acted like, which meant that I needed to harden myself to the small sadnesses and joys I witnessed in the daily lives of animals (attributing emotions to animals was anthropomorphic, a terrible scientific slur), that I had to travel "elsewhere."

Like women nature writers everywhere, I labored under the tremendous weight of the Thoreauvian model—men leaving society and going alone to the wilderness, men involved in feats of bravery in the natural world. Though I love much of this writing, Thoreau's writing and that of many men after him often centered on nature encountered in a world separate from our daily one, separate from society.

Eventually, I realized that today's relentlessly objective world of traditional science and the isolated world of nature as separate from my daily life were not enough for me, and so I became a writer of the natural world. There should be no walls or gates between the domestic and the natural worlds: the house flows into the garden, the garden into the wilderness, and all are connected. There is a whole other way of being in and interacting with the natural world, one that doesn't rely on *just* the rational and logical mind of science or the world "away" and not "here" at home. These other ways of knowing spoke to me as much as the scientific one and eventually even more: intuition, integration, relationship, metaphor, emotion, the heart and body. As Rachel Carson said, "It is not half so important to *know* as to *feel*."[5] Knowing won't change the way we view nature, though it may help. It is feeling as well as knowing; it is honoring and respecting our kinship with all other life. It is standing up and speaking for the snakes.

Notes

1. Humane Society of America, http://www.humanesociety.org/issues/rattlesnake_roundups.html; D. Bruce Means, "Effects of Rattlesnake Roundups on the Eastern Diamondback Rattlesnake *(Crotalus adamanteaus)*," *Herpetological Conservation and Biology* 4, no. 2 (2009): 132–41.

2. Karen Armstrong, *A Short History of Myth* (Edinburgh: Cannongate, 2005), 10.

3. "In the Year of the (Fake) Snake," *Salon* magazine, October 19, 2000, http://www.salon.com/2000/10/19/snakeyear/; Marija Gimbutas, *The Language of the Goddess* (London: Thames and Hudson, 1989), 121–27.

4. Loren Eiseley, "The Illusion of the Two Cultures," in *The Star Thrower* (New York: Times Books, 1978), 275–76.

5. Rachel Carson, *The Sense of Wonder* (New York: Harper & Row, 1956), 45.

4 Managing Apocalypse
A Cultural History of the Mormon Cricket

Christina Robertson

A Convulsion of Nature

They ravage farmland, rangeland, and gardens. They form migrating bands, miles deep. They are voracious to the point of cannibalism. They are a plague, a blight on the Western landscape. And they are on the march by the millions, headed for your backyard. A newspaper headline declares, "Mormon crickets showing no signs of making retreat." Another intones, "Big, ugly stinky bugs taking over Nevada."

Locusts have been humankind's bane since biblical times. Exodus reads, "The locusts came upon all the land of Egypt . . . a dense swarm of locusts as had never been before. . . . They ate all the plants . . . and all the fruits of the trees . . . nothing green was left."[1] In the Bible's sixty-six books, grasshoppers abound. They appear as locusts, palmerworms, cankerworms, and caterpillars. The Old Testament alone contains forty-two references to locusts. In the book of Joel the Lord promises his people, "I will repay you for the years that the swarming locust has eaten, the hopper, the destroyer, and the cutter, my great army, which I sent against you."[2] The image of a landscape "black" with grasshoppers recurs, a symbol for the wrath of God.

Natives of every continent, insects belonging to the order Orthoptera—grasshoppers, katydids, and crickets—appeared roughly 230 million years ago. Back then the supercontinent Pangaea's dominant feature, besides its new spine of mountains, was arid land supporting drought-tolerant vegetation. Orthoptera still thrive in arid landscapes, and the katydid *Anabrus simplex* is no exception. Known in the American West as the Mormon cricket, the insect earned its name in 1848 when a plague threatened settlers' crops. The legendary story goes that flocks of hungry gulls flew in to eat the insects, save the crop, and become Utah's state bird. Thus, through cultural association an age-old grasshopper came to be linked to the Mormon settlers who reviled it. Anglo settler cultures now dominate landscapes native to *Anabrus simplex;* yet, ironically, the insect's nickname invokes only its status as a pest.

By most accounts the western United States remains under siege. The last widespread Mormon cricket outbreak lasted seventeen years, from 1931 through 1948. At its 1939 peak in Nevada, several counties were declared disaster areas. Over the next several decades, isolated infestations occurred throughout the West. Then, an early spring in 2000 ushered in another cricket population surge that has continued to the present. A June 2006 *Reno Gazette Journal* story by Jeff DeLong reported Nevada's cricket infestation was "expected to cover 10 to 12 million acres by the end of the summer." Reporting from Austin, Nevada, a cricket stronghold, DeLong writes, "Last week, they invaded the town's park and public swimming pool, covering the complex in a shifting blanket of milling, ravenous, 2-inch-long bugs."[3] Less vivid yet no less emphatic, a story in the February 23, 2006, issue of the *Lovelock Review-Miner* declares, "The crickets pose a severe threat to crops, often eating everything in their paths as they progress across the land."[4] A June 15, 2003, Reuters headline reads, "Mormon crickets, the plague of the western United States, are on the march again, ravaging farms and turning roads blood red."[5]

Hardly descriptions of a sporadic spike in an insect population, these accounts read like harbingers of all-out mayhem. "Invasions" and "marches" and "blood" echo the rhetoric of war, whereas "plagues" of anything "progressing across the land" invoke biblical times. What the hyperbolic language of these stories shares with historical accounts and, significantly, government documents is a tone presaging the end of time, or apocalypse. This widespread fear and loathing of the grasshopper raises intriguing questions: Why have insects such as the Mormon cricket been cast as agents of doom? How has our apocalyptic reaction to grasshoppers shaped our management practices? Finally, what are the implications of these practices?

"Apocalypse" comes from the Greek *apokalypsis,* meaning "an uncovering, a revelation." Apocalyptic literature deals with eschatology, the branch of theology focused on predicting the ultimate fate of all humanity. Typically, a prophet conveys a vision of cosmic destruction wherein forces of good and evil collide. In such stories, the final judgment of God vanquishes all sinners and a postapocalyptic Christian era awaits the faithful. Dependent for its effect on poetic imagery and fantastic symbolism, the genre reaches its apotheosis in the New Testament's final book, Revelation. There the fifth angel trumpets the emergence of a plague of grasshoppers from a "bottomless pit." Dutifully, the prophet John describes the locusts of the fifth woe:

> In appearance the locusts were like horses equipped for battle. On their heads were what looked like crowns of gold; their faces were like human faces, their hair like women's hair, and their teeth like lion's teeth; they had scales like iron breastplates, and the noise of their wings was like the noise of many chariots with horses rushing into battle.[6]

This fantastical portrait illustrates the intensity of God's wrath. Agents of destruction, the locusts descend upon the heathens with supernatural, hybrid ferocity. The locusts' "human faces" make them more fearsome yet, forcing the reader to confront the specter of the beast within himself. Indeed, John leaves no doubt this plague will afflict only the wicked: the locusts harm "those people who do not have the seal of God on their foreheads."[7] The hyperbole that animates this horde of locusts aims to evoke fear and observance and to strengthen the reader's faith in the Second Coming. Moreover, the stylized and exaggerated depiction of the swarming grasshopper as a grotesque "convulsion of nature"[8] has persisted over millennia in the Judeo-Christian imagination. Thus, what originated in biblical decree gained credence as a metanarrative driven by a priori reasoning that reinscribes our cultural perception of grasshoppers as harbingers of woe. To this day, to witness Orthoptera in their swarming phase is to witness destruction.

From 1848 Utah to the present day, accounts of grasshopper outbreaks have been framed in cataclysmic terms. The bugs "take over" the land. They "threaten," "ravage," and "bloody" fields and roadways with their "stinking" corpses. Nevada senator Harry Reid, who by 2003 had secured 6.7 million dollars over a five-year period to fight Nevada's infestation, proclaimed, in a July 11, 2003, news conference, "The Mormon cricket infestation is devastating Nevada's rural communities."[9] The towns that Reid refers to are, in fact, sustained by mining, but ranching and farming define the character of the American West. Regardless of the actual damage that swarming crickets inflict, public perception deems the insect a menace. During cricket season's peak, says Jon Carpenter, a pesticide regulatory inspector for the Nevada Department of Agriculture, "We get 80 calls a day, maybe more."[10] To settler populations who see themselves as rightful masters of the land, spikes in Mormon crickets take on cosmic importance.

Cosmic by nature, apocalypticism is rooted in dualism. Virtue and vice, beauty and beastliness—such binaries shape the historical representation of animals. If a creature doesn't serve humankind, it falls prey to demonization. Indeed, this philosophy is plainly stated in Genesis 1:28: "And God said to them, 'Be fruitful and multiply, and fill the earth and subdue it; and have dominion over the fish of the sea and over the birds of the air and over every living thing that moves upon the earth.'"[11] In an anthropocentric, hierarchical universe, an animal that competes for human resources offends our sense of entitlement. Given the unimpeachable status Judeo-Christian settler cultures have assigned to their own presence everywhere, including the desert, the only possible role for the swarming, ravenous cricket is that of the evil foil, the destroyer pest.

Countless reports cast Mormon crickets as interlopers bent on destroying the livelihood of hard-working farmers and ranchers, like seventy-two-year-old Utah farmer Duane Anderson, who summed up his plight saying, "They've raised hell with my livelihood."[12] Farmers and ranchers aren't alone in adopting the tone of the righteous. As suburbs spread into deserts surrounding cities such as Reno and Salt Lake City, more people experience crickets migrating through "private" property. Carpenter says, "You get people calling, 'The crickets are five blocks from my house. I need some spray!'"[13]

Symbolic outsiders, the grasshoppers approach from lands beyond—open rangeland and "unimproved" land—and breach the borders of farms, ranches, towns, and suburbs. Their hordes "denude" the landscape. Reporting for the *Lovelock Review-Miner*, Michelle Willms informs us, "The crickets . . . have voracious appetites, eating as much as 38 pounds of grass, alfalfa, and various other types of forage per acre, with a density of just one cricket per square yard."[14] Even the insect's life cycle bolsters its reputation as a foreign threat that comes out of nowhere. By late September mature crickets die off, and all winter eggs lie dormant in the soil. In the spring they hatch, and in warm, dry years, the population "explodes." The reappearance of the Mormon cricket is thus perceived as an "invasion," all hell broken loose on the landscape.

Apocalyptic literature highlights despair. A landscape vulnerable to "infestations" of a swarming, buzzing, dank-smelling, two-to-three-inch-long grasshopper is, to Judeo-Christian sensibilities, a landscape forsaken. What Mormon crickets have come to symbolize—the end of the world, the loss of human control over the landscape—is far more significant than the damage even large numbers of the insects typically inflict. As human development spreads into western deserts, the probability that we will encounter swarming insects increases. In response, we cast them as interlopers. The moral outrage underlying Anglo settlers' reaction to the Mormon cricket justifies its eradication. Thus, government-funded "pest management" programs targeted at grasshoppers such as *Anabrus simplex* have become tantamount to a promise of deliverance.

Fighting Our Insect Enemies

The social construction of grasshoppers as agents of destruction is evident in the war waged against them. Against all evolutionary odds, for the past century and a half batteries of pesticides have been sprayed on millions of acres throughout the West to eradicate grasshoppers. A Clemens University pesticide information Web site, "Fighting Our Insect Enemies: Achievements of Professional Entomology 1854–1954," offers a history of the development of insecticides and "control equipment."[15] Several events on the time line stand out for how they revolutionized the war against grasshoppers, including the Mormon cricket.

In 1876 the hopper dozer was invented to "scoop up" grasshoppers from fields. Bran baits laced with poison were introduced in 1885. In 1908 nicotine sulfate, used extensively on Mormon crickets for the next thirty years, was patented. In 1917, hand-bait spreaders, invented expressly to control grasshoppers, joined the arsenal. In 1932, aerially distributed "wet poison baits" were brought into combat. Dry-bait spraying began in 1940. By 1951, a century after the Mormon cricket's debut in Utah, 24 million acres nationwide—an area almost as large as the state of Mississippi—were sprayed annually with aerial insecticides.

Within twenty years of Utah's 1848 Mormon cricket outbreak, arsenical insecticide came into use. By the late 1930s arsenic had become a mainstay of cricket programs. In "Pesky Little Critters: Crickets in Elko County," Howard Hickson, director emeritus of the Northeastern Nevada Museum, recalls the "cricket invasion" of 1935–39. He notes that sodium arsenic dust was spread on affected land by federally funded "cricket gangs." Hickson explains, "Sodium arsenic dust with banana oil attracted the young one[s]. . . . The poisoned dust did not penetrate the hard shells of the crickets, but when they cleaned themselves they went to cricket heaven."[16]

In a 1935 photograph taken in Elko, Nevada, six men abreast, a cricket gang, pose in a field of long grass. Behind them the land slopes upward and the horizon stretches wide, unfettered against a cloudless sky. The men wear fedora-style hats, aprons, long pants and sleeves, boots, and dust masks. Each carries a hand-bait spreader strapped to his chest, ready to disperse arsenic dust. The camera catches the gang midstride, as if to show them advancing on the crickets. In 1934, 80 to 90 million pounds of arsenicals were spread onto land "infested" with Mormon crickets. Inhaling the tasteless dust could be lethal. That the open sores suffered by cricket gangs after exposure to arsenic didn't strike the public as worse than a plague of crickets should astonish us. Yet, for untold creatures sharing cricket habitat, ecological Armageddon was still to come.

Decade by decade the war against "pests" like the Mormon cricket gained steam, powered by World War II and the development of synthetic pesticides. "In the course of developing agents of chemical warfare," Rachel Carson notes in *Silent Spring*, "some of the chemicals created in the laboratory were found to be lethal to insects."[17] By 1948, a wartime stockpile of chemicals had turned chlorinated hydrocarbons such as dieldrin, aldrin, and heptachlor (all more toxic than DDT) into household names of a postwar industry. According to the "Fighting Our Insect Enemies" time line, in 1953 a Mormon cricket outbreak was "eradicated" on half a million acres by aerially spraying aldrin, diluted to one-tenth of an ounce per acre. In *Living Downstream*, Sandra Steingraber explains that, as it breaks down, aldrin converts to dieldrin. Dieldrin poisons soil and water and penetrates tissues of plants and animals, persisting indefinitely in the environment.[18] Oregon State University entomologist Michael Burgett reports that in 1954 Klamath County, Oregon, sprayed dieldrin over 10,000 acres to control swarming locusts.[19]

In 1962, 33,000 acres in Harney County, Oregon, were treated with dieldrin to combat hoppers, among them the Mormon cricket. That was the same year that *Silent Spring* indicted the chemical industry. Carson documents the devastating impact of the 1959 spraying of aldrin (in essence, dieldrin) on nontarget species such as birds, bees, foxes, chipmunks, cats, fish, and humans over much of Michigan. Of this chemical's effects, Carson writes, "Birds picked up in a dying condition showed the typical symptoms of insecticide poisoning—tremoring, loss of ability to fly, paralysis, convulsions."[20] A known immune system suppressor and a kidney and liver toxin, aldrin was banned in 1975. Proof that dieldrin—aldrin's alchemical twin—persisted in the environment came in 1986. Steingraber reports, "It was still turning up in milk supplies because the soils of hayfields sprayed more than a decade earlier remained contaminated."[21] Such damning evidence of ecological harm eventually led government agencies to use other, less deadly chemicals.

By 1966 Oregon's grasshopper control program had replaced aldrin with malathion. A nerve gas developed in Germany during World War II, malathion is now used against mosquitoes, fruit flies, household insects, lice, and grasshoppers. Its broad-spectrum action makes it effective on contact against molting and mature Mormon crickets. Unlike dieldrin, malathion's half-life in air is short (1.5 days), as is its persistence in soil (1–25 days).[22] Nonetheless, malathion's water solubility makes it very hazardous for use near wetlands. Yet from 1965 through 1995 malathion was a mainstay in grasshopper control programs across the West.[23] Malathion is "moderately toxic" to birds and "highly toxic" to aquatic life and nontarget insects such as honeybees, butterflies, and moths.[24] In 1972, Burgett claims, seven counties in northeastern Oregon sprayed 689,850 acres with malathion to combat a locust outbreak. Famous for its wetlands, southwestern Oregon's Klamath County treated 49,665 acres with malathion in 1982.[25] That same year the United Nations voted 111 to 1 to establish the "World Charter for Nature." Its fourth principle insists human management of the land must "not endanger the integrity of those other ecosystems or species with which they coexist." The United States alone voted against the charter.[26]

Utah State University entomologist Edward W. Evans notes, "Malathion and carbaryl in liquid form are relatively non-toxic to humans, and may be sprayed along roadsides and fence rows by following label directions."[27] Since the early 1990s the insecticide carbaryl—an ester (salt) of carbamic acid—has been used to combat the Mormon cricket. Pesticide regulator Jon Carpenter says, "As far as pesticides go, carbaryl is one of the least toxic to people. It's very toxic to aquatic organisms. And I hate to say 'one of the least' because all pesticides are toxic."[28]

Like malathion, carbaryl interferes with the nervous system. Despite its "relative nontoxicity," Evans concedes, malathion and liquid carbaryl "are broad spectrum insecticides that kill many beneficial insects (e.g., predators, parasites, and pollinators) in addition to grasshoppers." For this reason, he notes, dry bait (wheat bran laced with carbaryl) is preferable. "Spread evenly throughout the habitat," he explains, "the bait selectively kills only grasshoppers and those other insects that consume it foraging on the ground."[29]

Evans's acknowledgment that "those other insects that consume" carbaryl bait also die begs the question: *what of the migratory and native birds that consume poisoned insects?* Back in 1939, biologist Ira La Rivers witnessed birds eating crickets poisoned with arsenic, among them a yellow-headed blackbird. In "The Mormon Cricket as Food for Birds" (1941), La Rivers writes:

> Poisoned crickets lay thickly on the ground . . . most of them killed by direct contact with the insecticidal dust, the remaining ones secondarily killed by eating the carcasses of their more strongly-poisoned fellows. . . . I came upon the solitary "White-wing" . . . feeding on the cricket. The bird flew off . . . upon inspection, the insect appeared to have been dead for some time. . . . since I failed to see the bird again, [I] have wondered about the effect the small amount of arsenic might have had.[30]

As a biologist researching crickets *in relation to* their avian predators, Ira La Rivers voices the concern that a poisoned insect becomes poison food. Speaking half a century later as a state university entomologist, Evans's focus on the more selective yet nonetheless lethal effects of carbaryl in dry-bait form precludes the wider angle of La Rivers's study. Yet Evans's narrow lens unwittingly reflects entomology itself, whose development as a field of study is intertwined with the chemical management of insects and the concomitant dispersal of millions of pounds of pesticides on lands inhabited by nontarget species.

Malathion and carbaryl may not persist in soils, water, and vegetation indefinitely, as do arsenic and dieldrin. Yet if the remains of the millions of birds, mammals, and fish poisoned by such chemicals occupied a mass grave, the war against "our insect enemies" would reveal, instead, ecological genocide. A hundred and fifty years of insect management, driven by industrial capitalism, the Second World War's chemical stockpiles, and our Judeo-Christian disdain of six-legged insects, has hardened us to the scattershot use of pesticides. By pitting human prosperity against nonhuman nature, by conflating swarming insects such as the Mormon cricket with apocalyptic destruction, we have set the stage for ecological Armageddon.

Bugmaster

In "Toward a Philosophy of Nature," Robert H. Harrison ventures, "A great deal of the destructiveness in our dealings with nature arises, it seems, from a stubborn refusal to come to terms with our finitude, to accept our fundamental limitations."[31] In the West our fundamental limitation is a scarcity of water. Indeed, it's no coincidence that the seventeen states prone to grasshopper outbreaks lay west of the one-hundredth meridian. If the 1902 Reclamation Act—conceived to "make the desert bloom"—was, as historians claim, a welfare act, today's government-funded cricket programs are its grandchildren. Indeed, the government intervention that made western agriculture possible by legislating water for the desert has created successive generations of people who likewise depend on government intervention to eradicate pests.

Western ranchers leasing government land, along with farmers who grow crops like alfalfa, look to government agencies like the Bureau of Land Management and Animal and Plant Health Inspection Service for protection against Mormon cricket outbreaks. Carpenter notes that such agencies fund 50 percent of the cost of spraying private lands, a situation he likens to handing out "government cheese." He concedes, "Two crickets per square yard can do economic damage. One every five or six square yards is more usual." He adds, "There's in some cases a legitimate need [for spraying], where you have seedlings, a young crop, but established alfalfa isn't getting destroyed. All you'll see is a little damage at the edges of the fields."[32] Yet federal agencies foot the annual bill for spraying millions of acres with chemicals to eradicate the Mormon cricket from hardscrabble range and farmland.

To make the desert bloom we've drained lakes and turned rivers into canals or flumes. We've drowned canyons, calling the aftermath reservoirs. We've replaced grasslands with rangelands. Our determination to reclaim land from the grip of a perceived hostile force—aridity—reveals a sense of entitlement at odds with the welfare of the nonhuman natural world. Owens Lake, Hetch Hetchy, the Colorado River, Glen Canyon: all are object lessons borne of this sense of entitlement. The West once supported myriad native species and many indigenous peoples. Is it, in part, the settler culture's tenuous foothold in the desert that makes us view Mormon crickets as an isolated blight, a scourge on the land? Indeed, according to Carpenter, among ranchers and farmers "there's the misconception that they're going to march out of the mountains and take everything, right down to the ground."[33]

Positing crickets as a chaotic paroxysm of nature that thwarts our rightful (that is, Judeo-Christian) stewardship, we remake history to reflect the remade landscape. In *Wild Echoes* (1990), Charles Bergman claims, "Animals are only partly biological creatures. They are also symbols in which we can read who we are."[34] The Mormon cricket, thriving despite the onslaught against it, is an apt symbol of our failure to control nature, particularly arid lands unsuited to agriculture. We are not hapless victims of a scourge. Instead "who we are" can be read in the apocalyptic rhetoric that dubs swarming grasshoppers a "convulsion of nature." This rhetoric has driven the insect's management.

"The goal of the Animal and Plant Health Inspection Service (APHIS) grasshopper program," states a May 2003 Fact Sheet, "is not to eradicate them but to reduce outbreak populations to less damaging levels."[35] Further, a March 2006 "site specific environmental assessment" of the "Rangeland Grasshopper and Mormon Cricket Suppression Program" prepared by the Animal and Plant Health Inspection Service (APHIS) for Klamath County, Oregon, allows, "In rangeland ecosystems in the Western United States, grasshoppers are a natural component of the biota." The report notes that grasshoppers are "native" and "perform beneficial functions by recycling nutrients and serving as food for other animal species." Yet the following fifty-two pages outline the "suppression" of grasshoppers and crickets when their numbers reach "economically damaging levels." The assessment addresses the environmental impact of applying pesticides such as malathion and carbaryl to land "infested" with grasshoppers and crickets. APHIS's report further acknowledges, "The proposed action could cause changes that may affect the behavior or physiological processes of some federally listed Threatened, Endangered, or Proposed species."[36] An apt example of institutional rhetoric, this statement's passive construction and euphemistic diction distance the "proposed action" (dispersal of malathion and/or carbaryl) from actors (those applying the pesticides) and from "changes" to (poisoning of) multiple-species habitat. Stated plainly, "changes that may affect the behavior and physiological processes" would more accurately read, *These pesticides will poison the nervous system of all nontarget species, resulting in neurological damage or maiming or death.*

Nontarget, "Threatened, Endangered, or Proposed species" in Klamath County, Oregon, include the Canada lynx, bull trout, Lost River and shortnose suckers, the bald eagle, the northern spotted owl, and Applegate's milkvetch. Add to this list those "pollinators occur[ring] within and near the proposed suppression area" and assume that (along with grasshoppers such as the Mormon cricket) bees, birds, butterflies, moths, and beetles will be poisoned. Still, the report notes, if APHIS takes a "No Action" approach, ranchers and farmers could apply "a large amount of insecticides, including those with a greater risk to human health . . . in an effort to suppress or even locally eradicate grasshopper populations." Thus, "economic levels" of grasshoppers must be controlled by the "suppression program," in part to limit the "risk to human health."[37] The tacit and certain risks to nonhuman, nontarget species posed by this grasshopper suppression program amount to an institutional admission of collateral damage.

Moreover, this language used by government agencies such as APHIS distances cause from effect, pesticide use from ecological damage. Its euphemisms—"economic levels," "management," "suppression area," "changes that may affect," to name just a few—belie an us-versus-them attitude rooted in anthropocentrism. At once economically expedient, at least in the short term, and culturally consistent with the West's religious metanarratives, our environmental engagement has long been governed by our insistence on dominance. The apocalypse that the apostle John promises in Revelation is a battle to be waged and won against the nonrighteous, the non-Christian, and the nonhuman. Creatures outside the fold, swarming grasshoppers serve as a touchstone of our righteousness, ignorance, and fear. As the object of such suppression programs, the Mormon cricket symbolizes an ideology rooted in dualism, hierarchy, and conquest.

Trade names for the routinely used pesticide carbaryl reflect this hegemonic perspective. Playful names mask carbaryl's toxicity while underscoring our attitude toward insects like the Mormon cricket. One product, Bugmaster, comically iterates humankind's God-given dominion over plants and animals. Crunch, another carbaryl trade name, conjures the sound of stomping with a big-soled shoe on a hard-shelled cricket. "Try it," Crunch seems to say, "It's onomatopoeic. It's fun."

A third brand, Tornado, suggests fighting like with like, matching one convulsion of nature—the swarming cricket—with another, a man-made funnel cloud. A fourth carbaryl pesticide, Adios, carries more freight, only half of it intended. The company clearly hoped to sell their pesticide by making the customer chuckle. We imagine waving "adios!" to hordes of pests who eat the bait we spread. What the marketers didn't intend to highlight, given carbaryl's unrivaled popularity as an insecticide on a broad range of crops, are the migrant Mexican farmworkers most likely to come into direct contact with the chemical. Carbaryl is classified as "moderately toxic" to "highly toxic" depending on the formulation. Its side effects include burns, nausea, stomach cramps, diarrhea, blurred vision, and convulsions. Our thin skin offers us less protection than a Mormon cricket's shell; unlike us, to be poisoned it must eat the carbaryl-laced bran bait.

Ecology of a Grasshopper

While working on the Nevada cricket control program during the 1939 invasion, biologist Ira La Rivers cataloged bird–cricket relationships. "The Mormon Cricket as Food for Birds," published in the *Condor* in January 1941, relays his observations. "The list of birds which eat the Mormon cricket is sizable," La Rivers begins, "and these species constitute a potent natural control of the insect." Bird by bird, La Rivers illustrates the Mormon cricket's significance in high desert ecosystems. Nevada and green-tailed towhees, he writes, "were found feeding on the small, third-instar [immature, or nymphal] crickets in the Bull Run Mountains, southwest of Mountain City." In contrast, La Rivers witnessed American magpies, Brewer's blackbirds, horned larks, sage grouse, and Nevada loggerhead shrikes feeding "exclusively" on mature crickets. Still south of Mountain City, he observed the sage thrasher "feeding not only on the migrating crickets, in company with grasshopper mice and shrews, but also digging up crickets from partly finished wasp burrows."[38] Here, La Rivers offers anecdotal evidence of the mouse named for its prey and the bird named for its habitat both feeding on a grasshopper that shelters, suns, and molts in sagebrush. Here, too, we glimpse a web of relationships—between birds and grasshoppers; mice, shrews, and grasshoppers; birds and rodents; grasshoppers and wasps—that predate *Homo sapiens* by at least 150 million years.

Not only do birds eat Mormon crickets, they also eat the insect's eggs. La Rivers observed that Brewer's blackbirds feed exclusively on female crickets, "which the birds covet for their eggs." Western meadowlarks, he tells us, "have been reported at various times as destroying entire, vast cricket egg-beds." A native Great Basin bird, meadowlarks are the cricket's "ablest" predator, La Rivers explains: "Because a bird can consume up to two hundred eggs at a time, but only, at most, 8 or 10 adults, egg predators are generally more efficient against a species than animals which eat only adults." He concludes, "This wholesale destruction of the eggs becomes increasingly important in any human scheme to control the insect."[39] Human schemes notwithstanding, La Rivers's detailed observations of bird–cricket relationships reveal the workings of a nonhuman story set in an arid and well-inhabited landscape. Swarming crickets may illustrate nature's extravagance, even its chaos, yet their ecological niche is irrefutable.

In the millennia preceding the arrival of settler cultures and the concomitant rise of industrial capitalism, indigenous peoples coexisted with *Anabrus simplex.* Robert E. Pfadt, emeritus professor of entomology at the University of Wyoming, notes in a 1994 Agricultural Experiment Station bulletin that "among the artifacts discovered in a cave inhabited by humans near Ten Sleep, Wyoming, the cooked remains of several hundred Mormon crickets were found in a roasting pit. Charcoal from the hearth gave a radio-carbon date of 222 ± 150 B.C."[40] As late as the 1850s, while Mormon settlers despaired, Paiute tribes dug trenches thirty to forty feet long, covered them with straw, then drove bands of crickets into the grass and lit it on fire, thereby roasting the insects. These cricket drives were useful for more than just control of outbreaks. In "Some Insect Foods of the American Indians and How the Early Whites Reacted to Them," entomologist Gene R. De Foliart notes that charred crickets were collected, dried, and then ground into flour to sweeten bread.[41] In recognizing these insects as a valuable food source, indigenous cultures not only accommodated but also capitalized on spikes in grasshopper populations.

In contrast to such traditional grasshopper management strategies, the U.S. Department of Agriculture's online Economic Research Service reports that "pesticide use on major field crops, fruits, and vegetables more than doubled from 215 million pounds in 1964 to 511 million pounds in 2001."[42] Is it merely a widespread failure of imagination that has led to the current regime of insect management? Or does our cultural revulsion to grasshoppers and other "pests" justify waging chemical warfare against them?

During a Mormon cricket outbreak in the late 1980s in Colorado and Utah, entomologist Charles MacVean researched damage done to food plants by swarming crickets. Examining the "gut contents" of immature and mature crickets, MacVean discovered that, contrary to popular belief, "over 90% of the adults' diet was made up of sagebrush, with only traces of grasses, forbs, or other crickets. Thus, the adult insects, which are potentially the most damaging, fed on one of the least desirable plants." MacVean's field observations counter the myth of the horned locust. By determining what plants the cricket actually does eat, he illuminates insect–plant relationships. His research also suggests that by cultivating nonnative crops in prime cricket habitat—thereby plowing under sagebrush—settler cultures may, in effect, leave swarming grasshoppers with little else but these introduced crops to eat. MacVean concludes that the cricket's reputation as a voracious pest "stems more from inaccuracies in the literature and historical legend than from current facts. . . . These insects are native to North American rangelands and have coexisted successfully with range plants for centuries." Not averse to managing outbreaks of the insect, MacVean notes that where range conditions dictate cricket control, he sees "promise" in using a naturally occurring parasite, *Varimorpha,* on immature crickets. Unlike chemical agents, he notes, the parasite "does not threaten non-target insects, wildlife, water sources, or human safety."[43] MacVean's research challenges the rhetoric that has defined grasshopper management for the past 150 years. In advocating the use of a nontoxic, organic technology—an endemic parasite—he recasts the Mormon cricket as a biological creature vulnerable to environmental pathogens. With ample evidence that this long-horned grasshopper wreaks much less havoc than widely imagined, we might ask how, exactly, to dismantle the massive and misguided system of control that has come to be called insect management.

In the summer of 2006, not far from the Mountain City site of La Rivers's 1939 cricket observations, a hopper infestation spurred residents of Tuscarora, Nevada, to bait crickets with carbaryl. In a July 25, 2006, e-mail message, local artist Elaine Parks explained, "We are provided bait by the county and have been baiting [crickets] ourselves to keep them from coming to town. Last year we had a terrible infestation. The crickets were crawling all over our houses, by the ten thousands—literally." Weeks of such close contact with the crickets allowed Parks to observe their "various habits."[44] This led her and fellow resident, Sidne Teske, to construct a Mormon cricket float for Tuscarora's Fourth of July parade.

In a photograph printed in the *Elko Free Press* in July 2006, their super-sized Mormon cricket perches atop an ATV rolling along in the parade. The chicken-wire and burlap-mâché cricket is about four feet long and eighteen inches high. Shiny black eyes protrude from its huge blue head. An emerald green crown extends down to the insect's purple thorax. The cricket's shield, vestigial wings that run the length of its thorax, is fuchsia. Three sets of jointed, anatomically correct, purple legs form elegant triangles with the roof of the ATV. Parks and Teske's simulacrum, despite its surreal, larger-than-life proportions, accurately portrays the cricket's colors in its most beautiful instar, a mature and breeding grasshopper. The bright colors celebrate a cricket in the prime of its five months of life, its shell shimmering like a prism in a beam of sunlight. Yet the cricket's perch is a camouflage-green four-wheeler flanked by two women. One pushes a wheelbarrow containing a box of carbaryl. The other pushes a bait spreader. In her e-mail Parks admits that the float "was inspired by our successful baiting."[45]

Our cultural revulsion to swarming insects makes it easy for us to empathize with the residents of Mountain City. Envisioning legions of grasshoppers crawling all over our own houses, we envision apocalypse descending. Taking up arms—or carbaryl—against the insects, as Parks and her community did, strikes us as justified, necessary, even natural. For parade-goers, the cricket symbolizes destruction, while the ATV—doubtless more destructive than a native insect to the desert ecosystem—bears the grasshopper aloft like a trophy. Technology, in the form of poisons, enables humans to turn the tide in their favor. Yet Parks's float also uncovers the ironies inherent in baiting crickets with poisons that bio-accumulate in the soil and water, posing a long-term threat to humans, nontarget plants, and other animals. In casting the grasshopper as that which we must destroy, we fail to see our impact on the landscape, to imagine ecological complexity.[46]

Environmental historian Carolyn Merchant suggests that North America has become the stage for the Euroamerican "recovery plot . . . the long, slow process of returning humans to the Garden of Eden through labor in the earth."[47] The arachnids, crustaceans, and insects that compose the phylum Arthropoda account for roughly 80 percent of all known species. Yet because insects like the Mormon cricket have not been successfully yoked to Western civilization's plow, we have discounted their place in nonhuman nature. Our attempt to banish them from Eden illustrates an either-or hierarchical dualism rooted in biblical doctrine, and this doctrine blinds us to an ecological worldview. In our zeal to destroy those insects we deem pests, we do not deliver ourselves from evil. Instead, we visit ecological destruction on the earth and on ourselves.

The scribe in Isaiah 40:22 proclaims, "It is he who sits above the circle of the earth, and its inhabitants are like grasshoppers; who stretches out the heavens like a curtain, and spreads them like a tent to live in."[48] If likening human beings to grasshoppers is meant to humble the reader and reinforce the authority of God, these lines might also be read ecologically. Humankind inhabits the same tent as grasshoppers. We live and die under the same sky. The gulf between us and them is a human construct predicated on a great chain of being, inspired by Christianity and driven by capitalism. Clearly, there are other biblical metanarratives that can guide us. Apocalypse almost always necessitates some kind of redemption—a remnant is saved from destruction, hope rises from the ashes, life somehow begins anew—with a deeper understanding of the human actions that led to destruction. Our interactions with nonhuman nature need not follow a script that wreaks havoc. We can forgo the notion that the desert is merely the backdrop against which we work out our human salvation and choose, instead, to see ourselves as one part of an interconnected and dynamic living world.

Notes

1. Exodus 10:12, *Oxford Annotated Bible* (New York: Oxford University Press, 1994), 81.

2. Joel 2:25, ibid., 1167.

3. Jeff DeLong, "Mormon Crickets Showing No Signs of Making Retreat," *Reno Gazette Journal,* June 20, 2006, D11.

4. Michelle Willms, "Mormon Cricket Infestation May Have Peaked," *Lovelock Review-Miner Newspaper Online,* February 23, 2006, http://nevadarancher.com/rminer/rm2006/rmfeb23c.htm.

5. James Nelson, "Mormon Crickets Devour Crops, Turn Roads Blood Red," Reuters News Service, June 14, 2003, http://www.cnn.com/2003/US/West/06/14/Mormon.crickets.reut/.

6. Revelation 9:7, *Oxford Annotated Bible* (New York: Oxford University Press, 1994), NT373.

7. Ibid.

8. Ibid.

9. "Senate Approves $20 million to Control Mormon Crickets," Environment News Service: International Daily Newswire, July 11, 2003, http://www.ens-newswire.com/ens/jul2003/2003-07-11-09.html.

10. Jon Carpenter, interview by author, July 21, 2006, Reno, Nevada.

11. Genesis 1:28, *Oxford Annotated Bible,* 3.

12. Nelson, "Mormon Crickets Devour Crops, Turn Roads Blood Red."

13. Carpenter interview.

14. Michelle Willms, "Mormon Cricket Infestation May Have Peaked."

15. Clemson University, "Fighting Our Insect Enemies: Achievements of Professional Entomology 1854–1954," http://entweb.clemson.pesticid.history.htm.

16. Howard Hickson, "Pesky Little Critters: Crickets in Elko County (1935–1938)," Howard Hickson's Histories, May 7, 2002, http://www.gbcnv.edu/howh/index.html.

17. Rachel Carson, *Silent Spring* (New York: Fawcett Crest, 1962), 24.

18. Sandra Steingraber, *Living Downstream: A Scientist's Personal Investigation of Cancer and the Environment* (1997; Cambridge, Mass.: Da Capo Press, 2010), 10.

19. Michael Burgett, "Online Lecture Notes: The Year of the Locust," 2002, http://www.ent.orst.edu//burgett/ent.300_lecture11.html.

20. Carson, *Silent Spring,* 88.

21. Steingraber, *Living Downstream,* 10.

22. EXTOXNET, Poison Toxicology Network, "Pesticide Information Profiles: Malathion," http://extoxnet.orst.edu/pips/malathio.htm, revised in 1996.

23. Burgett, "Online Lecture Notes: The Year of the Locust."

24. EXTOXNET, Poison Toxicology Network, "Pesticide Information Profiles: Malathion."

25. Burgett, "Online Lecture Notes: The Year of the Locust."

26. United Nations, "World Charter for Nature," http://www.un.org/documents/ga/res/37/a37r007.html.

27. Edward W. Evans, "Chemical and Biological Control of Grasshoppers in Utah," Extension Entomology, Utah State University, Fact Sheet No. 73 (December 1990), 2, http://www.extension.usu.edu/files/factsheets/grassho2.pdf.

28. Carpenter interview.

29. Evans, "Chemical and Biological Control of Grasshoppers in Utah," 2.

30. Ira La Rivers, "The Mormon Cricket as Food for Birds," *Condor* 43 (January 1941): 68.

31. Robert H. Harrison, "Toward a Philosophy of Nature," in *Uncommon Ground: Rethinking the Human Place in Nature,* ed. William Cronon (New York: Norton, 1996), 436.

32. Carpenter interview.

33. Ibid.

34. Charles Bergman, *Wild Echoes: Encounters with the Most Endangered Animals in North America* (Washington: Alaska Northwest Book, 1990), 10.

35. "Fact Sheet: Plant Protection and Quarantine: Grasshoppers and Mormon Crickets," Animal and Plant Health Inspection Service, USDA, May 2003, http://www.aphis.usda.gov/lpa/pubs/fsheet_faq_notice/fs_grasshoppersmc.htm.

36. "Site Specific Environmental Assessment: Rangeland Grasshopper and Mormon Cricket Suppression Program, Portland, Oregon," Animal and Plant Health Inspection Service, USDA, EA Number OR-06-02, March 2006, 2, 2, 1, 20.

37. Ibid., 23.

38. La Rivers, "The Mormon Cricket as Food for Birds," 65, 69, 67.

39. Ibid., 68.

40. Roberts E. Pfadt, "Species Fact Sheet: *Anabrus simplex Haldeman*," Wyoming Agricultural Experiment Station, Bulletin 912 (September 1994), 3.

41. Gene R. De Foliart, "Some Insect Foods of the American Indians and How the Early Whites Reacted to Them," *Food Insects Newsletter* 7, no. 3 (November 1994): 3.

42. "Agricultural Chemicals and Production Technology: Pest Management," USDA, 2005, http://usda.gov/Briefing/AgChemicals/pestmangementUSDA.

43. Charles MacVean, "Mormon Crickets: A Brighter Side," *Rangelands: Society for Range Management* 12, no. 4 (August 1990): 235.

44. Elaine Parks, "Mormon Crickets," e-mail to author, July 25, 2006.

45. Ibid.

46. Since the events detailed in our e-mail correspondence, Elaine Parks has reexamined both her relationship to the Mormon cricket and the insect's place in its own ecosystem. Her artist's installation, *Swarm,* was on display at the Nevada Museum of Art from December 2008 through March 2009 (see http://thisisreno.com/2009/12/). An interview with Parks was also featured on CBC Radio's DNTO (Definitely Not the Opera, episode 2010/04/21/) on April 25, 2010 (see http://www

.cbc.ca/). Moreover, since 2006 the community of Tuscarora has turned to playing loud music to keep the Mormon crickets at bay (see http://online.wsj.com/article/SB124052112850249691.html).

47. Carolyn Merchant, "Reinventing Eden: Western Culture as a Recovery Narrative," in *Uncommon Ground: Rethinking the Human Place in Nature,* ed. William Cronon (New York: Norton, 1996), 133.

48. Isaiah 40:2, *Oxford Annotated Bible,* OT918.

II. THE NATIVE TRASH ANIMAL

5 One Nation under Coyote, Divisible

Lisa Couturier

All that we are arises with our thoughts.
—Buddha

UNTIL THIS MOMENT—when I am walking quietly through fields of long grass, vines, mud, trees, thickets, and the pale gray air of March—the day has been ordinary. Like millions of other mothers across the country, I sent my child off to school, accomplished some work, and ran errands. Now not far beyond the field I am in, rush hour is winding down, stoves warm dinner, families relax inside their homes—in the country, the suburbs, the city—where the nightly news lights up dens along the East Coast. Parents kiss and play with giggling children they've missed all day. The family dog or cat scratches repeatedly at the door, asking to be let out into the peach-lit sky and then to come in, again and again. But just as the news ends and the dishes are cleaned, things will change. For outside, beyond the dens of humans, in the scattered winds of owls and near gatherings of wild geese, is the eastern coyote, the coyote stretching into the evening and, I hope, into the slowly darkening moments ahead.

Walking beside me is Rob Gibbs, a wildlife ecologist with the Montgomery County Park Department in Maryland, where, on the outskirts of Washington, D.C., sightings of coyotes have increased over the past few years. Behind us is my husband, who, during our half-hour drive from D.C., described how his boss, in Manhattan, believes our excursion to find coyotes is not all that interesting. This man's indifference, or lack of enthusiasm, is due to the fact that he lives in Westchester County, New York, which has been infiltrated by coyotes that, it is said, wound their way down the Adirondacks. As my husband spoke about his boss, I remembered once again the coyote that ventured out of Westchester through Yonkers and then headed south into the densely populated borough of the Bronx, from whence it had to cross the Harlem River, by swimming or by bridge, to arrive on the agonizingly populated shore of Manhattan. Naturalists theorize that, once in Manhattan, the coyote made its way south through Riverside Park and then scratched its way east along the streets of the Upper West Side to arrive, finally, in a landscape the coyote surely believed was, at the very least, some approximate rendition of wilderness: Central Park. But before long, on April Fool's Day 1999, the thirty-five-pound coyote was stalked by urban park rangers and hit with a tranquilizer dart a few blocks from the famous Plaza Hotel on the park's southern edge. This occurred not long after I arrived in Washington, and ever since I have wondered, How did I leave New York, travel through gray walls, south, when coyotes were coming closer toward my life, from the north?

This does not mean coyotes were not already in Maryland, because they were, out in the fringes, in the foothills west toward West Virginia. But just as water dripping from a faucet grows into an overflowing puddle, so too has the coyote population grown and begun to stream east through the state. The fact is that right now Maryland has the fine distinction of being, along with Delaware, the state in which coyotes from the north and coyotes from the south are converging. So it seems, after all, that I have arrived in just the right place at just the right time. As Rob, my husband, and I move on, I picture in my head a map of the United States and imagine on it two shaggy arrows of gray and reddish-brown fur, one curving down the East Coast, one curving up, until, in Maryland, the arrowheads meet along the Potomac River, virtually on the doorstep of the president of the United States, where in the nearby woods of dusk and dawn, the country's foremost canine predator is forming a new native American nation: the Nation of Eastern Coyote.

One way to find a coyote, Rob has told us already, is to search deeper into McKee-Beshers Wildlife Management Area, the official name of this brushy, thicketed, wooded, and swampy landscape along the Potomac River that is one of the wildest spots in all the state, although it is only thirty or so minutes outside of Washington, D.C. As the sun drops closer to the horizon, Rob will set on the ground a tape-recorded predator call, the voice of an animal in distress. Tonight, the distress will be that of a rabbit, since coyotes enjoy eating rabbits. Coyotes also are one of the best mouse chasers working today; and when rabbits and mice are unavailable, moles and voles are preferred. The curious and smart coyote, which is all coyotes, will, we hope, awaken to its nocturnal day and—eagerly anticipating dinner or, depending on how one twists time, breakfast—come to investigate the call of the distressed rabbit. We will wait, crouched down, our backs against brush and trees, behind the sound of the rabbit's crying, and downwind of what I imagine will be fields of emerging coyotes.

I have, in my life, glimpsed the silhouette of a coyote just once. It was two years ago, and it occurred so fast that had I been tuning the car radio or glancing left instead of right, I could not be claiming to have seen what I believe I saw. In fact, my conclusion that the animal actually was a coyote has come to me with increased confidence only recently, which often leaves me to tell a still somewhat hesitant-sounding story, depending on who is listening. After all, a coyote is something like a UFO in these parts: some people believe in them, some don't; and so you make midcourse adjustments as you speak, knowing instinctively who is which, or at least, who desires to believe in the mysterious.

There are not many more facts to tell, except that I was driving down a well-traveled, yet dark, two-lane road at 10:15 p.m., just three minutes beyond the city limits of Washington, into Maryland, when not far from one of the sporadically lit street lamps there stood, like a shadow, like a ghost, a German-shepherdish creature. In the split second that my mind registered *dog*, I questioned what was no longer visible: *the legs were too long; the body was too thick; it disappeared too quickly.*

It is useful to know, however, that at the time of my questionable coyote sighting I had recently had a baby. A related thought is that I wasn't out much at night back then, and so, when by chance I did get out, I was operating in that depleted state of exhaustion known as the constantly-nursing-baby syndrome. Women in this realm drown fast in what we mothers call "mother muddle." A "muddle" is forgetting words midsentence, phone numbers as you are dialing them, and many other ordinary, common things that previously kept us on track and believing we lived in the human world. Positively identifying, while in muddle, an animal on the side of the road, in the dark, virtually in the city, as a coyote? *Nah.*

But it kept at me, this coyote. When I took my infant daughter down to the Potomac River's muddy paths in her SUV-like stroller, I looked for coyote tracks. If it was not spring and the time of coyote birth, when coyotes spend their days by the den in a side of a hill, there was a chance a coyote would have settled near rock piles, in a hollow log, under ledges, in a drainage pipe—of which there are several along the river—or in the woodsy and grassy sides of the path. For some reason, perhaps because I myself was sleep-deprived, I fantasized about finding the coyote's bed. Locating the private place of a coyote, where it dreamed and secretly cycled through the same stages of sleep as I once had, held an inexplicable allure. Though I never deluded myself with the idea that I heard a group of howling coyotes, sometimes I stopped the stroller fast, thinking, mistakenly it would turn out, that what was a bird or a squirrel had been a coyote's yelp or yip. By the end of our walks, I'd pointed out to my baby the red-eared sliders sunning on the water, the whitewash of owls, a great blue heron or two, gulls, kingfishers. No coyote.

Until eight months later when, in my mother's group one Friday morning, wherein seven or so mothers—and their plump, rosy-cheeked, crawling babies—came to my house for banana bread and coffee. It was then, between bouts of babies crying, that one of the mothers brought up an article about coyotes that she had read in the local weekly paper. This news ended any discussions about weaning babies, disciplining kids, sex, or the lack of it.

In one moment, the mere mention of a word—coyote—changed everyone. Some of the excitement dangling in the air was leavened with protective instincts and with fear of a foreign creature, a predator, in our suburban midst. Though I wondered, too, how much each woman inherently understood how close the perceived personality of a coyote matched her own psyche as a mother. For what is a mother in the modern world—as she juggles children and work and life—if not a coyote: a spontaneous creature by necessity; a creature defying fixed roles; one who looks for shortcuts and realizes the essential health of playfulness over seriousness.

Whatever each of us individually and silently thought, it was clear that for this morning at least nothing was more important in the world than coyotes. A new story had arrived in the lives of these women, and it was not only about the birth of their awareness of the coyote but about the real wild animal itself. This was when I began thinking of the presence of the coyote as something of a request—a request that we create our own new eastern stories, different from the western ones, for this predator, stories that necessarily might begin with: coyotes, what could they mean to me?

My sister lives in Virginia's horse country, where she keeps her horses and the stray dogs she has rescued. On her large landscape of fields and woods live owls, foxes, crows, hawks, snakes, fence lizards, and one day, she dreams, coyotes. Every so often she calls to let me know she heard something in the night, although what, exactly, she is unsure. A man who lives near my sister, a man who talks to horses and whose horses listen, says that for several years now he has seen coyotes, up on the dusty gravel road leading to his ranch, at twilight. Without much hesitation, he says he may shoot one. Once, when this man handed me a beer and welcomed me into his home, he detailed the sordid story of the stuffed raven I noticed sitting on his coffee table, the raven he'd shot long ago, when small pockets of the birds still flew east of the Mississippi. Another man declared recently that if he had sheep and a sheep was killed, he would blame coyotes and shoot one. He doesn't have sheep, so perhaps he's joking, but it's hard to tell, especially since the idea of killing is spoken with such ease, while smiling.

I want to say to those willing to shoot at the unknown—to shoot at what is perceived as a threat—that perhaps certain explicit information would calm their fears. For instance, a coyote's main diet is not sheep but rabbits, mice, voles, moles, woodchucks, fruit, corn, and carrion. A coyote's overall temperament and behavior are not vicious; it will not attack, in packs, the lone person out for a walk; and it has been known, when captured, to roll belly-up, like a dog. Coyotes can be affectionate and sociable, or solitary and seemingly lonely. Some coyotes mate for life, and the male, female, and their offspring constitute the "pack." Pups from this pack may, instead of venturing out on their own, stay for a while with their parents to help raise babies born in the following year.

Knowledge—does it make it any easier to redirect one's rage?

In the complicated eastern landscapes where humans mix with coyote, it is helpful to remember Emerson, who said, "You shall have joy, or you shall have power . . . you shall not have both." In the end, I wander south to my sister's land in Virginia because her open fields nip at me, reminding me of the agricultural landscape where we spent the later years of our childhood and where my sister, on one of her walks, found Brandy, a wounded but *sonsy* wild husky that so resembled a wolf we believed she had brought one home.

Sonsy, which means "attractive and healthy," comes from the Irish Gaelic *sonas*, which means "good fortune." Brandy brought good fortune, if it can be considered as something other than wealth, as something that instead brings one a sense of living authentically. For some months before we found her, Brandy had lived outside, in woods, in wind. She drank from the little brown-water creek. She slept curled in a perfect circle, her head wrapped around her legs and her tail over her nose. She brought to us the earth that had settled in her, the earth's ease with solitude, and after she healed and could have run, she stayed. Afternoons, we followed her through sun or rain as she trotted, nose up in the air then down to the soil, hoping to catch a mouse's scent or movement. When day turned and the sky's upper edges darkened, Brandy sat by the sliding glass door, looked into the world with her eyes of crystal blue light, and howled, singing of something eternal that, when she was free like a wolf, or like a coyote, had inhabited her, inhabited her still, and over time came to inhabit us so much that we would run our hands over her thick furred back, rub our cheeks on her snout, and beg, "Brandy . . . howl, girl." We wanted to be taken. We wanted accompaniment, as though Brandy's howling was a song, a ballad, a peaceful greeting to the unknowns of the dark night ahead.

My old coyote-silhouette story came to mind when I first asked Rob to take me on what could be called a predator search, since a variety of predators other than coyotes—owls, for instance, or foxes—might appear. But I wasn't shy; I had a lust for coyote. The silhouette—it had just not been enough. Seeing a coyote for longer than a moment was, to be honest, an experience I felt I deserved. A need, really, the origins of which, it is my hunch, had grown from the attempts we all make to understand the misunderstood creatures in one's life, whether they be people or animals.

My desire cut deep into that vein of longing that stretches between a person and the cosmos for things you think you never will have and keep asking for—silently, anyway. For everyone, there is always something. In our private moments it is an almost childlike urgency: "I wish, I wish upon a star . . . to see a coyote, near or far." Two years after I'd seen the coyote silhouette, newspapers were running a coyote article here and there, and I increasingly felt it unfair that people who perhaps never wanted to see a coyote, who had not wished upon any stars, nonetheless had been visited by a coyote: in the garage, reported one local newspaper; eating a squirrel in the front yard, described by another; and the veterinarian who in the *Washington Post* cited the story of his client, a farmer who had his "barn swept clean of nearly ten barn cats by coyotes."

Then, too, there had been those who had not seen but heard coyotes and described the coyote howl as "haunting," reported the *Post,* as "very chilling," "troubling," and "creepy," reminding me of what Jung said: We are "afraid of anything new because it contains unknown powers, indefinite dangers. . . . Everybody is afraid, nobody likes new ideas; they always throw people into a panic, and where there is panic, there is bloodshed."

Bloodshed is the predominant American story of the western coyote as well as its cousin and old foe, the wolf—the predator our twenty-sixth president,

Theodore Roosevelt (for whom the teddy bear is named, with reference to his bear hunting) called "the archetype of ravin, the beast of waste and desolation." Early Americans came to the shores of this country with an inherited European hatred for the wolf, which grew vehemently to include the coyote. Although I'm an easterner, I don't think I'd be remiss if I said that many westerners think of the coyote (or "Song Dog," "God's Dog," or "Little Wolf") as the symbol of all that is wild and free, but that some consider the coyote, who like the wolf has at times been known to prey on goats, chickens, and lambs, an eliminable nuisance. Through what is currently and euphemistically called Wildlife Services (WS), and what for many decades was more realistically termed Animal Danger Control (ADC), the U.S. government has, since the early 1900s, destroyed the millions of coyotes, wolves, mountain lions, and bears that ranchers condemn as livestock killers. This service costs the American people ten million taxpayer dollars per year, and it continues to this day despite a U.S. Government Accounting Office report issued fifteen years ago that found ADC kills coyotes even when damage to livestock has not occurred.

Surprising as it sounds, as early as 1906 the renowned nature writer John Burroughs claimed that the predators in Yellowstone "certainly needed killing," a comment likely directed at wolves. Lisa Mighetto, in *Wild Animals and American Environmental Ethics* (Tucson: University of Arizona Press, 1991), calls them "the quintessential predators." Though by now the majority of Americans understand wolves as shy, reclusive animals that are not a threat to humans, Mighetto says, "the *idea* of the wolf . . . has been more terrifying than the behavior of the actual animal." Coyote, being such a close cousin to wolf, suffers from the same antipathy. "Throughout the twentieth century coyotes in this country have suffered numerous atrocities," writes Mighetto, "including being ignited alive and left to starve with their mouths wired shut; some have even been scalped."

Over the last twenty-five years, WS/ADC has destroyed seventy-five thousand to ninety thousand coyotes *per year* in, mostly, seventeen western states. This management tactic successfully accomplishes two things. First, it elevates the risk of overabundance of the rodents and other small mammals coyotes are so important in controlling. Look, for example, at an old black-and-white photograph courtesy of the Idaho State Historical Society, Boise. Published in Mighetto's book, it depicts five men, a few of them in suits, standing by a large cart drawn by two horses standing on a wet, muddy or snowy, road. The year is 1912. It is daylight, morning perhaps, and each man is holding, upside down and by one leg, a dead jackrabbit. In the cart, piled high and sliding off of one another's furry torsos, are the bodies of the other

1,195 jackrabbits the men had shot, "representing one night's catch," reads the photo's caption. One night.

Second, killing coyotes simply makes more of them. When coyotes inhabit a landscape where hunting is not allowed, such as modern-day Yellowstone, they live in social groups in which, for the most part, only the dominant pair breeds; others in the group, the younger, less dominant individuals, are essentially behaviorally sterile. Lift this arrangement out of Yellowstone, though, and set it down in a landscape of relentless persecution, where virtually all coyote social groups have been dismantled, and the logical outcome is that, without dominant pairs, breeding is acceptable for all.

That the behavioral ecology of the coyote—arguably the most adaptable, successful, and incredibly intelligent midsize predator roaming this country today—is somehow overlooked allows WS/ADC to continue its mission. In addition to the aerial gunning (shooting from a helicopter) of coyotes and other predators, additional methods of sanitizing the landscape—poisons, gasses, snares, and leghold traps—consequently destroy many nontarget animals: dogs, opossums, foxes, skunks, vultures, badgers, and raccoons, to name several.

This is in sharp contrast to the Native American relationship to the coyote, an animal understood and admired for its intelligence, cunning, and joyful spirit. Navajo stories, for instance, served—says a gem of an old Interior Department booklet titled *Coyote Tales,* published in 1949—"to instruct the young with regard to right and wrong, and many times the characters [were] personified animals. . . . A story might illustrate the fact that the strong should not use their strength to take things from the weak." There are stories like "Coyote and Rabbit," wherein Coyote is "out-coyoted," so to speak, by Rabbit, coyote's main food. We have "Coyote and Crow," in which Coyote's mischievous and sneaky behavior leads to his own demise as he chomps down on a cactus instead of the yummy bluebird dinner that Crow had led everyone to believe was waiting under a hat. And we have "Coyote and the Fawn's Stars," in which a seemingly sweet deer mother resorts to tricking a gullible coyote father. In the story, Coyote admires the spots, or stars, on the backs of Deer's fawns and expresses a desire that his babies be adorned with stars. Deer appears quite civilized and helpful during the encounter, and she manages the situation thus: "When my babies are very little, I build a big fire. The sparks from the fire make the stars. You can do that for your babies," she directs Coyote. "Then they will have pretty stars too." Coyote misunderstands Deer and puts its babies straight into the fire. Deer watches, knowing this is wrong, but she does not prevent it.

When Coyote asks, "Have they been in the fire long enough?" Will they have pretty stars now?" Deer says, "Yes," and she runs away laughing, knowing that all the young coyotes have died. Coyote was angry, the story continues, and so chased Deer, and "still chases deer, but he never catches her."

Is "Coyote and the Fawn's Stars" meant to inspire belief in one's own beauty? Is it about revenge, since it is, after all, the weaker of the two personalities who has in the past had her beloveds killed by the stronger? Is it simply an attempt to explain why coyotes ever began chasing deer in the first place? Or might the meaning reside in something else altogether?

"Everyone is a moon," wrote Mark Twain, "and has a dark side," like the deer, "which he never shows to anybody"—except perhaps when it comes to coyotes. Then the moon may, at times, shine brightly with fear, aggression, and the loathing reserved for predators. As civilized as our nation is, coyotes make it clear that there is a wildness running through our landscapes and evidently through ourselves: Could it be we need to manage our own wildness more than that of the coyote's? Or could we say of coyotes what the poet Tanaka Shozo said of rivers: "The care of rivers is not a question of rivers, but of the human heart"?

In the way that "love, like death, changes everything," as written by the mystic Kahlil Gibran, so too does hate change everything. And it is within this emotional aversion that the story of the eastern coyote began. Imagine, if you will, the northeastern woods of the United States in the early part of the twentieth century, when the few remaining wolves—those rare descendants of wolves that had escaped the wrath of Roosevelt and Burroughs and outlasted nearly three hundred years of American abhorrence, three hundred years of being shot on sight—still roamed these deepest and most impenetrable places. With all other forests in the United States clean of wolves, western coyotes took to walking where they would. And so somewhere back then, a coyote arrived in the northeastern woods on, say, a March evening in the bitter cold hills of Maine or Vermont and ran into a wolf, a wolf long alone without its pack.

The two canines met. They sniffed and, one would have to guess, came to some sort of an agreement about their chance evening meeting. Who knows how long they ran together; if they shared prey; if they played, as we know they do; if they howled on the same nights, together, their own distinct howls. We have no human witnesses and are, therefore, some sixty to eighty years later, left with a mystery of cold nights, dark trees, winds, moonlight, and two canine species making themselves anew. If it sounds like a romance, maybe it was. If it sounds like two creatures driven by related biology, hormones, and instincts, maybe it was that as well. This is how the world evolves. As the Upanishads said, it is a time of being led "from the unreal to the real." It is mysteriousness moving into our lives like love—unrestrained and stormy, but gripping, until finally there is surrender and acceptance of it all as a gift, a present that each day will unwrap itself before us.

What is known, however, is that not long after this time the wolf permanently left the upper reaches of the northeastern United States and retreated into the Canadian wilderness, while the coyote, imbued with the wolf's genes, grew bigger than its western predecessor and trickled slowly into the rapidly developing East Coast.

Rob had been patient when, earlier as we were walking into McKee-Beshers, I thought I'd found a coyote track in the mud, which, I was absolutely convinced, looked like the picture of one I'd etched into my mind, the one with the defining claws on toes three and four, the center toes. "Paw size is perfect," Rob agreed as he bent down closer to take a look, "but it could just as well have been a dog's," he concluded, as he tipped down the visor of his olive-green baseball cap and rose to continue walking. Rob is wearing what he suggested I wear, greens and browns, camouflage-colored cotton clothing that, unlike synthetic clothing, does not, under your arms or between your thighs, annoyingly *swish, swish, swish*—the noise of humans easily detected by coyotes. In the short time we have been in the beige fields, I have watched Rob, who is cautious, like an animal. He senses when to stop; he spots things in the brush I would not see; he cups his hand to his ears and makes them more canid-like to funnel sounds of the fields into himself—a scratchiness to his left, the tousled grass to the right. He appears to notice, at once, the ground and the sky—pointing out a sharp-shinned hawk one moment and whispering, "deer, in the corner, there," the next. The land we walk through is state hunting land, and so here there are only a mere twelve white-tailed deer per square mile compared to the county's more densely overpopulated parks and suburban landscapes, where one hundred to two hundred deer live per square mile. Rob spends his days attempting to find solutions that would control the county's explosive deer population, and he hopes that, somehow, the growing number of coyotes might help thin the herds. There are no figures, though, for the population of eastern coyotes living in the area. We know only that they are here, that whatever their numbers might be it is estimated those numbers could be growing by 15 to 25 percent a year, and that, as Rob says, coyotes are viewed by more than a few in the area as "wolves in miniature," that is, as adversaries.

Spring peepers crank up the volume of their peeping as, thirty minutes into our coyote search, which is a long time for our intermittent rabbit's crying, the upper portion of the pale gray sky has turned a truer purplish blue. An endless stream of jets blaze toward the airports—Reagan National and Dulles International—not all that far from us. We are downwind and smell what the light breezes shed our way: pools of mud, dry late-winter grass, cool evening air, dead leaves. Ducks fly low over the darkening fields and head north. They must hear our injured rabbit below them, and I watch their wings overhead, trying to confirm my suspicion that the calls of the rabbit motivate them to fly faster. I believe that certain things matter to animals, and though it's just a guess, it seems that the squealing, unrelenting sound of a rabbit's pain would be one of those things. We are starting to feel that trying to use this sound to out-trick the biggest trickster—a live, frolicking coyote—might prove us fools.

My knees are aching from the pose of stillness I am attempting to hold—rock or tree stump, though I haven't the strength of either. Waiting for coyotes even in a place Rob guesses is prime coyote habitat will be, it appears, an enterprise of patience, hope, and exceedingly good luck. I distract myself by replaying in my mind the easy-to-come-by textbook facts about the coyote, an animal that is, one could say, through and through a true blue-blooded American since coyotes are native only to North America. The coyote is a fast runner, clocking up to forty miles an hour, which makes it the fastest of all North American canids patrolling its territory of anywhere from one to ten square miles. If it lives past adolescence, and 50 percent of coyotes do not, the animal I wish to see tonight could be eight to twelve years old, its lifespan in the wild. The coyote is a capable swimmer and an agile jumper, both of which give it an advantage over bobcats when hunting rabbits that, nimble and fast themselves, have been known to dive into water to escape—behavior that deters the feline, but not the canine. Including its bushy, black-tipped, foot-long tail, a coyote's grayish, reddish, brownish body is about four feet long; shoulder height is about two feet; and the eastern coyote, which is larger than its western counterpart, weighs generally anywhere from twenty to more than fifty pounds. This identifying information is something to grab on to, I think, as I squint through the binoculars, waiting for the fiery figure of a coyote that might match the sizes and colors I have in my head. Still, all of these facts are not unlike my saying

I am five feet, eight inches tall; weigh 130 pounds; that I have brownish, reddish, grayish, longish hair; and that my home range is about ten square miles east, north, and south from my den at Little Falls along the Potomac River. Certain facts provide certain knowledge. But what are our joys and privacies? What shapes our dreams; what have we lost; what do we desire? What, when night falls, would be the stories we would tell to those waiting to listen?

Though she died years ago, I keep looking for Brandy, for the movements of her wolf-like, coyote-like body in what has now become a moonlit field, dark except for the occasional passing of a red-tinted light Rob shines into the long grass and brushy trees. We search for the yellow eyes of coyotes that we hope are venturing toward our tape-recorded sounds and thus toward the answer to the question coyote carries in its own mind: *Rabbit? Dying rabbit?* If a coyote dares, Rob says, it will circle, like all great predators, and then dash, run, dart toward us, figuring *a rabbit in distress is being distressed by another animal—an animal,* thinks coyote, *that may itself be edible, if I can get to it fast enough.* Behavior not much different than my hurrying to the two-for-the-price-of-one-sale at Sears. Or, in coyote's—and McDonald's—reasoning: eat one, get one free! This is coyote cleverness, coyote consciousness.

A predator search being what it is, it does not include an actual incident of predation. I will not see the superb thinking skills of a coyote. I will not see a coyote ally itself with a badger, as one of the old myths has it. I will not see a badger (who does not live in these parts anyway) do all the hard work of digging up a rodent from its burrow only to have a coyote waiting at the other end of the rodent's underground tunnel where, when the rodent pops up to escape the badger, the coyote grabs it. I will not see a patient coyote sitting on a frozen lake by the hole of an otter fishing below the ice. I will not see the industrious otter poke its cool, wet head up through its icy hole and slap down its sparkling fish, when the coyote will instantly steal it. I will not see a coyote chasing a larger animal in circles, as it might a pronghorn antelope on the open plains of the West, until the coyote tires and gestures, somehow, to a buddy coyote to take over the chase, continuing until the antelope succumbs, whereupon the companions will divvy up dinner. I will not see a coyote glancing toward the daylit sky for the flight of crows or vultures, a hint of carrion on the ground below.

The truth is, I might not see anything at all out here. We have, after almost an hour, milked this first spot, Rob says. It is time to move on, especially before our poor old rabbit tape and our knees die out. We discuss heading farther into the countryside, toward a place called Poolesville, where reports of coyotes have been more numerous. Part of me wants to stay where we are, along the river, since I imagine that coyotes living here could be those that at night travel safely and secretly down the densely wooded, dark, and remote towpath of the C&O Canal, which borders the Potomac on the Maryland side of the river, and would lead a coyote, should a coyote decide to make the trip, right to my stone cottage overlooking the river. My sense is that my silhouette coyote, who disappeared into the woods, lives here in McKee-Beshers.

Another part of me thinks Poolesville is a better bet, not necessarily because of previous reports about coyotes, which to anyone else might be the more significant and rational reason to head out there, but instead, because of an old and unusable sterling silver fountain pen that in the 1800s belonged to Hettie M. Poole, daughter of Mr. Poole, founder of Poolesville, and that, on Christmas day in 1982, came to belong to me. There is a story of this pen, a spirit in it that, whenever I fail to attend to the mysteries of the nonhuman world—whenever, for instance, I walk without listening for sopranos in the trees or fail to turn my head toward the cries of the crows, whenever I dismiss the smell of rain and fire on a cold day or do not smile at angry squirrels, when I neglect noticing the blood of road-killed snakes and deer as the blood of sentient beings—then the story of my pen reminds me that it is not always the human world that shows us the way.

That Christmas day in 1982, when I was twenty, the man who is now my husband handed me his gift. I unwrapped an old, polished, smallish wooden box that once had belonged to his grandmother and in which she had kept her precious silver belongings. He had lined the box with golden silk and had fashioned, on the inside edge, a ledge. Upon this ledge, cocooned in yet more silk, was a fountain pen like none I had ever seen, a pen densely carved with flowers and intricate vines except for a smooth, plain space of oval on the silver in which were engraved the initials H. M. P.— Hettie M. Poole. I was told the history of this woman and the old wooden store in which the pen had been found and told that, alas, the pen did not work. We would need to fix it. And so I ran my fingers along the flowers and vines, as though they were braille for the natural world I so loved.

But you know Christmas day, or any important religious holiday, and how, when there are no children present or yet born to the family, there is abundant time to eat and talk, and after dinner when it is quiet, you return to the living room to gaze at gifts exchanged, to look out the window, or stare at the fire. This was when, as everyone left the chandeliered dinning room and headed toward the brightly lit Christmas tree in the living room, that I once again took out my pen. We passed it around the eight people present until someone suggested I try it. Maybe the salesperson had been wrong, maybe the pen, if dipped in ink, would actually work.

I opened a bottle of black ink, dipped the pen in, scraped the excess ink off the edge of the bottle and, just as the tip of the pen touched the paper, all the lights in the house immediately, magically, frightfully went out. The people who would one day become my in-laws, the men who would become my brothers and their girlfriends—all of us sat suddenly decorated in darkness. It was a mystery that seemed solvable, simple enough—*Here I am, folks, Hettie M. Poole. Don't even think of using my pen!*

But was that it?

In the years since, I have come to understand the mystery wasn't about death, about Hettie's death, but about birth: the birth of a new awareness on a night that was otherwise meant as a celebration of newness, acceptance, and miracles. It was Christmas night, and we'd been taken under the wing of a presence that, as I think of it now, was much like the presence of animals in our lives: does not the inaccessibility to an animal's mind and thoughts throw us into some state of darkness? I cannot ask anything of a wild animal. Instead, animals sprint across the backlit stages of our thoughts or in the literal darkness of our streets. We cannot ask what are an animal's experiences of generosity and devotion, of suffering, of nourishment and exile, what it is for them to have possibilities, to know terror and love, to understand possession, to bid farewell, to feel awe, to know loneliness and gratitude, starlessness, sorrow, and loss. But "the difficulty, or even the impossibility, of conveying to others the exact nature of something," writes Donald Griffen in *Animal Minds* (Chicago: University of Chicago Press, 2001), "does not rule it out of existence or deprive it of significance."

It seems, then, that the mystery of Hettie, of what she birthed into our lives that night, was an awareness of paradox: perhaps in not always asking for verification we come to know in our hearts something is true.

Eventually, at the requests of those with me, I lifted the pen, whereupon all the colorful lights miraculously fluttered back on. Many Christmases have since passed. I never did have the pen fixed and have never since put it to paper. I prefer simply to remember Hettie, who all those years ago embroidered mystery into my days, who crossed into light and then took it away to reveal that, even in the darkness of night, there is a world more decorated, ornamented, and interwoven than we may know. This was why, when Rob suggested we head to Poolesville, I though it might be Hettie, or the paradox of Hettie, that, more than anything else, would now lead us into vines of coyotes.

With the decision made about Poolesville, Rob asks if we can first stop along a road that cuts through fields of the nocturnal woodcock's singing grounds, fields in which songs of foreplay, songs meant to attract wood-cock hens, are sung. The fields become mating grounds from February to May and then, some three weeks later, transform into birthing grounds. Depending on whom you ask, a woodcock is also known as a timerdoodle, a big-eye, a bogsucker, or a mudbat—not the most attractive-sounding names, especially since the male woodcock is something of a romantic.

It will be good, though, to listen for a while to romance rather than to death, to listen for, as Rob describes it, the buzzing *peeent* sound of the male woodcock. Rob *peeents* the sound himself and explains that this is the song of the male while he is on the ground. After the woodcock's *peeent,* the bird takes off into the night sky, his wings composing a musical whistle as he ascends two or three hundred feet in the air. In the dark, he circles randomly, with what guidebooks describe as a "bubbly chipping," before he descends, spiraling and zigzagging his way back to the earth, back to his grassy field, singing his liquid and warbling *pee chuck tee chuck chip chip chip.*

It is this love song we want to hear—as though we are hens listening for the most beautiful boy in the grass—when we pull over and idle Rob's truck on the side of a lonely two-lane road within the territory of McKee Beshers's black fields of grass, woods, and thickets and under a moon still rising, which means it is still more dark than it is light. Quite unexpectedly, when we have not asked, when we have not positioned ourselves downwind on our miserable old knees for hours, begging with a taped rabbit call, this is when we hear not a *peeent* but what I am only able to describe as a hurt woman, a woman screaming from the bottom of her belly. She screams again, a primal, bone-chilling scream, from our left, in the darkness. Rob shuts off the truck. Another scream. We open our doors—another scream—step into the road, and gently close the doors, hoping not to frighten away whatever animal is out there calling. That I am describing to myself the sound of this animal as an injured, dying woman is, I feel, so unfair and unforgivable that I dare not mention it to Rob or my husband. I stand in the darkness thinking what a sucker I am, so capable of being influenced by newspaper reports that I cannot hear beyond the fear-ridden accounts of how others have experienced the coyote's howl: *bone-chilling, haunting, eerie.* This is not what I care to hear from anyone, most of all myself.

I remember then—as I stand against the truck waiting for Rob to pull out his tape-recorded rabbit and a tape-recorded coyote howl that he thinks might cause the creature in the field to call back—that a coyote's voice should sound higher pitched than a wolf's voice, which, thanks to Brandy, is a voice I know well, a lower, more monotone moaning. Rob is not quick to conclude anything. As he sets up the predator calls, there is a commotion of wild geese in what I can just barely make out as scattered clumps of brush and trees in the darkness. Wings flap riotously, chaotically; and in the blackness my body begins to feel what I cannot see, which is the uneasy and breaking feeling of dense feathers smashing up against feathers. There are geese honking, yelling, and then stillness, nothing, as though I am not only blind but have now gone deaf.

The woman in the field stops screaming.

Rob whispers in my ear that a coyote howls to be heard by another coyote. That is, they don't howl for nothing. Aside from revealing where each might be in the grass or woods, a howl also sends out information, the precise nature of which is privy to only coyotes but that may signal to a mate that prey has been located. A sort of *come on, honey, dinner's done!*

Rob plays the recorded version of a coyote, and in its beginnings at least, it is a voice quite different from the screaming woman I have just heard. There are doggish-sounding barks, yips, and yaps; and as I listen to them they remind me of the small talk of a husband when a wife wants deeper conversation. But then the recorded coyote breaks into a prolonged, wailing howl that, as the howl ascends toward its ending, sounds like a woman, like the woman in our field, in its tremulous, shivering way. The creature not silent in the darkness may be—Rob is beginning to concede—a coyote, a coyote that had essentially cut to the chase and moved right into the deep conversation. And I think, *well, this is just like a woman!*

Rob wants to be sure this is a coyote. But because we are not downwind of the animal, we will have, Rob says, immense difficulty convincing the creature to come any closer or even to head in the direction of our smelly humanness. Rob switches to the rabbit tape. Earlier in the night we were downwind and behind the rabbit's calling, which meant that any possible coyotes would have had to rely on and respond to their sense of hearing and sight, for the most part. Now we are sending out mixed messages to the coyote: a rabbit's calling with a human smell; indeed, we are making everything seem fishy.

Nonetheless, Rob, who himself has never seen a coyote, is determined. As he lifts the red-tinged light into our field of silence, we see through our binoculars that there are two round yellow eyes moving east and west, then a bit north toward us, back south, then east again, and west. The use of the red light from where we are, about sixty yards away, allows us only to see eyes and only works, of course, if the animal happens to be glancing our way. Bodies cannot be discerned at this distance until the light is replaced with a white light, which immediately startles animals into bolting away. Rob has seen the night eyes of fox, and these, he believes, are the eyes of a coyote— larger, more widely spaced, higher off the ground. By watching the animal's eyes, we see a coyote move across the field like a tennis player—up to the net, then back, across the court one way and then the other. It is clear that decisions are being made: coyote thinking, desiring; coyote responding to joy and sizing up the situation: *What are the possibilities of this rabbit? When is the time to run? What might be my loss?*

As this is going on, four sets of golden eyes, not all that far from the coyote, begin floating toward us. The eight golden eyes are like the distant lights of a ship in a calm night sea. Even higher from the ground than those of the tennis player, the lights are coming at us more deliberately and slowly until, with once glance back to see how the tennis player is faring, the ship's lights disperse and disappear into the ocean of McKee-Beshers. I search for them—the eyes of four white-tailed deer—but it is as though they were never here.

A barred owl hoots, we turn to the sound, and the owl bears down across the brown sky behind us to perch in a dead tree. No woodcocks are *peeent*ing. No howling, no screaming woman. Occasionally, a speeding country truck roars by, rattling down the main road. Breezes of wild grass, cool winter air, and far-off chimney smoke linger around us. The time has now come simply to be with the bright yellow eyes of an otherwise invisible coyote, the yellow eyes of the new story we will tell, the story of the eastern coyote as the sunshine of the night.

6 Prairie Dog and Prejudice

Kelsi Nagy

We have been trying to get rid of prairie dogs in South Dakota for over one hundred years and have yet to get the job done. It is estimated that there are more prairie dogs in Jones County, where I grew up, than there are people. Who is the real endangered species?

—Congressman John Thune

IT WAS A SUNNY DAY in Colorado in late March when I looked out over a pasture full of fat, yapping little rodents and thought, "There is no way in hell I am turning my horse out on that field." I was visiting a small, privately owned farm to see about leasing it with a friend for our collective four horses. The farm had all the amenities we required: an outdoor riding arena, a spacious four-stall barn, and a thirty-acre pasture our horses could spend their days grazing. Best of all, we could afford the lease.

As I gazed out over the pasture and contemplated letting Oscar loose on a field full of a hundred hoof-sized holes, I felt crestfallen. It was clear from the number of dried horse droppings around the mounded burrows that horses had recently shared this pasture with prairie dogs, but the thought of making a decision that would put Oscar at risk of breaking a leg was mortifying. My friend didn't seem as bothered by the prairie dogs as I was. She liked the farm but couldn't afford the lease if I backed out of the deal. "There were nine other horses on the field and I don't think they had any problems. We can fill the holes in if it really bothers you," she tried to reassure me.

I didn't want to let my friend down by backing out on the new lease, but I didn't want to turn Oscar out on the prairie dog pasture, and I didn't want to disturb the prairie dogs, either. I knew they were black-tailed prairie dogs, a species native to the area. As far as rodents go, they were cute, a gregarious cross between a squirrel and a guinea pig. They lived in colonies and appeared to communicate with one another. I had been distressed to see them poisoned or plowed under to make way for development throughout the Front Range. But at that moment I suddenly saw them as vermin. To regain my objectivity, I decided to research conflicts between livestock and prairie dogs before I made my decision. That night I slept fitfully with uneasy dreams.

The next day I went to the library and pulled all five books I found on prairie dogs off the shelf. I spent a lot of time searching Google and downloading things like *Report from the Burrow,* an annual publication about the status of prairie dogs in the United States compiled by the nonprofit WildEarth Guardians, an organization that has tried to overshadow Groundhog's Day by deeming February 2 Prairie Dog Day.[1] And I rented a documentary on prairie dogs titled *Varmints,* which my hometown paper, the *Coloradoan,* reviewed as "the Schindler's List of wildlife documentaries."[2] I soon wondered exactly what I had gotten myself into.

Though my initial concern was for my horse, I quickly became worried about the prairie dogs. My research revealed that each of the five species of prairie dogs that exist in North America meet the criteria to be considered an endangered species. In fact, the Mexican and Utah prairie dogs are listed as endangered under the Endangered Species Act (ESA), the Gunnison prairie dog is listed as a candidate species, and environmental groups have petitioned to have white-tailed and black-tailed prairie dogs listed under the Endangered Species Act. I also discovered that even though some prairie dogs have federal protection, it has made little difference as all prairie dog habitats continue to decline.[3] Public sentiment does not support the ruling, and even state agencies ignore the listing. For instance, the State of Utah still classifies the Utah prairie dog as "a pest species."[4]

Prairie dogs are communal ground-dwelling members of the squirrel family. Spending as much as 95 percent of the day aboveground, they are usually easy to spot.[5] The football-sized rodents build mounded burrow entrances, up to 2.5 feet high,[6] which both serve as a perch from which to spot predators and create ventilation for their underground burrows. To help spot predators, prairie dogs also clip short all vegetation around the colony, like a putting green. The combination of mounded burrow entrances and denuded vegetation can give the prairie dog colony a moonscape-like feel. When a predator is spotted, they alert each other to danger by "barking." Their "barks" earned them the name "prairie dog," given to them by French trappers who called them "petit chien," French for "little dog."[7]

More Chihuahua than German shepherd, the prairie dog bark to me sounds like a series of very loud chirps. The latest scientific studies reveal that these alarm cries are a system of communication akin to language. Con Slobodchikoff, a researcher at the University of Arizona, has made a career studying prairie dog calls[8] and has said, "At this point in time, prairie dogs have the most sophisticated animal language that has been decoded," including great apes, whales, and dolphins.[9] Slobodchikoff has documented one hundred different words, including verbs and adjectives. They have specific calls for predators like coyotes, badgers, and ferrets, and even a distinct call for humans.[10] His research has also revealed that prairie dogs can tell the difference between people, even when they wear different clothes,[11] and although they use similar warning calls, different colonies have different dialects.[12]

Their ability to communicate and keep each other from harm may be one reason they have been so successful as a species, even though compared to most rodents they have a low reproduction rate. On average, a female will have a litter of four pups each spring. Some of these pups may be the victims of infanticide, which occurs when rival females within the same family group kill and sometimes eat pups in a neighboring burrow. In one study done in South Dakota, infanticide was the greatest cause of death in young pups, accounting for half the deaths of all pups born.[13] Compare this modest rate of reproduction to rats. According to Robert Sullivan in *Rats,* one pair of rats has the potential of 15,000 descendants a year.[14]

Though prairie dogs do not reproduce rapidly, their colonies take up a sizable area on the landscape. Once miles long, the average size of a modern-day prairie dog colony is forty to fifty acres, and their colonies gradually move across the landscape as new prairie dogs seek more territory.[15] The facts that prairie dogs dig holes, trim grass, occupy significant portions of the landscape, and don't observe distinct territories have made them unpopular with many Americans who make a living off the land and have created the impression that prairie dogs are harmful pests and should be treated as vermin.

Prairie dogs peacefully shared the Great Plains with Native Americans and millions of bison, but they were perceived to be a threat by European pioneers who started farms and cattle ranches. Beginning in 1900 government campaigns targeted millions of prairie dogs for extermination, which resulted in staggering numbers killed in the last 150 years. In my home state of Colorado, from 1903 to 1912 poisoning killed 91 percent of the state's prairie dogs. A further 31 million prairie dogs were killed between 1912 and 1923. In 1923 alone poisoning devastated 3.7 million acres inhabited by prairie dogs. The goal of many of these early 1900s poisoning campaigns was complete extermination.[16]

While I initially thought the *Coloradoan* had been hyperbolic when comparing the eradication campaigns against prairie dogs to the Holocaust, it turned out to be a fitting analogy of the huge effort made to minimize the population of a species. When the Mayflower docked at Plymouth Rock, the black-tailed prairie dog may have been the most numerous mammal in North America.[17] It is estimated that before Europeans colonized North America over 5 billion prairie dogs inhabited between 40 and 80 million acres of prairie on the Great Plains, stretching from Mexico to Canada. Now their scattered colonies occupy 1 to 2 million acres within this region, and it is likely that the current number of prairie dogs is less than 2 percent of the number that Meriwether Lewis described as "infinite" two hundred years ago.[18] Like another prominent member of the Great Plains that was historically targeted for eradication, prairie dogs appear to be going the way of the bison.

Though far fewer prairie dogs remain today than in the early 1900s, some government agencies, ranchers, land developers, and oil and gas drillers still want prairie dogs eliminated. Wildlife biologists and wildlife advocates like Defenders of Wildlife, the Prairie Dog Coalition, and WildEarth Guardians feel differently. They view prairie dogs as an essential species for the health of the shortgrass prairie ecosystem. The debate over whether human enterprise should usurp the rights of a native rodent has made prairie dogs one of the most controversial wildlife species in the United States.

I found little evidence that my horse would be harmed on a prairie dog colony. My dread of turning Oscar out on that pockmarked pasture changed to a feeling of fascination with these unique animals and a willingness to trust my horse to keep his wits about him and his hooves out of burrow holes. I called my friend back and told her I was convinced the horses would be fine. We moved our horses to the new farm, walked the horses around the perimeter of the pasture, and set them free.

The Assumptions

Once I moved Oscar to the farm, I was curious what other people thought about prairie dogs. I found that people fell into two camps: prairie dogs were either cute or a nuisance. People loved them or hated them in equal measure with no middle ground in between, but the majority loathed them, finding them dangerous to livestock, disease ridden, or an impediment to development. Again and again I heard at least one of four beliefs about prairie dogs that I had learned were untrue. These assumptions were unsupported by recent scientific research but are pervasive among most of my friends, acquaintances, and some media outlets.

The first assumption is that *livestock have a higher likelihood of break-ing their legs on prairie dog colonies.* I found no data confirming this "fact." I was particularly frustrated by the lack of attention to this issue since it had been my own personal fear. In *Conservation of the Black-Tailed Prairie Dog,* the chapter "Do Prairie Dogs Compete with Livestock?" didn't even mention the issue of livestock stepping in prairie dog holes.[19] Other sources call it a myth.[20] The only person to support my fear was Mark Mason, a member of the Varmint Hunter Militia of Denver, Colorado, interviewed in the video *Varmints,* who mentioned his neighbor's miniature horse broke its leg in a prairie dog hole. But since he proudly sported a large button on his vest that read, "I explode dogs," I assume he is perhaps not the most reliable authority on the situation.[21]

Perplexed that my biggest fear was so quickly dismissed by my research, I decided to approach my conflict from another angle. Are there reasons why horses and prairie dogs might make *good* neighbors? I looked up the evo-lutionary history of each species and found that both evolved on the Great Plains of North America until horses were pushed out by the last ice age. The horses that crossed the land bridge to Asia and then Europe continued the genus *Equus.* After that, horses were extinct in North America until ten thousand years later when the Spanish conquistadors reintroduced them to the Americas. The fact that prairie dogs and horses had co-evolved with each other eased my mind when I turned my horse loose on the infamous field. Somewhere, deep in my horse's walnut-sized brain, existed the knowl-edge of traveling over a prairie full of ground squirrels and their ubiquitous burrows. It was a knowledge I couldn't begin to comprehend but I could likely trust.

Though I had addressed my biggest fear and most of my anxieties had abated, dispelling the first assumption only served as an initiation to the real prairie dog controversy. Ranchers don't have to spend sleepless nights wor-rying about waking up to find a field full of three-legged cattle, but the ma-jority of ranchers believe prairie dogs are detrimental to their livelihood. I soon discovered ranchers hate prairie dogs not because of their burrows but because of the perception that they compete with cattle for grass. The fact that these so-called varmints eat and trim the grass short around their bur-rows is obvious, and ranchers believe that their presence negatively affects the production of rangeland livestock. Ranchers also become frustrated that prairie dogs are often attracted to areas inhabited by cattle, especially when cattle overgraze their rangeland. This allows prairie dogs a clear and effort-less view of predators.[22]

This second assumption, that *prairie dogs steal grass from cattle,* does not have a cut-and-dried answer. Yes, without livestock prairie dogs naturally keep grass clipped short around their colonies, which means there is less grass on prairie dog colonies. But the process of clipping forbs and grasses short encourages plants to produce new growth, resulting in the constant production of tender protein and nutrient-dense plants on prairie dog colonies. We apply this same logic to keep our lawns lush and green. Ranchers and biologists have observed that cattle often prefer to graze on prairie dog colonies instead of grazing on taller, woodier grasses. By sampling the succulent garden of a prairie dog town, cattle get more nutrition for less work. Wild animals such as antelope and bison are also drawn to prairie dog colonies for the same reason.[23] Craig Knowles, a grasslands ecologist interviewed on the video *Varmints,* argues that rabbits and grasshoppers eat more prairie grass than prairie dogs but have not garnered the same enmity that prairie dogs have.[24] This is likely due to the fact that prairie dogs occupy distinct territories, and while their overall affect on the prairie is minimal, a colony at the local level of a paddock or a ranch has an obvious presence, and ranchers have a genuine concern for the welfare of their livestock.[25]

Only a handful of scientific studies have been conducted to analyze the impact of prairie dogs on beef cattle, and these studies have not been conclusive. Many of them have been criticized for small sample sizes or results that conflict with prior studies. For example, one study in North Dakota indicated that bison, and possibly other ungulates, may benefit by being allowed access to colony sites.[26] Another estimates that a prairie dog town produces only half the forage of a similar acre off the town.[27] And while this study advises ranchers to double the amount of pasture a cow-calf unit grazes when prairie dogs inhabit 20 percent of a pasture, another study found that there was no difference in body mass between cows that fed exclusively on a prairie dog colony than cows that grazed prairie dog–free pastures.[28] Perhaps the science is inconclusive because it is difficult to conduct a controlled study on open range where many factors can influence data. For example, the type and amount of forage differ from region to region and time of year.

Even if prairie dogs do reduce production, it may cost ranchers far more to poison prairie dogs than to leave them be. Randy Buhler, a Colorado State University extension agronomist, said that given the data, ranchers shouldn't bother trying to kill prairie dogs because "the expense of bait, poison and labor to eliminate them could be acutely hazardous to [a rancher's] profit."[29] The state of South Dakota even offers ranchers some compensation for leaving prairie dogs on their private lands. If ranchers agree not to poison or shoot prairie dogs on their own land, they can collect between $10 to $18 per prairie dog acre.[30] It appears that few ranchers take advantage of this program because they would rather have prairie dogs poisoned, which is also subsidized by the government.

An astounding amount of government money has been spent poisoning an equally astonishing number of prairie dogs. According to Slobodchikoff, if we use "the figure from the Nebraska National Forest Service as an estimate of average government spending, today's equivalent of at least $143,650,000 of taxpayer's money was spent on poisoning prairie dogs between 1916 and 1920." The most expensive federally subsidized poisoning campaign happened in South Dakota between 1980 and 1984. The U.S. government spent $6,200,000 to poison 185,600 hectares of prairie dogs. This cost taxpayers about $3 per prairie dog.[31] The government still subsidizes the poisoning of prairie dogs even though prairie dogs may not significantly threaten the profits of livestock owners.

Convincing ranchers that it is more cost-effective to leave prairie dogs alone than to poison them is another matter. Anyone can see that there is less grass on a prairie dog colony than the rest of the prairie. They also flourish when there is a drought, which further distresses ranchers worried about feeding their cows. The argument that bison would be a much more cost-effective alternative to beef is lost on the American rancher who raises beef to satisfy the American palate, which is accustomed to European beeves rather than native cattle species. Steak is considered as American as apple pie even though beef and apples are European emigrants. As Mark Mason, the varmint hunter on the documentary *Varmints,* states, "[Varmint hunters] are the true militia. We are called to defend these lands from the invaders, which in this case are the rodents. We are the first line of defense. When they poison them, well, that's the last line of defense." Like many Americans, Mason believes that humans have a right to utilize the landscape any way we see fit regardless of what belonged here before we did.

The prairie dog's maligned status is not helped by the fact that it is also viewed as a plague-ridden varmint. It is true that prairie dogs are susceptible to the plague, but the assumption that *prairie dogs spread the plague* is also untrue. Prairie dogs do not spread the plague because prairie dogs have virtually no immunity to the virus. The sylvatic plague, commonly known as the bubonic plague, has at least a 99 percent mortality rate in prairie dogs. Technically, prairie dogs are only an indication that plague fleas and the rats or mice that harbor them are in the area. Because the plague has only existed in North America for the past hundred years, prairie dogs have not yet become immune to it.

The plague was introduced to North America in the year 1900 when rats infected with plague fleas jumped off commercial ships from Asia and found refuge in San Francisco's sewers. The virus was carried east across the plains by a variety of mostly nonnative rodents with an immunity to the disease. Many native North American ground squirrels became afflicted with the plague, and prairie dogs have been especially susceptible. Even though there are currently more rodents harboring the plague in North America than there were in Europe at the time of the Black Death, most of these rodents inhabit rural areas where they are unlikely to encounter humans.[32] In the United States only ten to fifteen people on average each year are infected with the plague, which is easily treated if detected in time.[33] The Centers for Disease Control recommends that to avoid contracting plague, do not touch dead animals and make your home inhospitable to rodents.[34] Unless you are a teenage boy with a morbid curiosity, it seems relatively easy to avoid the plague.

It is clear the plague has a much larger effect on prairie dogs than it does on people. At times the plague is even viewed favorably by those who want prairie dogs eradicated from the landscape, like Mrs. Robert Taylor, a ranchwoman on the video *Varmints,* who prays for the plague to relieve her cattle from the rodents that are threatening to "starve" her livestock. At the other end of the spectrum, conservationists who strive to protect the last remnants of North America's native shortgrass prairie ecosystem are concerned about the plague's unpredictable and extreme effect on prairie dog populations. While ranchers fight to keep their right to poison prairie dogs, other people fight just as hard to have them protected under the Endangered Species Act.

There have been two serious attempts to list prairie dogs under the Endangered Species Act as a threatened species. In 2000 U.S. Fish and Wildlife Services designated prairie dogs as a candidate species, meaning that it was warranted for protection under the Endangered Species Act but precluded because other species were of greater importance. That designation was revoked in 2004,[35] because of new scientific evidence that prairie dog populations were on the rise. In 2008 WildEarth Guardians petitioned Fish and Wildlife Services to revisit the status of the species.[36] They argued that without federal protection prairie dogs would continue to be poisoned en masse. Fish and Wildlife Services conducted another survey of the species and in September 2009 ruled against listing the black-tailed prairie dogs. These decisions were a relief to many farmers, ranchers, oil companies, and land developers who were worried that a potential formal listing of the species would threaten their livelihoods. It is difficult for many people to see that a hole-digging, grass-eating, "land-grabbing" rodent could be anything but destructive, but its role as a native species and an abundant snack for a variety of predators complicates this perception. Though prairie dogs do create challenges for some human enterprises, the very behaviors that cause prairie dogs such disdain among ranchers and developers are the very traits that make them beneficial to the environment.

Indeed, the fourth and final assumption I have encountered about prairie dogs, that *prairie dogs destroy the environment,* is the most misleading. Prairie dogs happen to be among a handful of species that biologists consider to be keystone species. A keystone species modifies its environment in a manner that benefits a significant number of other species and if gone would likely cause the collapse of a unique ecosystem. In fact, more species of animals are found on prairie dog colonies than landscapes devoid of prairie dogs. As many as two hundred species may benefit from the habitat prairie dogs create, including insects, amphibians, birds, and mammals: the diminutive swift fox, the not-so-diminutive ferruginous hawk, and the burrowing owl, a creature that has such a charismatic appearance it could be a cartoon character.[37] These animals are more likely to be found on a prairie dog colony than off it and struggle to find suitable habitat without prairie dogs.

The black-footed ferret tops the list of endangered animals that depend on prairie dog colonies. This curious and fierce brown ferret has a black marking across its eyes that remind one of a 1950s superhero's mask and is often referred to as the most endangered mammal in North America. Populations of black-footed ferrets declined because of a rapid drop in populations of prairie dogs, their main source of food and shelter. Remaining populations are also susceptible to the plague and canine distemper. Never numerous in number, black-footed ferrets were declared extinct in 1974. Six years later, in 1981, a small population was discovered living on a ranch in Meeteetse, Wyoming. These ferrets were observed in the wild until they too were struck with canine distemper. Eighteen ferrets were captured, and U.S. Fish and Wildlife Services began successfully breeding them in captivity. Ten years later there were enough to begin releasing them back into the wild.[38] By May 2008, 750 black-footed ferrets were living in the wild. To date, the recovery of the black-footed ferret has been an inspiring success story, but the survival of the species is by no means secure, largely because the creature that provides nearly all of its food and shelter is considered an animal enemy to most of the people that share its habitat.

The relationship between prairie dogs and black-footed ferrets and the history of the management of each species reveal that our attitudes about animals that are seen as pests, vermin, and varmints can villainize a creature that is also essential to a unique and thriving ecosystem. While black-footed ferrets are protected under the Endangered Species Act, the black-tailed prairie dog, their only source of food and habitat, is not. This has placed the prairie dog in an odd position for land managers who are under pressure by both ranchers, who would like to see the prairie dogs managed as an invasive species, and environmentalists, who want the prairie dogs managed as a keystone species. The unique and strange status of prairie dogs, simultaneously a hated animal enemy and an important native species that is crucial to the survival of the most endangered mammal in North America, has incited two national controversies that have tested the very limits of the protection that the Endangered Species Act can provide for animals.

The first controversy occurred over wildlife management in the Conata Basin, an area in Buffalo Gap, South Dakota. In this vast and largely deserted landscape sprawls one of the largest prairie dog colonies in North America and the largest population of reintroduced black-footed ferrets, which at nearly three hundred individuals is a third of all ferrets living in the wild. In 2007 ranchers who lease the Forest Service lands in this ecosystem convinced the Forest Service to poison up to two-thirds of the prairie dogs in this colony. The controversial Forest Service decision made headlines on a CNN news program that rightly pointed out that taxpayers were simultaneously paying to have the three hundred ferrets managed and the prairie dogs poisoned in the same ecosystem.[39] The Endangered Species Act could only stop direct poisoning of the ferrets and did not protect habitat they did not immediately occupy. Despite protests from several environmental groups, the Forest Service was in the process of poisoning prairie dogs on lands bordering the ranches when the plague struck the colony for the first time in history during May 2008.[40] Thirty ferrets were lost in the initial wave of the plague. Efforts then turned to dusting the prairie dogs with flea powder instead of poisoning them and vaccinating ferrets with an experimental vaccine.

The second controversy happened in Logan County, Kansas, where two ranchers, Larry Haverfied and Gordon Barnhardt, harbor a ten-thousand-acre colony of prairie dogs between their two ranches. Their cattle are rotated on the pastures, mimicking the intensive grazing patterns of native bison, which minimizes conflicts between cattle and prairie dogs.[41] These ranchers like the wildlife that prairie dogs attract and see them as components of a healthy ecosystem.[42] Not everyone in Logan County shares their love of wildlife or prairie dogs. One neighbor enforced a hundred-year-old county law that allows the county to poison a rancher's prairie dogs if their neighbor complains about the prairie dogs encroaching on neighboring property. The landowner is then billed for the poisoning.[43] To protect their prairie dogs from the county law, Haverfield and Berhnart, in association with Fish and Wildlife Services and the Audubon Society, had several black-footed ferrets released on their ranch. They hoped that the ferrets would act as an umbrella species, a listed species that provides protection for other plants and animals that share its habitat, believing that the federal law would trump the county law. But the Logan County commissioners continued to poison the prairie dogs, regardless of the ferrets' presence, which nearly prompted Fish and Wildlife Services to remove the ferrets. Although the ferrets are unlikely to directly eat the grain-based poison, the threat of secondary poisoning from eating dead prairie dogs is significant, especially from the controversial new poison Rozol, which threatens to harm more predators than just the ferrets. Finally, in the spring of 2009 a Kansas judge ruled that the county commissioners could trespass only ninety feet into the property and no farther, creating an uneasy truce.[44] Like other issues that divide American citizens, it is easy for people to believe what they want to believe, and even though scientific evidence provides many arguments for prairie dog protection, their protection under the law will remain an uphill battle.

After overcoming my own prejudice and letting my dearly loved horse share space with these "varmints," I was perplexed by the prevailing deep hatred for prairie dogs even after science and logic reveal them to be mostly beneficial or benign creatures. When I happened to meet Jonathan Proctor, the Rocky Mountain/Great Plains representative for the Defenders of Wildlife, at a book reading, I voiced my concerns. Proctor is one of the most prominent prairie dog advocates in the country. He told me the most beneficial strategy for prairie dog conservation would be to preserve the colonies that are ten thousand acres or larger. That would safeguard prairie dogs as a keystone species and provide enough room for healthy ferret populations. It would take at least ten of these areas to rehabilitate ferret populations and ensure that enough colonies would remain if others were inflicted with the plague. "What we're asking for is that 1 percent of the prairie would be set aside for native wildlife. People often tell me that wildlife activists are unreasonable, but preserving only *1 percent* of the prairie doesn't sound unreasonable to me."[45] When I suggested that we convert cattle ranches to bison ranches and end all conflicts between native wildlife and ranchers, he laughed at the suggestion and said, "Well, that will never happen."

Ghost Towns

Back in my prairie dog pasture the horses made a well-worn trail between the burrows to get from the barn to the lush marshy area on the far side of the field and seemed unbothered by their diminutive neighbors. The prairie dogs soon became used to our benign barn activities and stopped running into their burrows and alerting each other whenever we came into the field to empty the wheelbarrow onto the manure pile. I looked forward to observing them and the other wildlife that lived in the field. In the spring I watched mothers teach their babies how to forage through the short grasses. Especially on breezy days, I often heard an eagle or a hawk call out over the field or saw them sailing over the farm on a high air current. One gray morning I observed a red-tailed hawk standing over a dead prairie dog near a burrow entrance in the field. Two other hawks watched it from a nearby tree. The air was often filled with the chatter of songbirds or the cry of the mountain plover. And even the flock of pigeons that nested in the overhang rafters of the barn seemed to spend an inordinate amount of time on the ground, picking at the dirt and short grasses on the prairie dog colony. Now that my fears had abated, I savored the prairie dog pastoral of the farm.

Walking though the pasture to catch my horse, I started to see everything from a different point of view. When a tumbleweed cartwheeled across my path on a blustery day, I remembered that tumbleweeds, the subject of a classic country western song, are actually an exotic species native to Russia. Cattle, for that matter, were European imports, and the cowboys that herded them across the continent were descendants of Basque, Celtic, and West African emigrants who devised new ways of mustering cattle in this vast and often hostile landscape. The days when cowboys drove large herds of cattle across the fenceless Great Plains among those tumbling tumbleweeds lasted a mere twenty years in the late 1800s.[46] Some of the most iconic symbols of being American are far from being native to this land or relevant to the landscape. When our sense of identity is rooted not in the landscape but in an imported ideal, it should be no surprise that we struggle against the land and its animals. No wonder it is so difficult to perceive the magnificence that existed here before we came.

I admit that before I learned about prairie dogs, I was blind to many beauties of the prairie. Since I have become educated in all things prairie dog, I am now inscribed in the landscape, in my home, in a way I wasn't before. Now when I walk through the pasture, instead of seeing a diminished landscape, I see the multitude of tiny flowers, shrubs, and grasses prairie dogs cultivate that I didn't know to look for before. I scan the sky for a raptor. I hope to see a killdeer or a mountain plover, ground-nesting birds that often nest on colonies. In the summer, my horse is fat and glossy, thriving on a pasture I once worried would cause his demise. When I walk across the pasture to catch my horse and see the prairie dogs scuttle back into their burrows and bark their alarm, I know they call me by name. This other prairie, the one that has been reconstructed on open areas around my town, only resembles a prairie. The silent ranches reserve their grasses for cattle; the land has no burrow mounds or fat yapping rodents. That prairie is a diminished landscape. A ghost town.

Notes

1. Laura McCain, *Report from the Burrow* (Denver, Colo.: WildEarthGuardians, 2009).

2. Kevin Cook, review of *Varmints, Coloradoan,* October 23, 1998, http://www .highplainsfilms.org/hpf/films/varmints/full-review_coloradoan/184.

3. McCain, *Report from the Burrow.*

4. Ibid.

5. John L. Hoogland, *The Black-Tailed Prairie Dog: Social Life of a Burrowing Mammal* (Chicago: University of Chicago, 1995), 1.

6. John Hoogland, ed., *Conservation of the Black-Tailed Prairie Dog* (Washington, D.C.: Island Press, 2006), 1.

7. Kim Long, *Prairie Dogs: A Wildlife Handbook* (Boulder, Colo.: Johnson Books, 2002), 18.

8. Con Slobbodchikoff, http://www.conslobodchikoff.com/.

9. Bill Blakemore, "America's Meerkat," video, in "How Would a Prairie Dog Describe You? Thin? Short? Just Ask One," http://abcnews.go.com/blogs/technology/2012/01/how-would-a-prairie-dog-describe-you-thin-short-just-ask-one/.

10. C. N. Slobodchikoff, Bianca S. Perla, and Jennifer L. Verdolin, *Prairie Dogs: Communication and Community in an Animal Society* (Cambridge, Mass.: Harvard University Press, 2009), 67.

11. Ibid., 74–75.

12. C. N. Slobodchikoff, S. H. Ackers and M. Van Ert, "Geographical Variation in Alarm Calls of Gunnison's Prairie Dogs," *Journal of Mammalogy* 79 (1998): 1265–72.

13. Long, *Prairie Dogs,* 61.

14. Robert Sullivan, *Rats: Observations on the History and Habitat of the City's Most Unwanted Inhabitants* (New York: Bloomsbury, 2004), 11.

15. Long, *Prairie Dogs,* 77

16. Hoogland, *Conservation of the Black-Tailed Prairie Dog,* 90.

17. Defenders of Wildlife, "Prairie Dogs 101," http://www.defenders.org/wildlife_and_habitat/wildlife/prairie_dog,_black-tailed.php.

18. Ibid.; Hoogland, *Conservation of the Black-Tailed Prairie Dog,* 1, 2.

19. James K. Detling, "Do Prairie Dogs Compete with Livestock?" in *Conservation of the Black-Tailed Prairie Dog,* ed. John L. Hoogland (Washington D.C.: Island Press, 2006), 65–88.

20. Maryland Zoo in Baltimore, http://www.marylandzoo.org/meet/meet-animals.aspx?AnimalID=64.

21. *Varmints,* directed by Doug Hawes-Davis (Oley, Penn.: BullFrog Films, 1998), VHS, High Plains Film.

22. Daniel S. Licht and Kenneth D. Sanchez, "Associations of the Black-Tailed Prairie Dog Colonies with Cattle Point Attractants in the Northern Great Plains," *Great Plains Naturalist* 53, no. 4 (1993): 385–89.

23. Detling, "Do Prairie Dogs Compete with Livestock?," 83.

24. *Varmints.*

25. Detling, "Do Prairie Dogs Compete with Livestock?," 65

26. Ibid., 83.

27. Marianne Stein, "Prairie Dogs, Adjust Your Stocking Rate," *Farm and Home Research* 56, no. 1 (April 2005): 17.

28. Detling, "Do Prairie Dogs Compete with Livestock?," 86.

29. Quoted in Katy Human, "Cattle Slimmer as Prairie Dogs Enjoy the Fat of the Land; a Study Concludes, However, That in Small Numbers Rodents Don't Compete with Livestock," *Denver Post,* January 4, 2007.

30. WildEarth Guradians, http://www.wildearthguardians.org/Portals/0/support_docs/report_pdog_from-the-burrow_2009.pdf.

31. Slobodchikoff, *Prairie Dogs,* 67, 156.

32. Sullivan, *Rats,* 162.

33. Centers for Disease Control, "Plague," http://www.cdc.gov/ncidod/dvbid/plague/index.htm.

34. Centers for Disease Control, "Protect Yourself from Plague," http://www.cdc.gov/ncidod/dvbid/plague/resources/plaguebrochure.pdf.

35. Hoogland, *Conservation of the Black-Tailed Prairie Dog,* 2, 171, 288, 2.

36. Melanie Dabovich, "Prairie Dog Suit Filed: Petition to List the Black-Tailed Prairie Dog under the Endangered Species Act Ignored," *Albuquerque Journal,* February 20, 2008.

37. Paul A. Johnsgard, *Prairie Dog Empire: A Saga of the Shortgrass Prairie* (Lincoln: University of Nebraska Press, 2005).

38. Defenders of Wildlife, http://www.defenders.org.

39. CNN, "Scorched Earth, Divided Government," broadcast August 11, 2008.

40. Defenders of Wildlife, http://www.defenders.org.

41. Rod Haxton, "Prairie Dog's Best Friend," *Scott County Record,* September 2, 2010, http://www.scottcountyrecord.com/news/prairie-dogs-best-friend.

42. Ted Williams, "Doggone," *Audubon Magazine,* November–December 2009.

43. Felicity Barringer, "In Kansas, a Line Is Drawn around a Prairie Dog Town, *New York Times,* December 11, 2006, http://www.nytimes.com/2006/12/11/us/11prairiedogs.html.

44. Mike Corn, "Judge Rules for Ferrets," http://www.hdnews.net/printstory/pdogruling022009.

45. Jonathan Proctor, Defenders of Wildlife Rocky Mountains/Great Plains representative, interview by author, February 20, 2008.

46. Laurie Winn Carlson, *Cattle: An Informal History* (Chicago: Ivan R. Dee, 2001), 63–65.

7 Nothing Says Trash like Packrats
Nature Boy Meets Bushy Tail

Michael P. Branch

"HONEY, GET THE CAMERA!" I've just peeled back the tarp covering a half-used pallet of granite to reveal the cutest thing I've ever seen. From between the slats of the empty part of the pallet pokes a furry little head with large, dark eyes, a tiny, sniffing nose, and twitching whiskers. Its big, rounded ears are backlit in the early morning summer sun, and its bushy tail is partially visible through the slats just behind its body. Then a second curious little head pops up, and a third, and a fourth! By now my wife has arrived with our two-year-old daughter, and with each furry noggin that pops up they both release a squeal of delight. "They're *so* cute!" Eryn says, smiling, as she snaps away with the camera. "What are their names?" asks Hannah, looking up at Mom.

"Packrats." It is the gravelly voice of my sullen neighbor and mason Charlie, who is coming around the corner of the house, finishing his third beer and getting ready to lay stone. In building this passive solar house at six thousand feet in the desert of rural western Nevada, we've employed mostly neighbors, and there have been some hardpan characters among them. Charlie the mason—whom my wife calls Charlie Manson—is an irredeemable desert rat, and though he's wild-eyed and surly I like him very much. He knows stone and he knows the high desert, which is good enough for me.

"Packrats?" Eryn asks. "Is that really a kind of rat? It looks more like a baby squirrel."

"Packrat," Charlie repeats, scowling a little from behind his beer. "Wood-rat. Traderat. Packrat. Rat. Deal with him." He's looking straight at me. My kid is still grinning, but my wife is now frowning. I reach over and slowly slide the glass door closed in front of them. I can see my daughter's lips moving but can no longer hear her voice.

I turn to face Charlie. "What do you mean 'deal with him'?"

Charlie takes a big step closer to me, crushing and dropping his beer can as he does. "You don't know him like I know him, Nature Boy." I hated when he called me that, but I tried never to show it. "One day you'll step out of your house to take a piss behind that woodpile, and when you come back inside you'll find your bottle of single-barrel empty and that rat bastard sitting up in bed with your wife, smoking a cig and grinning." Charlie is as earnest as a shark hunter and he's in my face, reeking and squinting as he growls out his apocalyptic warnings.

"Charlie, come on, it's just a little squirrely thing." I gesture toward the pallet, where the wee, timorous beasties are still peeping up at us, cute as can be.

"Deal with him," he says over his shoulder, as he walks back to his truck to get another beer.

That night I heard no hooting from the resident great horned owls, no yelping from the local pack of coyotes. Instead, strange scurrying sounds filled the darkness, unmistakably the acoustic trail of rodents, and the sounds were as loud as the jackrabbits out here are big. Scurrying on the deck, on the walls, on the outer sill of the window just behind the head of our bed—the scratching and scrabbling sounds of claws, so loud that it kept me awake most of the night.

In the morning I found small, sausage-shaped lumps of poop on the stoops of the house, with the greatest concentration on the doormats, as if the calling card had been left intentionally. Brownish-yellow streaks ran down the house's stucco walls, as if pints of porter or brown mustard had been spilled from the window ledges. The flowers in the pots on our porch had been clearcut, leaving sheared stems where colorful stalks had recently stood.

By breakfast I was already hunched over my field guides, reciting preliminary findings to Eryn. "Got to be *Neotoma cinerea*, the bushy-tailed woodrat," I concluded. "There are twenty-one species of woodrats, spread out across the United States and from Arctic Canada south to the jungles of Nicaragua, but this is the only one that fits: fairly boreal, widely distributed in the Great Basin desert, and has that big, fluffy tail. Nocturnal, good climber, likes to hole up in crevices in rock faces but also builds stick houses in juniper country like this. Will carry stuff off and pack it into its house. Generalist herbivore, but relishes succulent plants like, say, your snapdragons. *Neotoma cinerea.* That's our boy." Now I can answer Hannah's question. "He's named 'bushy tail,' sweetie," I say. She likes that.

In the days ahead the signs of a rodent invasion become increasingly evident. Every night brings the Mardi Gras of scurrying, and every morning a new harvest of the signature greenish pellets and the proliferation of nasty yellow streaks down the house. The potted plants are soon completely gone, and their stems invariably show the distinctive angular cut of rodent teeth, which gets the maligned cottontails off the hook. Bugs Bunny just chomps and gnaws, while rodents slash stems on a perfect angle, like a carrot sliced julienne with the precision of a sous chef's blade.

One morning I went to fetch our hidden house key to loan it to a neighbor, and it was unaccountably missing from its secret place. Then in the afternoon I opened the hood of my truck to add windshield wiper fluid and found that over a single night the bushy tails had built a respectable nest atop my battery, one that was not only cozy but also colorful. As I removed the nest I called out to Eryn: "Honey, I found your snapdragons." Of course the inevitable happened. Evolutionary programming told the packrats that our stucco house was the sheer face of a rock cliff and the cement roof tiles were the innumerable doorways to a honeycomb of crevices and cavities. Once under the tiles they had the run of the joint, and could at leisure chew their way into the attic space, where they proceeded to gnaw insulation off pipes and coating off wiring. Now we had a critter issue that no amount of cute was going to fix. If something wasn't done soon, we'd be evicted from our new home by an army of furry little *Neotoma.* I'd have to "deal with him" and without delay.

But in a matter of twenty-four hours, before I could even formulate a strategy, something happened that should only happen in stories by Edgar Allan Poe: scratching, scrabbling, clawing sounds came from within the interior walls of the house. Now even Nature Boy admitted that things were getting out of hand. I winced, steeling myself for what I knew was necessary: a belly crawl through the dark, claustrophobic space beneath the floors of the house. If the rats were down there (at some point I had stopped calling them "bushy tails" and started calling them "rats"), then the levee was breached, and they would not only be under the roof and in the walls but would have access to a labyrinth of ducts.

I drained a glass of single-barrel before strapping on my headlamp and dropping through the trap hole in the floor. It was immediately clear from the acrid smell that something was down there, and the stench wasn't coming from the black widow spider that was the first thing illuminated in the beam of my small headlamp. With less than two feet of clearance, I had to commando crawl across the vapor barrier on the ground, where I soon discovered that the plastic sheeting was littered with turds and sticky with the same grey poupon that streaked the walls of the house. They were down here, all right, but I didn't know where, or what I'd do if I found them. How many would there be? What diseases would they carry? Would they julienne my fingers with their razor-sharp choppers, leaving me with ten perfectly angled stumps?

As I pulled myself forward with my forearms, I began to identify trash that had been collected from around our property: bottle cap, tinfoil, coyote scat, wood screw, dog hair, flagging tape, masonry nail, owl pellet, snapdragon stalk, can tabs from Charlie's beers, and, yes, my spare house key. There were clipped juniper twigs everywhere, mostly still green. It was my house but their world, and since they were accustomed to crawling around in the dark in the choking ammonia stench of urine, they had several important advantages over me. In the dusty beam of my headlamp I saw a pile of sticks a few yards ahead, tucked against a foundation wall and behind the elbow of a large duct. This had to be it. Nudging forward in the dark I expected at any moment to feel a rat run across my back or tangle itself in my hair. At last I eased up, close to the duct behind which the stick nest was hidden, and then slowly craned my neck down and around the duct, turning my head to allow the beam of my lamp to fall onto the bundle of sticks. There he was, a foot from my face and exactly at eye level, and he was all attitude, glaring straight at me and ready to rumble. I had somehow assumed that if I found the beast he would scurry away like, well . . . like a rodent, but clearly this bruiser had no intention of stepping off. Which of us would blink first? It was in the next moment that I reached the turning point in my troubled relationship with *Neotoma cinerea*. As I tilted my head a little, the headlamp revealed the treasures he was defending in his nest. Nestled among juniper berries and beer can tabs rested Hannah's pink pacifier. Now I could feel my jaws clench. "Listen here, you wife-stealing rat bastard," I said aloud, "you are *not* going to drink my good bourbon." He didn't move a whisker, and he didn't look at all scared.

Since moving out here I've dealt with plenty of critters. Once a swooping great horned owl tried to nab our cat. Once a colony of winged harvester ants came down the chimney, filling the woodstove until you could see them writhing a foot deep behind the glass door of the firebox. Once I intercepted a scorpion as it crawled along the rail of our daughter's crib. Once I had my truck towed to the shop only to have the mechanic call to say he couldn't work on it because there was a four-foot gopher snake snoozing on the engine block. But it was the pacifier that finally pushed me over the edge. In a way that perhaps only a father can understand, that was going too far. Nature Boy was on the warpath.

I started by doing a lot of research quickly. I reckoned that to defeat an enemy you must first know his strengths and weaknesses, and compare them to your own. What would make my adversary hungry, thirsty, tired, cold, worried, existentially despondent? What would a bad day for a packrat look like? I read what I could find on woodrat social biology and then made a two-column list by which I constructed a point-by-point comparison of the relative strengths of "Rat Bastard" and "Mike." I expected, given my status as a member of the species widely celebrated (albeit only among ourselves) as the pinnacle of evolution, that I'd have impressive advantages over my foe. As the list shaped up, I saw that the opposite was true. Rat Bastard was such a dietary generalist that I could never stop him by cutting off his food supply—he'd eat almost anything, from plants, berries, seeds, twigs, and bark to small invertebrates, fungi, and even his own feces. I couldn't chase him down, as he could climb like lightning up vertical and even inverted faces, and I couldn't shoot him because he was nocturnal and, besides, he was always crawling across my damned house. I couldn't track him, as he could navigate by kinesthetic memory and scent markings—detailed maps I couldn't even see to take away. Because he was hydrated by the plant matter he ate, he could go his whole life without taking a drink while I, by contrast, couldn't go a day without whiskey, let alone water. When I was roasting in summer he'd be chillin' in a cool rock crevice, and when I was freezing in winter the master of thermoregulation would be toasty in the heart of his insulated den, curled into a ball and wrapped snugly in a long, furry tail designed especially for the purpose.

As for breeding, it's no wonder he's a threat to people's wives. Bushy tails produce one to three litters of two to six young each season, so they can feed plenty of owls and still fill your crawl space with the next generation. Their social structure is polygynous, which means that each male shacks up with a harem of several females. The females, for their part, are capable of running up vertical walls even with young dangling from their mammary glands, and they will often begin copulating within twelve hours of giving birth (two facts, it turns out, I'd advise against bringing to the attention of human mothers). Finally, packrats are meaner than they are cute—we aren't talking mice here. Because of sexual dimorphism in the species, a male *Neotoma cinerea* can weigh in at a whopping 600 grams, which is about the size of a really big burrito—a ferocious burrito with razor-sharp claws and teeth. In fighting with other packrats, which he does viciously and from a young age, he'll stand upright on his hind legs and bite and scratch for all he's worth, even leaping into the air to use his powerful hind claws to slash at and lacerate his opponents.

So what advantages are on the "Mike" side of the column? Not many. I have a ridiculously overdeveloped cerebral cortex, which is proving virtually useless in the current conflict. I do find that I have some things in common with Rat Bastard, who is described as "unsocial, solitary, and strongly territorial," but identifying his weaknesses is another matter. I did locate a few general sources devoted to how to get rid of rodents, but all the prescribed methods had attendant perils. "Exclusion" sounded obvious but assumed that I knew exactly where they were getting into the house, which I didn't. "Toxicants" wasn't a great option, as packrats will carry poison bait away and cache it in their dens, sometimes not eating it for weeks or even months; besides, my collateral damage assessment suggested that, considering both the domestic and wild animals around, there were plenty of non-target species to be concerned about. "Biological Control" for packrats is more or less limited to cats, and our cat, which in any case spends most of his time trying not to become dinner for a coyote, was too fat and slow to dream of going to the mat with a big, mean burrito; indeed, he's the kind of feline who would have his paws full in a smackdown with an actual burrito. "Ultrasound Repellers" sounded encouragingly high-tech but had been shown to be completely ineffective after a very short period. This left only "Trapping," which had plenty of complications. Rat Bastard was too big for a glue board, which seemed cruel anyhow, and a conventional snap trap would certainly catch me or my kid or my obese cat before it ever caught him. And anyway, think of the splatter. My father-in-law, an impressively resourceful guy, suggested enthusiastically that we make a steel mat and rig a system by which we could electrocute the rats. I imagined myself standing in front of the charred remains of my new home, explaining to my insurance agent how this happened.

It was then that the owls helped me to see the light. Eryn and Hannah and I went away for a single night, mostly to avoid my ratty nemesis, and when we returned it looked as if a 55-gallon drum of Wite-Out had been spilled on the peaks of our roof and on the ground below. "That's bird doo-doo,"

I explain in answer to Hannah's question, though it seems inconceivable that anything smaller than a pterodactyl could muster crap this voluminous. "Yay, the birdie went poopie all by his self!" Hannah screeches, hopping up and down. And then I notice that there is no packrat poop on the porches—not one pellet. Aha! *Rat Bastard, you have a weakness.* My presence here has disrupted a predatory cycle and has given Rat Bastard prime digs—not only a good place to hang out but also protection from predation by Ye Olde Nocturnal Raptor. Now, combining what I learned from reading about woodrats with my feces-induced epiphany about the vulnerabilities of my furry antagonist, I rededicated myself to getting something other than my frontal lobes on the "Mike" side of the power tally.

How does the genius detective catch the genius criminal? By *thinking* like the criminal. If I were Rat Bastard, what would I want and what would I fear? He's got plenty of chow and women and he doesn't even need to drink, but he has the willies about being out in the open. He needs deep cover to nest, to cache food, to thermoregulate—and to avoid that silent-winged death from above. And packrats are fiercely territorial and agonistic. Like alligators, they'll live close together but they don't like each other much, and they'll fight hard for cover when it is scarce. As one study I read put it, "Possession of a house is so important to woodrat survival that a high level of aggression and solitary house occupancy are basic to the genus." A glance around our property suggests that I've inadvertently created packrat heaven. There are pallets of rock everywhere, old PVC pipe lying around the foundation of the house, heaps of scrap lumber, junk left over from construction. And because we heat primarily with wood, there is a pile of stove wood the size of an RV—at least six cords that I've bucked, split, and hauled. How many rats might be living inside there? At the top of Rat Bastard's column of advantages over me is the superb cover that my own trash has provided him.

Heartened by these new observations, I decide to run my insights by an expert, if I can find one. After a number of phone calls, I track down a guy named "the Ratman" at the state wildlife office. I don't catch his real name, but everybody I talk to says he's the packrat guru in Nevada. When I finally reach him, he turns out to be another of these quirky, knowledgeable desert rats that I enjoy so much.

"You up in the juniper? Yeah, *cinerea* for sure. Cute, aren't they? Ever seen them climb? They're amazing!" The Ratman is not only knowledgeable and friendly but also perfectly evangelical about the wonders of woodrats. He talks like a guy with nowhere to be, which is oddly pleasant, and he clearly wants to educate me as well as help solve my problem. I go over my observations and options with him and he concludes that he can help, but first extorts from me a promise that in exchange for his help I'll bring him a frozen packrat, "and not one that's poisoned," he specifies. I reluctantly agree, though I haven't the slightest idea how I'll keep my promise.

"First, you've got to stop them from getting in," he says. "Then, you need to deprive them of protective habitat around your place—that's their real vulnerability. They've got a small home range, so four or five hundred meters is plenty. Then, you need to trap like crazy. Listen to the Ratman."

Passing over his creepy use of the third person, I proceed to resisting the apparent complexity of his plan. "I can't figure out where they're getting in, Ratman, and I have about six or eight cords of wood I'd have to move, and I'm really not the hunter-trapper type."

"If they're getting in under the roof tiles, stick steel wool or blow foam in there. If they're coming in around the foundation, mortar it up. You *have* to move all the wood—that's ideal habitat. And the best trap for *Neotoma* is the two-foot, two-door Havahart." I'm comforted that he's suggested a live trap, but then he follows with: "And for crying out loud, don't release them! Best to drown them in a trashcan." This from a guy who likes pack-rats enough to want to be called "the Ratman."

"I know it's hard to tell over the phone," I reply, "but I'm really not the killing type. I'm one of those warm-hearted environmentalists. You know, peace to all creatures, live and let live sort of guy."

"Listen, Nature Boy, you've got to do it." This uncanny use of Charlie's language catches me off guard. "Nothing you do will dent the general population—we're just talking about making an NFZ, a '*Neotoma* free zone,' in a five-hundred-meter arc around your place. Besides, you're only icing some of this year's model, the young who are being kicked out of the nests by the adults. The home nests will still be out there in the scrub. You've got to tear up that woodpile like a coyote and hunt them at night like an owl. Listen to the Ratman. Peanut butter in the trap, then swimming lessons in the trashcan. You have to deal with them." I thank the Ratman for his help and, at his insistence, renew my pledge to bring him a bushy-tail Popsicle.

Then, over a solid week of summer, I set out to do everything the Ratman recommended. First I spent several days up on my roof, broiling in the sun as I lay on my belly, spraying foam into every rat-sized gap. The remainder of the backbreaking week is devoted to moving stove wood and debris to another part of the property—eighteen pickup loads in all. As I did so, I found no less than a dozen individual packrat nests in the woodpile alone—downy soft, palm-sized cups of shredded juniper bark, more delicately woven than a bird's nest. And every night I set a trap, and almost every morning I had a hopping mad incarcerated packrat to deal with. At first I allowed my tender green mercies to trump the Ratman's directive, and I drove my catch out into the desert each morning for its ritual release. But soon I admitted that the scarcity of quality habitat, the fiercely agonistic nature of *Neotoma,* the extreme climatic conditions, and the summer's bumper crop of dispersing, aggressive young packrats made this approach a death sentence for the animal, as well as being a very stinky and time-consuming prebreakfast activity for me each day.

And that is how I became a cold-blooded killer of my fellow creatures. Every morning I would wake up, drink a big mug of strong java, trudge off to my improvised trashcan water-tank death chamber, and use the unfortunately named Havahart trap to give terminal swimming lessons to animals that, even if they are shameless stealers of baby pacifiers, are handsome, intelligent creatures that really just want a peanut-butter cracker. And when the awful deed was done, of course, I'd have to empty the trash.

Perhaps it was my guilt about the fact that my furry pupils universally failed their swimming lessons that fueled my fascination with them, for as I became a murderer I also became an admirer. Once I had evicted the bushy tails from our house and had, after repeated failures, managed to keep them out, I read more about packrats—both in books and in the landscape. I perused scientific studies of woodrats, gleaned what I could, and then hiked out into the desert to make my own observations. I looked for packrat bones in owl pellets, and I climbed cliffs to examine *Neotoma* nests in the granite notches. I identified many packrat stick houses, which I visited regularly and watched closely, noticing if they had been built up, lined with fresh juniper, or disturbed by predators. Based on exposure, cover, and vegetation, I learned to anticipate where packrats were likely to live, and eventually I became a fair hand at locating packrat houses by following their distinctive odor across the sagebrush steppe. I made regular visits to inspect the urination "posts" that packrats visit repeatedly as a way of sharing olfactory information, and I watched the artistic patterns of their urine streaks emerge on rock faces after rain washed organic materials away, leaving expressionistic striations of dissolved calcium carbonate behind.

The packrat is no Johnny-come-lately, like the Old World rats whose pedigree dates only to the *Mayflower* and that now infest the sewers beneath every city in America. *Neotoma* is a native, and there are fossil packrat nesting sites in the West that have seen more or less continuous use for fifty thousand years. As a result of this long residency—and because packrats have not changed their basic social behavior since the last ice age—we have learned amazing things from them. Of special value is the packrat's powerful but indiscriminate penchant for collecting and storing things, often caching them deep within cliff faces and protected within stick houses, where the worst weather never reaches. Better still for posterity, it is often the case that generations of *Neotoma* have urinated on the collected materials, causing them to be encased in a virtually impervious, amberlike gem of crystallized pee—a substance the earliest western explorers couldn't identify but thought looked a lot like candy (some who took the confectionary appearance literally reported that the stuff tastes sweet but causes a bellyache). Because it is a collection of not only food but also trash, a packrat's midden (the pile of material that usually guards its nest) is a wild miscellany of objects that functions as a time capsule of the local environment at the time of collection. But what some of us call "trash" an anthropologist calls an "artifact" and a paleoecologist calls a "macrofossil." It is in the packrat's trash that we have discovered answers to some of the most important questions of the past that we have.

How do we know what level ancient lakes in the West reached, and how have we managed to chart their rising and recession over tens of thousands of years? By documenting the elevations of fossil packrat middens, the ages of which are determined by studying the easily dated materials they contain. How do we know whether martens or jackrabbits or pikas or diamondback rattlers lived in a certain place ten or twenty thousand years ago? Because packrats collect and store small bones, as well as coyote scat and owl pellets in which bone fragments of larger animals are found. How do we know that here in the Great Basin subalpine conifers once grew 1,000 meters below their lowest distribution today? Because the twigs of bristlecone and limber pine are found in ancient packrat middens that are far below the areas where those trees now exist. And this sort of information is important not only to paleogeeks. Knowing the relative distribution of various plant species over a period of thirty or forty thousand years allows us to extrapolate changes in climate during that period. Because this, in turn, provides a paleoclimatologic baseline against which we can measure current rates of climate change, it might be said that the packrat's appetite for trash provides a crucial means to gauge the degree to which the human appetite for fossil fuels is contributing to global warming. And we know all this for very simple reasons: packrats gather trash, and they gather that trash near their house, and they store that trash safely. The packrat is the ultimate trash animal, which is precisely what makes it a preservationist of the first order—without its collections of scat and berries and bone we would be hard-pressed to understand the environment of the late Pleistocene and early Holocene periods.

It is no doubt true that one person's trash is another's treasure, but to the packrat all trash is treasure—and I have discovered that in this treasuring of trash, as well as in the trash itself, treasures are sometimes found. *Neotoma* and I are still cohabitants of sorts. Although he no longer lives within my house, he has houses nearby, and we visit each other from time to time. And in this truce we both seem to prosper, even if my way of "dealing with him" doesn't involve the apocalyptic extermination Charlie advocated. I realize, of course, that there is blood on my hands. Indeed, I've remembered my debt to the Ratman and have in the back of my freezer, where Eryn isn't likely to notice it, a package clearly labeled "NOT A BURRITO." Despite this, my relationship with my bushy-tailed neighbor is mostly peaceful, and détente has its blessings. I still have my wife and my single-barrel, and he still has his wives and his beer can tabs. If my spare key vanishes occasionally, I trust that my friend won't use it to let himself in.

III. THE INVASIVE TRASH ANIMAL

8 Canadas

From Conservation Success to Flying Carp

Bernard Quetchenbach

The wild gander leads his flock through the cool night;
Ya-honk! he says, and sounds it down to me like an invitation.
—Walt Whitman, *Song of Myself*

A JUNE MORNING IN BOSTON. A quiet tributary greenbelts its way through Riverside Park toward the Charles River. A pair of large Canada geese balance forward across the path as I walk by, preserving their dignity through a kind of aloof disdain. Geese appear at intervals in pairs and groups of three or four. Some don't lift their heads from under their wings when I pass.

Two old men are sitting on a bench, tossing bread crumbs in the general direction of several Canadas. Conversing, they seem hardly to notice the geese, which approach the men slantwise, not out of wariness but as if they find their benefactors uninteresting. They are simply going about their business, including, in this case, sampling the bread that has appeared in the grass before the bench.

Urban historian Sam Bass Warner points out that the Charles, where Bostonians go for a green reprieve, is in fact distinctly artificial, the original watercourse altered beyond recognition by the designs of municipalities, landscape architects, even rowing clubs. The geese aren't much different from other city dwellers.[1] Not looking too closely at the source of their well-being, they integrate benches and bread, reservoirs and the Olmstead philosophy of city planning, into their "natural" habitat. Like the landscape that surrounds them, they have become civilized.

Boston is not alone in hosting a resident population of Canada geese. Over the past few decades, the big goose with the black neck and white chinstrap has become a fixture in city parks and suburban neighborhoods throughout much of temperate North America. And Canadas have not always been welcomed with the easy equanimity of the men on the Boston bench, especially in suburban towns where fatalistic urban expectations are replaced by a quixotic belief that, in the midst of rapid unregulated growth, a homogenous neatness is both attainable and desirable.

The appearance of wildlife in cities and suburban towns anchors us to the earth but also shows that our control over these environments is tentative, illusory, maybe a little dangerous. There's something vaguely disconcerting about Canadas sauntering through northern parks in June. Obvious changes in the behavior of neighborhood animals undermine a deep if unspoken faith that the actions of our elaborate human communities have little connection to the world at large and no consequences beyond those desirable, even mandatory, results claimed by advertisers: convenience, green lawns, a dependable flow of summer jobs, and cheap consumer goods. We call the shots within the gates, but the world goes on around us as it always has. God's in his heaven; all's right with the subdivision.

The year-round presence of the once almost-exclusively migratory Canada goose testifies that our actions have far-reaching, unpredictable effects, causing apparently permanent disruptions in what we like to think of as serene, dependable nature.[2] One consequence of the growth of the resident flocks is that our view of Canadas has changed as the geese have adapted to us. Might we forget, might *they* forget, that the migration of Canada geese has been one of North America's most vivid and universal reminders that the everyday demands and dramas of our lives are set in and surrounded by grand and resonant natural cycles and rhythms by which we all, geese and humans alike, really live?

The line, a temporary sky form long enough to link horizons, at least as the village allows for horizons, extends across the clouds, both ends lost in trees. It ripples softly like a curtain of northern lights, puts forward broad points, breaks off trailers only to absorb them elsewhere.

It is early morning and I am twenty-one, walking across a parking lot at a state college in Upstate New York. Perhaps I'm on my way to class, or home from a long night full of the vague angst and ecstasy of that period in my life. I'm looking up, of course, have been for perhaps a minute or two, because the line snaking across the morning sky was not first a visual phenomenon. Its initial manifestation was an equally undulant laughter, or maybe a single bark ahead of the flock like a stray raindrop in the heavy April air.

Looking up. Such behavior—cocking the head spaniel-fashion, then standing transfixed waiting for the line to cover the sky, then slowly spinning under it as it passes—does not go unnoticed in a small town like Brockport, New York. As a creative writing student, I wrote about Canadas often enough so that goose imagery became a kind of trademark idiosyncrasy. But for me there was no question. One watched geese because—well, who wouldn't? They talked to me. They talked to everyone. Aldo Leopold calls the geese that migrate through Wisconsin "a wild poem dropped from the murky skies upon the muds of March."[3] Poet Galway Kinnell says that poetry is "a paradigm of what people might wish to say in addressing the cosmos."[4] It seemed pretty clear that something important was in those voices. I wasn't the only one looking up. At least for a moment, when the first *ya-honk* broke the horizon like a distant train whistle, it changed everything, carrying the garden back into the machine, affirming the breath of the continent. It was as if time itself were arching across the sky, hauling lilacs, fresh grass, and long days inexorably northward, and in the process of that journey opening the doors of perception closed by the quotidian blinders of habit. "Geese ring over the bell tower," I wrote in one of my undergraduate poems, words that strike me as overdramatic today.[5] But at that time, with the experience of those great lines of geese fresh in mind, they seemed not quite strong enough.

For northerners like Leopold, the music of springtime geese has been the very embodiment of something beyond blank mechanism at work in or through the soul of the earth. By force of beauty and essential truth, the spectacle of migration justifies a moral imperative to do right by the planet; Leopold's hard-headed scientific realism runs on a parallel track with Emerson's extension of the romantic link between truth and beauty, each leading to the sphere of ethics and morality.[6] The necessary rightness of natural cycles shows the way to appropriate human conduct in Paul Annixter's 1950 novel *Swiftwater*. In that story of a father and son's efforts to provide a Northwoods sanctuary for migrating Canadas, a biologist encourages young Bucky Calloway by telling him, "It doesn't take long for geese to adapt themselves to man."[7] There would be no argument from the managers of Iroquois National Wildlife Refuge near my family home in Western New York, where migratory geese have long accepted human agency in matters of food and habitat. Even so, the migrants remain themselves visitors with their own appointments and priorities, Leopold's "wild poem."

April, sometime in the mid-1960s. I would have been around nine or ten, searching with my family for the immediate source of those incredible all-across-the-sky lines that crossed our bland suburban horizon each spring.

That source, we knew from the newspaper, was a staging area out in the ever-so-slightly undulating lowland woods and fields west of Rochester. Eagle Harbor was not much more than a steel-deck Erie Canal bridge and a few houses, just a dot on a map, but since our directions called for us to turn off "the Ridge"—Route 104—at Eagle Harbor Road, the wetlands complex known to local geographers as the Alabama Swamp and to wildlife managers as the Iroquois National Wildlife Refuge and its satellite state game management areas, Oak Orchard on the east and Tonawanda on the west, became known to my family as Eagle Harbor, a name my parents used for the rest of their lives, though the refuge itself is about ten miles south of the hamlet.

"Eagle Harbor" was only about an hour from our home in Rochester, but anticipation and uncertainty had stretched the miles. Finally, after a couple of brief detours where our directions failed to warn of forks in the road, we rounded a gently curving rise and swung into a gravel parking lot overlooking a shallow bowl occupied by Stafford, or Goose, Pond. And there we looked out on—nothing. Just a quiet, unassuming, and evidently empty body of water lapsing into a narrow fringe of marsh with woods and fields beyond, all under the gray sky of early spring.

And so we discovered the importance of timing in what was, after all, a great demonstration of the life of time in the world. This was the first of many visits to the geese, but even later when we supposedly knew what we were doing, it was not uncommon for us to try the refuge a little too early or late. Local and continental weather patterns shifted the migration by a few days this way and that. Other, more ominous changes in climate and goose behavior were already underway, though we didn't know it at the time. We did find quickly enough that the swamp was a pretty interesting place even when the goose migration was short of its peak. There might be a few tundra swans (called whistling swans then), the jaunty flash of a deer's tail, a garter snake sliding across the road. The ride itself became a vernal ritual—the subtle contours of the muddy fields, the rich agrarian tang of Podunk Road and Johnny Cake Lane, the coots and wood ducks in the shallow swales.

We also found out soon enough that the geese had daily as well as seasonal routines. They would vacate Stafford Pond early in the morning to forage in fields subsidized for their benefit (and for the benefit of hunters) and return en masse late in the afternoon, around four o'clock to be just about exact.

Four o'clock, like magic. One spring day some years later, some college friends and I were returning to Brockport from Niagara Falls, driving past fields of water and last year's stubble. On impulse I said something to the effect that in five minutes, the sky would be full of geese. And just in time, the fields exploded with the flight of hitherto unseen presences, probably bound for Stafford Pond or elsewhere in the refuges. At four o'clock on an April afternoon, the time was ripe for geese.

The marshes, woods, and pools of the Alabama Swamp were the local wildlands of my youth. I have rarely been there since I left Upstate New York in the early 1980s and had not, until recently, been there at all since late in that decade. But the swamp inhabits my memory as a place too wild to be pastoral, overgrown to the point of escape—an image that is, in one sense, profoundly illusory. Iroquois was at best a compromise between bureaucratic order and the deeper resonance of primeval nature. The original glacial wetland had been cleared and drained, albeit imperfectly, generations of farmers earlier, and, like so many of our designated "wildlife areas," Iroquois was a mosaic of second-growth hardwoods, impoundments flooded and dried in accordance with managerial schedules, grain dutifully planted by state employees or farmers picking up a little extra cash from the government. The Oak Orchard section of the refuge complex was a site for New York's successful bald eagle hacking program—an eagle harbor in fact—and for a while a bizarre wooden structure loomed at the edge of Stafford Pond across from the gravel lot, looking not unlike the skeleton of a dilapidated farm outbuilding, except, of course, for the eaglets that flopped about the enclosure, testing their wings. They, too, were an artifact of the wildlife managers. Once I saw an eaglet careening through the trees at Swallow Hollow, a roadside stop on the Oak Orchard–Iroquois border where picnic tables and a boardwalk trail were all that the refuge had to offer as an official recreation area. The young bird was already a couple of miles away from the treehouse-like flight platform, but the experience hardly seemed like a real encounter with a wild eagle. For that matter, the name Swallow Hollow itself seemed like it was invented from whole cloth by a public relations specialist, perhaps the same one who tried to achieve a measure of authenticity by applying conceptually neat Iroquois nation names to the recently constructed Seneca, Cayuga, Onondaga, Oneida, and Mohawk pools.

Sometimes, though, artificiality was easy to forget. One April evening, as a teen with fresh access to a car, I found myself more or less spontaneously racing nightfall to the Alabama Swamp. Stafford Pond had already exchanged the day's last sun for the rising moon. There was just enough light through the bare trees to make out where the Swallow Hollow boardwalk dipped into flooded woods. Somewhere close a barred owl called. There were rustlings of small creatures near the trail, the occasional crash of something bigger—fox? deer? And over it all, goose voices from out in the ponds, the nervous expressions of resting birds mingled with the announcement of new arrivals.

As with most birds, the migration of geese often occurs after dark, and their calls in the night are especially evocative. One evening, perhaps a decade earlier, a migrating vee had passed low enough over my elementary school to catch the parking lot lights. It was probably the first time I saw birds flying at night, and the experience made the world bigger, stranger, and the movements across it by wild creatures somehow less predictable, more mysterious. Goose calls heard at night through a tent flap or open window took on an interrogative tone, posing a question that I could never begin to answer (though I tried, insufficiently, to phrase the question itself as "Canada? Canada?" in a poem written shortly after my evening run to the refuge).[8] It was the same quality I heard when I stood on my grandparents' cobble beach and listened as disembodied voices drifted in over Lake Ontario from, I thought, great rafts of geese beyond the horizon, though maybe they were really coming from smaller, closer gaggles tucked in valleys and pockets of the waves.

And that night on the moonlit Swallow Hollow boardwalk, goose calls were both intimately close and immersed in the incredible distances of the flyway.

Despite its location between Rochester, Batavia, and Buffalo, the Alabama Swamp really was remote, or at least neglected, a ragged loose end of American enterprise. Its few "towns" seemed to exist mostly on maps. Two farmhouses for one, three for another. None had a gas station or store. There were still some working farms, but they lacked both the mystique of the apple country north of Ridge Road and the calendar appeal of the tidy, bucolic landscape to the south, where the escarpments of the Allegheny Plateau folded into the pastoral sweep of ridges and valleys that Western New York is known for. In the Alabama Swamp, most of the farmers had given up long ago, leaving empty barns, old trucks peering from swayback garages, farmsteads owned by city cousins. I suppose the swamp was really no more destitute than other northeastern rural areas. What seemed unusual, though, was the sense of obscurity, houses perhaps occupied, maybe not, the shades always halfway. One almost never encountered anyone on the refuge roads or trails. For a kid from the suburbs, it was *Deliverance* country.[9] Iroquois had a headquarters, but there never seemed to be anyone there. The interpretive materials were few. The Swallow Hollow boardwalk just appeared. Even the eagles seemed to have arrived on their own, as if they had built their treehouse themselves. It was better that way, of course. The annual newspaper feature made it clear that the geese were noticed, but most visits were innocent of refuge staff, birdwatching tourists, anyone, though there was evidence—an occasional pickup leaned mysteriously into the grass on the side of the road—that the place was not really abandoned.

Like most waterfowl refuges, Iroquois and its satellites catered primarily to fall hunters. Migration was for me a spring phenomenon, as October flocks kept high in the sky, risking descent into shotgun range only when absolutely necessary. The geese were quieter during autumn, "their calls / dried to whispers" in yet another old poem.[10] What was heard in fall was mostly shooting, a more fulfilling sound for participants than for spectators, no doubt. In spring, the place was just about empty except for wildlife, except for geese. But spring or fall, the mere presence of the refuge complex, a cooperative venture between state and federal entities with enough modesty to stay mostly out of sight, was itself significant. The world was going about its business, and even its noisiest, most disruptive species could, at least sometimes, ply its meddlesome, manipulative ways in harmony with those larger planetary rhythms.

The Alabama wetland constituted a soggy backwater, a liminal space between better-known, more appreciated places. When I attended college at Brockport, just a half hour drive to the east, I went there as often as I could. Sometimes I slipped away when I should have been in class. Sometimes I went alone, sometimes with a friend or two, occasionally a girlfriend who shared at least somewhat in my enthusiasm. Now and again, I would still go with my parents. On one of these occasions, on a late summer morning, I saw my first egrets. At other times, a redhead or a pair of blue-winged teal in the Feeder Canal might mark a visit. But it was usually geese we came to see. The refuge, like Montezuma to the east, now highlights the success of its eagle program—no wonder, as bald eagles appeal to people's patriotism and to the perhaps more earned pride in at least one major conservation victory. But the adoption of an alternative flagship species also shows that what the Canada goose means to people in temperate North America has changed. Obvious all year in cities and suburban towns, geese have become less viable as a sublime embodiment of planetary rhythms. In fact, they are increasingly lumped with raccoons and gulls in the category of "nuisance animals": ubiquitous, inconvenient, maybe downright unnatural. "It doesn't take long for geese to adapt themselves to man," says Annixter's biologist, innocent of his words' double edge. Today, that tendency to adapt has compromised the Canadas' image to the point that, even in the remote Yaak Valley of Montana—nowhere near, one might think, the nearest neighborhood goose—Rick Bass feels obliged to establish that the birds he's praising in an *Audubon* article are "not backyard, yearlong golf course geese, but the wild migrators."[11]

The Atlantic population of Canada geese rides the flyway twice each year between Northern Quebec's muskeg and Chesapeake Bay, some birds continuing south of the Chesapeake, especially during hard winters. Even the most jaded suburbanite would probably admit that Canadas are handsome creatures, more swanlike in proportions than the other wild geese in North America, and for that matter, most geese elsewhere. The larger forms are the world's biggest geese. Canadas excel at a kind of avian triathlon—they swim like ducks, walk with an ambling but not undignified gait, and with just a short runway, can lift their ten-pound weight, quite substantial by bird standards, and take clean, direct, powerful flight. And then there's the "falling leaf" maneuver. The slightly elevated Stafford Pond parking lot was an ideal place to watch geese break formation. As a great rippling line would reach the pond, a few birds at a time would simply drop, drifting this way and that like leaves caught in the wind. Then somehow, when they were maybe a hundred feet above the water, they would right themselves, easing into a long glide that ended in a graceful, wake-producing splashdown, wings poised for a few seconds in a folding arc above each now-swimming goose. Then they would be at rest, as if they had been there all day, and always—this was the part that was hard to imagine—in a clear spot, no matter how many (and there could be thousands) had already gathered at the pond.

Maybe one reason neighborhood geese lack charisma is that they are not often seen in flight, and when they do take to the air, bustling to and fro like harried shoppers, the cramped glimpse between houses isn't much of a substitute for the wide-ranging freedom and uncanny wisdom of the flyways. How could they have given up such freedom, such a life in the great world? How could we? Resident Canadas face a kind of double bind. On the one hand, they are wild enough to be nuisances; on the other, they remind suburbanites that, like the neighborhood geese, we too, or at least our grandparents, must once have lived more natural, more adventurous, maybe more genuine lives.

In the suburbs of Rochester, one year-round home to Canada geese is Mendon Ponds, a county park built around a series of glacial eskers and the namesake kettle ponds, one of which is a popular swimming hole. Some years ago, during a summer visit when my son was ten, we joined my friend Chris's family there on a hazy, humid, overheated afternoon.

Just past the beach was a gathering place for park waterfowl—white domestic ducks; half-mallard, half-something-else dabblers; a few Canada geese. After swimming, we took a sack of leftover bread, not the most nutritious fare but an enduring tradition with people and park flocks, to throw to the ducks. The Canadas, aloof but also more aggressive than the smaller birds, were stalking along the perimeter of the group, snaking their necks forward to chase the ducks away from choice bits of bread.

As we stood by the pond, one big Canada that had been resting peacefully—listlessly?—at the edge of the milling congregation of birds suddenly shook violently in a kind of seizure, flipped over, and died. That's all. It was like nothing I had or have ever seen before or since. Our small group of witnesses stood and shifted for a moment before parents began ushering children back toward the swimming area. Chris, who had seen a similar occurrence at a golf course, guessed that the bird had suffered a heart attack.

We learn about death from our pets, the common wisdom goes. But these birds weren't pets. They were park waterfowl—part wildlife, part scenery, perhaps part surrogate barnyard stock for suburbanites indulging a kind of semiconscious nostalgia for the farming life. But in their own right, they were individual organisms who had found a place in the world that worked for them even if we didn't understand why they would give up all that wild sky and golden marsh. Their lineages, apparent in unnatural amalgamations of breed and species traits, suggested that each had traveled a different route to Mendon Ponds. The domestics, or their ancestors, were perhaps dropped off in the dark of night a few weeks after Easter. The half-mallards descended, maybe, from wild birds that found life among the domestics both cushy and satisfying. The Canadas spent their days in a testy but largely workable association with their distant relatives, snapping up bits of stale bread in a place that must have seemed like a kind of miracle, goods and services provided without ever leaving the neighborhood. Paradise. Shelter from the vicissitudes of life in the wild for them, a break from stress and heat for the human swimmers. And then, one of the geese we had been feeding met the fate of all things, the only creature I ever saw die of natural causes. Right there, in front of the kids.

Mostly, though, the geese have meant life.

At least, they did. Life and wildness, a visitation in our sky from some far-off better world. The cover of the 1949 edition of Leopold's *Sand County Almanac* features an image of Canada geese, their heads tilted upward, releasing those evocative calls that struck, well, something atavistic and irresistible within, I like to think, most people. But those were not the Mendon birds, or the Boston birds, or any of those "sky carp" that have taken to decorating or infesting parks and golf courses.[12] In fact, at least in the Northeast, flyway and neighborhood geese are really not the same birds. Although all are genetically *Branta canadensis,* migrants and residents represent discrete populations that generally interact little and interbreed hardly at all.

There isn't much agreement in matters of Canada goose taxonomy on the subspecies level. Most sources, at least those geared for a general audience, used to posit about eleven subspecies ranging from larger, lighter birds in the East to smaller, darker Westerners. But the biggest of these subspecies, the Giant Canada, was an exception, native to the Upper Midwest and Prairie Provinces. No matter, since the Giant Canada was believed to be extinct. Until, that is, a small group was discovered in Minnesota (a minority opinion holds that it was in Colorado, in Denver's City Park). Decades later, however, the Giants are said to be a primary component of the resident nuisance flocks that inhabit subdivisions, schoolyards, and mall retention ponds. There are doubters, including shooters' groups and animal rights activists, who, depending on their perspective, hold that the subspecies divisions are designed either to prevent or promulgate hunting. But hunters and their foes are not alone in their skepticism. The American Ornithologists' Union, which develops the standard lists of North American birds, has only recently endorsed the Giant Canada as a subspecies in a 2004 shake-up of goose taxonomy. David Allen Sibley's highly regarded *Sibley Guide to Birds* claims "at least six recognizable populations," but if the obviously different Aleutian and Cackling Geese—assigned to a new species in 2004, after the *Sibley Guide* was published—are removed from consideration, Sibley's divisions are modest indeed.[13] Whether the Giants and the nebulous "Western Canadas," which make up the bulk of the Northeast's year-round goose population, represent verifiable genetic distinctions or arbitrary lines drawn by overzealous taxonomic splitters, there is a general consensus that the resident and migratory, or "wild," birds are clearly different in behavior and lifeways, and that the resident population is a relatively recent development.

How did these birds come to be ensconced in park lakes and mall drainage ponds? Apparently, the residents are descendants of more or less domesticated geese from decorative flocks, especially birds used as live decoys early in the twentieth century. This practice struck later generations of hunters and wildlife managers, their collective consciousness raised by Teddy Roosevelt, Aldo Leopold, and the like, as unsporting and was outlawed in many places in the 1930s. As a result, birds that had been kept captive for this purpose were dropped off in park "wilds" to mingle with the motley assortment of Easter ducklings. Other Canadas were released at refuges to augment migratory flocks for the benefit of hunters. Whether because they were raised in captivity or because relocation compromised their migratory instincts, the freed birds showed no inclination to join the vees of the Atlantic flyway, preferring the easy life of city parks and especially suburbs, where malls, office lawns, and subdivisions provided an attractive combination of amenities.

In New York, according to the state's Department of Environmental Conservation (DEC), the ancestors of today's resident geese were set loose in the general vicinity of Long Island and the Lower Hudson Valley, still a hot spot for resident geese and a likely source for the Boston birds as well. Their numbers presumably augmented by aggressive restoration efforts on behalf of Giant Canadas, residents spread gradually across the Northeast, and the New York population increased further when the state released more birds, perhaps including Giants, "north and west of Albany."[14] The White Game Farm in the Alabama Swamp was one site where geese were introduced into the wild (I distinctly remember seeing pens filled with big Canadas, apparently awaiting release, while riding past the game farm on one of my childhood visits). It was generally assumed that the newcomers would blend with existing populations, creating bigger flocks of bigger geese for the benefit of sportsmen up and down the Atlantic coast.

But that's not what happened, at least not exactly. Migratory geese—Atlantic Canadas to the taxonomic splitters—continued their long-distance flights while the released birds settled into local habitats where the living, often assisted by park-bench patrons carrying cracked corn or stale bread, was easy. Not only that, but since the 1980s, the residents, despite diets packed with human-generated junk food, have done considerably better than the migrants, constituting an ever-increasing percentage of the species' regional population.

According to New York's DEC, the number of resident geese rose from a "handful" at the beginning of the twentieth century to about 120,000 by the mid-1990s. But while the residents prospered, it eventually became apparent that something was amiss with migration. Breeding Atlantic Canadas in Quebec declined to 29,000 pairs in 1995 from over 100,000 just seven years earlier. At Iroquois, numbers of migrants dwindled by 70 percent, forcing New York to suspend the traditional fall goose-hunting season in 1995.[15] Since then, the DEC has tried to alter the timing of the hunt so that it occurs either before or after migration, when mostly resident birds are present. Even with these belated adjustments, the most common face of the species in its interactions with New Yorkers is now that of the residents, classed with landfill gulls as degenerate, lazy freeloaders that should be out "in the wild" earning an honest living. Goose calls may still stir one's soul when filtered through the bare trees of April, riding a brisk wind along with a few phantom raindrops, but the same sound coming from the fussy confines of a suburban neighborhood may instead call up decidedly prosaic images of soiled lawns and—apparently a bum rap—health hazards. A 1999 DEC brochure lists goose-related threats as "over-grazed lawns, accumulation of droppings and feathers on play areas and walkways, nutrient loading in ponds, public health concerns at beaches and drinking water supplies, aggressive behavior by nesting birds, and safety hazards near roads and airports." The State recommends strategies to "discourage" the birds, a far cry from Cam and Bucky Calloway's heroic efforts to entice them, which included, in Cam's case, taking a fatal shotgun blast intended for a flock of migrant Canadas.

Leopold's essay "Goose Music" compares golf and hunting, concluding that, while golf is "sophisticated exercise," the enjoyment of wildlife is fundamental to the human experience. "A man may not care for golf and still be a man," he asserts, "but the man who does not like to see, hunt, photograph, or otherwise outwit birds or animals is hardly normal." Such a person, says Leopold, is "supercivilized." Ironically, what's sauce for the human may be sauce for the gander, too. There seems to be a widespread sense that geese on the links are a different matter from geese in the marsh. And Leopold's conclusion about the supercivilized human, "I for one do not know how to deal with him," is echoed by suburbanites concerning the resident Canadas.[16]

Why have the residents done so well, and why have the migrants struggled? One reason is that the mid-1980s through the mid-1990s were bad years for breeding in Quebec; although Atlantic Canada numbers have rebounded some, the drop in the migratory population, corresponding with a period of expansion for the residents, shifted demographic proportions significantly. And in general, all other things being equal, the migratory life is more demanding than, say, hanging around a golf course, especially since mild, "open" winters have become increasingly frequent. But hunting is also implicated. After all, goose hunters, immersed in family tradition and Aldo Leopold, want the romance of the marsh, the music of migration, which beats popping out of a sand trap, camouflaged, perhaps, in golf shoes and a Nike visor, guns in a golf bag slung over a shoulder. For that matter, hunting is generally not allowed in cities and suburbs, so shooting between park bench slats is out of the question. Also, the general abundance of the species may have led managers to forget about the cultural as well as the alleged taxonomic differences between populations, concluding, both rightly and wrongly, that the Canada goose is hardly declining. And there's some indication that the increasing number of geese has translated into an increasing number of goose hunters, hunters who, it seems, have taken a disproportionately high number of migrants.

The swimming pool, an aboveground pool attached to a nondescript yellow 1950s-era house, is still there. It's been almost twenty years since we—my friend Tom, who now lives in Texas, and myself—last visited the Alabama Swamp, but the landmark that we traditionally used to make the left off Route 31 west of Brockport is intact and, as near as we can tell, unchanged. I resist the two wrong forks, and there's the curve, then the gravel lot. Stafford Pond is more marshy, less open than we remember it, perhaps because of the mid-August season, perhaps due to a scheduled maintenance drawdown, maybe, probably, a little of both. There are other changes. Plant succession has turned open marsh into soggy woods, while managers have reversed the process elsewhere. The Swallow Hollow boardwalk is gapped and overgrown; a sign proclaims it "dangerously unsafe."[17] Nearby, an eagle-viewing tower already shows considerable signs of wear, a chain-link barrier, bulging and loose, slung around the top platform as an afterthought nod to liability. In an eccentric touch, someone has affixed computer keycaps onto the wooden stairs, one on each step.

We don't see any eagles from the tower. Other typical birds of the area do make appearances. In the sumac and wild grape near the tower's base are catbirds, song sparrows, yellow warblers, and a nondescript brownish bird, perhaps a female yellowthroat, though it's hard to say from our elevated perch. A pair of great blue herons stalk through cattails at the water's edge, far below the tilting turkey vultures. In the distance, blue-winged teal flash their powder-blue namesake patches against the Swallow Hollow trees. And there are the geese, residents no doubt, in small, probably family groups, adding the distinctive sound that, even out of season, makes this place so memorable to me. Fittingly, there are few people, though it is a fine, breezy summer Sunday. However, there are empty cars—mostly pickups and SUVs—by the roadside, suggesting that local people are off somewhere in the refuge, maybe fishing.

The brick visitor's center is appropriately empty, evidently closed for the weekend. Elsewhere on the refuge, there are a couple of new trails and overlooks, heralded by rustic signs. Leopard frogs are everywhere. Near the Onondaga trailhead, turtles bask and joe-pye weed blooms. At the Cayuga Pool overlook on the west side of the refuge, several great egrets are hunting, heads and necks tensely waving among black willows; it might have been at this same impoundment that I saw my first egrets in 1982. Today they are accompanied by a couple of cormorants and the day's only eagle, a young bald hunched at the top of a snag undoubtedly flooded by the managers when the pond was expanded.

After leaving Iroquois, we head north, toward Lake Ontario. We wait for a turkey hen and seven half-grown chicks to cross Griswold Road (over the past few decades, wild turkeys have been recolonizing northwestern New York). We pay our respects to the lake, then find ourselves somewhat unexpectedly at the farmhouse where a friend—actually the mother of two friends from college—and retired Brockport professor lives. She relates her daughter's adventure in the New York City subway during the previous week's power blackout and tells us about her dog's Frisbee accident. When we say we have been at the refuge, she tells us that when she first moved to the farm about twenty years ago, large flocks of springtime geese used to feed in the fields across the road. In recent years, they have been absent, but there has been a family of residents on a nearby farm pond.

The evening before my return visit to the refuge, I was cooking out with Tom, Chris, and Dave, friends whom I have known since my Brockport days. We were at Dave's home in a prosperous, pleasant neighborhood of shade trees and gardens, streets with names like Red Fox Lane and Hunter's Run, at the far edge of Rochester's suburban sprawl. It was a reunion of sorts; it had been many years since the four of us had been in the same place at the same time. There were steaks sizzling on the grill, potatoes baking in foil, corn on the cob boiling in the kitchen. Summer. Shortly after sunset a voice in the distance, then several. Goose music. The two of us who live away stopped our conversation immediately to listen. As for Upstaters Chris—with whom I had watched the goose die at Mendon Ponds some years earlier—and Dave, the last thing they wanted to hear was those damned geese, not in August, not in town. The birds were residents, annoying their neighbors in prime suburban style with the classic suburban weapons—noise, dirt, bad timing. Acting inappropriately, out of control, dangerously unsafe for all we could tell. "Aggressive behavior by nesting birds." Then again, wasn't that spontaneous, vibrant flash of the unpredictable what we used to like about the untamed presences living—and dying—at the edges of our towns: the deer that could, did, erupt onto the highway; the potentially rabid raccoons; and the cat-eating owls? Well, yes, but—

It's tempting to think that mid-twentieth-century Americans moved to the suburbs to recapture the agrarian world of their grandparents, as if the suburbanite were a kind of homesteader from the city. But this isn't the truth—at least not the whole truth. The fact is that the suburbs were populated by newly mobile urban families seeking refuge from the cities with their mixed races, their motley juxtapositions of presences—urban expats freed from, among other things, sharing parks with strangers. But since the suburbs were built for city people on land that was recently rural, danger could also come from the hinterland, where wild animals and disreputable inbred persons abound. The Alabama Swamp. *Deliverance.* Encased in a paranoia of interchangeable streets and pedigreed shrubbery, suburban gentry engage in a constant low-intensity struggle to maintain an inherently unstable secured zone between the bad schools and crime of the city and the feral countryside. Whether they hail from an urban reservoir or from White Game Farm, resident geese have moved in on the burbs from less desirable real estate, less desirable in part because there are folks like them there, folks who don't know how to act around people. Like newly arrived cousins from farm or inner city, not quite supercivilized enough to appreciate the putting-green perfection of a suburban lawn, they park on the grass. And they come to stay. Leopold's wild poem rings like Walt Whitman's barbaric yawp or Allen Ginsberg's *Howl* or like the neighbor kid's music through the windows and streets, parks and parking lots, of little worlds carefully constructed to keep everything in its place and everything else out.

Homesteaders with no more respect for preexisting claims than their human counterparts, Canada geese throw down stakes at malls and schoolyards, insinuating themselves between the tame and the wild, the city and the country, moving in on turf marked and prepared by suburban development. Like the city hoods and rural hillbillies that haunt suburban dreams, they squeeze the subdivisions from both sides. Clambering up from greenways or dropping from the sky without the permission of the Neighborhood Association, they represent the world outside the gate.

But that's not all. Resident geese remind us of newer, deeper threats to the insular quality of contemporary American life. Year-round Canadas have, in effect, released the species from its seasonal cage, undermining our sense of the orderliness of nature, giving voice to the profoundly troubling sense that those natural rhythms that the geese embodied are themselves unraveling. The resident population is, after all, a result of human meddling—meddling with geese, meddling with habitat, even meddling with the climate. "It doesn't take long for geese to adapt themselves to man." An accusation? It is at least a reminder of the law of unintended consequences, an unpleasant law: in self-contained neighborhoods constructed for safety and control by a culture increasingly dedicated to the assumption that, at the "big picture" level, our daily actions don't much matter. Don't worry, the slogan says, just do it.

Better not get too close. Those wild things'll go for you, sure.

At dusk, the old men pack up what's left of their picnic supplies and abandon their Boston park bench. Perhaps they fold a checker or backgammon board under an arm. At Iroquois, several hundred miles inland to the west, fishermen are returning to their cars with stringers of bass and sunfish. In the far north, Atlantic Canadas are raising the future of the flyway. From where I stand at the farmhouse near Lake Ontario, none of this is visible. But if I listen I might hear distant goose music, a question on the night air, from across a pond, across a continent. I still can't claim to know much of what the song or poem is saying. But I think it might mean, at least to me, that *we're still here, we're still alive. The world changes. It changes you. It changes us. We adapt, we abide. You can't live on the earth and fence yourself off from us. Listen. In this place, at this time, you are not alone.*

Notes

1. Sam Bass Warner's observation was made in an address to the Association for the Study of Literature and the Environment conference at Boston University in June 2003.

2. In *The End of Nature* (1989) and elsewhere, Bill McKibben has addressed the implications of the loss of faith in nature as a self-regulating system impervious to human actions.

3. Aldo Leopold, "March," in *A Sand County Almanac with Essays on Conservation from Round River* (New York: Ballantine Books, 1966), 25.

4. Galway Kinnell's comment about poetry comes from the introduction to the bibliography entry on him in A. Poulin Jr.'s anthology *Contemporary American Poetry*, 8th ed. (New York: Houghton-Mifflin, 2006), 627–28. Poulin, incidentally, was a long-term member of the English faculty at SUNY-Brockport.

5. "Brockport—March 1978," in the chapbook *In the Distance* (Rochester, N.Y.: Mammoth Press, 1979), 21.

6. Emerson's first book, *Nature* (1836), outlines the romantic connection between beauty and truth, already linked in Keats's "Ode on a Grecian Urn" (1819), and ethics.

7. Paul Annixter, *Swiftwater* (New York: Hill and Wang, 1950), 158.

8. "Geese Calling in Darkness: Two Poems from Oak Orchard," in *In the Distance*, 22.

9. James Dickey, *Deliverance* (New York: Dell, 1970).

10. "October at the Orchard," in *In the Distance*, 7.

11. Rick Bass, "Flights of Spring," *Audubon*, March 2004, 32–35.

12. In "Honk if You Love Canada Geese," first published in *E Magazine*, November–December 1996, Judy Waytiuk notes, "Wildlife biologists have taken to calling them 'sky carp'—carp being 'junk' fish nobody wants." Information concerning goose taxonomy and the history of New York's geese was gathered from several sources, including publications of the New York State Department of Environmental Conservation. The quoted source is *When Geese Become a Problem* (Albany, N.Y.: New York State Department of Environmental Conservation, Division of Fish, Wildlife, and Marine Resources / U.S. Department of Agriculture Animal and Plant Health Inspection Service, 2007), 1. Other sources used include Jay B. Hestbeck, "Canada Geese in the Atlantic Flyway"; and John W. Grandy and John Hadidian, "Making Peace with Canada Geese," formerly available on the Web site of the Humane Society of the United States. Concerning subspecies, the traditional division into eleven subspecies is echoed by David Drake and Joseph Paulin, *A Goose Is a Goose? Identifying Differences between Migratory and Resident Canada Geese* (New Brunswick, N.J.: Rutgers Cooperative Extension, 2003). A contrarian opinion comes from Gerry Rising, "On 'Subspecies' of the Canada Goose," *Kingbird*, 2003. Sydney Landon Plum's *Solitary Goose* (Athens: University of Georgia Press, 2007) offers a slightly different interpretation of some aspects of Canada goose taxonomy and history, establishing, for example, that mid-twentieth-century New England wildlife managers intended to develop local nonmigratory populations at wildlife refuges to replace extirpated ones, rather than assuming that the released birds would merge indistinguishably with the migrants.

13. David Sibley, *The Sibley Guide to Birds* (New York: Alfred A. Knopf, 2000), 75.

14. New York State DEC, *When Geese Become a Problem*, 1.

15. Atlantic Canada population figures are from "1998-9 Canada Goose Hunting Seasons Announced," press release, New York State DEC, August 27, 1998. The GORP Web page for Iroquois National Wildlife Refuge says that annual numbers of migratory geese have declined from 88,000 to about 20,000, at http://www.gorp.com/parks-guide/Iroquois-national-wildlife-refuge-outdoor-pp2-guide-cid9099.html.

16. Aldo Leopold, "Goose Music," in *A Sand County Almanac*, 227.

17. Thanks to the efforts of a local community group, the Friends of the Iroquois National Wildlife Refuge, the boardwalk has now been repaired and reopened.

9 The Bard's Bird; or, The Slings and Arrows of Avicultural Hegemony

A Tragicomedy in Five Acts

Charles Mitchell

Act 1: Shakespeare in His Natural Habitat

It was 1890 and Shakespeare was in trouble in America. Though still a production staple of the major metropolitan theatrical companies, performances of his plays had declined significantly in number since before the Civil War. One critic, writing in 1882, reached a distressing conclusion: "Shakespeare was heard ten times in New York then [1840] for once that he is heard now."[1] The statue of Shakespeare in Central Park's Literary Walk was planned to commemorate the 1864 tricentennial of his birth, but the work was not completed until 1872. Leading Shakespearean actors had so thoroughly personalized their performances that theatergoers familiar with the texts of the plays were left disoriented. In 1884, Mark Twain committed virtual blasphemy by relegating the performance of Shakespeare to the King and the Duke, those unscrupulous rapscallions who hijacked Huck Finn's raft trip down the Mississippi River.

The setting of Twain's novel—in that putative golden age of Shakespearean performance, the 1840s—neatly captures the Bard's shifting place in American culture. To be sure, engagements like those lampooned in *The Adventures of Huckleberry Finn* composed a large share of prewar performances whose dwindling the critics mourned. Before he became Shakespeare-of-the-English-Department he was Shakespeare-of-the-stage, and for most of the nineteenth century the stage was a popular democratic medium. In urban theaters, working-class toughs mingled with more refined patrons at performances that interspersed scenes from Shakespeare with contemporary farces and other entertainments, in a setting more evocative of vaudeville than Shakespeare in the Park. Rural audiences throughout the South and

Midwest—like those in Twain's novel—were familiar enough with Shakespeare to know when they were being hoodwinked. Alexis de Tocqueville, that most indispensable of nineteenth-century chroniclers, famously observed: "There is hardly a pioneer hut in which the odd volume of Shakespeare cannot be found. I remember reading the feudal drama *Henry V* for the first time in a log cabin."[2]

In the decades after the Civil War, Shakespeare disappeared from those log cabins as his plays evolved from broadly popular performances before diverse audiences into a staple of elite, didactic culture. By the end of the century he was the property of those connoisseurs of taste and decorum for whom high culture was both a signifier of upper-class status and a means of civilizing the barbaric masses. The process was subtle but severe and unfolded as a kind of domestication. First, Shakespeare was to be rescued from the grubby clutches of those unworthy masses who provided an environment too hostile for the delicate flowers of iambic pentameter. Then, he was to be safely installed in the gilded palaces of the elite, surrounded by the well-dressed, the well-coiffed, and the well-heeled. Like the flowers and animals transplanted from the wild into private gardens and menageries, Shakespeare was plucked from his natural habitat—the raucous, topsy-turvy world of Elizabethan theater reconstituted in America's nineteenth-century public entertainments—and secured within a carefully managed and manicured House of Culture.

This disappearance of Shakespeare from the popular stage prompted the critic A. C. Wheeler to publish "The Extinction of Shakespeare" in 1890.[3] Yet while Wheeler and other critics longed for Shakespeare to regain his former popularity, they did not envision a return to the truncated, mixed entertainments that had been the foundation of that popularity. If the vulgar Shakespeare of the working-class playhouse was extinct, then good riddance. It was the Shakespeare of the black-tie theater, the newly enshrined icon of highbrow culture, whose endangered status was a cause for concern. This was the great paradox of cultural hierarchy. For the masses to enjoy Shakespeare on their own terms was to diminish him: popularity was the very opposite of refinement, and by 1890 Shakespeare was the embodiment of refined taste. But the masses nonetheless needed to be exposed to the moralizing force of Shakespeare and other incarnations of high culture in order to be rescued from a life of eternal grubbiness. Like Frederick Law Olmsted's Central Park and Andrew Carnegie's Music Hall, Shakespeare would help to civilize those masses—if only they would clean up, put on a tie, and buy a ticket.

Act 2: The Bard's Birds

In the same year that A. C. Wheeler warned of Shakespeare's endangered status (and the same year that construction began on New York City's Carnegie Hall), Eugene Schieffelin did his small part to ensure that Shakespeare's rumored extinction was not forever. A German immigrant who had established a prosperous drug manufacturing business in the Bronx, Schieffelin devoted his extracurricular energies to two pursuits that, in a moment of quirky synergy, would dramatically alter the North American landscape. As a committed patron of New York City theater, Schieffelin would certainly have been troubled to read Wheeler's account of Shakespeare's looming extinction. Strapping on his tuxedo before heading downtown for a performance of *Hamlet,* he might have reflected ruefully on what his less fortunate brethren were missing as they indulged in the inferior diversions of beer halls and other such pastimes. Schieffelin's civic participation also included his role as head of the New York branch of the American Acclimatization Society. With branches throughout the country, the society's modest goal was to introduce, at the local level, select species of old-world birds and plants in order to create a more familiar and comfortable environment for recent immigrants. Surrounded by some of the sights, sounds, and smells of home—at least those emanating from the species that had been successfully acclimatized—the immigrants themselves would adjust that much more easily to their new surroundings, or so the theory went.

Enter the starling, stage left. Under Schieffelin's guidance, the New York Acclimatization Society adopted as its special task the introduction of all the birds mentioned in the works of William Shakespeare. This was facilitated by the publication in 1871 of *The Birds of Shakespeare,* an exhaustive survey, with engravings, compiled by James Edmund Harting. Clearly, the goal here was not to provide a more familiar environment for recent immigrants from Elizabethan England. Rather, Schieffelin hoped to fashion an avian context for a fuller appreciation of Shakespeare's plays. The creation of Shakespeare gardens in the late nineteenth and early twentieth centuries had a similar purpose: to make Shakespeare's work seem less foreign to a modern audience by providing a picturesque showcase of all his featured flora. But Schieffelin, it seems, was aiming for something more than a park full of Shakespearean tableaux. If the masses could not be induced to hear Shakespeare in the theater, then perhaps they might be seduced by the sounds of Shakespeare's birds in the park.

In March 1890, Schieffelin released sixty European starlings into Central Park; the next year he released an additional forty. Unfortunately, he was a meticulous reader of Shakespeare, or, more likely, of Harting, for while several species of birds enjoyed starring roles in the metaphors and similes of Shakespeare's verse, the starling is given a single, obscure cameo in *Henry IV, Part I.* Here is Hotspur: "The king forbade my tongue to speak of Mortimer. But I will find him when he is asleep, and in his ear I'll holler 'Mortimer!' Nay, I'll have a starling shall be taught to speak nothing but Mortimer, and give it to him to keep his anger still in motion" (act 1, scene 3). Despite this eminently forgettable beginning, the starling would go on to dominate North America's avian stage, speaking "Mortimer" and more across four time zones and nearly thirty degrees of latitude. The noisy batch of starlings that evicted the pigeons from under my neighbor's eaves, the starlings I watched from my bathroom window this morning build their nests with the freshly severed stems of my tomato and pepper plants, are direct descendants of Eugene Schieffelin's effort to bring the soothing, civilizing music of Shakespeare to New York's huddling masses. *Sturnus vulgaris* indeed.

Act 3: Go West, Young Starling

In Shakespeare's time it appears that starlings were fairly widespread in Europe, if not exactly numerous, ranging from northern Italy to Scandinavia and from Russia to the not quite United Kingdom. Hotspur's reference to their ability to mimic human speech would suggest a significant degree of contact between the two species, with the likelihood that starlings were kept as a kind of pet in the centuries before the trade for exotic birds from South America would have displaced them. Even before their importation as cultural ambassadors to the United States, starlings were particularly well adapted to landscapes shaped by human activity. An omnivore preferring a diverse diet of insects, seeds, and fruits, the starling was a familiar denizen of the urban and agricultural regions of its eponymous continent. Unlike the eagles, kites, and falcons gliding through Shakespeare's more prolific avian references, the starling was most likely a bird with which the Bard was personally familiar: a squawker outside the doors of the Globe Theatre, a nester in the eaves of his gatehouse in Ireland Yard. Indeed, it may have been this very familiarity, this commonness, that restricted the starling's role to that of a bit player.

Upon their arrival in the United States, Eugene Schieffelin's wards found an environment much to their liking. Making their nests at first in the nooks and crannies of the Museum of Natural History, the starlings quickly acclimatized themselves to their new home. Most of the other in-troduced Shakespearean species died off; the starling has enjoyed what is effectively the longest-running and most widely traveled show in American theater history. It was wintering in Florida before Prohibition and followed many Americans across the border into Canada shortly after the Eighteenth Amendment took effect. By the end of World War II, starlings had reached the West Coast; they were in Alaska by the time Richard Nixon resigned the presidency. In less than one hundred years the European Starling had spread over North America and reached a population of more than 200 mil-lion, something it took the European American nearly half a millennium to achieve. A modern-day Tocqueville would find more starlings perched on the rain gutters of American homes than copies of Shakespeare in the parlor. Indeed, in what Schieffelin would likely consider a Pyrrhic victory, more Americans have heard the song of Shakespeare's bird than have heard the music of Shakespeare himself.

The secret to the starling's success in the New World is really no secret. Equally comfortable foraging for dinner in freshly mown grass, grain fields, and trash-strewn streets, it has found an abundance of culinary offerings in its adopted home. Its bill is equipped with muscles that both pry and clamp, allowing it to spread apart thick clumps of grass to locate reluctant prey: a much more efficient hunting technique than that endowed to most of its competitors. Starlings have also benefited from an abundance of ready-made housing locations. Indiscriminate cavity nesters, they have made full use of the buildings, bridges, and edge-of-clearing trees that are omnipresent features of the North American landscape. Their migratory patterns—first to arrive and last to leave—allow them to compete successfully with other cavity-nesting species, an ability greatly enhanced by their aggressive usur-pation of nesting sites already claimed by the natives.

And they breed like, well, starlings. Laying clutches of four to six eggs, mated pairs regularly produce two broods a season and occasionally three. For all their fecundity, starlings experience strikingly low rates of nestling mortality. In part this results from a form of colonial breeding, where un-mated males assist in the care of the young. Starlings are also highly skilled and efficient housekeepers. Perhaps the most effective of their domestic tech-nologies is the timely application to the nest of fresh foliage, like the stems of tomato and pepper plants, which serve as an antiparasitical fumigant. Not only does this protect the health of nestlings, it also frees up time and en-ergy for feeding that would otherwise have been spent on nest maintenance. With such competitive advantages—healthier homes, more and better-fed children, a willingness to trample on the rights of others—the starling's rapid colonization of North America appears to be nothing less than its manifest destiny.

Act 4: There Goes the Neighborhood

History, of course, is written by the winners, and the tribe of starling can proudly boast of its successes. However, just as the Iroquois and the Sioux might wish to add a qualifying footnote or two to Thomas Hart Benton's celebration of the destiny of his race, the red-bellied woodpecker, northern flicker, and eastern bluebird have ample reason to resent their European cousin's triumph. While the skies over North America are not a zero-sum world, the explosive growth of starling populations has inevitably come at the expense of other residents. Competition with starlings for food and, most important, nesting sites has contributed to significant population declines among more than a dozen species, though it remains difficult to isolate the effect of starlings from the role played by habitat loss and pollution. Woodpeckers in particular have a compelling grievance since starlings regularly claim the homes they have assiduously labored to excavate. Of course, European Americans established a precedent for just such an act of appropriation when Andrew Jackson forcibly removed the Cherokee not simply from their land but from the modern homes they had so dutifully constructed. Perhaps starlings mimic more than the human voice.

While certainly regrettable to those who watch birds, hug trees, and recycle rainwater, the starling's impact on avian ecology is a minor blip on the radar of national concerns. Far more worrisome is the threat starlings pose to frequent flyers, farmers, and the outdoor wedding industry. The 1989 film version of Robert Harling's *Steel Magnolias* opens with Tom Skerritt's character firing his gun into a tree in order to disperse the starlings poised to spoil his daughter's wedding reception. While the thought of Julia Roberts getting pelted with guano on her big day might be enough to drive even the most fervent pacifist to take up arms, the problem of roosting starlings is not merely a lifestyle nuisance for the eccentric and glamorous. Flocks of starlings numbering in the thousands are common, and some have been estimated to include more than two hundred thousand individuals, enough to induce Hitchcockian nightmares in Roger Torey Peterson.

Especially outside of breeding season, when females join the males, large flocks of starlings regularly return at night to roost in the same trees. Naturally, this poses a sanitation problem if the roosting tree happens to be adjacent to a public area. Along the two-block Commons in Ithaca, New York, green-haired adolescents and tweed-jacketed academics share the common plight of dodging the droppings of the thousands of starlings that perch overhead. Many an alfresco dinner has been disrupted by the telltale plop in the glass of chardonnay. Plastic owls and live hawks have provided no deterrent to the starlings' simple insistence on treetop tenement living. Roosting starlings also contribute to noise pollution, given their propensity to break into a cacophony of screeching at dawn and dusk. Finding the twice-daily din outside his bedroom window to be unbearable, a friend of mine spent hundreds of dollars trying to drive the nightly roost out of his backyard trees. He tried thinning the branches, installed netting, and set up solar-powered owls to frighten the starlings off. In the end, he cut down the trees and now complains about the lack of shade.

What has earned starlings an official "nuisance animal" designation from the federal government, however, has been their impact on aviation and agriculture. Between 1990 and 2001, according to the Federal Aviation Administration, there were 1,704 reported "strikes" of aircraft with flocking blackbirds. Exactly half of these reports identified starlings as the culprit while the majority of the remaining half refer only to generic "blackbirds." Apparently, a copy of the *Audubon Society Field Guide to North American Birds* is not standard-issue equipment for pilots. Nonetheless, it is likely that starlings were involved in most of the other incidents as well. The number of blackbird strikes over that time grew at a steady if modest pace, from 100 to 160 per year. While collisions with larger species, such as Canada Geese, are far more costly and occasionally result in crashes and fatalities, starlings have still been responsible for close to two million dollars' worth of damage to the civil aviation industry since 1990. Appearances to the contrary notwithstanding, starlings have not been trained by terrorists to disrupt air travel in some bastardization of *Day of the Dolphin*. Rather, they find airports to be naturally attractive homes. Often surrounded by fields or marshes and providing ample structures for nesting and roosting, the modern airport might well have been specially designed to meet the needs of this feathered frequent flyer, offering them the kind of amenities that make those of us who fly coach jealous.

Agriculture, however, is where starlings do the most damage. While there is some evidence that they contribute to insect control, they more than make up for that benefit in their taste for grain and sunflower seeds. They are also voracious raiders of feedlots for beef and dairy cattle, having developed a taste for the easy calories available in enriched feed corn. Given the size of their population and their prolific breeding success, containment rather than rollback is the only practical approach to controlling the starling menace. One popular method available to private citizens is the application of a detergent solution to roosts of winter birds. With the insulating power of their feathers compromised, the birds succumb to exposure. However, this is a difficult and, especially in temperate climates, not always effective method. For a more efficient approach, America's farmers and aviation authorities can turn to the U.S. Department of Agriculture.

The USDA's Wildlife Services division is responsible for managing a wide variety of broadly defined problem animals. In 2004 it reported killing 2,767,152 individual animals, from anhingas and badgers to weasels and wolves; methods used included shooting, trapping, poisoning, and "non chemical other." "Starlings, European" accounted for 2,320,086, or 84 percent, of the total number of animals killed. While more than 17,000 of Shakespeare's birds were shot and over 66,000 cage-killed, the vast majority—2,234,571—were dispatched courtesy of DRC-1339, which the USDA describes as an avian toxicant. Since there are no established tolerances for DRC-1339—which means nobody knows what effect it might have on humans—its use is, we are assured, carefully regulated to minimize the chance of its entering the food chain or affecting "non-target species." Shakespeare, Schieffelin, and the starling might find it a dubious honor that DRC-1339, when freed of its bureaucratic nomenclature, is known as Starlicide. It is a wonder that conservative academics, who have made something of a cottage industry condemning the Modern Language Association for its eradication of Shakespeare from the curriculum, have not expressed outrage at this murderous conspiracy.

Act 5: Starlings Are Us

I like bluebirds and flickers; while I have never seen one, I am sure I would like gila woodpeckers, whose numbers are declining at least in part because starlings evict them from the homes they have carved into saguaro cacti. As much as the next guy, I hate seeing a good glass of wine spoiled by starling poop. I had plans for those tomatoes and peppers: gazpacho, maybe, or a roasted salsa recipe I have been looking forward to trying. For these and many other reasons I could rage against the imbecility of Schieffelin, the arrogance behind his peculiar blend of cultural and ecological imperialism. What would my yard, my park, my skies look like if he had not been such a fool? What else would the Wildlife Services division be doing with its time and my tax dollars? I could offer the obvious condemnation of the starling as an invasive species, though in this case the invasion was by invitation. I could say, simply, that starlings do not belong here and allow the righteousness of my outrage to be the final word. But the fact is that starlings are here, and all the Starlicide in the world will not change that. And, as I learned from my German American grandmother—whose parents were released into New York City in the late nineteenth century—one should be cautious when deciding who does and who does not belong. If starlings do not belong here, then neither do I.

Starlings are here in North America because they mimic human speech. Had they not attached themselves to *Homo sapiens'* coattails and started chattering in English, Shakespeare would have had to come up with a different line for Hotspur and the starling would never have passed through Ellis Island. Once they arrived on these shores their success was guaranteed because they were so much like us in other ways as well, willing to live where we live, eat what we eat, and follow us wherever we might go. Unwillingly and unwittingly we have played Squanto and Sacajawea to the starling invaders, helping to pave the way for a success we have come to regret. The only two landscapes they have not successfully colonized are forested wilderness areas and open desert, the two landscapes with the lowest human population density (one by definition, the other by default). In short, where there are people there are starlings. And it is not just the opportunism and adaptability of their behavior that defines our kinship. During nesting season, while mom spends the night on the nest, dad flies off to join the boys in the roost, whooping it up like a convention of Promise Keepers at a monster truck rally. You can't get any more American than that.

To complain about starlings would be hypocritical and ungenerous, but it would be irresponsibly glib for us to dismiss the damage they have done with an Alfred E. Neuman shrug. Of course, I could spend pages unpacking, repacking, and unpacking again the meaning of the word "damage" in this context, and my unauthorized use of the first-person plural pronoun is bound to raise some postructuralist eyebrows. At the very least, the folks at starlingtalk.com—a Web site devoted to championing the starling's virtues and defending its honor—would find both "damage" and "us" to be fighting words. But if controlling starlings falls somewhere between the impractical and the impossible—and all but the hard-core Dr. Strangeloves at the USDA have admitted as much—then all that may be left to us is to learn to live with them. While I don't share the enthusiasm of the folks at starlingtalk.com for keeping starlings as pets, their uncomplicated acceptance of the reality of starlings is refreshing. Even Rachel Carson, in a 1939 essay for *Nature Magazine,* wondered whether it was time to grant the starling citizenship papers, an argument that has much to teach today's "immigration reform" advocates. The space we make for starlings may say something about the space we allow ourselves, all of our selves.

The starling came to us as a character in a tragedy, and the tragedy is that efforts to mitigate the impact of starlings on native species are unlikely to be more than nominally successful. A few carefully designed and tended nest boxes might lure a few more bluebirds, but isolated local victories may be all we can hope for. That is the nature of tragedy. Things did not work out too well for Hotspur and Mortimer, either. But Shakespeare was not all tragedy. His comedies suggest that merriment can be had, and happiness won, even under the least idyllic of circumstances. Hermia and Lysander avoid the path of Romeo and Juliet thanks to a midsummer night's frolic in the woods; Bottom's ass finds love with Titania. Any extraneous detail can be accommodated, any alien creature can find love, with a little imagination exercised under the open air. Balance is not so much restored as reimagined.

Epilogue: Oh Brave, New World That Has Such Starlings in It

It is a dreamy midsummer day. I am midsummering in a hammock in my friends' backyard in northwestern New Jersey, a backyard that includes ten acres, a barn, and a pond. Struggling to stay focused on James Fenimore Cooper's *The Pioneers,* which I will soon decide *not* to teach in the fall term, I turn frequently to watch the barn swallows (what were they called before we invented barns?) skim their lunch off the surface of the pond. Above the tree line two hundred yards away I see a handful of blackbirds crossing from stage right. Then a bucketful. Through binoculars I identify starlings. They keep coming. Soon, thirty degrees of my sky are filled with starlings. Renegade pockets angle out of the mainstream, circle back, and then seamlessly reintegrate themselves like water in an eddy. This goes on for seventeen minutes. I know that there are experts somewhere who could calculate the number of individual birds I saw that afternoon, but I do not care to know. What is of interest to me is that for those seventeen minutes I could imagine what it might have been like to stand with Natty Bumpo under a sky full of passenger pigeons. I know that starlings are not passenger pigeons. They do not make up for the extinction of passenger pigeons any more than the New York Mets make up for the loss of the Brooklyn Dodgers. But they are what we have now. And, at times, they can be amazing.

Notes

I first came across the story of Schieffelin's starlings in chapter 3 of Annie Dillard's *Pilgrim at Tinker Creek* (New York: Harper's Magazine Press, 1974), 35. Dillard credits Edwin Way Teale as her source. The story appears—with minor variations regarding the number of pairs released, the exact date of their release, and whether there were one or two releases—in environmental history texts, field guides, and online birding sites. After completing this essay I found accounts in Peter Cashwell's *The Verb "To Bird"* (Philadelphia: Paul Dry Books, 2003) and Kim Todd's *Tinkering with Eden: A Natural History of Exotics in America* (New York: Norton, 2001). Todd identifies her source as F. M. Chapman, "List of Birds Found within Fifty Miles of the American Museum of Natural History" (*American Museum Journal* 6, no. 3, 1906) and "The European Starling as an American Citizen" (*Natural History* 25, no. 5, 1925). These appear to be the original sources for the story.

Information on starling demographics and behavior is readily available in standard field guides and other birding resources. You might also just go for a walk in the park. The USDA and the FAA maintain meticulous records of their interactions with starlings and other problem animals (though I would love to know whose job it was to count the 2,320,086 starlings dispatched in 2004). The American Acclimatization Society is a dissertation topic waiting to be discovered. While basic information is available through its published charter and by-laws, I was unable to discover any narrative history of this oh-so-interesting organization.

1. Richard Grant White, quoted in Lawrence Levine, *Highbrow/Lowbrow: The Emergence of Cultural Hierarchy in America* (Cambridge, Mass.: Harvard University Press, 1988), 34. Throughout this first act I draw on Levine's discussion of Shakespeare's shifting place on the nineteenth-century stage.

2. Alexis de Tocqueville, *Democracy in America* (1840; New York: Library of America, 2004), 538.

3. Levine, *Highbrow/Lowbrow*, 45.

10 Fly-Fishing for Carp as a Deeper Aesthetics

Phillip David Johnson II

SINCE I QUIT THE FLY SHOP, I've been wading through miasmic absurdity with a six-hundred-dollar fly rod, chasing carp. Yes, I said carp. For a fly-fisherman and former guide living on Colorado's Front Range, choosing the ignoble carp over trout seems a travesty, or at the very least some kind of ingratitude. At this point, however, carp fishing, or "carping" as my friends and I like to call it, has become a compulsion, because it drives to the very marrow of all things angling.

So today, while SUVs sporting kayaks, coolers, and mountain bikes head west into the mountains, I go east through Fort Collins to Riverbend Ponds, a park picturesquely situated between a defense contractor, a dental tool company, the airport, and an overtapped urban stretch of the Cache la Poudre River. The ponds began as pits, a by-product of the state's need for road-building gravel, that filled with water and became home to ducks, geese, eagles, and ospreys. Of course, carp moved in as well—they always do. The state stocked the ponds with bass, bream, walleye, and occasionally rainbow trout, and the city began managing the place as a wetland, or what they call a *natural area.*

After parking the truck, I get out and go through the pre-fishing ritual of organizing and arranging gear while I occasionally look up to admire the Colorado-blue sky brushed thin with stratus clouds. (Admiring beauty is just part of the regimen.) The Indian summer sun warms my shirt and begins to burn my neck, and although the weather is probably warm enough to allow fishing without waders, I pull them on anyway. The temperature always drops sharply near dusk, and in November that's about dinnertime. As I check my gear one last time, joggers and dog walkers pass without saying anything, but they keep glancing at me and my waders, as though they're wondering if I'm from Mars.

Meticulously prepared for the best and worst of fishing circumstances, I head toward the pond along the raised wooden walkway that cuts through cattails and bulrushes. I stop to check out the message board—ANIMALS I MIGHT SEE; RULES AND REGULATIONS FOR ENJOYING MY NATURAL AREA— and notice a new laminated sign that reads, in large red letters:

CAUTION!

PUBLIC HEALTH ADVISORY.

PUBLIC HEALTH OFFICIALS HAVE IDENTIFIED THE DISEASE
TULAREMIA IN AREA WILDLIFE.

TULAREMIA IS A ZOONOTIC DISEASE THAT CAN BE TRANSMITTED
FROM ANIMALS TO HUMANS.

A numbered list warns me not to approach or handle living or dead animals; not to let pets come in contact with animal carcasses or drink surface water; to use gloves when handling fish and to cook them thoroughly; to wear DEET to deter ticks and deerflies that spread the disease; to stay on established trails; and not to enter rivers, creeks, or ditches. *Damn.*

I guess I could turn around now and follow the SUVs up into the mountains, but I'd be rubbing elbows on the river. The more I think about tularemia, or rabbit fever as it's called on the Plains, the less it worries me. Antibiotics are a reliable cure. There's no dog with me. I haven't played with dead animals since I was twelve, unless you count fly tying. We've had a couple of hard freezes already, so the biting bugs should be pretty much gone. And although I'll be leaving the trails and getting into the water, I'm wearing waders—I'm effectively wrapped in a Gore-Tex body condom. And, of course, I'm a catch-and-release fisherman, particularly when fishing for carp. I walk on.

As I walk toward the water, this November's unusual warmth reminds me of another Indian summer day when I was fifteen. My friend Andrew and I sat on a gravelly bank of East Texas's San Gabriel River on a Saturday morning, watching the tips of our fishing rods and talking in low voices. We had sunk treble hooks weighted only with doughball—a mixture of crushed corn flakes, vanilla extract, Big Red soda, and flour—into the far side of the river, where the water drifted imperceptibly over the limestone bottom. Because the San Gabriel River sluices through the Granger Dam, a Civilian

Conservation Corps project, before it gets to where we fished, and because of the time of year, well after the spring rains, the river seemed not much of a river at all, just limestone pools connected by trickles. Silt and muck choked eddies and cutoff channels; the water grew algae in dense mats. This was the perfect place for carp.

Our lines hadn't been out for very long when both rod tips began flexing slowly down and then up. Andrew, my self-appointed carp-fishing expert, advised me to wait before setting the hook.

"They're just sucking on the bait," he said. "Wait till they carry it off."

Pretty soon, we were both playing large carp somewhere in the range of twenty pounds—bigger than any catfish or largemouth we'd caught all season.

We spent most of the morning catching carp, putting all of them on a chain stringer, not necessarily because we wanted to keep them, but simply because we were serious fishermen—we kept fish. After my fourth or fifth carp, my Wal-Mart reel was gear-stripped, our lines were stretched, and we were tired. But we had a stringer full of carp, most weighing in the range of nearly eight pounds all the way up to twenty (we were sure). After admiring our catch, I looked at Andrew, "Now what?"

When I was younger, maybe five, I rode with my dad in his old blue Chevy pickup to town. On these trips, we passed a swampy area near the Highway 79 overpass outside of Taylor, Texas. The marsh had been a pond, dug out for fill to raise the road's grade over the interchange, but time and silt had turned the pond into a mudhole, and scrub oak, willow, and other undesirable trees had choked access to the water. Still, I asked my dad why we never fished there.

"That place is full of carp—no bass or catfish," he said.

When I pressed him about carp, he told me "they weren't much for fiddlin' with" and "they were trash fish."

"You have to throw 'em away?"

"Well, they're not worth eating."

"Does anybody eat them?"

"No, not really—they're full of bones, and you have to pressure cook 'em. They taste like mud."

"Have you ever eaten carp?"

"No—never, but I hear black folks like them."

Sometime later while my dad and I fished the tailwaters behind Granger Dam on the San Gabriel River, we inadvertently hooked a large carp and landed it. I was immediately sent downriver to where two African-American men sat angling with long cane poles to ask if they wanted a big carp. In light of racial and social hierarchies in Texas, this was my dad's way of being polite.

I took it for granted that carp were a worthless species, and on that fall day when Andrew suggested that we go carp fishing on "the river" (our term for the San Gabriel), I didn't know why anyone would want to. You can't keep them, you can't eat them, and, echoing my step-dad, they're just a "trash fish" (although we regularly fried flathead catfish in a big grease pot in the backyard—in some circles, another trash fish).

Andrew and I had promised his uncle we'd return in the afternoon to help with a few projects in the shop, so Andrew hooked the stringer of carp to a willow sapling that grew over a shallow pool. We'd come back for the carp later . . . for some reason or other. When we returned to the river to check on our carp, we walked up and down the bank where we left them.

Gone.

Noting the exact spot, we saw that the willow sapling was stripped of its branches and bark, exposing its green-tinted inner flesh. Those carp had escaped like a chain-gang who'd hatched a plan on work detail. I don't re-member being disappointed about losing the fish; in fact, we laughed. In that moment, our seriousness for fishing gave way to the inklings of parody and irony. Irony was the not the term I would have used then, but I knew I had touched on some form of *deeper* hilarity, maybe the absurd, where comedy can cut to the very soul of things. For a moment, I understood there could be nothing serious about fishing, and somehow a stringer full of carp had shown me this. Those carp had become dissemblers of cosmic proportions. And it definitely was not because fishing needed such significance; I'd dis-cover later in life that the opposite was true.

At the end of the walkway I see three city trucks and a group of workers standing around holding shovels. I offer a friendly *howdy,* and a muscular young woman with cropped hair says, "Hi, going fishing?" Before I can an-swer sarcastically, she says, pointing, "Hey, that's a nice setup. How much does that rod cost?"

I hesitate to answer. Am I being ridiculed? I mean, it's obvious I'm going fishing, and there's something about her tone. Do these hard-working folks think I'm some yuppie obsessed with consumer gadgetry—expensive rods, English reels, handmade wooden nets, Gore-Tex waders? Of course I *do* own all that stuff, but should I defend myself? Do I tell them of the simple pleasures of holding a fish—ego-tripping equipment be damned? Nah. Instead, I chuckle and try to appear friendly.

By now I'm surrounded by three other workers standing so close I can make out individual threads in their city-issue work shirts. It's beginning to feel like the start of a few bar fights I remember losing, but they're smiling, so I keep cool and smile back.

A tall, skinny guy grounds his shovel with a clank and moves closer. "Hey, she's serious. She just bought a fly rod, and I'm trying to unload one on eBay."

"Six hundred," I say to collective gasps. I decide not to tell them that six hundred dollars for a graphite rod is the high end of average these days. "But you really don't have to spend that much on a rod; I have a fifty-dollar job that I use just as much." And that's true.

The tall, skinny guy backs off, smiles, and asks what I'm out here fly-fishing for.

"Carp, big ones," I say.

He laughs, then furrows his brow, trying to figure out if I'm serious. "So carp bite flies?" he asks a little incredulously.

"Yeah," I reply, a trifle self-righteously, "they'll take any trout fly."

Everyone's still quiet, but they begin to back away. They look like I just told them I enjoy playing with dead animals. To break the silence I say, "Well, it's a good day to be outside." The tall, skinny guy looks over and grins to his buddy, reaches down for his shovel, and says with the slightest tinge of sarcasm, "Yeah, very nice. Good luck."

In my early twenties, I moved from Texas to the Rocky Mountains of Colorado and Montana to pursue the life of a fishing writer (or concrete day laborer, depending on how I choose to remember), and I too began to extol the virtues of trout over other species. In a conscious effort to forget my working-class childhood of hunting, fishing for catfish, setting jug lines, and the like, I let the image of rainbow trout (Orcorhynchus mykiss) become my highest object of pursuit. That image adorned my fishing vest, my coffee mugs, and a bumper sticker on my car, and even a lamp and a few Christmas ornaments. The rainbow trout was, in my mind, the synecdoche of fly-fishing,[1] of clear, "pure" water from snowmelt, and of flower-bedecked mountain meadows cut by glaciers in the deep past. The rainbow trout and the cold creeks and rivers where it could be found stood in sharp contrast to the muddy backwaters I grew up fishing in Texas. I had been converted not just to fly-fishing but also, more importantly, to aesthetic commitments. In this world, my step-dad's reasons about why we did not fish for carp were the rungs on a ladder, which ultimately reached high above to enlightenment—

like the not-so-subtle class distinctions between NASCAR and Formula One racing. High in the mountains, with a vintage bamboo fly rod and (later) a degree in philosophy, I was prepared to intermingle in the beauty of the Rocky Mountains. I stood streamside in a tattered fedora, smoking amaretto tobacco in a Peterson's Scholar's pipe, a small notebook and pen stowed in the breast pocket of my breathable, Gore-Tex waders, awaiting inspiration, casting ponderously for "solitude,"[2] a purity of experience, a directness of understanding, that somehow all the mysteries of the universe would gather focus—you know, "eventually, all things merge into one, and a river runs through it."[3] However, as I whipped bamboo rods throughout the mountain West, trying to fuse the lives of two great American myths—a cowboy who didn't ride horses and Norm Maclean's protégé, a more accurate conception of the American Western experience was quickly catching up to me in an invasive, carp-like fashion.

Through the years, as I studied the history of fly-fishing, fish stocking, and riparian ecology, and, more important, clerked in fly shops, the irony of those carp in Texas began to pollute my high notions of angling—historically, ethically, and most damaging of all, aesthetically. To see fly-fishing as beautiful or rivers as churches (a haggard trope of twentieth-century fly-fishing writing), you had to ignore quite a bit of history and you had to, above all, not fish for carp.

I always thought it peculiar that those who had seemingly little invested in the angling life were the most upset by the comedy of carp fishing. I leave the city workers with puzzled, chagrined looks on their faces. Offering a quick backward wave, I walk on down the trail, following the two-track as it rises to a point overlooking the main pond. Ahead, trees line the far side of the river, but I can hear an industrial hum when the wind lulls. The air smells like pond water mixed with cedar and juniper. Sometimes in the summer I can smell the sewage-treatment facility with a westerly wind, and when the wind blows from the east I can smell the cattle stockyards in Greeley—a concentrated, soggy odor sometimes so intense it registers on my tongue. Above the trees on the western horizon, the foothills jut up into the sky, and behind them rise snow-crested mountains. The air is remarkably clear, and I can distinguish individual trees on the nearest foothills.

From the point, I scan the water for shadows. The water is so clear it looks sterile, dead. Pockmarks in the shallows show where carp have been rooting, but that could have happened last summer. As a semi jake-brakes on the road, something catches my eye. At a spot where overhanging grasses shelter a tiny inlet and the water has undercut the bank, I see a shadow with the right size and shape. I stay as still as possible. If it's a carp, I know it's already seen me. I think I see a tail move. The shadow begins to drift toward deeper water. Yes, carp! I continue watching, but my excitement wanes a bit when I realize it's just doing the midday carp thing: drifting and watching. Not quite the attitude for getting caught.

Looking toward the eastern shore, where people fish from lawnchairs and let their dogs swim, I see that no one's out today. The western side, where I prefer to fish, is a large marsh broken and braided by remnants of roads, gravel piles, and old irrigation canals. This place is a carping paradise.

Below the point runs an old canal ditch I usually cross to get to better carp water. The ditch is clogged with tumbleweeds piled head-high, but I figure I can just push through them. Skidding and hopping down the bank, my felt soles lose traction, and I land square on my butt. I check my waders for damage, look around to make sure no one saw me fall, and then I force my way through the tumbleweeds to the ditch.

Thanks to the prevailing wind, the shore here is a cultural stew of soda pop bottles, Wal-Mart bags, red-wiggler cartons, and Skoal cans. The canal is clogged with purple loosestrife and cattail culms. Crossing a small island, I scrape through undersized Russian olives, and go deeper into the marsh. The thorns scratch my neck and arms, tangle my landing net, and grab my fly line. Around the tree trunks, the remains of toadflax and thistles carpet the soil. Everything is drab tan except the Russian olives' maroonish-brown branches. Then olives and thistles give way to cattails, and where the water stands ankle-deep, tamarisks take over—hundreds of them. They weren't here last year, or at least they weren't this far out into the marsh.

In the very center of the marsh, a shallow cove adjoins the deeper, eastern portion of the pond. The cove spans about two fly-casts, and the water, masked by cattails, willows, and Russian olives, appears unfishable from the trail above. You'd have to be standing right where I am to see its possibilities.

I wade slowly out into the cove, pausing to scan for carp, the mud feeling spongy under my boots. I take care to avoid pushing water into waves, alerting the carp. But some things I can't help, like the sucking sound of each footstep or the *gwallop* of bubbles that boil to the surface and smell of methane. I remove the fly, a blood-colored marabou leech, from the hook keeper on the rod and strip line off the reel while I await a sign—a cloud of silt, a ripple, a wake, a rise, a back and dorsal fin bouncing like a lost Red Grange bobber.

Nothing.

Although I've caught a few carp blind-casting, which means casting randomly into open water, I'd rather sight-fish for carp. It's one of my own rules, and I don't mind waiting. The waiting, the relative silence after you get used to the road noise, this manufactured wetland, and even the carp themselves make me wonder how it's come to this.

I learned to fly-fish when I was eight years old under the tutelage of a West Texas oil man who was an associate of my father's. There on a tributary of the South Platte that runs through Alma, Colorado, I vividly remember the poorly tied gray drake pattern dimpling the surface of the tiny stream. Brook trout, like drops of metallic paint in a Winslow Homer watercolor, splashed spastically after mayflies and caddis flies. The image of that gray drake floating through riffles in Alma stayed with me. I dreamed about the experience throughout my childhood, mostly during times away from the mountains, and it served to intensify my longing for trout and trout rivers. Closing my eyes, I could see brook trout nosing the gray hackles, leaping with flies in their mouths; I saw swallows darting after summer mayflies and returning to their mud nests in the alcoves of the old schoolhouse near the river, and all of this was backdropped by the Rockies towering above me.

When I was eighteen, I wanted to relive the experience, so I drove to Alma and my brook trout stream to find a twelve-foot, chain-link fence and strands of razor wire surrounding piles of mine slag. The once-vacant schoolhouse had become the new municipal building for the town. There were more liquor joints and convenience stores than I remembered. I looked south to a valley filled up, used up. I pulled my car to the side of the road to get a good look at it all, but I didn't really stay long enough to think about what it meant. At the time, I didn't know what to think. Since then, I've wondered if I should hate the mining company that turned a freestone river into an iron-stained industrial sluice. Part of me does, but my feelings have been tempered by the fact that most of my fishing equipment is made of metals. Eventually, I came to realize my concepts of nature and wilderness were deeply flawed, and later carp would subtly change my perspective about what fishing was truly about.

I started dabbling in carp fishing when I lived in the Midwest and slowly came to realize that fly-fishing for stocked trout really *sucked*, in carpian terms. Back in Indiana, a stocking truck would back up to a river and dump fish while anglers chucked red wigglers and garlic-flavored marshmallows.

To borrow the late Gary Lafontaine's term, this was a "Disneyland with fish," though perhaps Disneyland is too elevated. More like a catchpenny carnival—a mockery not just to the fishing but to the fish. Izaak Walton said anglers were peaceable, contemplative, and honest. He'd never seen put-and-take trout fishing. So, hating crowds and carnivals, I moved on to other species, and in a secretive kind of way this included carp. Once, on a white-bass trip to the Wabash River, I happened on a slough filled with enormous carp sipping algae and mulberries. I tied on a red-yarn salmon egg that looked close enough to a mulberry and caught a carp that ran my reel into its backing.

After that I started looking around for carp—in irrigation ditches, in farm ponds, in inner-city waterways, anywhere I thought they might swim. And I found something besides carp, something missing from most good trout waters: solitude.

"Excuse me, sir." Someone's yelling behind me. I turn and see the tall, skinny worker waving a pink sheet of paper. He's on the trail on the far side of the ditch, maybe sixty yards away. He seems to want me to come and get the paper.

"Did you see the posting back on the sign, the tularemia warning?" Farther up the trail, a woman walking her dog stops to watch.

"Yeah," I holler back, "but I thought it was just a problem for dogs and cats."

"Well, it's been tested positive in the water. You should be okay with your waders and all—I think."

"Do I need to be concerned about open wounds, things like that?" This just slips out before I could think of something else to say. I try to remember if I've cut myself lately. "What are the symptoms?"

He almost yells something, but stops and looks down at his piece of paper. A small plane circles overhead—a twin turboprop—and we look at each other, waiting for the droning of engines to quiet.

When the plane disappears over the trees, he yells louder, "Uh, rash, flu-like symptoms."

I nod emphatically, "Okay, I'll be careful. Thanks." I don't know what else to say.

He shakes his head and starts walking toward the trucks. "Yeah, I'm an idiot," I mutter as I watch him go. The woman walking her dog has disappeared. I turn to the cove and wonder what the hell it is I'm doing. Risking bubonic plague in pursuit of the lowly carp must suggest a travesty of values or, more likely, a kind of insanity. I wonder how long the water has been infected—most likely longer than the city knew about it.

I turn back to scan the cove, and a carp darts into deeper water, leaving an Evinrude-sized wake. "Twenty-pounder," I say out loud. Another pause. I guess I might as well stay for a while. Then I mouth the word *tu-la-re-mia*. How did he pronounce that? Probably shouldn't let the kids touch me when I get home.

I stand there for a moment, scanning the cove for another fish. The wind is rippling the surface, rasping at the loosestrife, fluttering dried-up leaves. I scan the shallows for any anomalies in the surface film. When a carp sits in shallow water, the waves directly above it subtly change shape—something you learn to see after a few years of carp fishing. But nothing is happening here, so I work my way farther into the marsh. My boots drag long strands of moss out of the cove up across a thin island and through more Russian olives and willows. On the far side of the island, I scare a carp out of some reeds. Judging by the amount of silt in the water, it was feeding. Good sign.

Kneeling on the bank, I strip line from the reel to cast. The reel clicks loudly, and as I move the rod two plumes of silt materialize right in front of me. The carp that made them are instantly gone, like piscine magicians disappearing into puffs of smoke. The cattails are molting everywhere in the marsh. Tiny wisps of cotton drift in the breeze. A breath of wind pushes them low over the water and then up like a hatch of *Ephoron* mayflies. A Cessna flies over. A honeybee scouts my sleeve for a place to land, then thinks better of it.

I raise my rod and begin working out line, and I send the fly toward a carpy-looking shadow. When the leech pattern hits the water, a plume of silt blossoms like a miniature mushroom cloud. One of the challenges of sight-casting to carp is laying weighted fly down softly. In shallow, clear waters I have been using longer leaders, sometimes up to sixteen feet long, which makes casting in the wind a challenge. But carp won't move far for a fly, so the best chance of hooking one is to plink a fly down gently within a foot of its head.

Something else that makes or breaks carp fishing is noise. A carp's hearing organs are connected to their swim bladders, so everything they hear is amplified. I once brought a guiding buddy from Estes Park out to this very spot. He was so nervous about wet wading—there were lots of snapping turtles skittering around in the shallows—that he started every time he bumped something underwater. He sounded like a cow blundering through the marsh. Carp bolted for deep water before we got close enough to cast. Finally I said, "What the hell do you think you're doing, trout fishing?"

Behind the silt clouds, I see another carp shadow. I cast, twitch the fly twice, pull in line, and it tightens. I get excited until my carp turns out to be a section of rubber hose. As I strip it in to remove the fly, I scare four more carp I'd been casting over and hadn't seen. My hands are shaking a little now, and it dawns on me that not only do I have more to learn about spotting carp, but I've also gotten a bad case of fish jitters from something most people call a "trash fish." This is a feeling I share with only a small and select group of other anglers—or idiots, depending on your viewpoint.

On the far side of the pond, some mallards and teal crash into the water, scattering carp in all directions. I turn and slowly scan the marsh. On my left I see a lone carp feeding methodically, its back bobbing through the muddy shallows, moss and algae draping its dorsal fin. I watch to figure out which way it's moving, then I cast, setting the line down too hard. It flushes.

I feel a tingle on my hand and look to see a mosquito, its abdomen swollen red. I'd assumed they'd all be dead by now. Is all the blood mine? Maybe she just filled up on a rat, dying of tularemia. I smack her dead. I think about the health advisory and the long-distance conversation with the tall, skinny guy, who seemed genuinely concerned. I imagine rashes, sores, vomiting. I decide on a hot shower immediately after stripping off my waders tonight.

I begin casting again. The fly line whips water into the air, and a droplet lands on my beard. I wipe it carefully away from my mouth with my shirt sleeve and think a bit more about fishing in what might be liquid plague. In this part of the marsh, dead cottonwoods stand in the stagnant water, their barkless branches outstretched like the arms of doomsdayers. A black-green sludge floats in the coves. There's a subdivision to the north, and I'm sure it supplies the pond with a healthy dose of fertilizer and pesticides. Across the road to the south is the old landfill. I expect it's a source of leachate from the buried garbage. And of course there's the road, slick with all sorts of leaking automotive fluids, a vector, if you will, for those who see natural areas as a kind of nocturnal dump.

I'm not surprised anymore when I find new piles of trash. The reasons carp found their way into the Cache la Poudre and then to these ponds is because of the ways people treated their watersheds. There is a much longer tradition of mistreating rivers than a history of protecting them.

In the decades following the Civil War, Congress was inundated with complaints of anglers and professional fishermen around the country who claimed that fish stocks were dwindling. To many, overfishing and pollution, the inevitable consequences of industrialization and population growth, were the culprits. Congress, feeling desperation, a sense of responsibility, and magnanimity, turned to the developing science of fish culture, mainly practiced by amateur pisciculturalist and scientific organizations like the American Fish Culturalists (AFC). The AFC, a private organization of anglers, commercial fisherman, and scientists, supplied the bureaucrats for a new government agency, the U.S. Fish Commission (USFC).[4]

As the story is popularly told, Congress, through the USFC, sent Rudolph Hessel to Holstein, Germany, to procure carp. In 1877, his second attempt (the first batch died in a rough winter crossing), Hessel ferried 345 carp across the Atlantic and placed them in Baltimore's Druid Hill Park. These founding fish proliferated with lascivious fecundity, and Congress approved the USFC's request to move the overflow to Babcock Lakes in Monument Park, Washington, D.C. The carp soon overran Babcock Lakes, and, as George Laycock writes in 1879, 12,265 carp were "happily spread out over twenty five states and territories,"[5] and by 1883 Congress authorized the USFC to distribute carp around the country in cooperation with state fisheries agencies. According to Laycock,[6] the number of fish shipped that year totaled 260,000. In 1879, 12,203 carp fingerlings were shipped from Baltimore and Washington, D.C. In 1880, 31,332 carp were shipped to 1,374 applicants. In 1881, 143,696 carp were shipped to seven thousand applicants. "From 1879 to 1896, the Fish Commission distributed approximately 2.4 million carp" altogether.[7] While some of these fish did go to other countries, most were sent to state hatcheries for propagation and to private citizens hoping to profit from pond culture.

Even my home state of Texas fell into collusion with the carp scheme. On December 2, 1879, the USFC supplied Texas fish commissioner J. H. Dinkins with 151 carp,[8] and these were followed by more federal shipments in the following years. Both the state of Texas and the USFC actively supplied carp to public and private waters across the state. The carp that Andrew and I angled out of the San Gabriel were descendents of those founding fish,[9] railroaded to Texas from 1879 to 1883.[10] Historian Robin W. Doughty reports that by 1881 Texas may have "received 15 percent" of all the carp propagated by the USFC at the Washington, D.C., fish ponds. However, Texas was by no means unique in the history of fish culture. Carp were shipped all over the United States to "improve" and create markets for freshwater fishing. And USFC records indicate that farmers living around Laporte, Colorado, requested carp. When the markets dried up, or never materialized, I imagine those fish were turned loose in the Cache la Poudre River or, like many of their counterparts, escaped in a spring flood.

From the standpoint of the USFC and other carp proponents in the 1870s and 1880s, the carp's impressive reproductive abilities only showed its reliable investment potential. In addition to rapid reproduction, fish commissioner Spencer F. Baird, New York state senator Robert Barnwell Roosevelt, and Hessel also reported that the carp was a "vegetable feeder," which assured its place on the bottom rung of the food chain and would be no threat to "game" species. It could thrive in warm, muddy, or brackish water when other fish could not, and it had been successfully cultured in Europe and Asia for centuries. In an interview with a *New York Times* reporter, in April 1878, Baird qualified these impressive abilities by saying the carp was mainly intended for Southern waters to be used as food fish for the poor of the country. When asked about the carp's use for sport, he conceded that the carp "affords no sport whatever to the angler that I am aware of, but its flesh is delicious."[11] And so the story of carp introduction, after the enterprise was considered a massive debacle,[12] would transform the carp's attributes of hardiness and fecundity into reasons to fear its unchecked spread across the continental United States. More important, those who told the carp's story would also fail to mention the overfishing and pollution problems that led to the founding of the USFC in the first place. As a result, carp introduction would later be portrayed as an "improvement" on nature arising from hubris, instead of a mix of complicated political and environmental reasons, including the government's attempt to save fisheries.

Today the carp is a valueless nonentity or pest, and a shadowy inhabitant of urban park ponds and polluted lakes and rivers. Most who encounter carp don't think much of them, unless they feel revulsion. If they notice carp, they see only an ugly bottom-feeder, classed with suckers, chubs, and other primordial fishes of little interest, aesthetic or otherwise. Anglers and scientists, for the most part, those who know something about the carp's biology or its foreign origins, denigrate the fish as a threat to more desirable species, as foul tasting, as "biological pollution," and as a "trash fish." It's the practice of many anglers, when fishing for bass or trout, to throw a carp on the bank of a river or a lake to die—a matter of principle, or good environmental stewardship. Scientists along with fisheries managers have employed a host of methods from poison to dynamite to rid lakes and rivers of carp. These attitudes and actions toward the carp, however, have not affected the fish's populations or its ever-increasing range—nor even have we come around to accepting the carp's presence as the inevitable consequence of other environmental attitudes or problems. Carp eradication is merely a utopian pipe dream, and even if eliminating all the carp in North America were possible, there would be plenty of other human-caused environmental problems left. But carp are a convenient culprit for degraded watersheds. Their resilience, once the reason they were prized, is now the reason they're damned.

There is no freshwater fish stronger and more resilient to human *management* than carp, but without the aid of humans, without the gargantuan fish-stocking project of the late nineteenth century, carp could not have spread so effectively across North America. Carp and other invasive species present a complex problem, a dilemma that is not quite as simple as killing off the offending animal or plant. As an expert on weeds explained it to me, "It's not a war; you can't just kill them. You never know what will take the invader's place, and what replaces it could be far worse." In spite of admiring carp, I don't really find this comforting. I really want to weep, or get angry and punch someone's lights out, for the native species we've lost and the places that will never be the same. Change isn't easy to understand, but our emotional response to it can seem clear and righteous. The distinction between pristine and developed (sometimes destroyed) landscapes has led a lot of people to take no notice of places like Riverbend Ponds as wilderness or, by virtue of historical ignorance, to imagine untouched landscapes where they never existed. These ponds, *artificial* wetlands if you will, are nature, and they too are a kind of wilderness that has been uncared for and mostly overlooked.

About three hundred feet over my head, a Piper Cub flutters its ailerons and veers off toward the airport. On the bank, I see a submerged fisherman's trail that looks like wagon ruts. Do carp travel here in high water? I decide to follow and see. The trail circles the edge of another little cove and ends at the eroded remnants of an irrigation ditch. Just beyond I see a circular disturbance, like an upwelling. I step carefully and deliberately, then false-cast. The carp stops moving, but I'm sure it didn't swim off. I decide to wait and let the fly line fall behind me without looking back. I kneel and wait for some indication that the carp is feeding again. After a minute, a circular boil produces concentric ripples. I raise the rod, false-cast to measure the distance, and set the fly down as lightly as I can near what I hope is its tail. I pull the leech pattern slowly past the fish's head. It stops rooting and swims after the fly. The leader moves slightly, and I set the hook.

The line snaps from the water, forming a straight line from the arched rod tip to the fish's mouth. As the carp turns for deep water, the line cuts the surface film making a sound like polyester ripping, and my reel revs with that whine fly anglers dream about in happy sleep. I judge the carp to be maybe eight pounds, just a little one, but it takes me down to the backing in just a few seconds. When the fish gets close to a sunken tree, I palm the spool, and the line grows taut and ticks for a few seconds. The carp pulls with throbbing tail thrusts, and I wait for the leader to snap.

It holds. The carp turns toward me, swimming hard, and the line falls slack between us. I wind the reel spool furiously, then the carp turns again, making one more blistering haul for deep water. I lower the rod tip and work the reel when I can. Each run is shorter and weaker than the last, and I'm able to wrench the fish toward me. When the carp circles in close, I slide it onto the moss-covered bank.

Removing the hook, I notice the fish's flanks, covered in scales like overlapping coins, reflecting copper and gold in the sun. Looking closely, I see prism-like lines in each scale that resemble tree rings. Under a magnifying glass, a fisheries biologist could determine this carp's age. Everybody always talks about how ugly they are, but this fish is anything but ugly. As beautiful as a rainbow or a brookie? Hmm.

I can appreciate that it is a species from the largest taxonomic family. In my hands, I am holding living stuff from the Caspian and Aral Seas, places I have never been, places where carp are still respected and even revered as spiritual symbols.

For me, fly-fishing for carp is an engagement with nature, nature where fences and prescribed ethics don't matter and where a constructed landscape becomes a wilderness again—or, at the very least, a wild place. Fisheries management, worn-out nineteenth-century landscape aesthetics, the fly-fishing industry, and rampant development have made angling for carp inevitable. This is what I'm doing out here; I'm embracing the future, something ancient, but entirely new. Carping with a fly rod signals the precariousness of the *not-long*-established tradition of fly-fishing—the clumsiness of sacred cows, what is not supposed to be questioned. Because if many did consider the ironies and absurdities here and admit their existence, then like me they're all heretics—uncommitted, unpatriotic, and irreverent. A fishing writer once suggested that if you find yourself overanalyzing fishing, then you should probably just give it up. But that sounds like another form of fundamentalism, like the hollow aesthetics I'm trying to understand. The carp is itself a meddlesome, ugly question for anyone who looks deeply into water, anglers especially.

I hold the fish for a few moments, admiring it, and then I lower its belly to the water. The fish rests in my hands, half submerged. Its eye roves from the water back to me, and I wonder if there's some kind of truth to see in the fish's eyes. The wind has died down, and the water in the marsh looks like stretched plastic. The sun will set soon, and the light is changing, diffusing across the pond and soaking the dried-out vegetation with electric pink and orange. I notice more boils and ripples from feeding carp. I figure it's time to go home. When I straighten up, the carp thrashes its tail and trucks on for deeper water.

Notes

Parts of this essay first appeared as "Heroes of the Underworld," *Gray's Sporting Journal,* May–June 2006.

1. I owe this idea of trout as synechdoche to David Quammen's "Synechdoche and the Trout," in *Wild Thoughts from Wild Places* (New York: Scribner, 1998).

2. See Robert Traver's "Testament of a Fisherman" in *Anatomy of a Fisherman* (New York: McGraw-Hill, 1964).

3. See the ending to Norman Maclean's novella, *A River Runs through It* (1976).

4. Checklist of U.S. Public Documents 1789–1909, 3rd ed. (Washington, D.C.: GPO, 1911), 1:406. The U.S. Fish Commission was established on February 9, 1871, and was later incorporated into the Department of Commerce and Labor on July 1, 1903.

5. George Laycock, *The Alien Animals: The Story of Imported Wildlife* (Garden City, N.Y.: Natural History Press, 1966), 163.

6. Laycock gets a number of his facts wrong, including placing Babcock Lakes in Boston instead of Baltimore. Intent on telling an "invasive alien species" story much akin to that of Satan entering the Garden of Eden, he illuminates very little of the historical and cultural context surrounding the USFC's efforts, including the optimistic spirit of nineteenth-century science and the deplorable state of North American fisheries.

7. Arnold W. Fritz, "Commercial Fishing for Carp," in *Carp in North America* (Bethesda, Md.: American Fisheries Society, 1987), 18.

8. Robin W. Doughty, "Wildlife Conservation in Late Nineteenth-Century Texas: The Carp Experiment," *Southwestern Historical Quarterly* 84, no. 2 (1980): 173.

9. I borrow this term from the title of John McPhee's *The Founding Fish* (New York: Farrar, Straus, and Giroux, 2002), which explores shad fishing's cultural lore through memoir and historical nonfiction. I should note that the USFC was instrumental in the restocking and protection of shad in New England waters during the late nineteenth century. When popular sporting writer Alexander Starbuck wrote a

four-part diatribe against the USFC and the carp in 1905, he did acknowledge that the USFC's efforts to improve the shad fishery had been a success. See, in particular, Alex Starbuck, "The Dominating Carp: Second Paper," *Forest and Stream: A Journal of Outdoor Life, Travel, Nature Study, Shooting, Fishing, Yachting* 65, no. 20 (November 11, 1905): 397.

10. Robin W. Doughty, "Wildlife Conservation in Late Nineteenth-Century Texas: The Carp Experiment," *Southwestern Historical Quarterly* 84, no. 2 (1980): 172–73, 176–77.

11. R. F. B., "Fish Culture: An Interview with Prof. Baird—Cultivation of Carp—The National Carp Hatching Establishment—Some Facts about Their Habits, Culture, Value, etc.," *Forest and Stream: A Journal of Outdoor Life, Travel, Nature Study, Shooting, Fishing, Yachting* 10, no. 12 (April 25, 1878): 214.

12. The public's reaction to carp during this time follows a rather comedic rise and fall—though that's a typically tragic plot trajectory. Through a series of *New York Times* and *Forest and Stream* articles and a few other miscellaneous publications, one can see how the public fervor for carp reached a fever pitch from 1875 through 1881, then grew strangely quiet with occasional mentions of a single auspicious carp turning up where to the best of anyone's knowledge carp were never stocked, to questions and more silence, and then finally to vitriolic rants against the government and the USFC for the letting loose of such a "plague" on its citizens.

IV. THE URBAN TRASH ANIMAL

11 Metamorphosis in Detroit

Carolyn Kraus

ONE SUMMER MORNING a raggedy shadow darted out from under the old black-and-white television set on my kitchen table, plopped to the floor, and disappeared. A maverick beetle in from the garden, I reasoned, or maybe a mutant ant. The next day my six-year-old son Nicholas trapped something in a pickle jar. Grinning up at me from beneath his Detroit Tigers baseball cap, he announced he was taking it to show-and-tell. I stared through the glass at the flat yellowish-brownish creature: six hairy legs, long flickering antennae, two big wraparound eyes, the bulging brow of a philosopher. It was grooming itself, one leg up, like a cat.

"Take it outside," I told my son, "and don't talk about it."

Skittering continued behind the TV for a week before my reluctant attention was drawn to a well-dressed matron peering out from the screen, her eyebrows raised in an expression that mirrored my own confusion and horror.

"I won't tolerate them in my house!" she wailed.

"We'll get rid of the cockroaches," came the reassuring voice of the Orkin man, easing the burden onto his own broad shoulders. It sounded so simple.

But I am a pacifist, a vegetarian, an ecofeminist. I cradle moths in my hands and carry them outside. I share the planet humbly with all creatures great and small, though I'd had no real dealings with cockroaches. I knew them only indirectly, as the ultimate underdogs of literature. In Don Marquis's 1927 chronicles of *Archy and Mehitabel*, Archy the cockroach has the transmigrated soul of a poet and writes free verse from the underside of a world full of giant mop buckets and evil-eyed exterminators. Diving furiously at the keys of an old typewriter, too small to work the shift key for the capital letters, he declares that "expression is the need of my soul"[1] and announces his intention to convey the cockroach point of view:

> of all
> the massacres and slaughter
> of persecuted insects
> at the hands of cruel humans[2]

My views were formed, as well, in solidarity with Kafka's Gregor Samsa, a humble clerk metamorphosed into a giant bug among human predators. Poor Gregor is content to creep up and down the wall or to dream in a corner as his sister plays the violin. But even this faithful sister eventually disowns him, declaring, "This disgusting animal"—tellingly, readers assume it's a cockroach—"obviously wants to occupy the whole apartment and force us to sleep in the gutter."[3]

I'd always sided with the bug. Given humanity's sordid history, I was even inclined to agree with the English professor in Jane Smiley's 1995 novel, *Moo,* that "being turned into a bug is a step *up*" for Gregor.[4]

So, theoretically, I was all for the cockroaches and against their human oppressors. But now my roaches marched from kitchen table to refrigerator to bathroom sink with the authority of doom, testing my principles and calling up some nastier characters from the cockroach canon: a decades-long parade of cinematic frankenbugs, roboroaches, goo-dripping cooties from outer space—and *The Cockroach That Ate Cincinnati.*

With trembling fingers I leafed through the Detroit phone book and found eleven yellow pages devoted to pest control. Competition was fierce. Six listings came before I even got to Aardvark Exterminators ("We use unmarked cars"). Appeals ranged from the euphemistic "Pestorest" to the metaphorical "Call Dr. Jess. All his patients die . . ." to the literal "We Kill."

To dignify their trade, some companies had chosen names like Christian Exterminators and Phoenix Environmental Systems, names hinting cryptically at resurrection. An outfit called Atlas boasted, "All work supervised by university graduate."

As I set down the phone book to make breakfast, I could hear my two sons, Nick and eleven-year-old Alexander, keeping score in the bathroom:

"Over here, crawling in the bathtub!"

"Hey look, a bunch of 'em under the sink!"

I shushed them and told them to get dressed for school. As I poured their orange juice, the toast popped up, and a cockroach zipped out from under the toaster, apparently unsinged. I picked up the butter dish and beheld a squashed specimen, wings spread in the figure of a crucifixion.

During the first troubled week of my cockroach invasion, I confided my secret to trusted friends who whispered back tales of their own roach-ridden lives. One depended on Mr. Roach of Ypsilanti. Another swore by the crew at Men in Black. A third friend had a monthly arrangement with Slug-a-Bug. But each told a tale of ubiquitous chemical dust, of heavy expenditure, of route men who never appeared twice.

I wanted to retreat from the problem—like a Southern belle of my acquaintance. Her husband tells how he first set eyes on her, standing in the shadow of a six-foot-long plastic roach revolving on a pole above the Terminex office in Austin. Racking his brain for a pickup line, he'd pointed up at the megaroach, done up in florescent purple and green paint, and asked his future wife if they got many cockroaches in Texas.

"Oh, we don't have roaches here," she'd drawled, "just li'l ol' palmetto bugs."

I lack my friend's cool Southern assurance, but when I noticed an ad for Pied Piper Pest Control, an acceptable strategy sprang to mind. While chemical warfare is not in my nature, I have nothing against reasoned argument, even gentle coercion. Why not lure the roaches out? This would require research into their passions and preferences—acquiring their language, so to speak. I resolved to track down the essentials at the Detroit Public Library the following Monday morning after I dropped the kids off at their elementary school.

It was pouring rain as I drove my rust-pocked Ford Escort down Woodward Avenue through a landscape of human dereliction that dwarfed the effects of my cockroach invasion: the abandoned White Castle, the crumbling hulks of Victorian mansions, the Stone Adult XXX Theater. I pulled up to the school, nestled between a boarded-up Chinese restaurant and a homeless shelter on Detroit's drug-infested Cass Corridor. Why did I stay in the city, when families from my neighborhood—an enclave of neat brick flats and bungalows—were taking off for the suburbs in droves? I'd convinced myself that it wasn't mere necessity. True, I was a single-mother survivalist without many options. But there was also a principle behind my staying. Like my children's teachers, soldiering on at their posts in the troubled city, I didn't want to be someone who bailed. I had always sided with the underdog. I would stubbornly hold to my principles. Yes, even about cockroaches.

I drove back down Woodward to the library and parked illegally in the circular drive by the entrance. Covering the top of my head with a newspaper, I dashed into the rain, through the revolving door, and up the white marble steps to the science section. Consulting a library computer, I gathered a tower of books—including some entomology tomes that hadn't left the building in decades—and learned the rudiments of cockroach history.

Cockroaches adopted their way of life during the Carboniferous age, a period so rich in cockroaches—perhaps eight hundred different kinds—that paleontologists have labeled it the "Age of Cockroaches." The first specimens twitched onto the scene some 55 million years before the first dinosaurs. They saw *Tyrannosaurus rex* come and go. Among all insects known from that epoch, cockroaches alone have endured through fire and ice for at least 300 million years, essentially unchanged. Darwin referred to them as "living fossils." Indeed the venerable cockroach you admire, frozen in amber in the natural history museum's display case, closely resembles the intruder you stomped flat that morning on the kitchen floor.

The high cost of downtown parking fines slipped my mind, as I sat hunched over my books at a polished oak table all morning, moving deeper and deeper into the cockroach condition. There were yellowing pictures of specimens with distinguished names worthy of their ancient lineage—like *Blaberus cranifer Burmeister,* largest of American roaches; *Cryptocircus punctulatus,* the wood roach; and *Gromphadorhina portentosa,* the giant Madagascar hissing cockroach, which, according to entomologists, can live for seven years and grow to three inches, hisses loud enough to scare a dog, and is highly recommended as a hardy and docile pet, good for beginners. Currently at least four thousand kinds of cockroaches are recognized, with countless more, presumably, lurking undiscovered in the planet's cracks and corners. A team of international scientists recently spotted a monster cockroach, four inches long, in the mountain caves of Indonesia and, no doubt to the dismay of local householders, launched a campaign to protect it.[5]

With a touch of disappointment, I identified my cockroaches as the most common household variety—*Blattella germanica,* the German roach. He apparently originated in Africa, not Germany, but cockroaches tend to get named for whomever you'd like to crush under your foot at a given historical moment. "During its spread across Europe," writes former Harvard Insect Curator Howard Evans, "the German roach was called the Prussian roach by the Russians, the Russian roach by the Prussians, thus paralleling the history of syphilis, which was known as the 'French disease' throughout much of Europe, but the 'Italian disease' by the French."[6]

Political, ethnic, and interest groups have similarly demonized outsiders by nicknaming them after the local pest. *Las cucurachas* was a disparaging term for female camp followers of Pancho Villa's army during the Mexican Revolution (1910–1920). These women were memorialized in the folk song, "La Cucuracha," with its baffling chorus about a stoned cockroach:

La cucuracha, la cucuracha,
ya no puede caminar
porque no tiene, porque le falta
marijuana que fumar

The cockroach, the cockroach,
is unable to walk
because she has none, because she lacks
marijuana to smoke[7]

The song apparently evolved—not only from legends surrounding Pancho Villa, but also from multiple threads of oral tradition—into a patchwork of political satire, romance, and drug imagery. I wondered if this jumbling of sources and themes had spawned the association of drugs and cockroaches that eventually led to "roach" as the name of a marijuana cigarette butt; the "coke bugs" and stoned "belly dancing roaches" in the novels of William S. Burroughs, who once worked as an exterminator; and such reggae classics as "Weedy Weedy" and "Mi Brethren Roach" by Jamaican singer Eek-a-Mouse.

Further examples of roach exploitation and slander? In the eighties Rafael Eitan, an Israeli chief of staff known for his blunt language, referred to the Palestinians as "roaches in a jar."[8] And at his 1992 extortion trial, New York mob boss John Gotti, lapsing into underworld dialect, denounced the "miserable cockroach" who ratted him out and could expect to be squashed for it.[9] In what is surely history's most egregious cockroach appropriation, Hutu Power fanatics in Rwanda labeled the Tutsi people "inyenzi," cockroaches, and promoted the language of disgust associated with an infestation in order to convince an entire population to take up machetes in 1994 and slaughter a million of their neighbors. Echoing the logic of anti-Semitic Nazi propaganda, the extremists argued that Tutsis represented an incorrigible evil. Leave just a few inyenzi and the plague will return, because "a cockroach cannot give birth to a butterfly."[10]

Given the roach's evil reputation, his association with narcotics, his exploitation as a symbol of disgust and a rationale for genocide, I welcomed the occasional happier affiliation. Long before Kafka's Gregor Samsa, it seemed, the cockroaches of literature and lore had spoken for the outcast and the downtrodden. In the Classical Greek play *Peace*, Aristophanes had his peasant Trygaeus—besieged by the miseries of the Peloponnesian war—ascend to Mount Olympus on a man-size cockroach to plead for divine intervention on behalf of his wretched compatriots.[11] Cockroaches figured as tricksters in African folktales and reemerged to match wits with their tormentors in Caribbean folktales and African-American slave narratives.

Identification with the canny underdog also led a number of contemporary Latino writers to embrace cockroach pariahdom. Oscar Acosta's autobiographical novel, *Revolt of the Cockroach People,* pits East Los Angeles Chicanos against the Anglo legal establishment, and in Martin Espada's "Cockroaches of Liberation," Latino activists multiply, strike, and disappear in the dark, "too quick for stomping boots."[12] It remained only for the roach to be sainted, and indeed, Kilgore Trout, the hero of Kurt Vonnegut's novel *Venus on the Half-Shell,* learns the secrets of the universe from a cockroach sage named Bingo.

My research also uncovered some pleasant surprises of a more scientific nature. A cockroach won't bite you, but if there's absolutely nothing else around, he may nibble a bit at your eyelashes or fingernails. He keeps himself clean and his back continually polished while he lives off human filth and spreads it around in the process. Although he has been linked to polio, hepatitis, asthma, salmonella, leprosy, and bubonic plague, the cockroach actually considers *you* the hygiene problem. After exploring your hand or your sleep-quiet eyelids, he'll lick his antennae, hooking them with a front leg and pulling them through his mouth to remove your skin's oily residue. That explained the fastidious and distinctly feline ritual I'd witnessed last week in my son's pickle jar.

I was surprised to learn that cockroaches have been the lab animal of choice in a gruesome variety of scientific experiments worldwide, particularly in the United States where they are exempt from Animal Welfare Act protection because of "insufficient evidence that they are capable of feeling pain."[13] A team of international researchers at Tokyo University surgically implanted cockroaches with microrobotic backpacks weighing one-tenth of an ounce, about twice the weight of the roaches themselves. With handheld devices, the scientists delighted in steering the bugs around the lab like remote-controlled go-carts. Their enthusiasm did not, however, extend to the toiling roaches. "They are not very nice insects," one commented. "They are a little bit smelly, and there's something about the way they move their antennae. But they look nicer when you put a little circuit on their backs and remove their wings."[14]

I found a number of references to the high intelligence of roaches, as demonstrated by their ability to master complicated mazes. Once trained, they can even be convinced to run them headless, a popular diversion of sadists and science fair enthusiasts, apparently, since I found half a dozen references to the headless, maze-running roach. Beheading may not rob the roach of his memory because he has an extra brain in his tail—a mere ganglion actually—that not only remembers the path through a maze but also coordinates an efficient escape reflex.[15] This enables the cockroach, with or without head, to hurtle away at the first sign of danger and worry about the head problem later.

One source even included practical tips on how to decapitate the hapless subject (slow strangulation by dental floss) and how to verify a successful nonlethal beheading (tickle with a feather or toothpick). "The subject should be dispatched after the experiment," another source instructed. "How do you kill something without a head?" I thought as I glanced up at the clock and noted that it was nearly three in the afternoon. The kids would be getting out of school soon.

I struggled to the checkout desk with an armload of books and scientific journals. Ducking back into the rain beneath my newspaper umbrella, I lugged my books to the car and dumped them into the trunk. Pausing to snatch a soggy parking ticket from the Escort's windshield, I drove back to school and picked up the kids, then headed home, amid gusts of wind from a duct-taped window. Back on my street I passed houses with window boxes trailing licorice and scarlet geraniums, and porches lined with clay pots of multicolored impatiens—bright flags raised against the city's blight and sprawl. What if these neighbors got wind of my roaches? Four white ducks were displayed on one of the manicured lawns. I felt their disapproving plastic eyes upon me.

That evening as I was boiling spaghetti for dinner, I opened a cupboard and pulled out the colander. Gazing forlornly at its speckling of telltale brown dots, I knew I'd left the innocent and hypothetical roach in the sparkling white sanctuary of the library. For despite his adaptability, his persecuted and maligned status, his headless martyrdom, his heroic feats of endurance, you cannot love a roach. At the slightest failure of the human will, he's there, determined to stay. I tossed the colander into the sink and slumped into a chair at the kitchen table. During the following days I would sink into paralysis as my sons called out more sightings and the roaches advanced. At night I would flick on the light and catch the roaches momentarily stunned in the midst of maneuvers, then watch them take off like halfbacks breaking into open field. They made great leaps from table to floor, buoyed by rumble-seat wings. Roaches are the fastest runners among insects.

But survivalists live Spartan lives, I knew, and the cockroaches among us are no exception. A touch of warmth from the motor of your refrigerator or my TV, a little garbage or wallpaper paste to munch on—that's as close as they get to nirvana. My research had, however, turned up one compensation for being born one of the wretched of the earth: the male roach is the sexiest thing on six legs. The X-rated scenes in progress behind every crack in my kitchen wall were documented admiringly in my library books in line after polysyllabic line. The male comes on like a Swiss Army knife, equipped with an arsenal of prongs and serrated projections that he fastens onto the female so that she's utterly hooked. Their marathon sessions may last several hours and, in some species, all day long. Still, it's sex without love. Postcoitus, the male loses interest in the partner he has barely seen, since they mated posterior to posterior. Once fertilized, the female goes on bearing forty young a month for life, while the cad of a male moves from virgin to virgin.

A pheromone dubbed "seducin" starts things off, and scientists appear to be determined to get their hands on it. If it could be manufactured synthetically, the pheromone might be used to bait lethal roach traps. Thus, the errant male would—with a certain poetic justice—find himself trapped in a matchbox motel between two overwhelming urges: sex and survival.

Back in the early seventies, the U.S. Defense Department apparently got wind of this research and cooked up a scheme to use synthetic roach pheromones as a secret weapon in the Vietnam War. Though never implemented, the plan was to sprinkle the roach attractant around known guerrilla hideouts. The scent would remain on the guerrillas and give them away when villagers under suspicion were marched past a box containing a platoon of six-legged conscripts. When the roaches got excited, police would close in.[16]

I turned on the kitchen faucet full force and rinsed out the colander, then left it soaking in a sink full of soapy water. Meanwhile, my older son, Alexander, stood at the kitchen counter in his Star Wars T-shirt smearing peanut butter on crackers, a before-dinner snack.

"Don't leave the peanut butter on the counter," I warned him. "Put the crackers, peanut butter—everything—in the refrigerator, not the cupboard." I rinsed out the colander, wiped it dry, and shook out the dishrag. A roach fell into the sink.

"Why?" Nick asked.

"We got all these cockroaches," Alexander explained.

Nick sat munching his cracker, a thoughtful look on his face. "Mom said they're a special kind of ant," he told his brother.

"Actually, no, they're cockroaches," I interrupted, ashamed of my feeble attempt to contain the family secret. I reached into the spice drawer for the oregano and noticed some movement in an uncapped dill weed shaker.

"They're kinda interesting though," I added, slamming the spice drawer shut. "I'll tell you some stuff I learned at the library today." I preferred the abstract roach, and besides, I'd always encouraged intellectual curiosity in my sons.

As we ate the spaghetti, I recounted the major selling points of roach design: their ability to adapt to climate change, to withstand killer radiation and gravitational force, to survive without water for several weeks by reabsorbing moisture from their own droppings. I described a Cold War–era experiment in which scientists had observed roaches whizzing around unfazed by ten times the gravitational force that would flatten a human, and another study that established the cockroach's ability to withstand radiation at six times the lethal human dose. With the occasional visual aid skittering across the wall, my lecture held the boys' attention.

After dinner, while Nick built a fort out of cardboard boxes in the living room and Alexander lay on the rug in his pajamas doing homework, I was on my hands and knees in the kitchen, scrubbing brown flecks off of the yellow linoleum that peeled at the corners near the walls, in effect forming little roach entrances and exits. They were pretty well dug in, I could see. I thought of a poster that used to hang in my friend's college dorm room with the caption: "A nuclear war will not be won by the Americans, the Russians, or the Chinese. The winner of World War Three will be the cockroach."

I'd become so immersed in the cockroach condition at the library that morning, that I'd neglected my search for his Achilles' heel, but now it hit me: a roach will eat almost anything—cigarettes, soap, ink, or the insulation poking out of my kitchen ceiling. They're especially fond of bat guano, leather, corks, cigars, and their own shed skin. But they have a special passion for beer. Especially, according to a soberly worded study conducted at Oklahoma University, for Pabst Blue Ribbon. A roach will die for a beer.

That night before going to bed, I set a pan in front of the infested TV and filled it with beer. My roaches would gorge all night in front of the tube, fall into a pleasant stupor, and drown. No mess. No dangerous chemicals. No direct assault. The next morning, as I was sending the kids off to school, I noticed a few adventurous lightweights floating in the pan, but when I emptied it into the sink, every one of them revived and darted into the wall.

I considered acquiring a predator for my kitchen. Then I recalled that, as part of his campaign for immortality, a cockroach tastes terrible. Only a few predators will bite into raw roach: tarantulas, hedgehogs, certain lizards, and blindfolded fraternity pledges.

A lizard sounded best. I remembered spotting a doomed roach or two the last time I'd taken the kids to the Detroit Zoo's reptile house while we were watching the snakes and lizards revolve under plastic bubbles like cafeteria salads. I called the reptile curator, who told me diplomatically, "Our lizards probably do get an occasional cockroach, but not because we provide them." The zoo once considered releasing some lizards behind the exhibits to forage for themselves. Geckos, like roaches, are crevice dwellers and a good bet to keep intruders in check. But, the curator conceded, "How would we keep them back there?" The zoo-going public wasn't ready for free-running geckos.

But I was. Especially when I learned that a gecko is small, clean, quiet, nearly invisible, and hides himself all day—coming out only at night to clean out my cockroaches. Estimating that I had two thousand freeloaders in my kitchen, half females, producing forty offspring a month, I did some quick arithmetic and concluded I would need at least four hundred geckos, each consuming three to five roaches per night, just to stay even. Nevertheless, I decided, one pair would start me off nicely. Lizard sales are illegal in the city of Detroit since they can carry salmonella, so I called Pets R Us, located in a nearby suburb. "We got in a bunch of geckos last week," answered a female voice, "but they sold like hotcakes. I don't know why."

As I hung up, a cockroach darted across the phone cradle. I cornered it with a cupped hand, eyed it through two fingers, and froze. In just such a moment of truth, George Orwell writes in his essay "Shooting an Elephant," he too had found himself stuck between principles and experience. On one hand was his hatred of the oppressive British Empire he served as a policeman in Burma; on the other was his palpable, even murderous, rage against the Burmese, those "evil-spirited little beasts" who baited him, spat on him, tripped him up, laughed at him, and made his life impossible.

The roach crept out, stunned, from between my cracked fingers, but I nabbed it and eyeballed it again. The scales tipped.

I lobbed the roach against the wall. As it skittered away, I grabbed a can of Raid—purchased in a moment of doubt—from its dark and secret shelf and blasted the TV. Roaches spurted out like water from a split hose—zooming, leaping, stumbling. I found one upside down in a reeking pool of Raid, legs waving in the air, and crushed it between my two fingers, then went for another one.

All night long I was flicking on the lights in the kitchen and living room and crunching as many as I could underfoot before they regained their senses and zigzagged away. I batted at them with a fly swatter. I sucked them up by the dozens into a foul-smelling vacuum cleaner.

The exterminator arrived the following Monday morning at ten—a moonlighting Orkin man with an acne-scarred face, a chronic cough, and a briefcase display of roach samples encased in plastic. Dressed in navy-blue coveralls with "Ray" embroidered in red on the breast pocket, he sagged into a chair and sipped coffee from a Styrofoam cup as I emptied my closets and cupboards, piling dishes, canned tomatoes, boxes of Kraft macaroni and cheese, winter jackets, books, and stuffed animals on sheets spread over the lawn.

To demonstrate a newfound solidarity with my exterminator's trade, I thumbed a small roach flat onto the table.

"How can you do that?" he said, shuddering.

"Isn't that your job?"

"I kill 'em. I don't thumb 'em," he said. "When I started, I was working in Bloomfield Hills. Rich people. It's mostly ants there. Ants are okay. Roaches give me the creeps."

"Do you get jobs worse than mine?" I asked, smiling weakly.

"Are you kidding?" He leaned back, resting his feet on the kitchen table. His sad blue eyes met mine. "Last week I opened a door in Pontiac and roaches came streaming out by the thousands. It was like a horror movie. The lady told me they hadn't gotten that bad till a week before. I just nodded and tried not to smile. There were a million roaches in that house."

"How bad are mine?"

"It's not your fault," he replied, ducking the question. "They can come in from anywhere. All the grocery stores have them. I don't mind a job like this. It's the phobics I can't stand."

"The phobics?"

"People who don't really have bugs and think they do," he explained. "One morning I was going into a house just as the furnace man was coming out. He just shook his head and said 'good luck.' The lady said she had bedbugs. She was scratching all over and telling me about bees in the wall and giant roaches under the bed. There weren't any, but she insisted, so I gassed the house. What I sold her was basically peace of mind."

As my exterminator went about his work, ferreting bugs out of the electric clock, the water pipes, the picture frames, the gap between the wall and the bathtub, coughing all the while, he regaled me with secrets of his cutthroat trade. "I go through the trash cans of my competitors regularly. I have lists of their customers with addresses, phone numbers, appointment dates, and charges. When business slows down, I'll blitz 'em with calls and underbid for the jobs." He confided his horror of poisons, especially of a mysterious rat killer called Cyanogas. "If you have an accident with that in your car, you don't walk away," he said, shaking his head.

It was the roaches, however, that had defeated him. "They develop immunities to poisons," he said. "They even pass the immunities on to their offspring." One waddling pregnant survivor, it seems, can repopulate a decimated pantry and negate all his efforts. "I want to go back to college," he confessed, "and study computers."

A few weeks later, my roaches came staggering back, but by then I had lost my taste for extermination. I abandoned the old TV by the curb, and I sat staring at a crack in the wall. "I know they're in there," I thought. "Or am I becoming a phobic?"

Finally, my ideals did not stand the test. Pacifism is easy from a distance, but up close a roach is a roach. The virtues of this six-legged survival machine—speed, endurance, intelligence, adaptability, fecundity—become his sins when he sets up his Spartan camp in your cupboard.

Still, I've gained a kind of resigned respect for the vilified cockroach. He skitters through the maze of life with no hard feelings—even without his head—and wreaks his devastation without malice. It's only fair to note, as well, that we invaded his pantry long before he invaded ours. As Archy the cockroach poet reminds us:

insects were insects
when man was only
a burbling whatsit[17]

The cockroach existed for 300 million years before the flicker of human history, and he's likely, with some justice, to inherit the Earth.

Notes

1. Don Marquis, *Archy and Mehitabel* (New York: Doubleday, 1927), 14.

2. Ibid., 27.

3. Franz Kafka, *Metamorphosis* (New York: Bantam, 1972), 49.

4. Jane Smiley, *Moo* (New York: Ivy Books, 1995), 251.

5. "Giant Cockroach among Jungle Finds," *BBC News,* December 23, 2004.

6. Howard Ensign Evans, *Life on a Little-Known Planet* (New York: Dutton, 1968), 50.

7. Robert Gordon, "La Cucuracha," in "Old Songs That Men Have Sung," issue no. 246 of *Adventure Magazine,* 1923.

8. Robert Fisk, "When Journalists Refuse to Tell the Truth," *Independent* (London), April 17, 2001, 7.

9. Marian Copeland, *Cockroach* (London: Reaktion Books, 2003), 109.

10. Human Rights Watch Web site, http://www.hrw.org/legacy/worldreport99/.

11. Malcolm Davies, *Greek Insects* (London: Gerald Duckworth, 1986), 11–12.

12. Martin Espada, "Cockroaches of Liberation," in *City of Coughing and Dead Radiators* (New York: Norton, 1993), 23.

13. Neil McFarquhar, "Four-Footed Clients and Futile Cases: A Rutgers Law Professor Fights to Expand the Animal Kingdom's Rights," *New York Times,* November 11, 1995, D4.

14. Eric Talmadoe, "Japan's Latest Innovation: A Remote-Control Roach," AP Wire Service, July 16, 2001, at http://www.wireheading.com/roboroach/.

15. Nicholas Longo, "Probability-Learning and Habit-Reversal in the Cockroach," *American Journal of Psychology* 77 (1964): 6–18.

16. Michael K. Rust and Donald Reierson, "Using Pheromone Extract to Reduce Repellancy of Blatticides," *Journal of Economic Entomology* 70 (1977): 37.

17. Marquis, *Archy and Mehitabel,* 30.

12 Kach'i

Garbage Birds in a Hybrid Landscape

James E. Bishop

IN THE DAYS AFTER I MOVED TO CH'ANGWON, a small city on the southern coast of Korea, I started seeing everywhere a species of jay-like bird with a long tail, a black head, and wings splotched white and black with an outlandish turquoise gloss. It was—dare I say it?—an attractive bird. I saw them fluttering between rooftops, roosting in trees, hopping across parking lots, bobbing on telephone wires, and perching on the light towers of the soccer stadium across the street from my apartment. But I had no idea what they were. I had to look them up. I found them in a tourist guide I picked up one day at city hall: in Korean the birds are called *kach'i*. The Latin name: *Pica pica*. In English: the black-billed magpie. They are named in many languages because they are known from Brussels to Russia, from Korea to Kansas.

I grew up in Maine, more than a thousand miles east of the eastern limit of the magpie's North American range, so I'd never seen one before. I knew of them, but I knew little of their nasty reputation. I have since learned that farmers, particularly orchard keepers, have traditionally seen magpies as pests because they devour cherries and other fruits. The scourge of orchard-raiding magpies has been known for centuries; in 1618 William Lawson, in his *A New Orchard and Garden,* wrote, "Your cherries when they bee ripe, wil draw all the blacke-birds, Thrushes and May-pyes to your Orchard."[1] While the language in Lawson's account does not show outright contempt for these birds, he does suggest that they are a nuisance, one that farmers must account for if they are to have a successful harvest.

In later years, magpies have come to be disliked not only for their taste for orchard fruits but for their alleged propensity for idle chatter. Edmund

Burke, in a letter to Claude-François de Rivarol in 1791, derisively compared other writers to magpies, complaining of "the whole flight of the magpies and jays of philosophy" who "may fancy and chatter."[2] More recently, the word "magpie" has come to refer to obsessive collectors and hoarders: a 1985 cookbook by Lionel Blue proclaims, "There is a magpie in all of us, and . . . there is enough tucked away in our cupboards to supply church bazaars, tombolas and countless bring-and-buys."[3] In the parlance of behavioral psychologists, "pica behavior," named for the magpie's genus, is "the compulsive, recurrent consumption of nonnutritive items."[4] The language of judgment, even in the realm of science, is still very much with us.

In their disdain for the magpie's habit of eating the eggs and fledglings of other birds, sportsmen and gamekeepers have been even less circumspect in their negative portrayal of magpies. According to British writer Charles Alexander Johns, "Partridges and pheasants are watched [by magpies] to their retreat and plundered mercilessly of their eggs and young."[5] The contempt in which gamekeepers held magpies was no doubt intensified by their perception that the magpie is a cowardly bird, waiting until the adult partridge or pheasant leaves its nest unguarded before launching its predatory assault.

The most virulent complaints about magpies—and surely the most surprising—have to do with magpies' alleged attacks on livestock. According to naturalist John Keats Lord, writing from British Columbia during the mid-nineteenth century, magpies actually killed horses and mules. For Lord, "the magpies are dire enemies." He claims that sometimes, when a pack animal develops a gall, the magpies peck so persistently and vigorously at it that "the tortured beast rolls madly," and eventually "this repeated agony soon kills an animal, unless the packers [Lord's companions] rescue it." Lord's depiction of the magpie as a relentless and bloodthirsty scoundrel justifies the behavior of the other men on his expedition, who gain revenge against the magpies by poisoning a mule carcass with strychnine. When the magpies begin dying by the score, the men respond with "wild glee" as the dead birds pile in heaps beside the poisoned carcass.[6]

Of course, modern ornithologists have come to question many of these early assumptions about magpies. While magpies do eat eggs and young of other bird species, they are considered a much less serious threat than house cats. Magpies do sometimes pluck cherries from trees, but they are primarily carrion eaters. And the accounts of magpies molesting livestock are likely exaggerated; although magpies do occasionally land on the backs of farm animals, this is usually to remove ticks or other parasites, to take wool or hair for nesting material, or to use the larger animal as a handy perch while searching for food. One observer recorded that magpies sit on the backs of sheep not to harm them but to "observe the grasshoppers which the flock disturb as they feed, and on which these birds feed luxuriously."[7] Indeed, most ecologists guess that the magpie's benefits to agriculture—removing insects and small mammals that destroy crops—probably outweigh its offenses.

Nevertheless, the negative image of magpies has persisted to the present day. My former housemate Paul, upon seeing a close-up magpie photo that I took while I was in Korea, shook his head and pronounced matter-of-factly, "Garbage bird." It was the one photo, out of the dozens in my photo album, that elicited any sort of response. At the time it didn't occur to me to ask Paul—a Nevada native and lifelong city dweller—what in particular made the magpie a "garbage bird." Is it related to his sense of the magpie as a pest? Does he think they're ugly? Or is it an unexamined assumption, something he'd been raised with and never thought to question? He never did explain, and I never got around to asking.

My own introduction to the magpie was free of the baggage of the "garbage bird" stereotype that I might have inherited if I'd been raised in the American West. For this ignorance I am grateful. Especially for the first few months I lived in Korea, the magpie served as a source of inspiration for me: a reminder of the adaptability, wildness of spirit, and determination that I would need in order to live successfully from day to day in an industrial city of a half million people.

Ch'angwon is laid out in a rigid grid, bound on the north by a low escarpment, on the south by rice fields, and on the east and west by the cities of Masan and Kimhae. My walks through the city took me past block after block of nearly identical apartment buildings, all named for multinational corporations: Hyundai, Muhack, Lotte. I found it an alarmingly soulless place.

I had trouble adjusting. I had a good job and a functional studio apartment, but few friends. I slept poorly. My next-door neighbors often steamed eels, filling the hallway with a stench so powerful it made me gag. I grew annoyed at people staring and pointing at me every time I waited at the bus stop or went out for a bowl of *bi bim bap*.

But I kept noticing the magpies. In the afternoons, hiding in my bedroom and reading one of the seventy-five books I finished during my year in Korea, I could hear their *shik-shik-shik* calls through my window as they flew from rooftop to rooftop. On my way to work, I saw an abandoned nest—one that had once contained five to eight hatchlings, possibly multiple times, and probably would do so again in the future—built on a church's cross. Running on the track behind the soccer stadium, I sometimes got a close look at them as they hopped through the grass in search of beetles and worms. I was astonished by the exquisiteness of the iridescent sheen on their wing feathers, particularly for a bird that looks ordinary from a distance. I was tempted to stop one of my fellow joggers and say, "Take a look at that *kach'i*! It's a beautiful bird, isn't it?" The first problem, of course, was that my Korean was terrible. The second is that while Koreans have a deep appreciation for natural aesthetics, they tend to view magpies with benign indifference, dodging them on the track the way New Yorkers shun pigeons on Manhattan sidewalks.

I couldn't take my eyes off them. What impressed me most about the magpies was their ability not only to survive but to thrive in the urban jungle of Ch'angwon. Riding the bus one day, I saw a magpie place nesting material on the top of a telephone pole in the middle of a busy downtown intersection. I saw another magpie drop onto the playing field for an ice-cream wrapper during a soccer game. They are apparently undaunted by the large human population, and they find places to cache their food—scientifically speaking, this is called "hoarding," a term loaded with moral judgments—and construct their prodigious, bedraggled-looking nests. Magpies not only tolerate the presence of people but actually find ways to benefit from it, all the while living with a spirit of dignity and nonchalance and what Arthur Cleveland Bent calls an "utmost interest in their occupation."[8]

I vowed to apply the magpie's curiosity and adaptability to my own life in Ch'angwon. I made it my mission to discover what local people loved about their home, to try to understand their own survival strategies. I started with my coworkers, and as I became braver and as my Korean gradually improved, I began asking strangers at the grocery store or in the barbershop: what do you like best about Ch'angwon?

"I like jogging around Yongji Lake," said one man, referring to a small reservoir on the edge of town that usually teemed with joggers wearing headphones.

"The cherry blossoms are very beautiful in the spring."

"My family is here."

The most common response—"It's got all the amenities of a city, but it's just like living in a country town"—still puzzles me. Everywhere on the outskirts of the city were the footprints of new construction: D-9 earthmovers, bulldozers, jackhammers, giant gravel piles, orange barrels, and pink flagging.

In this way it reminds me of my current hometown of Reno, Nevada: one of the fastest-growing metropolitan areas in North America, its own outskirts teeming with new housing developments and strip malls, not coincidentally a habitat for another healthy magpie population.

As I move from one sprawling city to another, I find myself wondering: Does my appreciation for the magpie in some way compromise my values? If I like magpies, must I also approve of their habitat and the means by which it came to be that way? Is it possible to lament the soul-crushing monotony of Ch'angwon's endless rows of apartment buildings while also admiring a bird that has found a way to flourish there? Or does this place my aesthetics and ethics in irreconcilable conflict?

The magpie, of course, does not recognize such distinctions. For a species equally at home in natural and cultivated spaces, Ch'angwon provides an ideal habitat. There are chaotic community gardens on the edge of the northern foothills abutting Ch'angwon, and local people have alternately described these spaces to me as production gardens, public parks, meditation spaces, and wildlife preserves. The boundaries between these categories are permeable. In these gardens I have seen people weeding their plots, picnicking, socializing, meditating, sleeping, and sometimes birdwatching. It should be unsurprising, then, that magpies succeed in such places, for they are a species that thrives in the ecotones between wildness and domesticity, between beauty and squalor, and between admirable resourcefulness and greedy opportunism.

In one of my favorite poems, "Magpie's Song," Gary Snyder describes the middle zone where the magpie thrives. The poem's narrator is sitting on a pile of gravel near Interstate 80—the same Interstate 80 that runs through Reno—and between trucks passing on the highway he hears several coyotes howling and yipping on a nearby ridge. At the same time, he notices a magpie on a nearby tree, occupying that border space between the bustle of the highway and the wildness of the coyotes. The magpie speaks to him:

Here in the mind, brother
Turquoise blue.
I wouldn't fool you.
Smell the breeze
It came through all the trees
No need to fear
What's ahead
Snow up on the hills west

Will be there every year
be at rest.
A feather on the ground—
The wind sound—[9]

In the poem the magpie does for Snyder what it did for me during my time in Korea. It links the human and nonhuman worlds, bringing together what we think of as wild and what we consider tame. It offers reassurance. It reminds us to notice details in the present moment, "here in the mind." It serves as a model by which we could live, if we wished to live intentionally and attentively.

My last weeks in Korea were rich in discovery. Just a few blocks from my apartment, I found a small urban park. A narrow footpath led through a grove of hardwoods, winding toward the crest of a low hill where someone had thoughtfully left a small wooden bench. I never saw another person there, and somehow the place seemed immune to the sounds of traffic and urban bustle that I knew surrounded me. Here I could watch an astonishing variety of birds that inhabited the city: thrushes, woodpeckers, finches, and many more I couldn't identify. Although I never got used to living in Ch'angwon, I found the park to be a refuge not only for the birds but for my mind. It made me feel that wildness of all kinds was possible, even in the most industrial of cities.

Stuck in traffic on my way to the Kimhae airport for the final time before heading back to the United States for good, I watched a magpie delivering sticks to its nest, which it had built on a telephone pole on the edge of a rice field. The nest must have been used multiple times, as it was huge and had a haphazard appearance, with branches and twigs jutting out at odd angles. The bird delivered another twig, and another, and another. The third time, it hopped several times on the nest's outer rim, perhaps packing down some errant structural pieces. It seemed to me an act of such care, such love for its unhatched young—probably the eggs hadn't even been laid—that it could not possibly have been the behavior of such a thoroughly reviled bird.

Without a trace of irony, the magpie then fluttered down to the highway, landed beside an anonymous scrap of roadkill, scooped a bloody chunk of intestine into its beak, and flapped into the rice fields like a fugitive. Traffic began moving. As I rolled slowly forward, I kept looking for the magpie in my rearview mirror, perhaps for some last hint of wisdom or inspiration. I never did see it again.

Notes

1. Quoted in Tim Birkhead, *The Magpies: The Ecology and Behaviour of Black-billed and Yellow-billed Magpies* (London: Poyser, 1991), 217.

2. Edmund Burke, *Selected Letters of Edmund Burke,* ed. Harvey C. Mansfield (Chicago: University of Chicago Press, 1984), 244.

3. Lionel Blue, *Kitchen Blues: Recipes for Body and Soul* (Oxford: Clio Press, 1985), 79.

4. Lilian N. Stiegler, "Understanding Pica Behavior: A Review for Clinical and Education Professionals," *Focus on Autism and Other Developmental Disabilities* 20, no. 1 (Spring 2005): 27.

5. Charles Alexander Johns, *British Birds in Their Haunts* (London: London Society for Promoting Christian Knowledge, 1862), 626.

6. John Keats Lord, *The Naturalist in Vancouver Island and British Columbia,* vol. 2 (London: Richard Bently, 1866), 72, 73.

7. W. Hewett, "Note on Magpies and Starlings." *Zoologist* 1 (1843): 351.

8. Arthur Cleveland Bent, *Life Histories of North American Jays, Crows, and Titmice* (New York: Dover, 1964), 145.

9. Gary Snyder, *No Nature* (San Francisco: Pantheon Books, 1992), 147.

13 Flying Rats

Andrew D. Blechman

MOST DENIZENS OF NEW YORK describe their city's pigeons alternately as "dirty," "filthy," and "disease-ridden." Although pigeons attempt to groom themselves daily, they do in fact poo in their own nests. Combine that with the perilous life of scavenging in a grimy, sooty city, and you can understand why some city pigeons look less than manicured. One urban aphorism often applied to the rock dove is the regrettable moniker "rats with wings."

Although he probably did not invent the slur, Woody Allen popularized it in his 1980 movie *Stardust Memories* when he panicked at the sight of a pigeon in his apartment: "It's not pretty at all. They're, they're, they're rats with wings! . . . It's probably one of those killer pigeons. . . . You see? It's got a swastika under its wings."

Although a mere one-liner in just one of Allen's many movies, it was nevertheless the shot heard 'round the world, one that put pigeons and their perches in the cultural crosshairs. Urban pigeon haters finally had a rallying cry. Pigeons, of course, are not rodents and have few similarities to them besides. The only thing they may have in common, in addition to both being vertebrates, is their hankering for human leftovers and a tendency to live in large urban colonies. (No, pigeons do not carry plague.) Combine Allen's slur with Tom Lehrer's 1959 satirical song "Poisoning Pigeons in the Park," in which he waxes poetic about feeding them cyanide-coated peanuts, and you can see why these birds are badly in need of a public relations makeover. Hatred of pigeons has become so fanatical that one resident of New York City recently published a book graphically outlining 101 ways to kill a pigeon, including: "Grab a pigeon by the head. Twist until you hear a 'pop.' Grab another bird and repeat."

It's difficult to tell if it's the pigeons or their excrement that truly pisses people off. After all, it's the droppings, not the pigeons, that blanket cities with unsightly noxious splatter. And it's their acidic dung that eats through stone and metal, corroding buildings, monuments, and (gasp!) automobile paint. It's also fertile ground for dangerous parasites and infectious bacteria.

Yet there was a time when pigeon droppings were considered a semi-precious commodity. In ancient Egypt, they were a highly prized manure that worked agricultural wonders because of a high nitrogen content. For centuries in England, only the wealthy were allowed to raise pigeons for food, and the feces were declared property of the crown. The valuable dung was used to manufacture saltpeter, a critical ingredient for making gunpowder.

Far from being a carefully guarded royal wonder, pigeon dung is now considered a health hazard and aesthetic nuisance. It's not that the feral pigeon is a particularly prodigious pooer. It's just that, unlike most birds, it congregates in large gregarious flocks that call our cities their home. Pigeons are attracted to the sight of other pigeons, and their droppings rapidly accumulate, much like bats and guana.

As their name suggests, feral pigeons were once domestic, just like wild ponies or the parrots of Telegraph Hill. They are dovecote escapees and the descendants of escapees that have flown the coop. As sport racing increased in popularity, many homers either lost their way or called it quits and joined these feral flocks. If you look closely at the pigeons in your park, you just might see one of them wearing a racing band around its leg.

These pigeons are survivors and have done remarkably well for themselves. They are particularly well adapted to urban living. Buildings provide them with plenty of nooks and crannies for nesting, and humans' pathological carelessness with food provides them sustenance. Bagels, doughnuts, and pizza crusts are the mainstay of a modern feral pigeon's diet. Despised for the messes they leave behind, these birds actually act as spontaneous street cleaners picking up after human litterbugs.

Since the beginning of the industrial revolution, humans have flocked to cities, and as we go, so go the feral pigeons. They remain attracted to us and follow us wherever we go. To a pigeon, more people means more buildings and more scraps of food. Biologists term this behavior *commensal,* from the Latin "com mensa," meaning to share a table. Rock doves thrive in these conditions. But the more they prosper, the more they propagate and the more they bombard us with their excrement. The average pigeon produces over twenty-five pounds of droppings a year. At some urban nesting sites, the accumulated crap can be measured in tons.

As our culture becomes increasingly hygienic, we have less tolerance for this sort of mess. What consumer would eat at a restaurant or shop at a market whose awnings were splattered with dung? What employee wants to breathe in air from a rooftop ventilation system that's home to dozens of roosting pigeons? The peaceful coexistence between man and pigeon, which lasted for thousands of years, has deteriorated into a war of attrition. The urban pigeon, regardless of its remarkable past and incredible physiology, is now considered a feathered outlaw.

The general and foot soldiers in this pigeon war are the owners and employees of the multibillion-dollar bird control industry. As you might expect, they have few kind words for the rock dove. According to many in the pest control industry, the rock dove is nothing more than a filthy, bacteria-ridden, disease-carrying vermin with absolutely no redeeming qualities. If the industry could pin AIDS and bubonic plague on the pigeon, they'd do so in a New York minute.

They've helped foster an environment where, for the first time in human history, pigeons are routinely ridiculed, vilified, and persecuted. The pigeon hasn't changed one iota, but after decades of ridicule and bad press, the public's perception of the bird has gone from admiration for its unique history to fear and disgust.

When small outbreaks of West Nile virus whipped the American public into a near-frenzy not long ago, it was a boon for the pigeon control industry. Some saw their business nearly triple. Lost in the shuffle was the fact that pigeons don't transmit West Nile virus; mosquitoes do. Pigeons don't carry the virus, either, because their body temperature is too high to host the bacteria. Further studies have shown pigeons to be either resistant or minimally susceptible to avian influenza as well.

Here's the poop on pigeons: their droppings can be linked to more than sixty communicable (bacterial and viral) diseases, but then again, so can yours. Yes, they *can* pose a health risk, but one that is comparable to cleaning out Whisker's litter box. Cat feces can contain parasites that cause toxoplasmosis, a disease that can result in neurological damage. Feral pigeons are more susceptible to these diseases than racing and show pigeons, which are typically kept in cleaned and maintained backyard coops.

The two diseases most commonly associated with pigeon dung are histoplasmosis, which attacks the lungs, and cryptococcosis, which causes meningitis and encephalitis. It's important to emphasize that neither disease is *carried* by pigeons. Rather, they are caused by fungi that exist all around us, particularly in soil. Pigeon dung happens to be an attractive breeding ground for these fungal spores because it is highly acidic and acts as a fertilizer. Chicken shit, by comparison, rapidly becomes alkaline and thus fungus-unfriendly.

There is no ironclad evidence that pigeons spread disease to humans. However, Dr. Arturo Casadevall, director of the Division of Infectious Diseases at Manhattan's Albert Einstein College of Medicine, says he suspects that people with weakened immune systems are at risk around pigeon feces.

Casadevall is one of the world's foremost experts in pigeon poop, an area of study that he characterizes as "not particularly crowded." His work with AIDS patients suffering from cryptococcosis suggests that they may have inhaled the spores in the vicinity of roosting city pigeons. "The vast majority of people will never get sick," Casadevall says. "But if you're one of the unlucky few . . ."

The easiest way to get sick from pigeon excrement is from cleaning it out of an unventilated space, such as an attic. When you disturb the feces, it will turn to dust if already dry, and the spores will dangle in the air. Breathing in large quantities of doo-doo dust is not a recommended activity, which is why professional bird-shit removers wet the droppings first, ventilate the area, and wear respirators.

But picking on pigeons is unwarranted, Casadevall warns. "Pigeons are no different than other animals. When it comes to spreading disease, they don't stand out. Dogs can have worms; bats, rabies; cats, toxoplasmosis. . . . We're exposed to microbes everywhere. You can get diseases from any animal, even a cockatoo. To single out pigeons is unfair."

Dr. Nina Marano, an epidemiologist with the Centers for Disease Control in Atlanta, agrees. "Pigeons are no more filthy than any other wild bird or animal. The problem is that they congregate very near to us and in large numbers." Pigeon overcrowding leads to large concentrated quantities of feces. The accumulation in an area highly trafficked by pedestrians is not something health officials are likely to endorse.

Early attempts at pigeon control usually involved picking off the birds one by one with a rifle. Although cruel and ineffective, this method is still in use today. The first so-called humane bird control product to be commercially manufactured was developed in 1950 in the American Midwest. Invented by a lawyer with an entrepreneurial drive, Nixalite is the spiky metal stuff you see on many city ledges. You'll even find it on top of the Alaska pipeline and on Coast Guard buoys out at sea. It's still in use, although more effective variations, with fewer piercingly sharp needles, have also been developed. Another humane favorite is netting draped tightly over pigeon perches.

Succeeding decades saw an alarming rise in cruel and desperate products and practices. Ledges were covered in chemical gels that either irritated the birds' feet or released strychnine into their bloodstream. Other entrepreneurs developed high-voltage platforms that electrocuted any bird landing on them. Some of these products have been banned and are no longer in use.

One product still used in many cities is Avitrol, a pesticide-laden bird food developed by a man whose last name is Swindle. Approved for use by the U.S. government, Avitrol is designed to bait and disorient a small portion of a flock. Other pigeons in the flock are supposed to flee after seeing the poisoned birds in distress. But more often than not, Avitrol is used as an avicide. As Avitrol's own literature states, "Dead or reacting birds in public areas may be an alarming sight to the general public. It is best to gather and dispose of dead birds regularly, especially if adverse public reaction is anticipated."

Not only are avicides cruel, they're also indiscriminate. So-called desirable birds are lured to their last meal as well. These poisoned birds make for easy prey and can end up in the stomachs of endangered species, such as the peregrine falcon.

While the bird control industry has its share of warped entrepreneurs who malign pigeons and busy themselves devising death traps, the industry has its fair share of goofy suburban warriors and their even sillier slogans ("We're number one at number two!"). Jack Wagner, a bird control expert with an irreverent take on his profession, is a prime example. He's been in business for twenty-five years and has used just about every product out there.

A roofer by trade, Wagner fell into bird control by accident. While he was on the job in Washington, D.C., more and more clients asked him for help with roosting pigeons. At the time, bird control experts were few and far between, so Jack experimented and improvised with whatever products existed.

One of his first clients was a drugstore on Dupont Circle. Jack improvised an electrical wiring system and installed it while hanging precariously from ropes and scaffolding. When he saw the flock leave the drugstore only to roost on the building right next door, Jack knew he was on to something. He dropped roofing and took up bird control full-time.

"My job involves architecture and biology," Jack tells me. "How fascinating is that? I get paid to outwit nature but not harm it, and to make sure that it is done in an architecturally correct way. In a sense, I'm an artist, mechanic, and biologist."

Jack named his new company BirdBusters (after the recently released *Ghostbusters*) and was the first bird control expert to acquire an 800 number (1-800-NO-BIRDS). His flamboyant style attracted business from across the country and even the world. Not only has he pigeon-proofed sections of the U.S. Capitol, his work has taken him to the Sudan, the United Arab Emirates, Alaska, Hong Kong, and the Caribbean. "Pigeons are a problem everywhere. They're the mainstay of the bird control industry. If my business were a gas station, they'd be the pump: steady, steady, steady." (Woodpeckers, however, are fast pushing pigeons out of their first-place perch. Says Jack, "They're like a carpenter on speed with an ax.")

Jack has mixed feelings about pigeons. On one hand, he calls them disgusting birds that nest in their own crap. Conversely, he sees them as harmless loafers that have survived millions of years of evolution only to be hounded by modern humans. "Sure, they'll crap on your birthday cake, but they're pacifists," Jack says. "They don't mean any harm. They just want to eat and hang out."

Ridding an area of pigeons does have some painful but beneficial consequences, such as leaving more food for smaller birds. "It's sort of like *Sophie's Choice*—for every pigeon and starling I knock off, a sparrow or songbird lives."

Jack says he's disappointed with nearly every product he's used against pigeons. He's tried speakers that emit avian distress signals; deterrent gels ("We sell bird gel remover; that's how bad it is"); bird spikes ("You know how a Hindu can sit on a bed of nails? Well pigeons can too"); traps employed for later release ("They're not called *homing* pigeons for nothing"); lasers; and avicides ("A bunch of lies. Distress signal? Baloney. They're dying: That's the distress signal. It's poison"). Fake owls are so lame, they're a standing joke in the business.

These days Jack is touting something called the Firefly, a six-inch wavy length of reflective plastic that produces glare. He strings them from buildings and swears by the results. "It truly affects their vision. They stay away!"

David Kane, who runs a New York outfit called Bye Bye Birdie, is a good friend of Jack's but thinks Jack has gone off the deep end with his Firefly business. David is a traditionalist. He believes that the only way to rid a building of pigeons is to wrap it in spikes, electrical wires, and netting. In the back of his maroon Buick LeSabre, he keeps a wooden box displaying the tricks of his trade, with names like Bird Coil, Flex-track, and StealthNet, "a poly netting with a forty-four-pounder breaking point." It's this display and the knowledge behind it that differentiate David from the small-timers, he says. "All those guys know is spikes. That's it."

Although he works on jobs as big as airports and entire college campuses, today he's tooling around Brooklyn with a detailed street map, writing up estimates for small residential jobs. He's continually on his cell phone, calling clients. "Hi, I'm David Kane from Bye Bye Birdie. Rich from Queensway Extermination suggested I give you a call. Where's the problem? On the front of the building? I'll be by to take a look."

After a succession of these calls, David turns to me in frustration. "These little jobs? I'm over it. I basically do them as favors for people I know. Most of these customers don't want to spend the kind of money it takes to get rid of pigeons anyway. They think it's just a matter of putting up a fake owl. But when they see us show up at the crack of dawn with a sixty-foot boom truck, they know it's serious business."

The jobs David dislikes even more are when he and his employees spend a night in a high-ceilinged big-box store trying to capture a stray bird with big nets hanging from forty-foot extension poles. "You have to figure out the bird's flight pattern, agitate it with a laser, and then try to catch it in these giant nets. But you're always taking the nets back down and moving them again and again. It's a monotonous, horrible job. Nobody wants it." It once took four nights and $7,000 in labor to capture a little sparrow that resorted to hiding under the store's aisles to evade capture.

When we arrive on a job, David takes out a sketchbook and measuring tape and starts writing the estimate. The first thing he does is look down at the pavement for the telltale splatters of bird shit. Only then does he look up at a building's ledges and cornices. I watch as a pigeon poops on the hood of David's car and another soils his light green oxford, a sure sign that he spends his days pursuing pigeons.

After years of practice, David can spot the problem in minutes, if not seconds. He usually recommends that the owner pigeon-proof the second to fifth floors of a building, where pigeons tend to roost on ledges and cornices and under air-conditioning units. Pigeons favor these heights because they're elevated enough to offer protection from pedestrians, but not so high as to distance the birds from their sidewalk food source (which is why you're unlikely to see a pigeon on top of the Empire State Building).

When estimating a job, David ranks the degree of pigeon infiltration and puts it in one of three categories: low-, medium-, and high-pressure. A low-pressure job consists of a smattering of pigeons routinely sunning themselves on a comfortable southern-facing ledge. A simple application of spikes and coils will do the trick. A medium-pressure job means the birds are hanging out because there's a nearby food source such as a bus stop where people drop off their half-eaten bagels before boarding. This density can require electrical work.

A high-pressure job denotes an area where the pigeons aren't just loafing or eating but also nesting. "That's the hardest pressure to eliminate," David explains to me. Pigeons don't like to move. Once they're born in a place, that's it, they're committed for life. They're staying no matter what and will build a nest on top of spikes if they have to. The only way to keep them away is total exclusion. And that's what netting is for. "If nothing else, pigeons are persistent, and there's plenty of them." David says. "They're my bread and butter."

Unlike Jack, David started in pest control before specializing in bird control, and he says, "I think there's an untapped market in geese." So his next business project will be tackling the geese that congregate at corporate parks and crap all over the expansive lawns.

As Jack and David can attest, bird control is an addictive and obsessive career. On a trip to Paris with his wife, David visited the Louvre. Rather than admiring the *Mona Lisa* with his wife, he found his eyes wandering to an outside ledge covered in bird wire. "I can't help it. It's my business. It's what I do."

On his way to another estimate, David makes a short detour and parks his car across the street from the Brooklyn Museum of Art. He aims binoculars at the building's enormous classical pediment and Ionic columns. A competitor recently installed netting to protect the ornate facade from pigeons.

"Wow. Look at that. You can't even see the netting. It's so taut the pigeons probably bounce off it. Now, that's something to be proud of."

As honest bird control experts will tell you, their product is at best a temporary solution. Total exclusion works, but it protects only one physical location. The birds just relocate to another roost nearby. Ask David Kane what he does for a living, and he'll tell you he's in the bird relocation business.

You can't wrap an entire city in netting. So what's a city to do? Sadly, most still depend on the most primitive of methods—killing pigeons. It's an ineffective method, and most pest control companies know this, but they continue to push these profitable services anyway.

To howls of protest from pigeon lovers and animal rights activists, the mayor of London, Ken Livingstone, recently declared war on the pigeons of Trafalgar Square, using a brutal mixture of lethal and nonlethal methods. He shut down a vendor whose family had sold birdseed to tourists since World War II, banned the feeding of pigeons altogether, and hired a falconer to patrol the square daily. But it's not Lord Nelson's column or the National Gallery alone that attracts flocks of tourists to Trafalgar Square, it's also the birds. Days before I visited the square to gauge the situation for myself, Paris Hilton made a splash when police issued her a $100 summons for feeding the birds. "But I just love feeding the pigeons in Trafalgar Square," she said. "I could do it forever. I even prefer it to going shopping."

With fewer pigeons visible, Livingstone is seemingly winning the Battle of Trafalgar Square, but for how long and at what cost? Using falconry for pigeon control is cruel as well as unsustainable: pigeons return the minute the falconer leaves. And the sight of a falcon ferociously dining on a splayed pigeon is traumatic for the public, especially children. A policy built on hatred is hardly a recipe for success, and it has unfortunately blinded Livingstone to the basic facts of bird control.

A Swiss biologist by the name of Daniel Haag-Wackernagel has spent over a decade studying pigeon populations and how to regulate them in an urban setting. His work turned many basic assumptions upside down. First, killing birds only *increases* the size of the flock. The loss of life means less competition and more food for the rest of the flock. That, in turn, means that a new generation of young birds is more likely to survive.

Haag-Wackernagel surmised that the key to controlling a pigeon population was food. Pigeons breed only when there's food available. When food is overly bountiful, as was the case at Trafalgar Square, pigeons will mate as often as possible, up to six times a year. When food is scarce, the mating routine drops dramatically, because pigeons must spend their time anxiously foraging for food.

Haag-Wackernagel used the streets of Basel as his laboratory. Between 1961 and 1985, marksmen hired by the city killed approximately one hundred thousand pigeons. But the pigeon population grew over this time. The first thing Haag-Wackernagel did was to launch a civic campaign to educate the public about pigeon feeding. Overfeeding, he explained, is an artificial intervention in a city's ecosystem. It leads to overpopulation and overcrowding, which stress a flock and encourage sickness and disease. In effect, Haag-Wackernagel declared, overfeeding pigeons is tantamount to animal cruelty.

Next Haag-Wackernagel set up clean lofts at hidden locations around the city and encouraged the pigeons to nest there, in effect returning the birds to the dovecotes where they originated centuries ago. Volunteers visited the lofts weekly to leave feed and clean up after the birds and regularly replaced their eggs with wooden or plastic facsimiles.

Within four years, Basel's pigeon population was reduced by 50 percent. Interestingly, the city's largest bird control company saw its sales drop by an astonishing two-thirds during the same period. Haag-Wackernagel proved that pigeon populations, unlike rats, really could be controlled, and humanely. And as flocks thin, hatred for the bird subsides. It's not the bird itself that annoys most people, it's the *number* of them.

A British nonprofit organization called the Pigeon Control Advisory Service (PiCAS) developed a similar strategy that has shown impressive results. At one of its projects, a public hospital in Nottingham, PiCAS reduced the bird population by 50 percent in under a year.

PiCAS began as the brainchild of Guy Merchant, a willowy man in his fifties who has dedicated his life to educating the public about humane and effective urban pigeon control. He has consulted for cities as far away as Rio and Melbourne and never charges a fee for his services.

"We are the only independent source of unbiased information out there," Guy says. "By comparison, the pest control industries are only motivated by greed. They invest millions of dollars each year on anti-pigeon propaganda and misinformation. It's entirely unethical. In fact, there are no ethics involved at all. Believe you me, the world hates pigeons because of them."

I met with Guy over a cup of coffee at his tidy home in Cambridgeshire. Few people in the world have dedicated their lives so totally to pigeons, with the possible exception of Dave Roth in Phoenix. Like Roth, he basically *is* the organization.

"I care about all birds, but the plight of the feral pigeon is far worse than the others," Guy says. "They are abused and tortured more than any other bird, and usually for profit. It just sticks in my throat. They're the ultimate underdog." He works 365 days a year to help pigeons, including every Christmas for over thirty years. "For better or worse, I live, eat—figuratively—and sleep pigeons." He blames a recent stroke on his obsessive work habits, but it hasn't slowed him down.

A trained bird rehabilitator, Guy started PiCAS three decades ago after treating an onslaught of sick and dying pigeons—the result of lethal bird control methods. "Once I learned how appalling, cruel, and ineffective those methods were, I had to come up with a solution. I had no choice but to dedicate my life to it. That's what started PiCAS—the massive buildup of dead and dying pigeons."

Guy says the biggest hurdle of any urban pigeon campaign is convincing the skeptical public to limit how much they feed the city's birds. Residents often fear the birds will starve and complain that they miss their relaxing daily routine of bird feeding. To combat this compulsion, PiCAS recommends building attractive lofts and designating them as places where feeding is encouraged. Some cities have created contests in which artists and architects design the lofts, which double as public art. PiCAS also recommends a thorough bird-proofing of public buildings where the birds used to make their homes, to ensure that they don't return.

The Basel/PiCAS models have been embraced by many cities in Europe. Visiting Aachen, in Germany, I was amazed at how unobtrusive the pigeons were. Instead of foraging for scraps in the city center, they happily loafed at well-maintained lofts circling the city. City residents had reached a détente with their feathered friends.

Compulsive feeding by certain individuals remains the biggest threat to the European model. Compulsive feeders will dodge fines, absorb public humiliation, and even resort to secret night feedings to avoid detection. "A small number of persistent and deliberate feeders are wholly responsible for the pigeon problem throughout the world," says Guy. "They *are* the pigeon problem. Pigeons overbreed when people overfeed. There is no other explanation."

According to Guy, regardless of where they live, compulsive feeders share similar quirky personality traits and slip into the obsession in nearly identical ways. "They're a strange bunch, extremely eccentric." Although compulsive feeders view themselves as charitable, Guy thinks them selfish. It's not enough to simply feed the pigeons, he says. All that does is burden everyone else with cleaning up the resulting mess.

Manhattan is home to countless unusual and lonely characters who seek solace by feeding pigeons from park benches. It's a classic New York preoccupation, practiced by the elderly, the unemployed, the curious, the melancholy, and the lonely. After all, if the human condition is ultimately to be alone, then why not let a few pigeons help us pass the time?

Some of these folks have routinely fed pigeons for years, if not decades. But when it comes to compulsive feeding, they can't outshine the likes of Sally Bananas and Anna Dove.

Sally, an elderly but energetic woman with a fondness for tight leggings, floppy hats, and oversize sunglasses, changed her last name to Bananas in honor of her poodle, Charlie Bananas. After a long life, Charlie is now in doggie heaven, but Sally still gets his mail (from Victoria's Secret, nonetheless) and telemarketing calls (the phone is in his name). "I tell them he's traveling in Brazil," she tells me. "That usually shuts them up."

Charlie Bananas was part of Sally's now-deceased Banana Gang, an entity that she says she had hoped to legally incorporate. There was also Sandy-of-Oz (with hyphens, please) and little José Caliente, who served as the "caboose of the gang." And there were three cats: Subway Red, Willie Whiskers, and Choo-Choo. Sally treated Charlie to drinks at the Waldorf-Astoria and says the whole gang joined her for a cruise on the QE2. Sally's dream of marching down the Champs Élysées with the whole Banana Gang was thwarted by Charlie's untimely passing.

Sally says she prefers the company of animals to humans. "If a dog ran for president, I'd vote for him," she says. "I've lost faith in the human race." After the passing of the Banana Gang, Sally has lived alone. She considers the neighborhood pigeons her family now. Most days Sally lugs forty to fifty pounds of birdseed around her Upper East Side neighborhood and hastily spills large quantities of it at her "usual spots." It's become a habit, she readily admits, because the birds "need" her.

"They know me," she says of her pigeons. "No matter how I'm dressed, they know who I am. And they're always so hungry, the poor darlings. We've taken away their habitat. Imagine if you had to hunt around for a seed to survive. Remember, every animal was once a mother's child."

Sally Bananas is friends with Anna Dove, whose name used to be Augusta Kugelmas. She changed her name in honor of her pet pigeon Lucie-Dove. It occurs to me that the names are a bit too perfect and the women perhaps prefer the use of animal-friendly pseudonyms—noms de guerre, if you will—when interacting with the outside world. Anna lives alone with her menagerie of doves, parakeets, parrots, finches, and a rabbit. She runs a club that organizes bird playdates, although she confesses that she doesn't enjoy working with other people and prefers to keep to herself.

A few years ago she was arrested for allegedly assaulting a Parks Department volunteer who insisted that Anna (then Augusta) stop feeding the pigeons. The volunteer claimed it was illegal. Anna insists the volunteer was "a bitch with Mafioso ties" and that she merely threw birdseed at the woman to protect herself. "She grabbed my bag of food," Anna recalls. "There was . . . a scuffle." The charges were dropped, but not before the quintessentially New York story made it onto the pages of the city's dailies and weeklies: WOMAN ARRESTED FOR FEEDING PIGEONS!

Anna used the publicity to form a pigeon club of irate citizens looking to defend their right to feed pigeons. The group met at a local bagel shop but eventually disbanded over internal squabbling. "We discussed things like how we should feed the pigeons and what to do about people that harass us. But nothing ever got accomplished. It became all about ego and who was in charge of the group."

Although pigeon feeding is illegal in some cities, such as San Francisco, it remains legal in New York City. A casualty of bureaucratic logic, pigeon feeding falls under the jurisdiction of the city's Department of Health, which issues summonses only if the feeding creates a nuisance condition—basically, if it attracts rats.

Anna tells me that she sympathizes with the city's concern about rats. This year she found mice in her apartment and was, in her words, "devastated to the point that I could not live my life." She removed all sources of food from her apartment, even her refrigerator and stove, and slept in the hallway a couple of nights. She knew better than to ask her landlord for help. Earlier, when the ceiling above her bed erupted with several gallons of water from burst pipes, he suggested she sleep on the couch.

Anna was in the news again when she posted a $10,000 reward for a missing exotic parrot she was tending. Against the owner's wishes, Anna brought the bird down to the lobby to get some fresh air, and the parrot promptly escaped. (It was later recovered, unharmed.)

When it comes to feeding pigeons, Anna says she has been pushed, shoved, berated, and threatened by fellow pedestrians. But she refuses to back down. "I've taken a stand," she says. "If you wanna stop me, go buy a gun and shoot me, because that's what it's going to take."

One of her favorite stories is about a security guard who used to work just outside her building. One day he confronted her for feeding a peanut to a squirrel. "He tells me he's going to report me and starts shouting into his walkie-talkie for backup. All because I was feeding a squirrel! Can you believe it? What a sick bastard. Well, later on I found out that he dropped dead the very next day. You know what I said? 'Good, that's one less person I have to worry about.' Now I feed ten squirrels with a whole bag of nuts. And you know what? Nobody says a word."

I spent a sunny afternoon accompanying the two ladies on their feeding safari. It proved a far more difficult undertaking than I had imagined. Both women had the unnerving ability to speak to me at the exact same time, one in each ear. Sally compulsively interrupted Anna, and Anna just kept right on talking (as did Sally).

Our expedition begins outside a coffee shop on First Avenue, along Sally's main route. It starts with her giving a young couple a lecture about tying up their dog to a tree while they run in for a cup of coffee. "It is very dangerous," she says. "It's a hot sun. Many dogs are stolen. It's not safe, not safe at all. There's shade under that tree over there, but that's where two little puppies got killed." At first friendly, the couple eventually stare at Sally blankly before they walk to another coffee shop.

Meanwhile, Anna is busy feeding sparrows bread crumbs between her own bites. "Today I have Pepperidge Farm's crunchy grains bread. But I change it every day. I always have a bag on me and a bag of nuts for the squirrels. I know it's weird, but I feel like an outlaw carrying this stuff around."

We head to a supermarket on Eighty-ninth Street. Sally buys enough birdseed to fill two plastic shopping bags. I offer to carry one for her. She says no, she's used to it and likes to walk balancing equal weights. Her back is bent, her shoulders stooped, and the bags dangle just inches above the ground, but she moves surprisingly quickly. Anna and I can barely keep up with her. She won't slow down until all the birds are fed.

A block away, Sally cuts open a ten-pound bag with her apartment key and dumps it beside a fire hydrant. The seeds splash all over the curb and settle into thick piles. It's the avian equivalent of an all-points bulletin. Dozens of birds swoop in from blocks away, like people chasing after loose dollars blowing in the wind.

Sally doesn't stick around to watch the birds feast on her munificence. Instead, she hastily disappears back into the crowd. Her satisfaction seems to come from knowing that the birds have been fed. By comparison, Anna takes her time and tries to bond with each and every bird.

Sally decides to return to the supermarket for more seed. "I need ten pounds more. C'mon!" she barks. Waiting outside the store, Anna sees two sparrows sparring over a pizza crust and points them out to me. "Look at how hungry they are! Look! Look! I shouldn't feed them here right in front of the supermarket, but they look so hungry. Maybe I'll give them just a little something . . ."

On Ninety-sixth Street, Sally *bites* open a thick plastic bag of seeds and spills it onto the sidewalk. Pigeons arrive out of nowhere. "They wait for me," she tells me. Sally is scheduled for a hospital procedure, and she's worried about the pigeons surviving while she's gone. Anna volunteers to staff Sally's feed route.

We walk to a small park where Sally catches her breath before we slog forward once again. Sally then buys yet more birdseed, this time at a supermarket on Second Avenue. On the sidewalk, Anna spots a pigeon. "This little guy needs something to eat," she says, tossing him bread crumbs. More pigeons appear. Sally emerges with more bags of feed. "Okay," she says. "Let's march on!"

The expedition ends at a neighborhood park, where Anna feeds the squirrels. Inevitably, conversation returns to pigeons and Anna's conviction that more and more of them are disappearing. "One day there will be just one left, and we'll idolize it because it's the last one," Anna says. "I believe it's a strong possibility. Oh, God. How awful. And once they're done with the pigeons, they'll pick on the starlings. And when they're gone, they'll pick on the sparrows."

While Sally and Anna walk the streets of New York like pigeon pied pipers, another community of similarly obsessed pigeon lovers network for their favorite bird in the digital ether.

The plea for help was gut-wrenching. A flurry of increasingly desperate e-mails on the New York City Pigeon People listserv reported seeing a pigeon hanging upside down from a tree branch, five stories off the ground in a nearly inaccessible courtyard of an apartment complex. The pigeon's feet were tangled in a piece of string, and now that piece of string was tangled in a tree branch. The bird could be seen thrashing about, clearly unable to right itself, let alone break loose. Night was falling, and a fierce winter storm was fast approaching.

The virtual community sprang into action with their keyboards, but no one could think of a way to rescue the struggling pigeon. The Fire Department doesn't rescue birds, and a ladder truck couldn't access the courtyard regardless; a climber willing to scale the tree couldn't be located, and a helicopter would generate too much wind and cost too much. Could someone harpoon the tree from an apartment window and shuffle across the wire to retrieve the bird? Somebody suggested alerting the media, but who's going to write about a city pigeon trapped in a tree? A puppy, maybe. But a pigeon?

The snowstorm arrived and blanketed the city. The dangling bird swayed in the wind. The pigeon advocates were at a complete loss. Successive e-mails were filled with panic and dread. The exhausted bird's movements slowed to minute twitches. By morning it was covered in snow and ice, dead. The small group of New York pigeon lovers was devastated.

A year earlier, a red-tailed hawk by the name of Pale Male made international news when the owners of a posh Fifth Avenue apartment building attempted to relocate his nest overlooking Central Park. Thousands of people picketed the building and wrote letters of protest to media outlets around the city, keeping up a constant vigil.

The high-voltage scrutiny of being front-page news took its toll (it was a slow news week), and the building's management finally caved in. Pale Male's eviction was rescinded. To this day, hundreds of people continue to visit the site, not to protest but to peer up at the raptor's nest with telescopes and binoculars. Meanwhile, landlords and residents spend tens of millions of dollars to evict pigeons from well-established perches all across the city.

Most birds in the United States are protected by a series of federal laws and international treaties. The federal Migratory Bird Treaty Act of 1918, for instance, has been expanded to cover nonmigratory birds and now protects more than eight hundred wild species. Even the devious, egg-stealing blue jay is federally protected. Then there's the federal Endangered Species Act, which gives additional protection to birds such as bald eagles, condors, piping plovers, and the infamous spotted owl. Many of these birds and their habitats are additionally protected by the multimillion-dollar efforts of nonprofit avian charities such as the American Bird Conservancy and the National Audubon Society. (*Most* birds are popular. There are forty-six million bird-watchers in the United States alone.)

So where does the pigeon fit into these public and private avian safety nets? It doesn't. The rock dove is one of a small handful of commoners, such as starlings and sparrows, that can't gain entry into the exclusive club of desirable birds, leaving them without any legal protections. Local animal cruelty laws occasionally address pigeons, but more often than not, the birds are exempted from protection because of their status as nuisance animals. The Environmental Protection Agency terms the rock dove a pest, and Wildlife Services, a branch of the U.S. Department of Agriculture, actively participates in pigeon-control operations in urban and agricultural areas (pigeons like to feast on cattle feed). The department averages about seventy-five thousand pigeon kills a year, often with the aid of Avitrol.

Why the discrimination? It's a matter of how you parse the words "wild" and "native." The rock dove is not, strictly speaking, wild. Having returned to an untamed state from domestication, the birds are now technically feral and thus unprotected. Having sailed here with settlers (albeit hundreds of years ago and with no say in the matter) the rock dove can't be labeled a native species, unlike its cousin the passenger pigeon. Instead, it carries the stigma of being an introduced species. Unlike cardinals, blue jays, and robins, pigeons are designated an invasive species, much like the archenemy of any gardener—the dandelion. And how do we rid ourselves of dandelions and other hated weeds? We poison them. But unlike dandelions, pigeons are not actually displacing anything. Their only real crime is annoying another predominantly nonnative species—Americans—by crapping all over the place. In fact, no country claims the rock dove as a native son, nor does any country specifically protect the bird.

Even devoted rock dove enthusiasts, such as pigeon racers and fancy pigeon breeders, look down on the city pigeon as a trash bird that gives their thoroughbreds and genetic beauties a bad name. And bird-watchers? They view any artificially introduced species as unnatural and therefore undesirable. You won't find many birders donning binoculars for pigeons.

That's not to say the street pigeon is without its fans and supporters. The Internet is filled with global discussion groups about rescuing injured pigeons. The members compare notes on antibiotics, broken wings, flushing out poisons, and anti-pigeon zoning ordinances. They share electronic photos of recovering birds, pray together for the dying ones, and bemoan the bias against what they consider a beautiful and majestic bird. It's a tight community in which members post multiple daily messages from places as far-flung as Europe, the Middle East, and California.

In addition to rehabbing pigeons, members also return lost racing pigeons to their owners by decoding racing bands. To maintain good public relations, racing organizations often thank these listservs for their help. But sadly, it's mostly window dressing. Unbeknownst to many of these bleeding hearts, pigeon racers don't want their wayward birds returned. A homer that can't make it home has no value. Although the birds are shipped back to their owners with the best of intentions, their necks are often snapped upon arrival.

New York City is big enough to have its own pro-pigeon listserv, an underground network of kindhearted and somewhat reclusive individuals who view pigeons as sweet, lovable birds that animate the cityscape. They see themselves as the birds' caretakers, an underdog's buffer against the barbarian hordes armed with poisons, nets, and a vitriolic hatred.

They spot injured pigeons, frequently taking them home to their small apartments, where they spend countless hours and hundreds of dollars rehabbing them. A typical listserv posting looks something like this: "I spotted a pigeon with a hurt wing on 42nd Street and 9th Ave.—on the southwest corner—huddled up near the door of the Dunkin' Donuts. . . . I wasn't able to catch it because there was too much traffic. Can someone check up on him? He's obviously in need of our help."

At about the same time the upside-down pigeon was slowly dying of exposure, a somewhat senile man by the name of Willie was in danger of eviction from his Queens apartment, along with his hundred pigeon friends. The Pigeon People listserv quickly swung into action. They tapped into the pigeon-loving virtual community, locating homes across the nation for the pigeons and collecting enough money to buy shipping crates. One member even accompanied Willie to housing court and discussed the situation with his assigned social worker.

But after days of tedious coordination, Willie changed his mind and wouldn't let his animal friends be relocated to safe homes. Instead, he locked himself in his dilapidated apartment and wouldn't return phone calls or open the door. Willie was evicted, and after years of cozy domestication, the pigeons were let loose to fend for themselves. Most surely died.

You could say that the Sallys, Annas, and listserv communities are the soup kitchens, medical clinics, and civil rights activists of the New York City pigeon movement that lies just beneath the surface of the city's cultural consciousness. But dig a little deeper and you'll find a third and more radical movement—one that believes in other means to protect the lives of pigeons. They're a Weather Underground of sorts, fed up with writing editorials and helping one pigeon at a time. They've grown disenchanted with conventional means for safeguarding the lives of city pigeons, although they always remain within the boundaries of the law. While they strategize on how to topple the systemic persecution of pigeons, they also concentrate on what they see as the bird's greatest immediate threat: pigeon poachers.

Eduardo, a middle-aged New York City street vendor of knockoff watches and baseball hats, tells me how he befriended a young pigeon, named him Jimmy, and took him home to his basement apartment. Jimmy would eat out of Eduardo's hand but preferred to peck partially chewed crackers out of the soft-spoken vendor's mouth.

Every morning Eduardo would let Jimmy loose, and every afternoon the bird would be waiting for him when he got home. One day Eduardo, who sets up his table in the predawn hours, saw men exit a white van and toss birdseed at the pigeons. Moments later, the men threw a net over the birds, tossed them in the back of the van, and drove down the avenue.

Eduardo's eyes tear up as he finishes his story: that afternoon he walked home to an empty apartment. His beloved Jimmy was gone. "I know it was those evil men. They took Jimmy. They stole my little Jimmy." More likely than not, Jimmy ended up as a live target at a pigeon shoot in rural Pennsylvania. That is, if he survived the trip.

As if life weren't hard enough for a city pigeon, these survivors of inhumane traps and hungry predators must also contend with the profit-driven world of netters. In principle, netting is illegal. Feral pigeons are the property of the state and fall under the domain of the Department of Environmental Protection. According to state statutes, wild birds cannot be trapped without written permission, nor sold across state lines as shotgun fodder for gun clubs. But once again, the bird's feral status confuses the issue: are pigeons truly wild? Even if pigeons didn't fall through the cracks, it's hard to imagine the state enforcing the law to protect them anyway.

The netters have free rein as long as they keep a low profile. They work under the cloak of near-darkness out of nondescript vans, often with the tacit approval of landlords sick of cleaning up after "winged cockroaches." But a tiny fringe group of anonymous spies is diligently working to punch a dent onto the quasi-illegal trade. They call themselves Bird Operations Busted, or B.O.B.

It is a secretive organization run by a middle-aged Walter Mitty who fancies himself the 007 of the pigeon world. To protect his true identity, he also calls himself "Bob." He won't tell you how many "agents" belong to B.O.B. or their names. In fact, no member of B.O.B. knows anything about the other members, except, of course, Bob. They are assigned code names such as Space Bird, Native Bird, and Street Bird (I suspect the latter is Eduardo).

Bob tells me that these seemingly paranoiac precautions are for the safety of the organization's secret agents. "The netters are not happy with us," he explains. "They really hate us, because we spoil their profit margins. . . . We are putting ourselves in jeopardy. I've had death threats. Not just one but many. They want my head. We use code names so that if information falls into the wrong hands, no one person can compromise other members."

Agents stake out their neighborhoods and report any suspicious pigeon activity. They are armed with disposable cameras and a blank form for recording license numbers, makes of vehicles, number of netters, time, location, and the number of captured birds. "Rain, sleet, snow—it doesn't matter. We are out there every day, keeping an eye on things, ready to ring the alarm bells," Bob tells me. "We are foot soldiers, the hard-core element of the pigeon movement. We have become a central pivot point. Actions get taken, things get done."

According to Bob, several notorious netting locations are monitored by video cameras located in members' apartments. He says he has over seven terabytes worth of video and other covert information divvied up and hidden among an undisclosed number of servers in undisclosed locations around the city. "We prefer not to discuss those matters," he informs me. "We don't want to alarm the authorities." He does, however, keep in touch with a cadre of animal-friendly journalists. "I can get something on television or published in a newspaper on a moment's notice if necessary."

The information is meticulously collected and recorded in hopes that the netters will one day be prosecuted. The group has at least one pro bono lawyer working on its behalf. But as one of their lawyers told me, it's an uphill battle. State law prohibits trapping, netting, or snaring only of *wild* birds. Meanwhile, Bob and the rest of the agents continue spying on the netters, letting them know they're being watched. So far, only one pigeon poacher has been dragged into court, and that was for assaulting one of Bob's agents and stealing his camera. (Bob says the man pled guilty to stealing the camera, but he continues to poach pigeons.)

And just who is this enigmatic Man from B.O.B.? I met with him one spring afternoon on an Upper West Side street corner he has selected, not long after I interviewed Eduardo. As I wait, I have a sneaky suspicion I'm being watched. (Later, Bob would reveal to me that I was under video surveillance for much of the day.) A man dressed in black jeans, a black leather coat, and shaded bifocals approaches me. We start walking west. After a block, Bob glances around and then visibly relaxes.

Bob won't tell me his real name or where his foreign accent is from. When he orders French fries at lunch and dips them in mayonnaise, I suspect he is Belgian. But then Bob lets drop between bites that he spent much of his childhood on a Caribbean island that was a former European colony. Which makes him . . . Dutch? A camera flash goes off at a nearby table, and Bob eyes the room suspiciously before continuing our conversation. Does he suspect I brought the heat?

He tells me that he had an "impressive and very successful career" in electrical engineering, broadcast engineering, theatrical lighting, and computer programming. He says Ray Dolby, the inventor of the eponymous sound reduction system, knows him by name, and that the inventor of streaming digital audio is personally indebted to him, or at least should be. "I was on the Internet in the mid-eighties," he says, "back when we called it 'phone phreaking.'" Disgusted by the corporate world, he began to focus his energies on helping animals.

Bob says he works 24/7 for his group, setting up video cameras around the city, collecting data, backing it up, and carefully feeding pigeons. "I have certain pigeons I keep an eye on," he confides, pulling a plastic sandwich bag partially filled with birdseed from his jacket pocket. He stealthily sprinkles a small amount behind a park bench.

Bob has a soft spot for all animals and has turned his apartment into a sanctuary for dying cats and wounded birds. He has a network of veterinarians who help him at cost or for free. "The cats are all old and abandoned by their owners. They are all terminal cases. It's just a matter of time. We give them fluids, pills, and wipe their butts because they are too old to keep themselves groomed. It's always an ending road, but we try to do it in a way that's as comfortable as possible for the kitty."

He's sickened by animal abuse and provides me with reams of data suggesting that cruelty to animals inevitably leads to violence against humans. The people who net pigeons, he explains, are motivated by the desire to abuse animals and are likely to be child and wife abusers as well—animals are merely a first step. Numerous studies have shown that societies that mistreat their animals are often violent societies overall.

Bob says he will one day establish a large animal asylum somewhere in the world to which he can devote all his energies. "I am not bound by any country, and I don't have to live by their corporate rules," he says. "There is animal abuse everywhere in the world."

A lifelong pigeon fan, Bob learned about netting by accident. Early one morning he saw some men netting birds outside his apartment. Instead of accosting them, he befriended them to learn more. What he heard horrified him. The poachers lure pigeons with seed, throw a big net over them, and then toss them in a truck. They can collect as many as a thousand birds in a single morning and sell them to restaurants and shooting clubs for a few bucks each.

Like Guy Merchant and Dave Roth, Bob was surprised to learn that no one in the city was doing anything about this nefarious pigeon trade. That was when he sprang into action. "It's a war being fought live every morning," he says.

Bob views education as an integral part of his job. He's familiar with many of the city's compulsive pigeon feeders and tries to tutor them on proper pigeon care and safety measures. First, he encourages feeders to lure the birds away from popular netting areas. It's best to feed away from the curb, where the birds are easy prey for drive-by poachers, and even better to feed on rooftops. Feeders should also clean up after the birds. "Feeding and cleaning should go hand in hand," Bob says. He claims to spend several hours a day sweeping and scrubbing his own pigeon feeding areas.

Then there's the matter of feed. Pigeons given bread made from processed white flour tend to poo rock-hard droppings that can be so difficult to remove they practically require sandblasting. It is these concrete-like turds that give pigeons an even worse reputation, Bob says. He recommends feeding pigeons birdseed because it contains plenty of fiber. The resulting craps are bigger and perhaps more frequent, but they wash away easily in the rain, he explains.

"It's pitiful, but there are large populations of pigeons in this city who don't even know what birdseed is," Bob tells me. "All they know are bagels and pizza crusts. I've even seen tow hawks fighting over a jelly doughnut." In Bob's world, it's the humans who are the slobs and the pigeons that generously clean up after us. "The pigeons are the day cleaning crew, and the rats are the night cleaning crew. Without them, we'd die in our own filth."

We walk to Verdi Square, a park popular with pigeons. Once there, Bob informs me, "As of right now, there are four B.O.B cameras recording us." One of his projects is training this park's pigeons to stay out of harm's way: "We can train these birds. We have probably trained one million already."

According to Bob, "We're on this planet because of the pigeons. They were here before us." Asked to clarify, he adds, "Seventy percent of us can thank these birds that our family line has continued. They have provided us with nourishment and carried our important messages."

Bob's vision is of pigeons and people living in complete and humane harmony all across the country. His future plans are to set up underground cells in Boston and Miami.

But Bob has more immediate pressing issues. "We have a problem, and it's very dangerous," he confides, voice lowered. A compulsive feeder on the Upper East Side is attracting thousands of pigeons, as well as the ire of his neighbors. Worse still, he's feeding them white bread and it's a high traffic area.

"He's not helping the birds. He's only creating a public nuisance and pissing people off. It's people like him that are ruining the bird's reputation. And that leads to poisonings. It's just this kind of downward spiral that B.O.B is trying to reverse."

Abruptly, Bob informs me that the interview is over; pigeons are waiting. Mouthing good-bye, he quickly glides backward away from me. He trips over a fire hydrant. I avert my eyes out of embarrassment and look up seconds later. Bob is gone.

V. MOVING BEYOND TRASH

14 Kill the Cat That Kills the Bird?

Bruce Barcott

LAST SUMMER, even as he talked about facing jail time, Jim Stevenson couldn't stop looking for birds. "There's a couple yellow-crowned night herons," he said, pointing out his living room window. "They roost in that chinaberry tree." He rested his eyes on the blue-gray birds. "Anyway, the cops pulled me over and searched my van and found the gun, and—" A movement caught his eye. "Roseate spoonbill. And there's a male orchard oriole."

Stevenson is a bearish, ruddy-faced, fifty-four-year-old former science teacher who is known as the ornithological guru of Galveston, Texas. Ten years ago, he moved to this Gulf Coast barrier island because of its abundant shorebirds. Enormous flocks of American avocets, willets, sanderlings, dowitchers, and plovers feed in the shallow, fertile estuary of Galveston Bay. Stevenson built his house amid a clump of trees so he could always be watching birds; he lives in a bird blind. Birds are his obsession and his profession. He is the director of the Galveston Ornithological Society and publisher of the quarterly newspaper *Gulls n Herons.* For money, he leads bird-watching tours.

Stevenson apologized for the paucity of species that day. "This part of summer you don't have a lot of migration," he said. "There's still plenty to see, though. We go out tomorrow, I'll load your wagon." By that he meant he would show me birds I could tick off my life list. Serious birders compile a list of every species they have seen in their lifetimes. I hadn't come to Galveston to load my wagon, though. I had come to find out why Jim Stevenson had become the most notorious cat killer in America.

The story went something like this: On the evening of Tuesday, November 7, 2006, Stevenson took a break from watching the election returns to look at some birds at San Luis Pass, a ripply channel connecting Galveston Bay to the gulf. Stevenson parked his white Dodge van with "Galveston Ornithological Society" bannered on its side, near the end of the San Luis Pass bridge, a tollway that connects Galveston Island to Follets Island. He found a spot in the low, grass-speckled dunes and waited. Soon enough, he saw a handful of piping plovers, a federally listed endangered species. Then he saw something else: a scraggly cat stalking the plovers. A colony of about a dozen feral cats had been sleeping under the bridge. The cats liked to wander into the dunes for the same reason Stevenson did: the birds.

"Piping plovers are tame, abiding little creatures," Stevenson told me. "They roost in the dunes and can't see or hear a cat creep up on them."

Stevenson said he tried to protect the birds by capturing the cat. He failed and returned home frustrated. Late that night, he worried about the problem. "The American taxpayers spend millions of dollars to protect birds like piping plovers," he said, "and yet here are these cats killing the birds, and nobody's doing anything to stop it."

The next morning, Stevenson decided to act. He loaded his .22 rifle in the van and took off for San Luis Pass. He spotted the same cat under the bridge. Stevenson put the animal in his sights and pulled the trigger.

"The cat dropped like a rock," he said.

Up on the bridge, a tollbooth attendant named John Newland heard the shot. Newland, a quiet man in his sixties, often fed the cats under the bridge. He called them his babies. Newland bolted out of his tollbooth and saw Stevenson's van. "I got you!" Newland screamed. "You quit shooting my cats!"

Stevenson fled, but the cops caught up to him near his house. A Galveston police officer cuffed him, read him his rights, and threw him in jail.

With one shot of his rifle, Stevenson found himself cast as the Bernhard Goetz of birders. His cat slaying became a national flash point in the strange Sylvester-and-Tweety feud between birders and cat fanciers, which the resolution of Stevenson's case last month has done little to pacify. For more than twenty years, the two sides have exchanged accusations and insults over the issue of cats killing birds. Depending on whom you talk to, cats are either rhinestone-collared mass murderers or victims of a smear campaign waged by lowdown cat haters. The National Audubon Society has declared that "worldwide, cats may have been involved in the extinction of more bird species than any other cause, except habitat destruction." The

American Bird Conservancy, a smaller, feistier group, runs a campaign to persuade cat owners to lock up their pets.

Cat defenders respond: They're cats! They chase birds.

Much of the controversy focuses on the nation's population of 50 to 90 million feral cats (exact figures are impossible to ascertain), former pets and their offspring that live independent of humans. Feral cats may not have owners, but they do have lobbyists. Alley Cat Allies, a national organization founded by an ex–social worker named Becky Robinson, harnesses a fierce coalition of celebrities, cat experts, and feral-cat-colony caretakers to fight for the rights of wild cats. Her allies include Roger Tabor, a leading British naturalist; Jeffrey Masson, the outspoken author of *The Nine Emotional Lives of Cats* and *When Elephants Weep*; and, fittingly, Tippi Hedren, the actress best known for starring in the 1963 Alfred Hitchcock thriller *The Birds*, which, as you will recall, was a film in which Hedren spent two hours dodging attacks by murderous birds.

Both sides weighed in on Stevenson's shooting. Cat advocates called him cruel and criminal. The blog Cat Defender ("Exposing the Crimes of Bird Lovers") labeled him the Evil Galveston Bird Lover. The president of the Houston Audubon Society condemned Stevenson's "illegal methods of controlling these animals," but other bird-watchers hailed his actions. One Texas birder, a fourth-grade science teacher, suggested that Stevenson be given a medal for his actions.

Like Goetz, who sparked a national debate when he shot four would-be robbers in a New York subway in 1984, Stevenson fired his gun during a time of heightened fear and anxiety. Bird populations are plummeting worldwide. Earlier this year BirdLife International found that 1,221 of the planet's 9,956 bird species were threatened with extinction, an increase of 35 species since 2006. Although hopeful stories like the 2004 purported sighting of an ivory-billed woodpecker—a species long thought extinct—tend to capture the public's imagination, the larger story is a depressing and seemingly inexorable march toward oblivion. In June, the National Audubon Society reported that an analysis of forty years of data from its annual Christmas bird count showed an alarming decline in nearly two dozen once-ubiquitous American songbirds. Since 1965, the common grackle has lost 61 percent of its population. Eastern meadowlarks are down 72 percent, northern bobwhites, 82 percent.

The primary cause of those losses is well known. Habitat destruction—industrial and agricultural development and suburban sprawl replacing forests and fields—is by far the biggest threat to bird populations. What is less understood is the extent to which a complex combination of secondary factors contributes to the decline. Power poles electrocute tens of thousands of birds. Estimates of birds killed in collisions with automobiles and glass windows every year run to the hundreds of millions.

Where cats sit in this continuum is a huge point of contention. Over the past ten years or so, however, a growing body of research has implicated cats as a serious factor in the loss of native birds in specific habitats— mostly islands, often shorelines, and sometimes inland areas. The World Conservation Union now lists the domestic cat as one of the world's one hundred worst invasive species.

As a person fond of cats and fascinated by birds, I tracked the issue for years without joining either camp. Stevenson's situation seemed to present a perfect microcosm of the problem. Which was the higher ethical duty: to save the bird or to leave the cat unharmed?

At the center of it stood Jim Stevenson, unrepentant and sure. "What I did was not only legal," he told me. "It was right."

What are our obligations to cats and birds? It's a tough question even for some cat advocates. Jeffrey Masson, a well-known Freud scholar as well as a cat fancier, faced the predicament a few years ago when he moved to New Zealand. "Our five cats started to hunt, as cats will," Masson told me recently. "Our neighbor, a bird enthusiast, was furious. 'Your cats are decimating these birds,' she told me, and I had to agree. But I didn't know quite what to do about it. True, the cats should not be here. But the cats were only doing what came naturally to cats."

Masson, like Jim Stevenson in Galveston, found himself caught in a classic squeeze between two equal but conflicting values: the rights of individual animals set against the health of the overall ecosystem. It's a battle that rages in philosophy departments across the country. "From an animal-welfare perspective, confining cats and shooting the cat, in the Galveston example, is wrong," says J. Baird Callicott, a philosophy professor at the University of North Texas. Callicott, a past president of the International Society for Environmental Ethics, taught one of the nation's first environmental ethics courses in 1971. He went on to say, however, that "from an environmental-ethics perspective it's right, because a whole species is at stake. Personally, I think environmental ethics should trump animal-welfare ethics. But just as personally, animal-welfare ethicists think the opposite."

Out of curiosity, I boiled down the Jim Stevenson case and sent it to a few environmental-ethics professors. Most agreed with Callicott: shoot the cat.

"You're trading a feral cat, an exotic animal that doesn't belong naturally on the landscape, against piping plovers, which evolved as natural fits in that environment," reasons Holmes Rolston III, a Colorado State University professor who is considered one of the deans of American environmental philosophy. "And it trades an endangered species, piping plovers, against cats, which as a species are in no danger whatsoever. Suffering—the pain of the cat versus the pain of the plover eaten by the cat—is irrelevant in this case."

Ultimately, Jeffrey Masson sided with the animal-welfare school. Confining his cats indoors, he decided, would be unfair to the cats. "A cat needs to hunt to survive—that is, they have the instinct to hunt," he said. "Even if you could extinguish that instinct, should you? We already take their sexuality away. There are people who declaw their cats. How far do we take this before we completely destroy the animal?"

One point in the case against cats is undisputed: they destroy island ecosystems. A variant of the African wildcat, domestic cats probably first cozied up to humans in Egypt several thousand years ago. They populated the globe by riding the coattails of trade and empire. Cats were welcome members of sailing expeditions because of their small size, their agreeable temperament, and their talent for killing shipboard rats. The British navigator James Cook was a veritable Johnny Appleseed of the cat. Cook brought tabbies on his eighteenth-century voyages around the Pacific, many of which were dropped off or stolen along the way.

The newcomers came ashore teeth first. Most oceanic islands had no mammalian predators before human contact, so native birds evolved with little ability to elude cats. Many were ground-nesters. Some lost, or never gained, the ability to fly. In Hawaii, at least thirty species or subspecies of forest birds were decimated or extirpated between 1870 and 1930, partly because cats ate them. In 1894, a lighthouse keeper's cat on an island off New Zealand proudly presented his owner with dead specimens of a bird then unknown to science, thus discovering and extinguishing the Stephens Island wren in a single year. Forty years ago, when the Swiss ecologist Vinzenz Ziswiler added up the number of birds wiped out by introduced predators, he found that cats were implicated in seventeen of forty-three extinctions. The cat's only rivals were the rat (fourteen extinctions) and the mongoose (nine). As the naturalist Christopher Lever once wrote, "The list of species they have helped to exterminate or endanger reads like a roll call of avian disaster."

But continents and islands are different. Continental birds had defenses against clawed mammals, so cats weren't a problem. Or such was the comfortable conventional wisdom until recently in the United States, which has one in four of the world's cats. The idea was challenged in 1987, when two biologists found that cats in a small English village were killing a surprising number of birds—nearly three hundred by seventy-eight cats in a single year. American biologists followed up with a study of cat kills in rural Wisconsin. John Coleman, a wildlife ecologist with the Great Lakes Indian Fish and Wildlife Commission, and Stanley Temple, a University of Wisconsin professor, estimated that the state's 1.4 to 2 million rural cats were killing between 8 million and 219 million birds every year.

Though that range was so large as to be of limited value, alarms went off in the birding world. If cats were taking out that many birds in a single state, imagine the carnage nationwide! Conservation groups urged cat owners to keep their pets indoors. The American Bird Conservancy suggested cat leashes.

Cat defenders scrambled to stay ahead of the story. They pointed out deficiencies in the Wisconsin study and said, correctly, that the situation couldn't be simplified into a kills-per-cat formula. Some cats were expert hunters. Others didn't hunt at all. The Wisconsin study dealt only with rural cats, and the authors didn't look at whether the cats were taking down rare species or common starlings.

Cat advocates love to attack the Wisconsin study, but the more you delve into the scientific literature, the more the Wisconsin study looks like a red herring used by cat defenders to divert attention from more grounded research. In the past decade, at least a dozen studies published in top scientific journals like *Biological Conservation, Journal of Zoology,* and *Mammal Review* have chronicled the problem of cat predation of small mammals and birds. The takeaway is clear: cats are a growing environmental concern because they are driving down some native bird populations—on islands, to be sure, but also in ecologically sensitive continental areas. At hot spots along the Pacific, Atlantic, and Gulf coasts, cat predation is a growing threat to shorebirds and long-distance migrants. And as wild habitat becomes more fragmented by human development, even some inland species are under increasing pressure from both house cats and their feral cousins.

In southern New Jersey, feral cats are killing migrating shorebirds, including a number of endangered species. In the scrubland canyons of Southern California, researchers have found that where coyote populations decline, the non-bird-eating carnivores are often replaced by domestic cats. Cat predation then leads to a decline in the abundance of native birds like the California quail, the greater roadrunner, and the cactus wren.

On the big island of Hawaii, the problem approaches crisis proportions. The feral cats of Mauna Loa, the island's active volcano, are decimating Hawaiian petrels, a seabird that nests in the volcano's lava crevices and takes off on foraging runs to the Aleutian Islands—a round trip of more than 4,500 miles.

Several years ago, Fern Duvall, a wildlife biologist with the Hawaii Department of Land and Natural Resources, compared two Hawaiian islands: one with a high feral cat population, the other without any cats at all. He looked at fledging rates of seabirds, which measures the percentage of chicks that successfully leave the nest. On the cat island, only 13 percent of the chicks made it out alive. On the cat-free island, 83 percent survived.

Cats aren't the only bird killers in Hawaii. Mongooses prey on birds, too. The difference, Duvall says, is that mongooses tend to take one or two birds and be satisfied. Cats can go postal. "We've had as many as 123 wedgetail shearwaters in one colony killed by a single cat," he said. "Adult shearwaters are clumsy on the ground, and cats will come in at night and rip the skulls off the shearwater chicks. When you come upon the aftermath in the morning, it's pretty horrendous."

A few years ago, the State of Hawaii's Department of Health considered a feeding ban on public lands as a way to tamp down the feral population. Cat advocates descended on the state capital, and state officials quickly realized they were throwing rocks at a hornet's nest. "The public outcry killed it," Fern Duvall recalled. "The health department didn't realize what it was getting into. People who own cats are very emotionally attached to them—even feral cats that aren't their own—and they're extremely vocal."

The day after our initial meeting in Galveston, Jim Stevenson and I drove down the Texas coast looking for birds. San Luis Pass was our first stop. As we strolled through patches of spartina grass, it wasn't hard to see why birds and birders would flock here. Galveston Bay is a shallow, fertile, six-hundred-square-mile estuary where the Trinity and San Jacinto Rivers mix with the saltwater of the gulf to produce an eruption of life. The hourglass of one of the main North American flyways narrows to its waist here, and the bay provides a safe, nourishing pit stop for neotropical migrants making their way to and from Central and South America. Stevenson swung his arms in an arc and named the birds around us like a trick shooter nailing tossed cards: "Four stilts, two laughing gulls, three godwits, a flock of royal terns, clapper rails and—there he is—one piping plover."

We watched the plover dash across the sand in short spurts, hunting for insects and worms. Piping plovers live and breed on beaches from Newfoundland to North Carolina. They winter along the southern Atlantic and Gulf Coasts. Hat makers nearly wiped them out during the nineteenth century, but the passage of the Migratory Bird Treaty Act of 1918 allowed them to recover. Postwar prosperity brought vacation houses and beach resorts (and cats) to the Atlantic coast, disturbing millions of acres of plover nesting ground. At last count, the species' Atlantic population was down to fewer than 1,800 pairs.

"At night, the plovers tend to roost under the dunes against the bridge," Stevenson said. "They sleep on the ground. It's easy pickings for those cats." Under the bridge, I spotted an old plastic tray and a golf ball hanging down on a fishing line—a toy for the cats. A couple of gnarled ferals peeked out from some bushes.

Until the early 1980s, municipalities contained feral cats the old-fashioned way: they shot them. Or they trapped and killed them. "It was considered pest control," says Roger Tabor, the British biologist. Tabor helped change that in the 1970s with his research on feral cats in London. He found that ferals weren't loners. They lived in highly social colonies, and killing them didn't work. If you removed some cats, others simply took their place. Tabor called it the vacuum effect.

Other methods were tried. A cat birth-control pill failed because you couldn't control who ate it—set out a dish of spiked cat chow and you might affect the local raccoon population. Feeding bans were, as in Hawaii, shouted down or ignored. In the early 1980s, a number of cat activists began experimenting with a technique known as trap-neuter-return, T.N.R., which involved capturing feral cats, spaying or neutering them, then returning them to their colonies. T.N.R. seemed to work, and the movement spread. There are now several hundred groups that practice T.N.R. in the United States.

The problem with T.N.R., bird advocates contend, is that it doesn't eliminate the problem. "We appreciate the neutering," says Jim Cramer, a spokesman for the U.S. Fish and Wildlife Service's New Jersey field office. "The problem is the release. Even neutered, well-fed cats are hunters."

Stevenson said he tried to work with the local feral cat people. "People have dumped cats at San Luis Pass for years," he told me. "I've tried to have dialogue with the trap-neuter-return people, tried to tell them their cats are wreaking havoc with wild bird populations. A few years ago, we ran an ad offering to pay for an outdoor enclosure, to keep the cats in. We got no takers. I've encouraged city officials to do something about the cats out there, and they did nothing."

We talked about the drop in bird population. "We've lost 40 percent of our migrant songbirds in the last twenty-five years—a lot of this is why," he said, peering out at dozens of new vacation condominiums going up along the shore. "We've taken away their food source and their habitat. Double whammy. Then they get here, and those migrants, man, they're beat. For the cats, it's easy pickings. They're popping birds like they were M&M's."

In the late afternoon, we turned around and headed for home. Our route took us back past the San Luis Pass bridge just when John Newland happened to be out feeding the feral cats. Stevenson dropped me off—he wanted nothing to do with the toll taker—and I greeted Newland as he poured out about four pounds of Meow Mix. "I feed them twice a day," he told me in a Texas twang. The sound of the food hitting the tray drew cats from between the rocks.

"How many cats are there?" I asked.

"I'd say about fifteen to twenty," he said. "I can't keep up with the babies. But the babies don't last long. Maybe one out of ten survive. We got coyotes, owls, hawks out here. I've seen owls carry my babies off."

I asked him about Jim Stevenson.

"I've got pictures of the cats he shot," Newland said angrily. "He shot a mother and a baby in their bed, splattered all over the wall." Newland pointed to some grimy blankets strewn on a concrete shelf—feral-cat beds. "He shot one off the rocks here; you can see the bloodstain. The one he got caught doing was right there by that food tray. He shot her there, pregnant, and she died."

This was the first I'd heard of Stevenson shooting more than one cat. "This wasn't the first time your cats were shot?" I asked.

"Three days before he killed that pregnant cat, my coworkers heard four shots, saw a car going off toward the beach. It was his little Chevy compact."

I left Newland and caught up to Jim Stevenson and his Chevy compact a few hundred yards from the bridge. "The toll taker says that wasn't the only cat you shot," I said. "He says you've been shooting at the cats for a while."

Stevenson grew quiet. "What I would say to that," he finally told me, "is that if that's so, why doesn't he have any evidence to support that accusation?"

We drove along in silence for a while. Then Stevenson spotted a dead bird on the side of the road. He stopped to check it out. "It's a yellow-bellied cuckoo," he said. He held the dead bird tenderly in his palm, ran his fingers through its soft feathers and explained in great detail the cuckoo's fascinating toe structure.

Shortly after leaving Galveston, I traveled to Portland, Oregon, to see the Wildlife Care Center, an emergency room operated by the city's Audubon Society. Every year the center cares for three thousand injured and diseased animals. In the process, center officials have compiled a rare and significant set of data. Since 1995, they have analyzed how all the wild animals admitted have been injured. The results are remarkable. Estimates for cat-injured animals, mostly birds, accounted for nearly one-quarter of all admittances. Other causes paled: car accidents (14 percent), window strikes (5 percent), dog-caused injuries (3 percent).

"The biggest complaint we get is cats," Bob Sallinger, conservation director of the Portland Audubon Society, told me. "The statistics are actually misleading. We only record an injury as cat-caused if the person saw the cat injure the bird. I'm kind of a stickler on that. A huge number of the injuries we record as 'unknown' are consistent with cat injuries, and the birds recorded as 'orphaned' are often that way because their mothers were caught by cats. . . . We often say that up to 40 percent of the injuries we see are cat related."

On the morning I visited, a woman came in with an injured scrub jay. "One of my cats caught it," the woman explained. Glancing at a "Cats Indoors!" brochure, she said somewhat sheepishly, "My cats are indoor-outdoor. I half expected a lecture from the people here, but I felt responsible for the bird, so I came anyway."

Sallinger skipped the lecture and gave the bird to Karen Munday, an urban-wildlife specialist, who took it into an adjoining room and laid it out.

"This one's got a wing abrasion and puncture wounds," she said. That's likely a fatal diagnosis. A cat's teeth and gums contain enough bacteria to overwhelm a bird's immune system. "What usually kills the bird isn't the puncture; it's the infection," Munday explained. "A bird is more likely to survive a gunshot than a cat bite."

Despite the number of cat-caused injuries, bird and cat advocates have achieved a rare détente in Portland. Sallinger works with the Feral Cat Coalition of Oregon to keep cats in check near critical wildlife refuges.

Later that afternoon, I met up with Carma Crimins, a feral-cat-colony caretaker, in Portland's Sellwood district. Since 1995, the Feral Cat Coalition of Oregon has spayed or neutered more than thirty thousand ferals. Given the superfecundity of cats, a little back-of-the-envelope math shows that their T.N.R. program has kept at least one hundred thousand potential ferals out of the system. Crimins, a stylish woman in her early fifties, manages two colonies in the city. One is located behind a small grocery store; the other, in an abandoned factory.

Crimins led me to the grocery-store colony. A half dozen cats prowled around an open-air storage area, climbing up rusting grocery carts, and lying on flattened boxes. "There's Betty, Anita, Helen, the boys Tom and Vic, and mother Maybelle," Crimins said. This was a controlled population. A few years ago, Crimins said, forty to fifty cats lived here. Using the T.N.R. method, Crimins swept up the little kittens and put them into good homes. Feral kittens are easily socialized to humans. It's extremely difficult—some say impossible—for adult ferals to adjust to our presence. Crimins trapped the adults and had them spayed or neutered. Without constant batches of kittens, the colony stabilized at about ten cats, where it remains today.

As Crimins told me this, I noticed that the cats had all vanished. "Where'd they go?" I asked.

"They're still here, watching us," Crimins said. "They don't know you, so they're hiding out."

It occurred to me that this was the crux of the feral cat problem. If you came at the feral cat advocates with blunt force—with feeding bans or old-fashioned trap-remove-and-kill programs—they would fight, claws extended, in the political arena. But if they lost, they wouldn't give up. They would vanish into cracks and crevices, slinking out to feed their cats when the coast was clear.

As his court date approached, Jim Stevenson was confident that a jury would vindicate his decision. "The cat was chasing an endangered species," he told me. "I'd tried for years to get people to do something about those cats. So I decided that I needed to take that cat out." The charge against him, animal cruelty, carried a maximum penalty of two years in prison and a $10,000 fine.

The state's case hinged mainly on the contention that the murdered cat was a pet belonging to John Newland, the tollbooth attendant. "They're using the term 'feral cat,' but that's not the situation here," Paige Santell, the Galveston County assistant district attorney, told me. (Until recently, killing a feral cat was a legal gray area in Texas. State legislators, inspired partly by the Stevenson case, made it illegal earlier this year.)

If the state proved that the cat belonged to Newland, however, it could have devastating ramifications for T.N.R. programs across the country. Endangered birds are protected by the Endangered Species Act, and all migratory birds are protected by the Migratory Bird Treaty Act. If feral-colony caretakers are held to be legally responsible for the cats, they could conceivably be charged with violations of either act by aiding and abetting the killing of endangered or migratory birds. Before the trial, in fact, Stevenson's lawyer, Tad Nelson, considered reading John Newland his Miranda rights—just to make the point—but decided against it. ("He's just a sweet old man who loves cats," Nelson said. "There's no reason to beat him up over this.")

Bringing the Endangered Species Act into play could force states and the federal government to take a more active role in managing feral cats. It could potentially lead to the development of a new kind of wildlife management, one that recognizes the cat's half-domesticated, half-wild ecological niche and its unique political position in America. Industrial and residential development is carving the continent into islands of wildlife habitat. Birds are increasingly left with isolated patches of forest and seashore, surrounded by hostile territory. The feral cats under the San Luis Pass bridge are important only because the piping plovers have nowhere else to go. The rest of Galveston Island has been given over to vacation condos and seafood restaurants.

The same predicament is unfolding all over the country. Bob Sallinger told me about the loss of bird habitat in Portland, which is widely considered one of the greenest cities in America. "Habitat loss is the No. 1 problem, no doubt," he said, "but that's all the more reason to deal with these secondary problems. We don't have the luxury of saying, well, there's all this habitat out there, and the birds will recover. It's not, and they won't."

The cat killer's trial lasted a full week. Jurors heard testimony for three days and then retired to consider Jim Stevenson's fate. On November 16, the jury returned to the courtroom and addressed the Galveston County district judge, Frank Carmona. After two days spent struggling with Stevenson's act and the problem of cats and birds, the twelve jurors pronounced themselves hopelessly deadlocked. They simply couldn't decide. The case was dismissed.

The war between cats and birds—and among their protectors—continues.

15 An Unlimited Take of Ugly
The Bullhead Catfish

Kyhl Lyndgaard

> Water-eager eyes,
> Mouth-gate open
> And strong spine urging, driving;
> And desirous belly gulping.
>
> —D. H. Lawrence, "The Fish"

ON ONE OF THE FIRST TIMES I was allowed to go fishing without adults, my friend Oscar and I were dropped off at tiny Lake Sagatagan in central Minnesota. We used the classic combination of worm and bobber and began catching one fish after another. The fish were bullheads: black with muddy bellies, about eight to ten inches long, with whiskers and big mouths. We kept the largest ones in a five-gallon bucket to eat later. Oscar's father was disgusted when he came by an hour later to pick us up. He wanted to throw our prized catch onto the grass to die and rot like trash. Indeed, fishermen routinely toss bullheads onto the lakeshore to slowly suffocate, which is the first introduction many people have to these fish. I've walked along idyllic lakes, only to be startled by the smell and sight of rotting bullheads, and such a display must help persuade people that bullheads are ugly. A recent *Washington Post* article compares a belted kingfisher to a dead bullhead on a fishing pier, stating that "the beautiful and ugly go hand in hand."[1]

But on that long-ago summer day, Oscar and I prevailed, keeping the bullheads to eat for dinner. The fish were tasty, and Oscar's father grudgingly admitted they were edible. The aesthetics, physiology, and culture that surround the "ugliness" of the bullhead has occasioned many divergent interpretations of its worth and appearance. While ugliness is not necessarily in the eye of the beholder, the outward appearance of the bullhead should first be understood as a case of form following function. Nonetheless, the form is certainly arresting and has led to a surprisingly varied relationship between humans and this unique fish.

I'd like to start, as Lawrence does in his poem, with the eye. Bullheads are often thought of as being an ungainly, inelegant fish, and one preliminary reason for this aesthetic reaction can be traced to their eyes. Bullhead eyes are set low on a relatively large and wide head and can be accurately described as beady. By looking at Edmund Burke's ideas of beauty and the eye, we can see why bullheads are not always looked at with pleasure by humans. "The beauty of the eye consists, first, in its *clearness;* . . . none are pleased with an eye whose water (to use that term) is dull and muddy. We are pleased with the eye in this view, on the principle upon which we like diamonds, clear water, glass, and such like transparent substances."[2] The "water-eager eyes" of the bullhead are dull and muddy in appearance, yet the eyes of the bullhead are exactly as large as they need to be. Since bullheads rely on senses of taste, smell, and hearing more than sight, their eyes are not especially large or important.

If the eyes cannot be seen as beautiful, what about the waters the fish live in? Surely they are more transparent. The statue labeled the "World's Largest Bullhead" is at Crystal Lake, Iowa. Borrowing Burke's examples of "diamonds, clear water, glass," it would seem that a place named Crystal Lake should fit the bill. Created by Carl Frick in 1958, the bullhead statue is twelve feet from head to tail and is on a stone pedestal.[3] Perhaps the only book that discusses the statue is *Oddball Iowa.* This quirky travel guide is not exactly a work of art criticism, but it is certainly appreciative of what its subtitle calls "really strange places."[4] What of the lake itself? The water is shallow and muddy. Crystal Lake is a eutrophic—and at times hypereutrophic—lake, with a water clarity level that rarely exceeds a half meter.[5] In other words, if you wade into the lake, you are more likely to step on a bullhead than to see one.

Perhaps the appreciation of the people that live in rural Iowa for both bullheads and lakes points to the scarcity of both commodities—or an excellent sense of humor. Also, consider the small Minnesota town of Waterville, just north of the Iowa border. Waterville residents have dubbed their town the "Bullhead Capital of the United States." Since 1964, Bullhead Days has been celebrated as the town's community festival. Held the second weekend after Memorial Day, Waterville's not atypical small-town festival has such events as a tractor pull, parade, fireworks, and demolition derby. They put their own spin on the festival with deep-fried bullhead cuisine.[6] Hugh Valient, a fisheries supervisor, noted that some Waterville residents complained about a drop in bullheads after a new sewage treatment plant improved water quality in Sakatah and Tetonka Lakes.[7] Clearly, these people are fond of bullheads. I don't necessarily mean to suggest a link between the survival of small, out-of-the-way farming communities in the Midwest and bullheads, but these bullhead appreciators do seem to share a common landscape.

From the eyes of a bullhead, the muddy water of Iowa's Crystal Lake is more beautiful than that of a cold mountain stream. For one thing, the same reason the eyes are small explains why the bullhead prefers a stagnant habitat. Bullheads locate their food sources by smell and taste. Bullheads have been proven to lose much of their ability to locate a chemical signal if they are in flowing water, as they cannot continue their normal swimming patterns and food tracking. Furthermore, competition from other fish species that are "visually oriented and oxyphilic" is reduced in a habitat such as Crystal Lake, which is turbid and low in oxygen content.[8]

Bullheads not only have ugly eyes, they live in ugly waters, at least according to Burke. The places these fish populate include artificial wetlands such as dikes and seasonal marshes. Unusually varied and flexible in their spawning patterns, bullheads seem to thrive on human-caused disturbances that other species cannot adapt to as rapidly.[9] They also survive in grossly polluted places like Maryland's Anacostia River and South River. These two rivers have left bullheads with record cancer rates; 70 percent of the bullheads in the Anacostia suffer from liver cancer. In the Anacostia, a link to polynuclear aromatic hydrocarbons was established. These chemicals are in the river due to "urban runoff laden with car exhaust residue, pavement sealants and asphalt particles."[10] Addressing the lack of a fish consumption advisory in the South River, the rather alarming statement from a spokesman with the Maryland Department of the Environment was as follows: "If you catch any fish that looks strange . . . throw it back."[11] Of course, the level of chemical toxicity in a fish's tissues cannot be measured by a fisherman's gaze. The spokesman, who should know better, simply suggests that malformed, ugly fish should not be eaten. As bullheads are the focus of the article, the obvious meaning of the statement is that they should not be eaten due to their appearance.

Bullheads can even live in radiation-contaminated waters, as exemplified by the existence of bullheads in Pond B, Savannah River Site, South Carolina. A study of a population of yellow bullheads in this abandoned nuclear reactor reservoir examined the levels of cesium-137 in their tissues.[12] Yet bullheads—for all their value as a bioindicator species—are not found solely in the most impacted environments. They have naturally occurred in North American waters for hundreds of thousands of years and have a place in the diversity of local ecosystems. They reproduce in huge numbers, and are often the only sizable fish in shallow ponds, capable of repopulating lakes rapidly after a cold winter when most fish die from low oxygen levels in iced-over waters. In fact, this is yet another place to see bullheads rotting on the shore, as a portion of bullhead populations will succumb to winter-kill in northern ponds. Rather than seeing this as ugly, it could be taken as a reminder of the stark challenges of survival.

Seen as an annoyance by anglers who would prefer to catch other fish, the decision to revile bullheads for the simple act of survival in shallow, turbid waters that kill almost everything else seems to miss the point of their physiological traits. Perhaps some of the lack of respect for bullheads comes from official fishing regulations, which, unwittingly or not, reinforce cultural perceptions on the value fish have. Should a person decide to fish at the home of the "World's Largest Bullhead," an unlimited take of bull-heads is permitted by the state of Iowa. Other U.S. states have similarly liberal regulations, with many limits being set at one hundred. These numbers stand in contrast to game fish limits for various species of trout and bass, for example, which are often set in the low single digits. Also, bullheads are not normally differentiated between the various species that occur across the country.

Game fish bias has been dramatically played out in places such as Bass Lake, near Mankato in south-central Minnesota. In 1988, this lake was judged to be dominated by "a fish community of low-recreational value— black bullheads and carp."[13] Perhaps the name Bass Lake, which refers to a fish of high recreational value, was no longer as applicable as the residents wished. The lake association (home- and landowners) backed a Department of Natural Resources (DNR) plan to chemically "reclaim" the lake. There were no fishing limits that season, and then the fish were all killed by the application of the chemical rotenone. Bass Lake was subsequently restocked with game fish such as northern pike, largemouth bass, walleye, bluegill sunfish, and crappie. Yet within ten years, bullheads somehow became reestablished. Perhaps because bullhead are more resistant to low oxygen, and rotenone kills fish by reducing oxygen, a few bullheads were able to survive and were discovered only years later. When the DNR suggested another chemical reclamation, the lake association's politics had shifted and there was considerable opposition. Along with the stocking efforts, the DNR also worked to improve private septic systems along the lakeshore and to restore wetlands in the watershed. If the water is clean, bullheads will generally not dominate but will remain as a less noticeable part of the community.[14] But Bass Lake is far from alone, and other lakes continue to be chemically treated to remove bullheads.

North Dakota's Crown Butte Dam, west of Mandan, was treated with rotenone in September 2005. The fishery was then stocked with largemouth bass, sunfish, and trout. The local newspaper used phrases about the bullhead population and the reservoir such as "knocked back to zero," and "chemically renovated."[15] Fisheries supervisor Jason Lee said, "We will . . . take care of the bullhead problem."[16] Clearly, these evaluative words and connections are deeply ingrained in people's minds, and bullheads are subconsciously denigrated. Bullheads create "problems" that can be "treated" like a malady, "renovated" like a dilapidated apartment building, or "reclaimed" like an alfalfa field full of thistle.

At least in North America, bullheads are given some credit for being a native fish, unlike various species of carp or sea lampreys decried for their invasive alien status. Where they have been introduced, most notably Western Europe and New Zealand, bullheads are uniformly reviled. R. M. McDowell writes that in New Zealand "the importation of the North American brown bullhead . . . in 1877 was something of an enigma."[17] McDowell fails to find any commentator from 1877 to the present day that can explain a benefit to introducing bullheads. He suggests that the fyke nets that eelers used inadvertently allowed bullheads to spread widely across New Zealand, but the appearance of bullheads in additional lakes during the 1970s "defies any sensible explanation and must have been the action of some irresponsible biological hooligan."[18] Not only are the fish ugly, but the people who planted them are inexplicably misguided. Many studies have been conducted in the last decade around different methods of controlling invasive bullhead populations in New Zealand and in Europe, all with varying, but generally poor, rates of success.

The bullhead has many discordant features that seem anachronistic in modern times. It is a visual hodgepodge of whiskers, mouth, skin, and spine. Yet this very disunity gives hidden strength and presence. Mark Cousins argues for the undeniability of ugliness: "That the ugly *is,* is central to this argument."[19] Nobody is able to look at a bullhead and dismiss its appearance. The fish demands attention. Rather than a harmonic whole, bullheads feature a variety of highly specialized structures that are unusual, yet obvious, to the casual observer. I discussed the eye of the bullhead briefly, but additional physiological features that are integral to the successful adaptation of bullheads are worth a close look.

Bullhead catfish *(Ameiurus)* are represented by seven extant species, which had diverged from their common ancestor with other Ictalurids by the early Eocene.[20] Bullheads look similar to other catfish but their tails are squared-off instead of forked. All bullhead species are much smaller than most catfish, due in part to their relatively early evolutionary divergence, and rarely grow larger than ten inches long and a pound in weight. Their scientific name, *Ameiurus,* refers to their broad mouths—or what Lawrence calls the "mouth-gate." The common name "bullhead" was originally applied in the fifteenth century to a smaller fish in England that does not have whiskers, the sculpin. Eventually, "bullhead" was applied to this group of New World catfish.[21] Perhaps it is not surprising that people also had negative feelings toward the fish originally known as bullheads, due in large part to their ungainly appearance: "The Millers-thumb, or Bull-head, is a Fish of no pleasing shape. . . . It has a head big and flat, much greater than is suitable to his Body; a mouth very wide and usually gaping."[22]

The structures Lawrence poetically describes as "strong spine urging, driving" are critical to the success of bullheads. The barbed pectoral and dorsal spines are lockable and mildly venomous, making any threatened bullhead effectively larger in size than it really is and making it a more difficult quarry for predators. Early studies proved this hypothesis, showing that the spines of bullheads offered protection from herons.[23] Even for anglers, the task of taking a bullhead off the hook is much easier with thick leather gloves to ward off the spines and to get a solid grip on the slimy, scaleless body. My father recalls that he was told over and over when fishing southwestern Minnesota ponds in the 1950s to wear gloves when taking a bullhead off the hook or he'd get a partially paralyzed hand, like his Uncle Leonard.[24] People—often children—wading in shallow lakes in the spring have even been injured by stepping on schools of baby bullheads. The affects of coming in contact with a barbed spine are generally a white raised spot, not unlike a bee sting, accompanied by a stinging and even numbing sensation for up to fifteen minutes. While some debate continues about the venomous nature of the spines, the most comprehensive treatments add bullheads to the list of venomous catfishes.[25] Their defensive unpleasantness and ugly appearance has helped to push bullheads, in most peoples' minds, to a tier well below most game fish. Instead of a wealthy businessman fly-fishing a clean mountain stream in waders on the weekend, the people catching bullheads are farmers and children.

Although not beautiful, the bullhead is imbued with personality. This can be seen in the general argument by Cousins: "Monsters and characters from low life belong to a class of objects which are deemed ugly; it is that they are too strongly individual, are too much themselves."[26] Or to be more specific, as in a 1967 article in the *New York Times*: "The bearded lady at the circus receives much attention, not because she is pretty—she's not—but because she's interesting. All right, what is the ichthyological equivalent? What fish is so ugly it hurts, but is so interesting as to be lovable? Of course, one has to say the bullhead, the bearded one."[27] Others have made similar arguments, such as Rufus Jarman did in a 1954 *Saturday Evening Post* article, "Don't Sneer at the Catfish." Jarman suggests that catfish and bullheads have more personality than "normal" fish, and attributes to the magazine *Punch* the line that "the catfish is so ugly he is, in a way, attractive."[28] Bullheads are seen as highly individual in ways that populations of other fish are not. This personality can actually make bullheads attractive as pets.

Home aquariums sometimes feature bullheads, which, not surprisingly, are hardy tank residents. Their apparent ugliness is a deterrent to some, no doubt, yet other hobbyists find this ugliness lends bullheads a certain appeal. Monsterfishkeepers.com discuss bullheads as a good, if slightly small, option for raising in a fish tank. One hobbyist especially interested in the monstrous wrote in a 2007 online discussion about bullheads (a discussion that stretched to nearly one hundred entries): "I just caught a 11 inch bullhead its in my tank right now it had a hook in its mouth and a missing eye so I decided to keep him [sic]." The individuality that bullheads possess by dint of their unorthodox appearance was only enhanced by that particular fish's physical scars.

Despite the informal writing observed in online discussion boards, bullheads have been the subject of higher-quality prose. Writers similarly find bullheads to have a rich symbolic potential due to their appearance and other physiological traits. Michael Lohre, in his short story "Bullheads," from *Atlantic Monthly* (2005), chooses a fish for the elderly protagonist to identify with: "This was not a majestic muskie or a delicious walleye; no ferociously toothed northern pike or blue-bellied crappie. . . . No, this was a bottom-mucking bullhead, and damn if Leroy Johnson didn't almost come to tears for the spiny devil before he finally kicked it off the homemade dock."[29] Johnson, a retired Minnesota farmer, does not explicitly identify with the bullhead because of his own appearance, but he does have connections to the fish. Johnson had once rescued several bullheads from boys using them as the balls in a home-run derby. Throughout the short story, Johnson struggles to define his ethics and core beliefs, noting that he is not a "tree hugger" but that he respects animals.[30]

Johnson recalls moments from his life that were traumatic, including his wife's losing battle with lung cancer. The act of breathing is important to this story, and just as the bullhead on the dock struggled for air, she too struggles on her deathbed: "His wife meant more to him than the bullhead, so Leroy was confused to find them edited together in his memory's slideshow. . . . The bullhead had become mythic somehow."[31] Near the end of the story, Johnson jumps into a frigid lake to rescue his aged dog, who can barely keep her nose above the water and is unable to break through the rushes lining the bank. Johnson soon dies of hypothermia after rescuing his dog, and in his final moments pushes his fingers into the ground on shore, mirroring the act of emerging from an iced-over lake: "The ground was hard, but he had enough energy to break through its frozen surface."[32] The bullhead of the title is therefore given a plural form to emphasize the protagonist's connection to actual fish. Our common need to breathe and connect with others suggests that even the most humble—be they people or bullheads—are worth something. At the opening of the story, Johnson is moved to feelings about the bullhead because on the dock "its death was being prolonged needlessly."[33] As the story closes, his death comes quickly, as Johnson accomplished what he needed to in his life.

Bullheads are not necessarily beautiful, but they do have a depth that Lohre and others have appreciated. The Ojibwe people, or Anishinabeg, in the Midwest and Great Lakes regions chose the bullhead as a totemic animal based on the belief that this animal "symbolized an ideal to be sought, attained, and perpetuated."[34] Bullheads and other fish totems generally are seen as teachers: "fishes are hidden behind rocks, live unseen in the dark depths, but remain steadfast in the swirling currents."[35] Bullheads are particularly instructional, perhaps, because adult fish guard their eggs, and they even stay with the newly hatched offspring to protect them and keep them together until the young are nearly an inch long.

Schools of baby bullheads hatch when the water warms each spring, and the fish stay in large schools among the shallows for a couple of weeks. A parent can often be spotted, herding and protecting the school. At first, the young seem to be clouds of tadpoles, all head with thin, squirmy, pitch-black bodies. Up close, these small fry sport tiny whiskers and are quite endearing. Many children, with great delight, have caught baby bullheads from a dock with a cheap net. While those rather cute babies rapidly grow, losing some of their dramatic coloration and becoming muddier in appearance and slower in their movements, I believe the bullhead remains—at the least—an instructional animal for humans to study as it becomes uglier and larger. Indeed, my childhood fishing trip may have taught Oscar's father something about the worth of bullheads, or perhaps it was a lesson on the worth of bullheads to children that have not yet learned what ugliness looks like, which is of no small importance.

Notes

1. Bill Broadway, "Undoing the Damage to Sacred Banks; Interfaith Effort Plans Revival of the Anacostia River, Replenishment of Its Neighborhoods," *Washington Post,* October 30, 2004.

2. Edmund Burke, *A Philosophical Enquiry into the Origin of Our Ideas of the Sublime and Beautiful,* ed. James T. Boulton (1757; Notre Dame, Ind.: University of Notre Dame Press, 1958), 118.

3. Crystal Lake, Iowa, "Fun Facts," http://www.crystallakeia.com.

4. Jerome Pohlen, *Oddball Iowa: A Guide to Some Really Strange Places* (Chicago: Chicago Review Press, 2005).

5. Iowa Department of Natural Resources, "Iowa Lakes Information System, Report Year 2007: Crystal Lake, Hancock County," http://limnology.eeob .iastate.edu/.

6. Waterville, Minnesota, "Bullhead Days," http://www.watervillemn.com/.

7. Nathan Mathews, phone interview of Hugh Valient, August 2, 2005, sent to author via e-mail, August 4, 2005.

8. Etienne Baras and Philippe Laleye, "Ecology and Behaviour of Catfishes," in *Catfishes,* ed. Gloria Arratia et al. (Enfield, N.H.: Science Publishers: 2003), 2:543.

9. J. Cucherousset et al., "Habitat Use of an Artificial Wetland by the Invasive Catfish *Ameiurus melas,*" *Ecology of Freshwater Fish* 15 (2006): 589–96.

10. Elizabeth Williamson, "Catfish in Md. River Have High Cancer Rates," *Washington Post,* January 25, 2006.

11. Richard McIntire, quoted in ibid.

12. Clark D. McCreedy et al., "Bioaccumulation of Cesium-137 in Yellow Bullhead Catfish *(Ameiurus Natalis)* Inhabiting an Abandoned Nuclear Reactor Reservoir," *Environmental Toxicology and Chemistry* 16, no. 2 (February 1997): 328–35.

13. Mathews, phone interview.

14. Ibid.

15. Richard Hinton, "Bullheads in Crown Butte to be Eradicated," *Bismarck Tribune,* September 20, 2005.

16. Jason Lee, quoted in ibid.

17. R. M. McDowell, *Gamekeepers for the Nation: The Story of New Zealand's Acclimatisation Societies 1861–1990* (Christchurch, New Zealand: Canterbury University Press, 1994), 221.

18. Ibid., 222.

19. Mark Cousins, "The Ugly," *AA Files; Annals of the Architectural Association School of Architecture* 28 (1994): 61.

20. Michael Hardman and Lotta M. Hardman, "The Relative Importance of Body Size and Paleoclimatic Change as Explanatory Variables Influencing Lineage Diversification Rate: An Evolutionary Analysis of Bullhead Catfishes (Siluriformes: Ictaluridae)," *Systematic Biology* 57, no. 1 (2008): 116–30.

21. Robert A. Palmatier. *Speaking of Animals: A Dictionary of Animal Metaphors* (Westport, Conn.: Greenwood Press, 1995), 49.

22. Izaak Walton, *The Compleat Angler* (1653; London: Nattali and Bond, 1860), 288.

23. Michael L. Fine and Friedrich Ladich, "Sound Production, Spine Locking, and Related Adaptations," in *Catfishes,* ed. Arratia et al., 1:252.

24. David Lyndgaard, interview by author, August 8, 2005.

25. Claude Perrière and Françoise Goudey-Perrière, "Poisonous Catfishes: Venom Apparatus, Acanthotoxins, Crinotoxins and Other Skin Secretions," in *Catfishes,* ed. Arratia et al., 1:291–314. See 297–99 in particular.

26. Cousins, "The Ugly," 61.

27. Oscar Godbout, "Scientific Survey Shows Bullheads Use Chin-Whiskers in Scenting Food," *New York Times,* April 23, 1967.

28. Rufus Jarman, "Don't Sneer at the Catfish," *Saturday Evening Post* 227, no. 8 (August 21, 1954): 22.

29. Michael Lohre, "Bullheads," *Atlantic Monthly* 295, no. 3 (April 2005): 117.

30. Ibid., 118.

31. Ibid., 119.

32. Ibid., 130.

33. Ibid., 117.

34. Basil Johnston, *Ojibway Heritage* (New York: Columbia University Press, 1976), 53.

35. Ibid., 70.

16 A Six-legged Guru

Fear and Loathing in Nature

Jeffrey A. Lockwood

WITHIN MINUTES, our hands are covered in feces and vomit. Our quarry, the prairie lubber grasshopper, is surely one of the most disgusting creatures to subdue. The largest of all insects on the Wyoming grasslands, *Brachystola magna* is reminiscent of the chewed cigar butts that I used to encounter jammed into ashtrays when I was a kid. They're about the same size and equally appealing. This is no dainty grasshopper capable of lithesome leaps—it has the heft of a breakfast sausage. Every summer we collect a few dozen of these creatures from the weedy roadsides in southeastern Wyoming. They make outstanding specimens for dissections in my Insect Anatomy and Physiology laboratory. But this is not the primary reason for bringing my students into intimate contact with these repulsive beasts. My real motive is both much simpler and more complex.

Most of my summer encounters with rangeland grasshoppers involve some version of "applied ecology," the academic euphemism that I prefer to "pest management," which sounds like a listing in the Yellow Pages. Despite the otherwise pedestrian tone of my work, developing methods to suppress grasshopper outbreaks has a certain cachet in rural Wyoming. Most folks respect, even admire, my efforts to defeat a worthy foe. After all, grasshoppers—especially locusts, a particular kind of grasshopper that forms swarms—are formidable and legendary enemies of agriculture. Human-versus-insect battles have been recounted in Western literature ranging from the book of Exodus ("Then the Lord said to Moses, 'Stretch out your hand over the land of Egypt for the locusts, that they may come upon the land of Egypt, and eat every plant in the land.'") to Laura Ingalls Wilder's Little House series (*On the Banks of Plum Creek* recounts an infestation in terrifying terms) and to my childhood encounters with the stirring language and vivid photos in *National Geographic* (the August 1969 article "Locusts: 'Teeth of the Wind'" stirred a sense of martial righteousness in combating an invading army of insects). So a sense of cultural honor comes with adding my own chapter to the epic human struggle against an insect menace. But, alas, there is no such glory in my encounters with the lubber grasshopper.

This species has none of the qualities of a worthy opponent. It is not a pest of any consequence since it infests weedy roadsides of no economic value. The creature favors the juicy sunflowers in the ditches, but there's no record of the insect doing harm to the fields of these plants that blanket the Midwest. A blitzkrieg by this species is out of the question, given that the lubberly beasts are incapable of flight, having only stub-like wings. Even a credible, ground-based assault on agriculture is probably too much work for these lethargic insects. And if they threatened farmers' fields, mounting a control program would be tantamount to picking a fight with the fat kid on the playground or beating up the town drunk. If their economic importance is nil, their ecological value is not much greater.

The lubber is hardly a keystone species, given that no other life-forms seem to depend on them. They are not known to be common prey of the birds or mammals of the prairie. Our best guess is that the grasshopper's population is kept in check by a combination of their food supply, disease, and parasites—none of which would be much affected by the absence of the lubbers. If the ecological notion that everything is connected to everything else is true, then it's a damn thin thread linking this creature to the rest of the prairie. I'm not willing to say that we know enough to say that any species can go extinct without serious ripple effects on the ecosystem, but if I were forced to pick an organism that had to disappear or else some horrific alternative was assured (philosophers love these sorts of thought experiments), the lubber grasshopper would be pretty close to the top of my list. Of course, I'd lose a first-rate subject for students in my dissection laboratories.

The greatest virtue of this grasshopper, at least from the peculiar perspective of a professor of entomology, is its size. My students struggle to find the various organs in bumblebees and cockroaches, converting the specimens into homogenized masses of insect tissue by the end of the period. But a big ol' prairie lubber—particularly if it is fresh-frozen until we get to the dissections midway through the fall semester—has the potential of revealing an internal anatomy that is both eerily familiar (the insect alimentary canal is highly reminiscent of the human digestive tract) and curiously alien (the insect breathes without lungs and circulates its blood without veins or arteries). All of which brings me to this creature's second-greatest virtue.

The lubber is, in principle, the easiest species of grasshopper to catch. However, the only way to gather them is by hand. An insect net is an effective means of capturing grass*hoppers* that are willing and able to live up to their names, but the net snares few of these lumbering creatures. They are clumsy behemoths, hopping with the agility of insect sumo wrestlers, hence their name of "lubbers." Grabbing a fat, flightless beast—the dodo of the insect world—is a simple matter. But catching this grasshopper is not the same thing as holding onto it.

The lubber may look dim-witted and benign, but appearances can be deceiving. Lurking beneath the bulging exoskeleton is a cantankerous and wily creature. One must be careful when accosting these grasshoppers because their hind legs sport rows of spines that they rake across the flesh of a would-be captor. This might partially explain their minor-at-best place in the vertebrate cuisine of the prairie. However, a clever predator (or entomologist) can neutralize this defensive maneuver by grabbing them by their hind legs. But wait—as they say on the cable infomercials—there's more. At this juncture of the capture, the lubbers resort to their most noteworthy tactic. They become utterly repulsive.

Their first and most revolting strategy in this regard is to regurgitate copiously. Many species exhibit this defensive behavior, and as kids we referred to grasshoppers "spitting tobacco juice." Indeed, the cola-colored fluid resembles the expectorant of tobacco chewers in its capacity to stain whatever it hits. Of course, a grasshopper isn't spitting masticated wads of chewed tobacco. Rather, it is heaving up masticated and liquefied sunflower leaves—the contents of its foregut, which is the anatomical equivalent of our stomach. The prairie lubber manages to produce this material in truly impressive quantities, smearing itself and its handler with the dark brown fluid. For this grasshopper, however, the effort to repulse its assailant is not complete.

The restrained grasshopper next begins to defecate prodigiously. As opposed to vomiting, this offensive approach to defense is not widely practiced among the lubber's brethren. Perhaps it wouldn't be particularly repugnant for most species, as grasshoppers generally produce very dry, compact fecal pellets the size of sesame seeds. The lubber, on the other hand, can produce a dozen mushy, mouse-like turds in quick succession. Perhaps the sunflowers, being rather more succulent than prairie grasses, provide enough fluid to allow this grasshopper the luxury of a softer stool. Thus, an experienced collector avoids the rear end of the grasshopper and holds the insect at bay for a few seconds until it has exhausted its colonic arsenal. If one is too hasty in dropping the repulsive creatures into a collecting bag, the grasshoppers quickly foul the container with smeared feces, making any future handling a most unpleasant prospect.

The excretory behaviors of the prairie lubber suggest a rather profound and profane form of interspecies communication. The information is transmitted between grasshoppers and other creatures—humans in particular. It doesn't take Dr. Doolittle to decipher the meaning because the insect has translated the message—"Put me down!"—into a language that we can readily comprehend. Nature does not offer many opportunities to encounter a communiqué so compelling to us and originating in a creature so different from us. This grasshopper has come to understand—at least in evolutionary terms, if not with regard to individual consciousness—what regurgitation and defecation mean to us. Sometimes, I wonder if a few of these creatures might even possess a vague sense of what they're telling me. There's always one or two who seem to engage in excretion with a perverse gusto beyond that required by strict necessity—defecation with an exclamation mark of sorts.

But, one might fairly object, couldn't the emptying of gut and bowels serve some noncommunicative function? After all, many creatures defecate when accosted by predators. Animal behaviorists explain that this often is a tactic for lightening the load of the prey during the ensuing run for their lives. But the lubber isn't about to outrun anything. A meadowlark, coyote, or mouse that can't keep pace with a flightless grasshopper that leaps eighteen inches on a good day isn't worthy of being called a predator. So if the lubber is not preparing to sprint but is exuding a repulsive message, how do I know that humans are the intended recipients?

The prairie lubber comes from a long line of lubbers, many of which feed on poisonous plants and sequester the toxins. These relatives sport the classic warning coloration of nasty-tasting insects—reds and yellows on a black background. However, the prairie lubber is a mottled green-and-tan with muted pinkish highlights. Hardly a memorable pattern, but then their diet of sunflowers with a dash of hoary vervain, wheatgrass, kochia, and prickly lettuce is not a recipe for generating toxic exudates. The excretions do not irritate the skin, they don't seem otherwise functional as physical defenses against vertebrates, nor does the material affect their kin. Tumbled together in a collecting bag, the grasshoppers wallow blissfully, unfazed by one another's gunk. But perhaps regurgitation and defecation are evolutionary echoes.

When asked about the prairie lubber's propensity for emptying its innards, my zoological and entomological colleagues proposed that this behavior might be a vestige of a time in which an ancestor successfully defended itself with foul-tasting or toxic exudates—the idea being that today's harmless lubber has retained this behavior because there's no cost to regurgitating and defecating in the last, desperate moments when a predator has you in its clutches. It might just work. By this line of reasoning, the fact that humans are revolted is merely an accidental collision of evolutionary trajectories. We find vomit and feces to be disgusting, and the lubber serendipitously benefits from our response.

It's a bit like how a teenage boy communicated his hotness to girls when I was growing up. Driving a Boss 302 Ford Mustang (nobody I knew could afford a Corvette) sent the message that he was cool and a bit dangerous—all for a base price of $3,720. Today, a guy driving a classic '70 Mustang isn't sending a message of youthful virility. Rather, he's letting prospective mates know that he can afford an automobile that goes for upward of $80,000. Same behavior, new message. The analogy isn't perfect because for modern-day lubbers, humans don't represent much of a threat, so repulsing them isn't a great advantage.

The crossing of evolutionary paths makes a fine story, but there is an alternative account that doesn't rely on the last resort of evolutionary biology. Phylogenetic inertia is the continuation of a character by virtue of its having little or no contemporary benefit but only a nominal cost. What if regurgitation and defecation evolved as a means of disgusting other creatures?

There is a long, albeit somewhat sparse, literature on the nature of disgust. In the nineteenth century, Darwin argued for this being an instinctual response while Freud maintained that it was socially inculcated. Today, the nature-or-nurture debate about the origins of traits has been largely dismissed as an unproductive dichotomization—the answer is almost invariably "both." There remain some Freudians who propose, for example, that defecation is the prototype of castration and the "very first purpose to which feces are put [is] the auto-erotic stimulation of the intestinal mucous membrane." Now, I relish a good dump as much as the next guy, but I find that neither the loss of my penis nor erotic gratification crosses my mind during such occasions. And there are some rather silly postmodern anthropologists who insist that everything is "constructed" (presumably this would include postmodernism itself, so that the deconstructionist snake latches onto its own tail and swallows itself).

Science doesn't hold all of the answers to life's mysteries, but Jill Toronchuk and George Ellis have reconstructed a most plausible evolutionary account of disgust. They contend that this emotion (it is one of the seven universal human emotions, along with anger, contempt, fear, happiness, sadness, and surprise) originated in the ancient capacity for distaste, a response that is evident in organisms with chemosensory systems (i.e., almost every living thing). This capacity then gave rise to taste aversion—the ability of an organism to associate a novel taste with an adverse physiological state. Not all creatures exhibit taste aversion, but it is no great leap of intelligence given that slugs, snails, and even roundworms can learn to shun novel flavors.

Aversion was the predecessor of genuine disgust, an emotional response that is no mere reflex. This cognitive state is seen in an array of vertebrates, including rats (when presented with a taste that previously made them sick, they open their mouths, gag, retch, shake their heads, and wipe their chins on the floor), coyotes (they not only retch but kick dirt on the offensive offering), cougars (they shake their paws as if to expel the nasty stuff), and monkeys (their repertoire includes squashing the source of their disgust, flinging it away, and then wiping their hands).

In a sense, when it comes to disgust, ontogeny recapitulates phylogeny. Paul Rozin—the kingpin of disgust research at the University of Pennsylvania—notes that babies given foul-tasting food will make correspondingly terrible faces. This "proto-emotion" serves as the foundation for the later capacity to evince genuine disgust toward conceptually nasty substances.

Psychobiologists maintain that disgust functions as an avoidance of pathogens and their toxins. As for the social constructionists, there must be a global, physiological conspiracy because disgust universally produces changes in blood pressure, heart rate, respiration, and skin conductance. I'm betting on a biological basis because disgust is invariably elicited by contact with stuff that is likely to cause illness such as bodily secretions, viscous substances, vermin, and sick or filthy people. As such, disgust is not merely a feeling of nausea but an emotional response to the danger of illness or defilement. As Rozin and his colleagues put it, "Disgust is triggered not primarily by the sensory properties of an object, but by the ideational concerns about *what it is, or where it has been*," as in the mother's admonition, "Don't put that in your mouth, you don't know where it has been," which means, of course, "It's been somewhere gross." These concerns for contamination and contagion may be deeply rooted in the evolutionary past, but culture has certainly exploited our capacity to link sensations with thoughts.

Just as societies have manipulated anger and fear, they have shaped disgust to meet collective needs. We have conceptually elaborated this emotion into the experience of moral disgust—the somatic response that many people have to two men kissing, the practice of slavery, or acts of pedophilia and incest. Metaphors such as "moral decay" and "foulness of character" suggest that immorality can evoke nausea. Disgust is a psychovisceral affect that lies at the boundary of mind and body or, as Nietzsche argued, the interface of conscious conduct and unconscious impulse. But in the end, disgust trumps culture. Even in the 1700s, the philosopher Moses Mendelssohn recognized, "There is only one kind of ugliness that cannot be presented in conformity with nature without obliterating all aesthetic pleasure, hence artistic beauty: namely, the ugliness arousing disgust."

So what does all this mean for lubbers? For starters, lubber excrement bats a thousand in terms of the universal features of disgusting material, according to William Ian Miller, who wrote *The Anatomy of Disgust*. The insect's excrement is organic, animal, wet, squishy, sticky, and abundant. What's more, feces on the outside of the body is stuff that ought to be on the inside.

In terms of enculturated disgust, lubbers push our buttons. These grasshoppers embody most of the features that we've associated with disgusting human forms, according to Winfried Menninghaus in *Disgust: Theory and History of a Strong Sensation*. A lubber is fat, with deep wrinkles and folds (on the abdomen and ventral thorax), grotesquely swollen femurs (like the beefy legs of an obese person), spare buttocks (with its leg musculature concentrated in the thorax, the grasshopper tapers to a pathetically thin rear end), and a bald head (at least the grasshopper doesn't have hair growing in repulsive places). The human archetype of disgust is the "ugly old lady" with revolting habits. The lubber would make a convincing insect version of this character.

Add to the individual qualities of the insects the element of surfeit via their being found in immoderate excess, and we have the cultural epitome of disgust. In Aurel Kolnai's classic 1929 essay "Disgust," he refers to the extravagant profusion of "senseless, formless, surging" insect swarms. Kolnai's contemporary, the philosopher Otto Weininger, maintained, "All fecundity is simply disgusting." The seething abundance of a maggot-ridden corpse or of a lubber-infested roadside suggests an orgy of reproduction far beyond necessity. Likewise, Jean-Paul Sartre's character Roquentin in *La Nausée* refers to the profligacy of overgrown vegetation: "the garden, toppled down into the trees, all soft, sticky, soiling everything . . . Mounting up, mounting up as high as the sky, spilling over, filling everything."

Laura Ingalls Wilder described grasshoppers in terms that evoked the entire spectrum of disgusting qualities, from their obscenely teeming abundance to their grotesquely humanoid appearance, and finishing with their gooeyness underfoot:

> A cloud was over the sun. It was not like any cloud they had ever seen before. . . . Then huge brown grasshoppers were hitting the ground all around her, hitting her head and her face and her arms. They came thudding down like hail. . . . The cloud was hailing grasshoppers. The cloud *was* grasshoppers. . . . Laura tried to beat them off. Their claws clung to her skin and her dress. They looked at her with bulging eyes, turning their heads this way and that. Mary ran screaming into the house. Grasshoppers covered the ground, there was not one bare bit to step on. Laura had to step on grasshoppers and they smashed squirming and slimy under her feet.

The repulsive nature of grasshoppers may tap into our earliest aversions. Indeed, Rozin found that 62 percent of children under the age of two years would put imitation dog feces in their mouths, but only half as many would do so with a whole, sterilized grasshopper. Somewhat ironically, these insects are permissible fare in Leviticus 11:22, but it has been suggested that their hopping made them less repulsive than the creeping and slithering of their prohibited insect brethren. So things could be worse for grasshoppers, but not by much. No doubt we're disgusted, but what about other animals?

Coyotes, foxes, skunks, bobcats, deer mice, and a whole slew of birds eat grasshoppers. And these furred and feathered animals also have the capacity for disgust. So the possibility that lubbers evolved their tendency to regurgitate and defecate to tap into their predators' cognitive states seems plausible.

Doug Whitman knows more than anyone else in the world about lubbers (at least the Eastern lubber, which is the prairie lubber's brightly colored and noxious cousin). He acknowledges that disgust could lie at the core of the predator–prey relationship. Doug has published dozens of papers concerning lubber biology, including studies in which he fed Eastern lubbers to birds in his laboratory. The result was bird barf. And when he tossed fresh specimens to the birds a few days later, the poor things opened their mouths as if gagging, squawked, and tried to fly away. When I asked Doug about the prairie lubber, he sent me an e-mail that systematically assessed the various possibilities. He might not go so far as to suggest that nonhuman predators associate lubber regurgitation or defecation with their own bodily excretions but neither would he dismiss the yuck factor. Doug concluded, "I think that the bottom line is that no-one knows what is going on with BM" (meaning *Brachystola magna,* but a most appropriate acronym in light of the species' propensity for moving its bowels).

While we can't know what a predator is thinking, it can be supposed that revulsion is proportional to the assailant's capacity to experience disgust or, conversely, to value cleanliness. The lubber's behaviors and their resulting mess function as gestures of unambiguous meaning to animals with a sense of propriety. And many animals are quite sanitary, washing and grooming themselves to remove filth. In short, this species knows how to gross out other animals with a sense of personal hygiene. Even so, the excretory message from the lubbers seems particularly—if not solely—tuned to our senses and sensibilities.

Modern culture has crafted from our natural fastidiousness a variety of behaviors far more biologically inane than the biological spectacles that we deem absurd. The peacock struts and the packrat collects, but we spend hours scrubbing ourselves with an assortment of implements and subjecting our bodies to an array of purportedly purifying chemicals. And now, as if shampoos, detergents, and soaps weren't sufficient evidence of our technological devotion to the cleanliness–godliness principle, we have embedded antibiotics in our plastics, our meat, and our underwear. I would not be surprised if the models in biology labs will soon be molded from antibiotic plastics, completing our separation from the living world. Our genetic predisposition to avoid or at least to easily learn to shun filth makes an encounter with the lubber grasshopper profoundly compelling.

But at the same time, modern society inculcates a kind of affected tolerance when it comes to nature. Instead of judging organisms on our own terms, we're supposed to accept them for what they are. Rather than being perceived as the ugly old women of the prairie, lubbers are to be seen as elegantly colored, finely sculpted, noble creatures that put to scorn, as Walt Whitman said in *Leaves of Grass,* the most exquisite products of human engineering. However, a conflict arises as I realize that these awesome creatures can be absolutely awful.

When a humongous insect regurgitates and defecates (perhaps I should say "pukes and craps" to retain the earthy sense of these crude behaviors), no amount of cultivated sensitivity saves this from being a truly disgusting encounter. Mendelssohn was right, biology trumps culture, and there is no potential for aesthetic pleasure—or even neutrality. There is something true and meaningful about my instinctive reactions, and the grasshoppers

allow—indeed force—me to honor these sensibilities. I believe that the lubber grasshopper is being authentically gross because it intends to be. And it
is in my genuine biological nature to honor their revolting efforts, to issue
forth a guttural tribute to their nastiness, to twist my face into a mask of
revulsion.

As I kid, I turned over my fair share of decomposing critters and poked at
the edges of many fetid puddles. In fact, the latter yielded about the only
firsthand evidence of minuscule life that my ill-focused, under-illuminated,
one-hundred-power microscope was able to reveal. The offal of life provided
me with my introduction to animal innards and microbial worlds. The science of biology, however, tended to clean up such messes, ironically steril-
izing the living world. High school biology was aseptic, relying primarily on
models and pickled specimens. College teaching laboratories were neat and
organized. Likewise, the scientific research facilities where I worked as an
undergraduate were sanitized. I might never have discovered the ultimate
fate of those neatly bagged and odorless frozen cadavers—the refuse of biological research—without an unforgettable trip to the rodents' mass grave.

    That summer of discovery I was working in a laboratory where mice
were the subjects of investigation. In the course of a particularly busy series
of experiments, plastic bags of dead mice piled up. For reasons that I can't
recall, the normal pickup routine for the tiny corpses was interrupted, and
the professor told me and another lab tech to empty the overflowing freezer
and take the bags to the city landfill. Relishing an opportunity to get outside
and go for a drive, Ed and I loaded the bags into a large cardboard box (an
effort at discretion, as we had to carry the load across campus to his truck)
and headed out.

    At the dump, we were directed to the far end of the site, where a pit had
been designated for dead animals. To our dismay, we found that the summer
heat had caused the mice to thaw and a pinkish liquid was soaking the box.
Rather than trying to heave a few dozen chunks of dripping, semi-frozen
rodents from a discrete distance, we decided to make the delivery in one fell
swoop. We grabbed the bottom corners of the soggy box and staggered to
the edge of the pit—and that was our singularly unforgettable mistake.

    From where we parked, the thick vapors emanating from the half-
buried corpses of cats, dogs, and other decomposing creatures were un-
detectable. But somewhere within a few feet of the pit, we walked through
an invisible curtain of cadaverine, the chemical released during the decay

of animal tissue. Never have I been so instantaneously overcome by nausea. Putrefying tissue has been proposed as the prototypical object of disgust. And I can attest that my encounter was the purest revulsion that I've experienced. Swallowing repeatedly and inhaling through clenched teeth, we heaved the box into the pit.

Back on campus, I showered and crushed my clothes into the bottom of my laundry bag. But for the rest of the day, stray molecules of cadaverine would escape from a pore or be released from a hair. With the merest hint of that stench, my stomach would lurch. Our instinctual revulsion to this particular odor presumably evolved to keep us from the health hazards of rotten flesh. Rarely do we encounter such a deeply primal sensory experience, unaided by learning and unaltered by culture.

We have forgotten much as a species, having renounced our animalistic intuitions. To suppress life's most ancient form of communication— scent—we add fragrances, shave our bodies, and otherwise deodorize ourselves. But we cannot so easily censor our genetic heritage, and the ancient, emotional partner of disgust is fear. These two are the principal psychological reactions that allow us to defend ourselves; they are, according to Kolnai, "the standard modes of aversion." Both emotions trigger physiological responses and intense desires to separate from the stimulus. The difference is that with disgust, our pulse slows and we seek to remove the offending source, while with fear, our pulse quickens as we seek to remove ourselves from the threat. I've been told that our heart rate increases when we smell the odor of urine from a tiger or a lion. This atavistic reaction is the result not of conditioning but of the millions of years of experience encoded in our genes. Ours is the intuition of a naked ape that was once stalked by large carnivores. I cannot vouch for the instinctual response to a predator's odor, but I can testify to the no-experience-necessary reaction to the sound of a hungry cougar.

In college, I worked with a summer field crew of other students on a project to livetrap wild mice for physiological studies. A July afternoon in 1981 found us in our routine: hop-scotching along a trapline in the mountains above Magdalena, New Mexico. My future wife and I composed one team, and another pair of students systematically alternated with us in the task of baiting and setting traps. While working a cheekful of dry rolled oats into a sticky, semimasticated "bait ball" that the mice adored, I heard what seemed to be a low growl in the pines dotting the hillside above us. Dismissing this as a mistaken interpretation of a creaking tree (there was not a breath of wind, but denial has its own adaptive virtues), I continued on with Nan. We passed Ed and Val, and started baiting the next trap another twenty yards along the fall line of the hill. Again, I heard a throaty rumble, so deep as to be at the edge of audibility. "Did you hear anything?" I asked, feigning detached curiosity. "Yeah," Nan replied, "and I heard the same sound earlier" (the capacity for denial is well-rooted in both genders). Ed and Val caught up with us and agreed that they, too, had heard the ominous sound. "There's only a couple more traps on this line," Ed offered, "Let's stick together, set the last two, and get the hell outta here."

We cast furtive glances up the forested slope and stopped at the next trap. Above us was an outcropping of rock, splattered with grey-green and garish orange blotches of lichen. As Ed bent to attend to the trap, a shriek rent the stillness. The hunting cry of a cougar is a sound that resonates in the shadowy recesses of our evolutionary memory. This sound takes no more enculturation to understand than does the odor of a rotting corpse. Never before had I been an item of prey, but my long-forgotten ancestors had bequeathed me their experience. Primally encoded in neural pathways like roots that penetrate into the darkest depths, I knew instinctively and instantly what we had encountered. But I could not see the predator, which seemed impossible given the volume of the sound. Fighting the instinct to run—precisely the response that the cat intended to elicit—we turned our backs to one another, reflexively forming a box in the manner of other social animals assailed by predators.

We worked our way down the slope in this phalanx of adrenalin-fueled awareness. The aura of focused senses and clarity of mind was animalistic, unparalleled even in the midst of other imminent dangers that I've experienced. I recall all of the sensations and none of the perceptions, and even as I recount this event the hairs on the backs of my arms tingle. Only upon reaching the safety of the truck did keen awareness give way to the trembling-legged, loose-boweled hyperventilation of authentic terror. We never saw the mountain lion, although we found tracks the next week. Humans are profoundly visual creatures—seeing is believing. And those mute tracks transformed the sound of a phantom into the reality of a predator.

On the grasslands of Wyoming, the closest sensory experience to the cougar's cry is the buzz of a prairie rattler. In walking through our study sites, the possibility of a snake lies in a remote, unconscious corner of my mind.

I am usually busy contemplating the impending midday heat, the logistics of the project, or the dusty crispness of the ongoing drought. But before my mind can grasp the meaning of the dry buzz, let alone the direction from which it originates, I can leap a good six feet away from the menacing reptile. Like the desire to bolt from the poised cougar, flight from the coiled snake is an adaptive and instantaneous reflex but in this case completed before consciousness can intercede. This "snake dance," as my field crew has named the balletic leap, is performed maybe once or twice a summer. But it takes no practice and fails to improve with repetition—a pure and instinctual act of fear, honed by human experience before we were born.

These encounters with fanged creatures are too unpredictable and ultimately too dangerous to intentionally impose on my students. However, I know that I must provide them with authentic experiences, for these—not theories, principles, or techniques—are the lessons they will remember. All of my erudite lectures, red-scrawled corrections, and clever exams may help them learn the content of science. But the labors of the mind will only be valued and the self-discipline of scholars will only mature if they have a passion for their work. And passion can be evoked but never taught. So I take my students to visit the dusty roadsides of Wyoming in midsummer to play under the formal guise of a collecting trip. Here is our chance for a firsthand, utterly base encounter with a sublimely repulsive aspect of nature.

I don't know if my students are any more ethical for their encounters of disgust. In fact, I suspect that they may well be less moral, if we take this to mean a willingness to outcompete, kill, hunt, or otherwise violently engage other living beings. Having been vomited on by nature, they see the world in starker terms. Rather than the soft lap of a mythic mother, they understand that nature usually doesn't give a shit about us, and when it does, it is as likely to shit on us as to embrace us. Students who have a Disneyfied view of the world might well be more compassionate and gentle. A kind of insipid secondhand morality arises from *Bambi* and the proselytizing of organizations that claim to "speak for those that can't." When social norms are spoon-fed to an uncritical audience, people may do good things. But unless a person's reasons are their own, an individual is no more moral than the Labrador retriever that fetched the drowning kid from Colorado's Roaring Fork River a couple years ago. Through authentic experiences with the natural world, my students will arrive at values of their own making. For better or worse, their beliefs and actions will be rooted in their own lives. Perhaps they will even come to view cultural norms with a kind of disgust.

Kolnai was disgusted by the fawning, flattering speech of those currying favor. There's a good reason why we refer to such groveling in the modern era as ass-kissing or brownnosing—terms that capture the scatological aspect of disgust. Along similar lines, Mendelssohn argued that flabby flesh was the analog of a repulsive cultural softness. More than two centuries ago he expressed disgust with "sickly mollycoddling and moralization," but he'd likely find today's political correctness to be just as revolting. There is a repulsive hypocrisy in what Menninghaus called "faked non-disgust." The moral phony achieves a narcissistic victory over disgust: "Aren't I wonderful to be seen in public with this grotesquely obese person?" Extending this pseudovirtue to the natural world means pretending to be tolerant, even accepting, of other life-forms. Such biopolitical correctness sanitizes my students' gut feelings. Their primal sense of loathing is dulled, which might make them better neighbors for other people and other organisms but only through profound inauthenticity.

René Descartes elevated the intellect to being the foundation of humanity: *cogito ergo sum* (I think, therefore I am). Menninghaus proposed a visceral version of the claim. Adapting her notion, I'd contend that we can be sure about the existence of things other than ourselves by virtue of *fastidium movet, ergo est* (It is disgusting, therefore it is real). As the contemporary scholar Robert Rawdon Wilson, put it: The representation of filth is not filth. Only an *actual* lubber is disgusting.

Shock artists appreciate the power of real materials to evoke disgust. Their classic works involve music and dance in the midst of dismembered animal corpses, paintings in human blood, and sculptures of dung. These ventures are not new, the lamentations of cultural critics notwithstanding. For two hundred years, elements of Western society have sought disgust as a means of staving off the growing burden of banal information, the flood of empty stimuli, and ennui of passive conformity. The purpose of shocking artworks, according to Robert Wilson (the avant-garde playwright and director), is to "puncture conformity's protective balloon." Transgressing the boundary of social propriety forces the observer to face the "sad recognition of how much has been missed." I suppose that, in a way, I am a shock biologist. I want my students to see what they miss in nature documentaries, college textbooks, and computer simulations. Nor are my concerns new.

In 1914, William Hornaday (acclaimed naturalist and founder of the National Zoo) decried that "fully 90 percent of zoologists in America stick closely to their desk-work." A decade later Harvard's famed entomologist,

William Morton Wheeler, disparaged the "academic dry-rot" within the laboratory life of universities. And in 1951, John Steinbeck recounted in *The Log from the Sea of Cortez*:

> We sat on a crate of oranges and thought what good men most biologists are, the tenors of the scientific world—temperamental, moody, lecherous, loud-laughing, and healthy. Once in a while one comes on the other kind—what used in the university to be called a "dry-ball"—but such men are not really biologists. They are the embalmers of the field, the picklers who see only the preserved form of life without any of its principle. Out of their own crusted minds they create a world wrinkled with formaldehyde. . . . Your true biologist will sing you a song as loud and off-key as will a blacksmith, for he knows that morals are too often diagnostic of prostatitis and stomach ulcers. Sometimes he may proliferate a little too much in all directions, but he is as easy to kill as any other organism, and meanwhile he is very good company, and at least he does not confuse a low hormone productivity with moral ethics.

While grappling with kicking, puking, crapping animals, my students and I invariably laugh as heartily as Steinbeck's biologists. By some accounts, laughter is the negative complement of disgust—how can repulsion be funny? Humans laugh for many reasons, including the release of tension. Menninghaus contends that while vomiting is a sudden biological discharge, laughing at something is a psychic expulsion. I know that I prefer the latter, but it does seem true that in either case one feels much better afterward.

Although trained in the culture of science, the students who come with me to the field approach the lubbers like kids who are simultaneously attracted to and repulsed by a run-over cat or a fresh cowpat. In handling the messy lubbers we feel the push and pull of disgust—Kolnai's "macabre attraction." Immanuel Kant—arguably the greatest modern philosopher—developed his aesthetic framework using a triad of experiences: beauty, sublimity, and disgust. And like the sublime, disgust has the paradoxical capacity to simultaneously attract and repel. As we stand on the rim of a canyon, the sublime draws us perilously close to the edge, while a sense of dread pushes us away. However, disgust—the negative form of the sublime—is hidden away by nature guides and park officials who frame and interpret experiences for the public. The Grand Canyon may be a more powerful encounter of the sublime than is *Brachystola magna,* but what if we had not only lookout points for folks to contemplate the abyss but gross-out points with a decomposing deer seething with maggots, a pile of coyote scat, or a hawked-up owl pellet? For now, my students have to make do with prairie lubbers.

Come October, another group of students will encounter these creatures. Although many of the budding scientists will find the meaty insect carcasses to be grotesque, they will not know how nasty these specimens were a few months earlier. But I'll be able to tell their story. As the students cut and tease and probe, I can recount the dusty, sweat-streaked afternoons spent gathering these animals for their use. And in so doing, I hope to evoke not merely a sense of the living spectacle that is the lubber grasshopper but a sense of obligation—a duty to use well and learn much from this teacher. I want the students to share my sense of responsibility for killing a marvelously repugnant, authentically engaging creature.

Most of my summer work involves snuffing the life from enormous numbers of grasshoppers beneath blankets of chemicals—perhaps safer poisons in smaller doses, but toxins nonetheless. This might seem to be a terrible occupation, and mass killing is deeply troubling. But I find it easier to direct a spray pilot to rain neurotoxins over a field seething with grasshoppers than to wantonly crush a single individual beneath my boot. There is an anonymity that comes with taking life at inconceivable scales, billions upon billions of organisms in a single day's work. Joseph Stalin captured the callousness of wholesale slaughter when he said, "A single death is a tragedy; a million deaths is a statistic." The lubbers remind me of the tragedy.

The bodies thawing as the students arrive in the laboratory are the ironic ghosts of biology, a field of science in which students usually spend more time learning from dead organisms than from live ones and in which practitioners often take more lives than they save. But I prefer that the students dissect these insects because the lubbers are still real. The textures of their tissues have not been homogenized with chemical preservatives, but even a commercially prepared specimen—Steinbeck's "world wrinkled with formaldehyde"—is preferable to a plastic model or a pathetically simulated "virtual dissection" on a computer. The fat bodies of my specimens are still greasy, the muscles are firm, and the tracheae remain diaphanous. A thawed lubber retains the tactile potential to disgust—at least this authenticity remains. In reference to hunting, Thoreau wrote, "We cannot but pity the boy who has never fired a gun; he is no more humane, while his education has been sadly neglected." Likewise, I pity the student who has never cut into a fellow creature.

As the days grower shorter and the increasingly complex dissections stretch into the dusk of autumn, I share Steinbeck's concerns about "picklers who see only the preserved form of life without any of its principle." However, if I am attentive, the students will learn much about insect anatomy and something about life. I can't revivify the creatures pinned to the black wax of the dissection trays, repulsive for having been splayed open and disemboweled rather than for being disgusting on their own terms. But when a student opens the foregut to find a bolus of shredded leaves, I can recount the weedy roadside north of Torrington; and when one discovers the severed leg of a grasshopper within the crop contents of a dissected specimen, I can reveal that the lubber is an eager necrophage—an eater of the dead, a quality that deepens the sense of macabre wonder associated with this monstrous insect. If only those tearing into a death-stiffened body could have encountered the living, loathsome lubber grasshopper.

17 The Parables of the Rats and Mice

Kathleen Dean Moore

"A MOUSE WAS CRUSHED," Jon said as he loaded the tent bag into the boat. He and Frank and I had been camping on a gravel bar in the Willamette River, not far from home.

I looked up from my oatmeal.

"What are you talking about?"

"A mouse died under our tent."

"Of what?"

"Crushing."

Nobody talks this way.

"What kind of mouse?" I asked. "How crushed?"

"Deer mouse, I guess," Jon said. "Very."

I'm not the kind of person who won't kill if I need to. Slapping flies. Boiling crabs alive. Bashing a fresh-caught trout on the head. These things don't bother me all that much. But an innocent mouse ruptured like a water balloon under my hips while I roll around dreaming that we had adopted a baby girl named Guernica—this grieves me. I have no doubt I'm the one who squashed it. I'm dreaming of having too many committee obligations to take care of little Guernica. A mouse cowers under my hips. Then one more missed committee meeting and I roll this mouse flat as a cartoon.

"It was under my sleeping pad, wasn't it," I demanded.

Jon wouldn't answer. But Frank said it all by changing the subject. "Why did you name the baby Guernica?" he asked.

"I didn't name her. She came that way. But I was too busy to take care of her, so I was trying to think of a way to give her back," I said.

So many things you can't explain.

"Actually," Jon said, "it was pretty bloody."

I can understand how a gravity-drenched being can steamroller a mouse. What I have a harder time understanding is how human beings of goodwill can do so much harm. Not, how is it possible to do harm?—human beings have made a science of that. But how do we live with ourselves, go merrily on our little ways, knowing that we are destroying things we cherish?

A mouse was crushed, we say. The forest was cut. The birds were poisoned. An opossum was run over. A good time was had by all. So nobody's acting here, only being acted upon. A human being walks by and mice keel over, trees sever themselves at the knees and plop into the dirt, birds plummet from the sky, and opossums pop into the air, dissolve into fluids, and distribute themselves randomly over the asphalt. The passive voice, the sentence where the causal agent has gone missing. The facts are bad enough, but the grammar is terrifying.

Species go extinct, we say. But the fact of the matter is that species don't always go extinct, the way bananas go bad, or bombs go astray, or elderly uncles go crazy or go about their business. Human decisions sometimes drive animals to extinction. Human decisions extinguish entire species. Extinguish: to cause to cease burning. All the little sparking lives.

Shit happens, we say. And sometimes it does. But the fact of the matter is that sometimes, shit doesn't just happen. Sometimes, human beings deliberately create the conditions under which shit is more likely to occur.

Nobody says it's easy, knowing the difference between right and wrong. Is it what you *intend* that makes all the difference, or what actually *happens* as a result of what you do, no matter what you intend? Everybody makes mistakes, nobody can see into the future, and isn't too great an eagerness to lay blame a moral failing too? I think about this story and wonder what it means. One thing, I think is clear: I should go on full alert if I hear myself say, "I'm not the one who does harm; harm just happens around me." Like it or not, I own the consequences of my acts. They're mine. That mouse is mine.

In a mountain cabin in Colorado many years ago, when Frank and I were very young, we were annoyed each night by a packrat. It was a lovely brown rat with a softly furred tail, but it pooped on the dishtowels and skittered and crashed all night long, chewing up tin foil and Styrofoam cups. Plus, it was a prime suspect in the disappearance of a bike-lock key. Not really capital offenses, as I think about it now, but we decided to put out poison. In those days, rat poison was a waxy substance in bottle caps. Fools, we put out two.

In the morning, one of the bottle caps was gone, and in its place, the rat had left a quarter.

Western philosophy has made a whole moral theory out of trade-offs like this. "An act is right if it creates the greatest happiness for the greatest number," we assure each other: the famous Utilitarian Principle. So anything can be traded, as long as you're a sharper trader, always getting a balance of happiness over the long run. Dam the Columbia River, for example. Ruin ancient runs of lamprey and sockeye salmon, bury the places where native people have gathered for centuries to fish and to pray, as long as you can show on a graph how the benefits soar beyond the measured costs, irrigating orchards and sending cheap electricity to California. We do the calculation—this much pleasure, that much pain—and if the balance of happiness is in the black, we assure ourselves that we are acting morally.

Well, maybe we are and maybe we aren't. It's complicated.

Aren't there some things that can't be traded, not even for happiness? Some things are irreplaceable: too wonderful, too precious, too fundamental to be traded for anything. This is no secret. What parent would knowingly trade away her child's health? And what about other things we value for their own sake, not for what they can give us? The wild Sierras, and the wildflowers that flatten against the rocks in thunderstorms. The night sky. The turning of the seasons. An old man.

And even if everything could be traded, why is happiness always the most valuable of all the chits? The "greatest good" theory is built on the arrogant and dubious idea that human beings are the center of the universe and human happiness is the purpose of all creation. Human beings, imagining that the world and everything in it—the forests, the lakes, the great flocks of cranes—were made especially for them, the way ticks must think that hikers are their special gifts from God. Our temptation is to design arrogant policies and make dubious decisions, and then we end up doing to the natural world what ticks do to us, except that ticks have the good grace to drop off when their stomachs are full. I don't know. It's too convenient, that ethical theory should suddenly affirm the human race's single-minded search for happiness and forget about everything else we and the rest of creation might need and seek.

In the end, I don't think you can trade rights and wrong on the open market. I don't think it will do to say, I don't actually do anything wrong

in this place and time, as long as my act brings about happiness somewhere else.

My father was a boy during the Depression, in a family with never enough
money to go around. He saw economic opportunity in a matchbox adver-
tisement for dancing mice. Dancing mice are little house mice with a genetic abnormality that interferes with their ability to balance. So dancing
mice stagger and spin in a drunken tarantella—an entertainment, maybe,
in a grim time.

My father saved up his paper-route money and sent away for a pair.
The way mice breed, he was sure he'd have a dozen mice every few months
and could sell them door-to-door. Surely everyone wants a dancing mouse.
After a while, two mice came in the mail, as promised. But they didn't seem
to like each other, and within a week, one died. Hoping at least to recoup his
initial investment, my father went from house to house in his neighborhood,
giving mouse-dancing demonstrations, until he found a buyer—an elderly
woman who lived alone. She gave him a quarter and took the mouse.

"What happened then?" I asked my father.

"I don't know," he said.

One of the factors that makes moral reasoning difficult is that so many
of the consequences of our acts are invisible. What we care about the most
is often the hardest to locate and measure. How does beauty enter into a cal-
culus? How does forgiveness, or the grace in a rain-washed morning, or the
dignity of undisturbed land? What is the measurable value of a neighborhood? What unit of measurement do you use? Jeremy Bentham, the father
of Utilitarianism, suggested a "Utile," but that never quite caught on. The
industrialized economy has substituted the U.S. dollar. But if you have to
put a dollar value on everything, then before you know it, the dollar is the
only thing that has value. You make your charts, graphing out the benefits
and the costs, but the very fact of measuring and charting tips the scales
toward what can be measured and charted, or what can be traded for cash.

The moral of the story? I think it's this: it won't work to say, I don't do
harm if what I destroy has no dollar value, or if I have no way to measure
what happens as a result of my decisions. These are evasions, or denials.

This one is Jon's story. I wasn't there, but I'll try to do it justice. In the wilderness Alaska research camp where Jon works summers, a baby pine marten

turned up tangled in a fishnet in a storage shed. A pine marten is a large silky weasel, not a rodent, but close enough for this essay, I hope. And it's fierce—the hiss, the flashing teeth, the predator's slashing speed. Hearing the baby squeal, the two young aquatic biologists struggled to untangle it. They're used to releasing fish, but a panicked mammal was a different challenge. Add to the mix the frantic mother martin, crouching with her teeth bared and launching toward their ankles.

I can imagine the shouting and dodging, the strategic retreats and contingency plans, the clever use of long-handled tools, the quick reflexes and equally quick laughter, the relief and beers all around when the marten finally flashed from their hands and disappeared. What seems important to me about this story is that neither of the men wondered whether they should release the baby marten, whether they should risk the nasty bites to set it free. The only issue was how.

Philosophers say that you can't reduce an *ought* from an *is*. It's the old "is-ought problem" that has bedeviled Western philosophy since the eighteenth century, when David Hume explained that from a mere description—this is the way the world is—you can't infer a prescription—this is the way the world ought to be. In one sense, he's right: You can stare at the world as long as you want, examine it every which way in all its detail, and it will not reveal to you what ought to be. But that doesn't mean you can't infer what you ought to do, from a description of the way the world is. We do it all the time. Jon made that leap in a flash, the space of a synapse, so fast he was probably never aware of the jump: the marten is caught in the net; therefore, I ought to free it.

Logically speaking, the bridge linking "what is" and "what ought to be" is a hidden premise: if a marten is caught in my net, then I ought to free it. The premise is a description, not about the world, but about the moral convictions of the person acting in the world. To reason from facts to moral duties, a person has to take a stand: under these circumstances, this is what I ought to do. In taking this stand, in supplying the link between physical and moral worlds, he creates himself as a moral agent and defines his character.

Who is the person who would look at a squealing animal, rock back on his heels, say, "There is no moral obligation in this scene," and walk away? There may be no moral obligation in the scene, but there is a moral obligation in the presence of a person in the scene, a particular person stopped in his tracks by that set of facts, a particular person who embodies a set of unspoken principles about who he is and how he ought to act in the world. The quick judgment, the moral impulse, the silent premise affirming one's standing as a moral agent, the sharp knife against the tough strands of a net: this may be humanity's unique gift to the universe.

Last term, Viola Cordova came to my class to talk about taking moral responsibility. She was a wonderful person and a friend, a laughing, chain-smoking Jicarilla Apache woman with a philosophy doctorate from the University of New Mexico. Everything is connected, she told my students, and on the chalkboard she drew a stone dropping into a lake. The ripples spread out and out in widening circles and rocked the cattails by the shore. She paused to draw cattails, an arrow showing how they gently rocked. The students understood that every decision they make, every action they undertake, has spreading consequences in the real world, the world of water and sky and striving. And so they have to take responsibility, acknowledging that everything they do or fail to do creates the world in the next moment. They are co-creators of the universe, bringing into being the world where they will live.

A blood vessel burst in Viola's brain the week after her lecture, killing her and shaking my students to the core. They turned back through their notes to find the ideas she had given them, all finding the drawings they had copied off the board. Ripples reaching out toward shore.

One more story, this one with a happy ending. Our daughter Erin and her friend Jenny launched a canoe onto a lake in Wisconsin, after brushing out the pine needles that had accumulated over the summer. When they were well out on the water, a deer mouse squeezed from the bulkhead and started running up and down the length of the canoe.

"Before we could react, which means before we could climb onto the seats and dump the canoe," Erin said, "the mouse jumped into the drink. But it didn't know the direction to shore and it swam in tighter and tighter circles. So Jenny threw it one of those orange life jackets, and when she nudged the mouse in that direction with her paddle, the mouse climbed onto the collar."

Jenny pushed along the life jacket with its little passenger, Erin paddled the canoe, and the three of them zigzagged toward land. When they were close to safety, with the canoe between the life jacket and the shore, the mouse leapt onto the canoe, ran across a thwart, jumped into the water on the far side, and swam to the bank. What I like to think about, to picture in my mind, is a mouse dog-paddling between the cattails, pushing a tiny bow wave toward shore.

I can't say I always, or even often, know what is right. But I'm pretty well convinced that whatever I do—what I decide to do and what I do without deciding—shapes the world and shapes me as a moral agent. Perhaps humans are the only beings in the universe capable of regret and resolve. If this is so, then the most important question is how—by what sort of education or process of moral development—does a person come to grow these moral synapses, this strong sense that the world-as-it-is asks something of them?

Publication History

Chapter 2 was previously published as "Hunger Makes the Wolf" in *Wild Echoes: Encounters with the Most Endangered Animals in North America* (Washington: Alaska Northwest Book, 1990).

Chapter 5 was previously published as "One Nation under Coyote, Divisible" in *The Hopes of Snakes and Other Tales from the Urban Landscape* (Boston: Beacon Press, 2005). Copyright 2005 by Lisa Couturier. Reprinted with permission from Beacon Press.

Chapter 8 was previously published as "Canadas: From Conservation Success to Flying Carp" in *Ascent Literary Magazine* (2005).

Chapter 9 was previously published as "The Bard's Bird, or, the Slings and Arrows of Avicultural Hegemony: A Tragicomedy in Five Acts" on Terrain .org, Fall/Winter 2010.

Chapter 11 was previously published as "Metamorphosis in Detroit," *North American Review* 294 (Fall 2009): 38–44.

Chapter 13 was previously published as "Flying Rats" in *Pigeons: The Fascinating Saga of the World's Most Revered and Reviled Bird* (New York: Grove Press, 2006). Copyright 2006 by Andrew D. Blechman. Reprinted by permission of Grove/Atlantic, Inc.

Contributors

BRUCE BARCOTT is an American editor, environmental journalist, and author. He is a contributing editor of *Outside* and has written articles for the *New York Times Magazine, National Geographic, Mother Jones, Sports Illustrated, Harper's Magazine, Legal Affairs,* and *Utne Reader.* His books include *The Measure of a Mountain: Beauty and Terror on Mount Rainier* and *The Last Flight of the Scarlet Macaw: One Woman's Fight to Save the World's Most Beautiful Bird.* In 2009 he was named a Guggenheim fellow in nonfiction.

CHARLES BERGMAN teaches English literature and writing at Pacific Lutheran University. He writes extensively on wildlife and animals in academic journals and in national magazines such as *Audubon* and *Smithsonian.* He is the author of *Wild Echoes: Encounters with the Most Endangered Animals in North America.*

JAMES E. BISHOP is assistant professor of English at Young Harris College, where he teaches writing, American literature, and environmental literature. His scholarly work has been published in *Early American Literature, Nineteenth-Century Prose, Green Theory and Praxis,* and other academic journals.

ANDREW D. BLECHMAN is an award-winning journalist. He has been a reporter for the *Los Angeles Times* and the *Des Moines Register,* and his writing has been published in *Smithsonian* magazine, the *New York Times,* and the *International Herald Tribune.* He is the author of *Pigeons: The Fascinating Saga of the World's Most Revered and Reviled Bird* and *Leisureville.* He is managing editor of *Orion Magazine* and was elected selectman of his hometown, Great Barrington, Massachusetts, in 2011.

MICHAEL P. BRANCH is professor in the Literature and Environment Program at the University of Nevada, Reno. He is cofounder of the Association for the Study of Literature and Environment and coeditor of the book series Under the Sign of Nature. He has published five books as well as more than 150 articles and reviews on environmental literature; his creative nonfiction has appeared in *Utne Reader, Orion, Ecotone, Isotope, Hawk and Handsaw,* and *Whole Terrain.* His writing has been recognized as "Notable Essays" in *The Best American Essays, The Best American Science and Nature Writing,* and *The Best American Nonrequired Reading.* His monthly blog essay "Rants from the Hill" appears in the online edition of *High Country News.* He lives at six thousand feet in the western Nevada desert, where the Great Basin and the Sierra Nevada meet.

LISA COUTURIER is author of *The Hopes of Snakes and Other Tales from the Urban Landscape.* She was awarded a 2012 Pushcart Prize for her essay "Dark Horse" and was listed as a notable essayist in *Best American Essays 2006* and *Best American Essays 2011.* She lives with her family and six horses on an agricultural reserve in Maryland and is writing a memoir about her racehorse.

PHILLIP DAVID JOHNSON II is assistant coordinator for the Institute for Learning and Teaching at Colorado State University. He has written essays on metaphors of waste and degraded landscapes in the western United States. He writes about sports and sporting politics for *ESPN Outdoors,* and he has published essays about fly-fishing for carp as well as poetry about his experience as a working-class fly fisherman.

CAROLYN KRAUS is professor of journalism and screen studies at the University of Michigan–Dearborn. Her essays have been published in *Partisan Review, Threepenny Review,* the *New Yorker,* the *New York Times,* and *The Best Travel Writing 2011.*

JEFFREY A. LOCKWOOD was hired as an insect ecologist at the University of Wyoming in 1986 and since then has metamorphosed into a professor of natural sciences and humanities, with a joint appointment in the department of philosophy and in the MFA program in creative writing. He teaches natural resource ethics, environmental justice, and the philosophy of ecology, along with writing workshops in nature and religious/spiritual writing. His essays have been awarded a Pushcart Prize, a John Burroughs Award, the Albert Schweitzer Sermon Award of the UUA, and inclusion in *Best American Science and Nature Writing*. His most recent books are *Six-Legged Soldiers: Using Insects as Weapons of War* and *Philosophical Foundations for the Practices of Ecology*. He is working on a book that explores entomophobia and other psychological relationships between humans and insects.

KYHL LYNDGAARD is professor of writing and environmental studies at Marlboro College in Vermont. His wide-ranging work in the environmental humanities has been published in journals such as *Great Plains Quarterly, ISLE: Interdisciplinary Studies in Literature and Environment*, and *Ecopoetics*. His coedited anthology is forthcoming.

RANDY MALAMUD is the author of *An Introduction to Animals and Visual Culture, A Cultural History of Animals in the Modern Age, Poetic Animals and Animal Souls, Reading Zoos, The Language of Modernism*, and *Where the Words Are Valid: T. S. Eliot's Communities of Drama*. He is chair of the English department at Georgia State University.

CHARLES MITCHELL is associate professor of American studies at Elmira College in New York. He teaches U.S. cultural history and environmental history and studies. His essays have been published in *ISLE*, Terrain.org, the *Bloomsbury Review*, and *Isotope*.

KATHLEEN DEAN MOORE is best known for her books of essays about our cultural and spiritual connections to wet, wild places: *Riverwalking, Holdfast, The Pine Island Paradox*, and *Wild Comfort*. She has edited books about Rachel Carson and the Jicarilla–Apache philosopher Viola Cordova. Her most recent book is *Moral Ground: Ethical Action for a Planet in Peril*, which gathers calls from dozens of the world's moral leaders to honor our obligations to the future. She is Distinguished Professor of Philosophy at Oregon State University and serves on the board of directors of *Orion* magazine. She lives in Willamette Valley and in the summer writes at her Alaskan cabin, built where a stream and a bear trail meet the cove.

KELSI NAGY holds an M.A. in philosophy from Colorado State University and is a graduate student of anthrozoology at Canisius College in New York. She received a 2012 Culture and Animals Foundation grant for her research on cattle in human culture. She lives and works in Fort Collins, Colorado.

CATHERINE PUCKETT is a natural history and science writer whose work has appeared in literary journals, magazines, and newspapers. She focuses her research and writing on Florida and the southeastern United States and has participated in studies on crocodiles, gopher tortoises, and snakes. She is completing a book of natural history essays on Florida and a fiction book on panthers set in Florida.

BERNARD QUETCHENBACH is associate professor of English at Montana State University, Billings. His publications include essays, poetry, and criticism in books, anthologies, and journals. His essays have appeared in *Stone's Throw, Ascent,* and *Montreal Review.* "Canadas" was listed as a Notable Essay in *Best American Essays.*

CHRISTINA ROBERTSON was born and raised in British Columbia. She teaches literature, environmental justice, working-class studies, and gender, race, and identity studies at the University of Nevada, Reno. Her nonfiction appears in *Let There Be Night, The Pacific Crest Trailside Reader,* and *Lake: A Journal of Arts and Environment.* She is writing an environmental memoir.

GAVAN P. L. WATSON received his Ph.D. from York University in Toronto and is an educational developer with the Centre for Open Learning and Educational Support at the University of Guelph, Ontario. He is an experienced naturalist and environmental educator, and his research interests focus on the implications of informal environmental education practices for participants' perspectives toward the more-than-human world.

Index

rhetoric, 16, 24, 75, 95, 99
ring-billed gull, 12, 24, 31–37
rivers, 192; history of mistreatment, 192
Roberts, Christine, 11, 14, 86, 296
robins, 236
Robinson, Becky, 247
rock doves. *See* pigeons
rodents, 12, 15
Rolson, Holmes, III, 23, 249
Rome, 60
Romulus and Remus, 57
Roosevelt, Theodore, 13, 50, 113, 115,
    163, 194
rotenone, 261
Roth, Dave, 230
Rozin, Paul, 272
Rozol, 134
ruach (term for God), 75
rubbish, 5
Russia, 135, 174
Russians, 209

sage grouse, 97
saguaro cacti, 178
Sallinger, Bob, 254, 256
salmon, 24, 286
salmonella, 206
Salon (magazine Web site), 77
Samsa, Gregor, 202, 205
Sand County Almanac (Leopold), 4, 162
San Fransisco, 131, 233
San Gabriel River, 183–84, 193
Santell, Paige, 255
Sartre, Jean-Paul, 273
Saturday Evening Post (magazine), 263
scavengers, 1, 21, 24, 36, 66, 221
Schieffelin, Eugene, 173–75, 178
science, 3, 11, 12, 13, 19, 43, 48–49,
    51–52, 61, 84–85, 129, 134, 155, 193,
    209, 215, 272, 281–82; fish culture,
    193–94; history of, 54; male domina-
    tion of, 74; realism, 155; study of, 6;
    writing, 6

scientific method, 53
scientific model, 74
scorpion, 142
scrub jay, 254
seagulls, 13. *See also* gulls
settlers, 86, 90, 97, 113. *See also* Euro-
    pean immigrants; pioneers
Shakespeare, 40, 171–75, 178–80
sharp-shinned hawk, 116
sheep, 43, 60, 111, 113; Dall, 39
shepherds, 60
"shit hawk" (gull), 13, 34
"Shooting an Elephant" (Orwell), 210
Shozo, Tanaka, 115
shrews, 97
shrikes, 97
Sibley, David Allen, 162
Sibley Guide to Birds, 162
Sierra Club, 51
Silent Spring (Carson), 91
sinners, 87
Sioux, 176
skunks, 3, 114, 274
"sky carp" (geese), 162
Slobodichikoff, Con, 126
Smiley, Jane, 202
snakes, 1, 10, 14, 60, 67–85, 110; associa-
    tion with women, 75–77; cobra, 71;
    corn snakes, 81–82; cottonmouth,
    67; fear of, 6, 76; fer-de-lance, 74;
    gopher snake, 143; hog-nosed, 71; pit
    vipers, 80; puff adders, 82; worship
    of, 76
Snyder, Gary, 218–19
social norms, 279
society, 8
solitude, 190
*Some We Love, Some We Hate, Some
    We Eat* (Herzog), 9
Song of Myself (Whitman), 153
Sonoran Desert, 73
Sophie's Choice (Styron), 226
South Africa, 6